THE GAELIC ATHLETIC ASSOCIATION
1884–2009

THE GAELIC ATHLETIC ASSOCIATION

1884–2009

Editors

MIKE CRONIN • WILLIAM MURPHY
• PAUL ROUSE

IRISH ACADEMIC PRESS

DUBLIN • PORTLAND, OR

First published in 2009 by Irish Academic Press

2 Brookside,	920 NE 58th Avenue, Suite 300
Dundrum Road,	Portland, Oregon,
Dublin 14, Ireland	97213-3786, USA

This edition © 2009 by Irish Academic Press
Individual chapters © authors

www.iap.ie

British Library Cataloguing-in-Publication Data
An entry can be found on request

978 0 7165 3028 2 (cloth)

Library of Congress Cataloging-in-Publication Data
An entry can be found on request

Printed by the MPG Books Group in the UK

Contents

Editors' Preface

This book is the product of collaboration between the GAA Oral History Project and Sports History Ireland. The collaboration was born of an ambition to mark the 125th anniversary of the Gaelic Athletic Association by asking leading Irish and international historians to write on various aspects of the history of the GAA.

What has emerged – we believe – challenges assumptions and perceptions of the place of the GAA in Irish society. There will most likely be considerable disagreement over some of the arguments advanced by the contributors. This is to be welcomed. The GAA is an association beloved of generations of Irish people. Its contribution to shaping modern Ireland is immense and obvious. Nonetheless, nothing should be considered sacred in any analysis of the association's past.

It is a statement of the obvious to note that this book cannot claim to offer anything approaching a definitive account of every aspect of the GAA's history. Instead, it is conceived as a starting point for further scholarship. There are obvious lines of research. There is, for example, considerable scope for a major study of the relationship between the GAA and the Catholic church (and, indeed, the relationship between the GAA and religion in general).

The images reproduced in this book from the GAA Museum and Archive are intended to illustrate aspects of the history of the association which may not necessarily be covered in the chapters. We also acknowledge the following for images in chapter 8: Ken Loach/BIM (*The Wind that Shakes the Barley*); Film Company of Ireland (*Knocknagow*); Fergus Tighe/Circus Film (*Clash of the Ash*); Neil Jordan/Warner (*Michael Collins*); David Miller/MGM (*Hurling*); John Ford/Republic Pictures (*The Quiet Man*); Four Provinces Pictures (*The Rising of the Moon*); Rank Films (*Rooney*); and Paramount Pictures (*Three Kisses*). The front cover image, taken from Tadhg Saor Ó Séaghdha, *Dhá Sgéal* (Dublin, 1929), is courtesy of the Trustees of the Burns Library Collection, Boston College, and An Gúm.

Finally, we would like to thank everyone who contributed to the making of this book, including everyone at the GAA Oral History Project (www.gaahistory.com), and Lisa Hyde at Irish Academic Press for working so hard to ensure that this book saw the light of day. Particular thanks to the authors who responded to deadlines with diligence and forbearance. That this book has been published is a tribute to their scholarship and their interest in the Gaelic Athletic Association.

MIKE CRONIN, WILLIAM MURPHY AND PAUL ROUSE
Dublin, 2009

List of Contributors

Diarmaid Ferriter is Professor of Modern Irish History at UCD and is Burns Visiting Scholar in Irish Studies at Boston College for the academic year 2008-09. His books include the bestsellers *The Transformation of Ireland* 1900–2000 (2004) and *Judging Dev: A Reassessment of the life and legacy of Eamon De Valera* (2007), which won three Irish Book Awards. He is a regular broadcaster with RTE radio and contributes to a number of Irish newspapers on historical subjects.

A. B. Gleason is a social and cultural historian of the early medieval period. She earned her Ph.D. at Trinity College Dublin and is now a member of the History Department at Princeton University. Her current publication project is a book outlining entertainment and sport in early medieval Ireland. The study is based primarily on examination of early vernacular Irish sources such as law, literature, poetry and hagiography. Further research and publication interests examine the social and legal structures of early medieval socities, particularly Ireland, Scandinavia, Iceland and Russia.

Eoin Kinsella is currently working for the Royal Irish Academy on its Origins of the Irish Constitution project, to be completed in 2009. He is also undertaking research for his Ph.D. at University College Dublin, on Irish Catholic politics and society during the Restoration and Williamite eras. He plays hurling and football with Naomh Olaf GAA club, Dublin.

Richard Holt is Director of the International Centre for Sports, History and Culture at De Montfort University in Leicester, UK. He has written widely on the history of sport in France and in Britain, including 'Sport and the British' (OUP, 1989). He is currently working collaboratively on a history of sport in Europe.

Paul Rouse is a director of the GAA Oral History Project based at Boston College Ireland and a director of InQuest research group. He is also a lecturer at the School of History and Archives in UCD, where he teaches a course on the origins of modern sporting organ-isations. He has written extensively on the history of the GAA. A for-mer winner of Journalist of the Year with Prime Time Investigates. He continues to play Junior B football for his club, Tullamore, and is optimistic of securing an inter-county call-up.

William Murphy is a lecturer in Irish Studies at the Mater Dei Institute of Education, DCU. He is the co-founder of Sports History Ireland and author of the forthcoming book, *Political Imprisonment and the Irish, 1910–1921*.

David Hassan is Senior Lecturer with the Sport and Exercise Sciences Research Institute at the University of Ulster, Jordanstown. A recipient of a Distinguished Research Fellowship from UU in 2006, Dr Hassan has published extensively on Irish sport, specifically in the field of identity politics. In 2008, along with his colleague Dr Paul Darby, Dr Hassan published an edited collection entitled *Emigrant Players Sport and the Irish Diaspora* (Routledge).

Mark Duncan is a director of the GAA Oral History Project at Boston College Ireland and a co-founder of the InQuest research group. Working across a spectrum of media, publishing, education, public service and private industry, he has written several major research reports and books for a range of institutions including RTE, the Department of Education and Science, the National Archives of Ireland and the National College of Ireland and the Higher Education Authority. Prior to founding InQuest in 2005, he spent a decade as a freelance researcher and writer working mostly with RTE Current Affairs, exhibition design companies and various universi-ties. A former co-editor *High Ball*, the official magazine of the Gaelic Athletic Association, he is a frequent contributor to magazines and national newspapers.

Seán Crosson is a lecturer on Irish and world cinema and documen-tary with the Huston School of Film and Digital Media at NUI, Galway. His research interests include Irish film, sport and film, and the relationship between music and poetry, the subject of his recently published book *The Given Note: Traditional Music and Modern Irish Poetry* (Cambridge Scholars Publishing, 2008). He is a co-editor of the collections *The Quiet Man and Beyond* (Liffey Press, 2009) and *Anáil an Bhéil Bheo: Orality and Modern Irish Culture* (Cambridge Scholars Publishing, 2009).

LIST OF CONTRIBUTORS

Brian Ó Conchubhair is an assistant professor in the Department of Irish Language and Literature at the University of Notre Dame and a fellow of the Keough-Naughton Institute for Irish Studies at Notre Dame. In addition to articles on various aspects of nineteenth- and twentieth-century literature and culture, he has edited *Gearrscéalta Ár Linne* (2006) and *WHY IRISH? Irish Language and Literature in Academia* (2008), and a monograph, *Fin de Siècle na Gaeilge: An Athbheochan Ghaeilge agus Gluaiseacht Smaointeoireacht na hEorpa*, will appear in 2009.

Dónal McAnallen is an education officer at the Cardinal Ó Fiaich Library and Archive, Armagh. He took his B.A. in Modern History at Queen's University, Belfast, and his doctorate in History at the National University of Ireland, Galway. He has contributed articles to *Sport in Society* and several historical publications about the GAA, including three volumes of *The Complete Handbook of Gaelic Games*. He is still playing football for his club, An Eaglais, in Tyrone. He was formerly secretary of Comhairle Ardoideachais, the national Higher Education Council of the GAA, and editor of Gaelic games magazine *High Ball*.

Tom Hunt is a native of Clonea Power, County Waterford, and has been a long time exile in Westmeath, where he is a teacher in Mullingar Community College. He has had a lifelong involvement in the GAA both as a player and administrator. He played inter-county football for Waterford and was a member of the Munster inter-provincial panel from 1982 to 1984 and, unusually for a Waterford footballer, was a playing member of the UCD Sigerson Cup-winning team of 1973. He has also served his club Mullingar Shamrocks as a player, P.R.O., chairman and treasurer over the years. He has written extensively on aspects of economic and sports history and is the author of *Portlaw, County Waterford: Portrait of an Industrial Village and its Cotton Industry* (2000) and *Sport and Society in Victorian Ireland: the Case of Westmeath* (2007).

Paul Darby is Senior Lecturer in Sport and Exercise at the University of Ulster. He has written broadly on the history and politics of football (Association) in Africa and on the role of Gaelic games amongst the Irish Diaspora in the United States. He is author of *Africa, Football and FIFA: Politics, Colonialism and Resistance* and joint editor of *Soccer and Disaster: International Perspectives* (with Gavin Mellor and Martin Johnes) and *Emigrant Players: Sport and the Irish*

Diaspora (with David Hassan). His book on the history of the GAA in the United States will be published by University College Dublin Press in 2009.

Mike Cronin is Academic Director of Boston College in Ireland and the project leader of the GAA's oral history project. He is the author of *Sport and Nationalism in Ireland* (Dublin, 1999) and has written extensively on the historical and cultural significance of sport in Ireland.

Gearóid Ó Tuathaigh is Professor of History at the National University of Ireland, Galway. His interests lie in modern Irish and British history, and his publications include *Ireland before the Famine, 1798–1848* (1972); *The Age of de Valera* (1982), with Joe Lee; and (with others) *Irish Studies: A General Introduction* (1988).

List of Illustrations

1. This 1970 photograph shows Foireann na Gaeltachta from Conamara. The players are: *front row* (*left to right*) Al Ó Conghaile (An Spidéal), Tommy Keaney (Carna), Pádraic Corbett (Captaen) (Carna), Pádraic Kelly (An Cheathrú Rua), Pádraic Ó Conghaile (Leitir Mór/Naomh Anna), Máirtín Ó Flathartha (Leitir Mór/Naomh Anna), Micheal Breathnach (Leitir Mór), Micheál Tom Folan (Leitir Mór), Back Row (Left to Right): Christy Scanlon (Micheal Breathnach), Conor O'Malley (Leitir Mór), Frank Ned Ó Finneadh (Micheál Breathnach), Nioclás Ó Conchubhair (Leitir Mór/Naomh Anna), Joe Keane (Carna), Micheál Tim Ó Conghaile (Micheál Breathnach), Máirtín Ó Conghaile (An Spidéal), Joe Lydon (Carna); *missing from photograph*: Seáinin Ó Conghaile (Leitir Mór/Naomh Anna), Patsy McDermott (Micheál Breathnach), Maitiú O Domhnaill (An Cheathriú Rua), Johnny Mulkerrins (Carna). The photograph and names were supplied by Máire Áine beran Uí Choirbín, Carna.
2. A match between two unknown teams in Croke Park in the 1920s.
3. Maurice Davin, the first president of the GAA, was also the outstanding athlete of his generation. He is pictured here sporting the most important medals before he retired at the beginning of the 1880s.
4. The Cuchulainns camogie team pictured in 1904.
5. Michael Cusack, the founder of the GAA.
6. The great Kilkenny hurler, Lory Meagher, gives advice to a Kilkenny player during a match in Croke Park in the 1940s.
7. This picture of the Thurles team which won the first All-Ireland hurling championship in 1887 was taken at least twenty years after the match was played.
8. The Kilkenny team that won the All-Ireland hurling championship in 1911.
9. Still from the film *The Wind that Shakes the Barley* (Ken Loach, 2006).

List of Tables

Introduction

In 1996, when I was preparing a lecture on the impact of the GAA as part of a course on the social history of twentieth-century Ireland at University College Dublin, I was conscious of two things. Firstly, that there was a dearth of suitable analytical historical material to recommend to students on this subject; secondly, that some of my peers, steeped in the GAA as long as they could remember, regarded my tackling of the subject with suspicion. 'With you,' one of my historian colleagues and a GAA stalwart remarked, 'the GAA is not in a safe pair of hands.' It probably was not, nor should it have been; the lecture, as far as I was concerned, was not for the purpose of giving a sanitised and uncritical overview of the association's impact, but of emphasising its triumphs and mistakes and its fascinating complexity. The stern warning to me was a reminder that the GAA has not always been comfortable being subjected to scrutiny by those who have not experienced championship pain or been forced to the point of physical collapse on dark, dreary January nights as preparations begin once again for the summer.

In surveying the literature as it existed then, I was aware that one book in particular on the impact of the association stood out and sparkled. Breandán Ò hEithir's *Over the Bar*, published in 1984, framed life against the sporting backdrop. His reminiscences on his youth were skilfully interwoven with his recollections of Gaelic games and he was not shy in making dry, sometimes critical observations on the GAA and its role in modern Ireland. A certain melancholy sat alongside criticism and affection. His book was also a reminder that an analysis of sport and Irish society could go a long way towards revealing insights into that society's social and cultural fabric and value systems, and provide much information about facets of political and economic life. It was a book of added significance because the GAA, for all its influence on Irish culture and society and the huge level of participation it engendered at local and county level, had not, even one hundred years after its foundation, inspired an equally significant literature that contextualised the association and placed it at the heart of the community.

The essays contained in this book illustrate how that has changed profoundly. It is testimony to the emergence of objective, erudite and challenging scholarship on an organisation that has succeeded over the last 125 years in not only surviving, but also thriving.

Given its resilience and continuing relevance, it is easy to lapse into uncritical admiration of the GAA. I have found myself doing that on many occasions on the way to Croke Park. There is a justifiable pride in the ongoing success of the association and its exceptional contribution to our sense of community. As a Dubliner following the fortunes of its football team, I have often found it mesmerising to walk up O'Connell Street, on to Gardiner Street and past the Hill 16 pub, across Mountjoy Square and down to the throng outside Gill's pub on the corner of Jones's Road. The sense of expectation and the engagement is palpable.

There is no other experience like an All-Ireland final day and it evokes a pride that lingers long after the game. All-Ireland final days encapsulate what the late Nuala O'Faoláin once described as the 'feeling of the nation as an entity'. In 2007, when I was lucky enough to get a ticket for the hurling final, I talked to two natives of London who had travelled to see their first hurling match. They were awestruck, not just by the skill and athleticism they witnessed, but by the sheer scale of the stadium and the passion that emanates from amateur athletes and a crowd of 82,127 people. The Londoners had seen nothing like it before and were suitably impressed as they listened to impassioned post-match debates about whether or not Henry Shefflin is a better hurler than Christy Ring was in his heyday. One of the Londoners asked if it was possible to explain the essence of the appeal of the GAA to so many. I suggested he look not just at Ò hEithir's *Over the Bar* but also, aware that these visitors were more used to soccer, at Tom Humphries' assertion in his *Irish Times* column in May 1995: 'The GAA player who performs in front of 70,000 at the weekend will be teaching your kids on Monday, or he'll be selling you meat or fixing your drains or representing you in court. The soccer player who performs in front of 70,000 people at the weekend will be moaning about too many games and trying to sell you his personalised brand of leisure wear.'

The following year, in his book *Green Fields: Gaelic Sports in Ireland*, Humphries elaborated further: 'Its impact is emotional, visceral … the GAA is more than a sports organisation, it is a national trust, an entity which we feel we hold in common ownership. It is there to administer to our shared passion.'

It continues to do that handsomely. But administering passion, as this book demonstrates, is not a straightforward business. As an organisation it has at times been as frustrating as its founder, Michael

Cusack. In this book, Paul Rouse memorably encapsulates the essence of Cusack: 'At his best, he was extraordinary and brilliant, capable of great warmth, humour and generosity. His life's work is clearly that of a man of considerable vision. But Cusack's flaws were as outlandish as his talents. He was impetuous on a cartoonish scale. He thrived on confrontation and managed to find it in most quarters.' In my view, the same definition can legitimately, if provocatively, be applied to the GAA as an organisation. The GAA's relative silence about Cusack on the centenary of his death in 2006 was a reflection of its determination to keep the founding myths of the organisation intact. Cusack's tempestuous career and association with the GAA was inspirational but also messy, contradictory and full of rancour, as were many aspects of the GAA's early years, in common with some of the other political, sporting and social movements of the late nineteenth and early twentieth centuries.

Over the course of time, it is often easier to forget or ignore the divisions and feuds and present history in a neat and simplistic way. As I discovered in 1996, the GAA has been touchy about its history and unduly sensitive to criticism. To compound matters, Irish historians effectively ignored the place of the GAA in modern Irish life, apart from minimal (and sometimes speculative) remarks about its political function. As a result, for many years, publications on the GAA's history were uncritical and self-congratulatory, with the schisms and divisions papered over. This is of particular relevance to any assessment of Cusack, who became such a thorn in the side of the organisation he founded. It was perhaps easier for the GAA to forget him than to embrace his memory, warts and all. Despite a show of solidarity at the time of his death, and the naming of a stand at Croke Park after him, the GAA was notably quiet about Cusack and his legacy, probably because that legacy, as well as including foresight, energy, self-reliance and ambition, incorporates the themes of internal division, aggression and excessive centralisation, issues that, arguably, are common to all sporting organisations and should not be overlooked in a historical assessment of the GAA. This book succeeds in striking an admirable balance, and the GAA, to its credit, has in recent times welcomed a critical and inclusive engagement with its history in the form of its encouragement of challenging scholarship on its history and through its fulsome support, financially and intellectually, of an unprecedented and exciting oral history project to mark its 125th anniversary: *The GAA Oral History Project*.

When I was preparing my lecture in 1996 I was attempting to establish a framework of inquiry for students. In many respects it was a modest one that raised more questions than it answered, including the following: why was there such a lack of history writing on the GAA, particularly in view of the plaudits it had received over the years, including being described as the most successful of the original mass movements? I also drew attention to the importance of control, discipline and rules in the evolution of the organisation, and the extent to which it reflected a Victorian preoccupation with athleticism and manliness. I mentioned the various ways in which it had negotiated politics, its use by different interest groups, the challenges posed to it by emigration, how its games and philosophy were communicated, and the significance of the debates over the ban (rule 27) on its members playing so-called foreign sports.

I was also interested in how the organisation responded to the challenges of the 1960s; it seemed to be a crucial decade in terms of the association's ability to adapt to changed environments, particularly in view of some predications in that decade that the association was in danger of terminal decline. It was contended, for example, that the passionate attachment to hurling would die out because an individualistic urban approach to leisure would pervade rural areas and destroy the GAA's soul. In 1965 the GAA president Seán Ó Síocháin urged members to respond positively and imaginatively to the growing changes in Irish society and to clarify its social responsibilities, suggesting there was an onus on it to fulfil its purpose in Irish society. He concluded that a modern GAA 'would have to live all through the week and not only on Sundays'.

Clearly, the organisation faced many pressures: the continuing concern about the future viability of rural Ireland and its population, the growing emphasis on urban living, the increase in the popularity of soccer and the emergence of Irish television, which many believed would fatally damage attendances at Gaelic games. It thus had many reasons to be fearful, but it responded robustly and brought a focus to leadership while developing the social role of the association, and eventually, after much soul-searching and acrimonious exchanges, the ban on members playing foreign games was rescinded in 1971.

This book demonstrates how a much broader framework of inquiry can now be employed in relation to historical analysis of the GAA. It reflects how successful the association was on many levels, as well as its ability to periodically emit what Flann O'Brien described in 1956 as 'farcical drool', in responding to critics who were deemed to be engaging in conduct and rhetoric that was 'derogatory to the Gaels of Ireland'. There are many new and exciting research strands on display here; among others, a challenging of the notion that the GAA in its infancy 'swept the country like a prairie fire' in the words of Michael Cusack, and the extent to which the GAA was part of a much wider international phenomenon in the context of the codification of ball games, but was an organisation that ultimately created a unique blend of the traditional and the modern.

Attention is also devoted to the way the forces of tourism as well as nationalism have influenced how Gaelic games have been depicted through various media. The book sheds much light on the complexity of the GAA's relationship with nationalism and the Irish language, which was not acknowledged in the first histories of the GAA to appear after the creation of the Free State, as well as suggesting there were 'severe limits' to the GAA's power of healing after the civil war.

The book underlines the challenges and opportunities associated with keeping the GAA vibrant as a 32-county organisation and among emigrant communities, and how it has negotiated the tensions between its amateur status and the need for financial acumen. It was asserted by a committee appointed by the GAA's Central Council in 1971 that the association was an amateur one that prohibited 'payment or other material reward for participation in games and pastimes'. The relevance and meaning of that definition is an ongoing and controversial concern. There is also long overdue attention devoted to the social background of those individuals who became members.

Collectively, these essays encourage a questioning of often fiercely held and expressed assumptions about the GAA. By so expertly, fluently and searchingly probing the history, identity and culture of the association, they stand as a worthy monument to a unique, complex, successful and enthralling mass movement on the occasion of its 125th anniversary.

DIARMAID FERRITER
University College Dublin,
January 2009

1 Hurling in Medieval Ireland

A. B. GLEASON

Hurling as a pre-modern sport is necessarily a ghost. Sport in the modern sense is a construct of the nineteenth century. Hurling as an organised sport, with an overarching set of rules and regulations, is therefore no less so. Pre-modern hurling, that is to say ancient or medieval hurling, must be accepted then as a roughly defined game. It is a field game, a stick and ball game, but one whose history does not allow a concrete identification. The history of hurling demands wiggle-room for regional variants, substantial change over time and large gaps in knowledge. Accepted with such constraints, hurling is no longer a ghost, but it remains spectral.

Several comprehensive accounts of the broad history of hurling have been written over the last half-century. The largest is written in Irish and is astonishing in its breadth.[1] Those written in English are also commendable, and happily accessible to a much wider audience.[2] By necessity, and perhaps also by interest, these histories of hurling focus their attention on the sport's nearer past, primarily on the nineteenth and twentieth centuries. For the medieval and ancient periods historians have been quick to grant hurling an unquestioned popularity and frequency. In doing so they have rightly plumbed Ireland's rich corpus of medieval sources, but, as will be discussed, they have most often done so in translation. The result is a skewed report. The medieval Irish sources describe manifold contests and games, providing detail as to who played the games, with what equipment and where. Unfortunately, as much as the sources provide, collectively they remain rather silent on details a history of hurling needs to affirm an early existence. There is no doubt the modern game of hurling sprung from an earlier form. What remains uncertain, however, is just how far back that earlier form can be traced.

The following discussion highlights Ireland's range of early sources and the information they provide for the history of medieval and ancient field games, including, but not limited to, hurling. While there is little to be said definitively about the early history of hurling, there is much to be learned about early Irish field games in general. While hurling's ghost may elude us, there is still much to be seen.

The earliest reference to hurling, in this case 'horlinge', is found in the fourteenth-century Statutes of Kilkenny. The statutes, issued in 1366, outlined thirty-five acts passed to strengthen and secure Hiberno-Norman lordship in Ireland, a lordship in decline. The overall objective of the acts was to curb or prohibit 'native' Irish behaviour and tendencies. In relation to pastimes, the statutes banned several recreational activities, entertainments, performances and performers. Most notably, they took a firm stance against musical diversions and performances aimed at a Hiberno-Norman audience, including 'tympanours, pipers, story tellers, babblers, rhymers, harpers or any other Irish minstrels'. In terms of more active pursuits, 'horlinge' received specific mention, described as a game played 'with great clubs at ball upon the ground'. A justification of the ban was also added. Apart from the 'great evil and maims' incurred in the run of play, the game was seen to contribute to the weakening of the defence of the land, primarily by being a distraction and digression from more constructive physical pursuits such as archery and other 'gentlemanlike games'.[3]

Despite an obvious verbal connection, modern scholars have argued that the game the statutes deem 'horlinge' is not in fact a native one, and, consequently, not hurling. One such argument is based on two observations. Firstly, the 'ground game' of the statutes does not resemble the modern game of hurling, where movement of the ball is primarily in the air. Secondly, a provision in the considerably later Statutes of Galway, written in English and issued in 1527, also bans a stick and ball game, and with similar motivation and justification of the Kilkenny Statutes, but this time calling the game 'hockie'. The first argument presupposes early forms of hurling must have been played primarily in the air, which need not be the case. Among other possibilities, changes in the material of balls would prompt and favour increased air-play. The second argument assumes that the English term 'hockie' could not have been used in the sixteenth century to describe, or in fact merely stand for, a native Irish game, the same one that troubled fourteenth-century Kilkenny.

While very little description is provided for either 'horlinge' or 'hockie' as games, grounds for their mention in each of the respective statutes is clearly based on their popularity and appeal to Hiberno-Norman and 'native' Gaelic populations alike. The political and legal motivations behind both sets of statutes are conventional for a coloniser, namely to prohibit behaviour that tends to unify or foster solidarity among the colonised. The objectives behind the Kilkenny and Galway statutes therefore suggest that 'horlinge' and 'hockie' were in fact native games. At the very least, the games were clearly associated with the native Irish population and not that of Hiberno-Norman leadership. The games were moreover amusements that attracted and appealed to a mixed populace, and were seen to take attention and enthusiasm away from more valuable pursuits. Finally, the games were likely highly unregulated, prone to heady rivalries and generally troublesome for local authorities.

Unfortunately, there is no further definitive evidence for hurling contemporary to the two statutes. A medieval precursor to modern hurling must be sought after in physical and written evidence prior to the statutes. Such a search necessarily depends upon precision in translation, an awareness of literary and legal motivations, and a general lack of preconceived historical assumptions.

A search for the earliest evidence for field games in Ireland, particularly stick and ball games, also requires a glimpse eastward, to Britain, more specifically to Roman Britain. Ancient Romans played several stick and ball games. While all sections of Roman society enjoyed them, the games were in fact the special travel companions of the Roman army. Wherever Roman armies were posted the games were played, spread, and, most importantly, left behind.

Stick and ball games were current in Britain in the period of Roman occupation, starting in the mid-first century AD. Physical evidence suggests Britain's field games were in fact borrowed from the Roman world. Borrowing patterns are of course highly problematic. Popular games and activities are difficult to trace from one society or culture to the next, as lender and borrower invariably place their own unique stamp on what is exchanged. In relation to stick and ball games, this is compounded by the fact that the activity they share arises from a simple and universal impulse. It is human nature to strike an object with a stick. An impulse derived from a variety of means and moods; anger, boredom, competition and challenge, to name a few. Games and sports of every society and age have developed out of such an impulse. The universal nature of the activity then makes it difficult if not impossible to discern whether particular games were borrowed or were merely similar but culturally independent.

Several artefacts attest to the popularity of stick and ball games in Roman Britain. One such item, a small clay mould found in Northampton, dates to the second century AD. The mould depicts a figure holding a curved stick and what appear to be two balls, while a third ball is balanced on his knee.[4] While nothing can be said definitely on a proposed relationship between a stick and ball game from Roman Britain and a precursor to Irish hurling, the possibility of borrowing must be considered. Roman trade to Ireland was considerable. Much like soldiers, sailors and merchants were frequently the accidental vehicles of cultural exchange. Trade and contact between the two islands could easily have included the exchange of hockey or a game like it. The prospect that any Irish stick and ball game, including an early form of hurling, was borrowed from Britain can not be eliminated.

Unlike Britain, physical evidence for stick and ball games in ancient or medieval Ireland is lacking.[5] The search for the origins of hurling or its equivalent in Ireland depends solely on written evidence. Rather fortunately, Ireland's early sources are extensive, and impressive by any medieval scale. They survive from as early as the seventh century, before Viking, Norman or English influence, and boast a variety of genres including sagas, law, poetry, annals, chronicles and hagiography. The collection of medieval Irish sagas is especially large, with many stories and characters familiar to a modern audience. A considerable collection in themselves, the sagas represent only a fraction of what is a vast corpus of early sources.

The incredible wealth of historical detail locked inside the Irish legal sources is being slowly and methodically released. The information they provide stands to define, and substantially redefine, our understanding of the structure and scope of medieval Irish society. In the realm of games and sport, the laws provide especially helpful detail as to the participants, equipment, venues, injuries and strategy of early Irish amusements. Like all normative sources they most often provide information obliquely. Their picture of society is generally a photo negative, offering details as to what is not customary or accepted by society, rather than what is.[6]

Collectively, the Irish sources represent Europe's largest body of vernacular material for the early medieval period. In a surge of late nineteenth and early twentieth-century interest, the majority of texts were gathered and studied by a small group of dedicated scholars of Irish language and history. The group was spearheaded by Irish and German scholars who edited, translated and published the medieval material at a remarkable rate. Important to mention in this industrious undertaking is that the social and political atmosphere in which it was accomplished was the same nationalist atmosphere that prompted the formation of the Gaelic Athletic Association, and projects like it.

What this means to a study of hurling for the medieval period is that nineteenth- and twentieth-century translations of texts must often be re-evaluated. The atmosphere in which the texts were studied and translated necessarily prompted a heady blend of nostalgia and nationalism. With few exceptions, translations rendered otherwise simple and often unaccompanied terms for ball, stick, game, goal, or even hoop by the catch-all 'hurling'. This has inevitably led historians and fans alike to grant the sport of hurling an unassailable antiquity. By most accounts the game is taken to be the creation and pursuit of the pre-Christian Celts. Still others have suggested the game predates the Celtic arrival itself, stretching back into an even mistier era. There is no doubt the medieval and indeed ancient Irish sported and competed against one another. As any society, they invariably tossed and struck balls, tallied scores, contested rivalries and injured one another in the process. The sources tell us many things about the ways in which the early Irish sported and competed. What is once again left uncertain, however, is how far back the game of hurling, so recognisable in its modern structure, strategy and shape, takes us in the run of Irish history.

References to several different field games, including stick and ball games, are found throughout Ireland's early medieval source material. Clues as to the equipment and sometimes strategy of the games are offered in several legal texts composed in the language of Old Irish, allowing an existence as early as the seventh century. The saga literature likewise abounds with references to field games, and, as many of the surviving stories are clearly based on earlier written and oral versions, we can assume with reasonable confidence that the games themselves are considerably older than the texts in which they are found.

The most familiar saga to modern audiences is 'Táin Bó Cúailnge' ['The Cattle Raid of Cooley']. The story, surviving in several medieval versions, the oldest of which dates from the eighth century, outlines the extraordinary life and deeds of Ireland's epic hero Cúchulainn. While Cúchulainn is celebrated for many outstanding attributes, in modern sporting circles he is often considered Ireland's first great hurler. Whether or not the mythical hero's game is hurling, or a precursor to it, his knack for driving a ball with a stick earns him special recognition in Irish sports history.

The 'Táin' relates Cúchulainn's journey to a playing-field at Emain, modern Navan Fort, to challenge the boys of Ulster to a game. He brings with him a shield, a javelin, playing stick and ball. In the oldest surviving version of the story Cúchulainn's playing stick is deemed a *lorg áne*, literally 'driving-stick', while in a slightly later version he carries the more recognisable *cammán*.[7] *Cammán* of course survives in modern Irish as the term for hurley. Broken down, the term is a compound of *cam*, 'bent, crooked', and the diminutive suffix *án*, 'little'. Its meaning therefore aptly corresponds to its shape and function, namely a stick with small bend or crook. As attested by modern playing sticks, the shape remains the ideal choice for propelling a ball in play.[8] Modern sports such as field hockey, ice hockey, polo and indeed hurling support this.

A likely and readily available surrogate for a playing stick is the shepherd's staff. Medieval Ireland was dominated by agriculture. Sheep, cattle and pigs were herded and driven to and from nearby as well as outlying seasonal pastures. There is a natural development from the shepherd's crook to the playing stick. There is equally a natural suitability of stick and ball games to pastures, meadows and other landscapes suitable to grazing animals. Modern hockey derives its name from the Old French *hocquet*, 'shepherd's staff'. Similarly, lacrosse, the French term for the Native American game, takes its name from the shepherd's staff (*le crosse*) which resembled or doubled as a playing stick. Employing or replicating the shepherd's staff in stick and ball games is both a natural and universal consequence of both implement and environment.

Returning to the 'Táin', Cúchulainn sets out on his long and arduous journey and we are treated to his feats of dexterity and skill. His greatest trick involves striking the ball, throwing his stick after it to hit the ball again, tossing his javelin and running after all three to catch them before they hit the ground.[9] The description is a typical example of the frequent hyperbole applied to Cúchulainn's superhuman abilities. In this particular case, however, it is designed to foreshadow his impending success against the rival boys on the playing-field, and, by extension, against them later on the battlefield. For what it's worth, Cúchulainn's skilful use of the *cammán* suggests that it was customary to strike the ball into the air, rather than on the ground.

The *cammán* is mentioned elsewhere in the early medieval sources, lending further weight to its social frequency. An early legal tract lists the appropriate items a boy should be given upon entering fosterage. Among others, the son of a king is expected to have a *cammán* ornamented with bronze, while the son of a lord is expected to have a *cammán* ornamented with copper.[10] The bronze and copper are perhaps embellishments to emphasise and advertise the special privilege of the ruling class. Alternatively, they may represent structural enhancements to the playing sticks, as in the modern rings placed around the boss of the hurl for added strength and to prevent splitting. Regardless of the function of the added metals, or if in fact they can be believed, reference to the *cammán* as a customary possession of a foster-son points to its popular use. As a playing stick is required specifically for the sons of the ruling class, the reference may also hint to the role of the game as informal military training.

A further reference to the *cammán* in the legal material is found in a fragment concerning injuries and liability in field games. Concerning play with sticks and balls, the legal passage states that if a boy finds or takes a *cammán* which is not his own he is not charged with theft so long as he returns it.[11] In other words, the return of the *cammán* cancels out any offence or penalty. Such items were clearly valuable and players were responsible for providing their own equipment.

In terms of materials for medieval playing sticks, the most likely and certainly the most abundant was wood. Presumably nearly any type of wood was used as little more than a rod with a slight bend or boss at one end was needed. Native trees such as hazel, yew and willow are likely choices, as well as branches and trunks of hardy bush and scrub such as furze. Ash is mentioned in the medieval sources as a favoured choice for domestic implements and weapons. According to a law tract on farming, ash is preferred above all others for the 'half-material of a weapon', namely the spear shaft or handle.[12] The strengths and attributes of a spear's shaft would be the same as those required for a playing stick. The quasi-military nature of the stick and ball games may have added further natural parallels for its selection. Modern hurling sticks are made primarily of ash, still chosen for its strength and the straightness of its grain.

Balls are also often mentioned in the medieval sources, in a variety of games, tricks and amusements. While the materials for balls in medieval games is perhaps as predictable as that for sticks, the available evidence is less clear. A curious practice of removing the brains of slain opponents, mixing them with lime, and forming balls for use in games is a regular feature of the saga literature.[13] A modern reader no doubt hopes this is hyperbole. Human or animal brains mixed with lime would indeed harden to provide solid, if short-lived, playing pieces. As for more probable and durable substances, materials such as wood, leather and hair were likely used. Balls crafted mainly of woven cow or horse hair were used in Ireland from at least as early as the eighteenth century. The items were often considered gifts of favour from women to men.[14] In rural areas the balls were used into the twentieth century. The inherent craftsmanship and practicality of the woven balls suggest a long-standing folk tradition.

The settings for Irish medieval field games are varied and clear. Several references in the legal material mention games held on the neighbouring greens of a fort or enclosure. A passage from a law tract concerning negligence states that anyone who causes damage to property or injury to humans or animals from striking a ball on such a green is immune from prosecution, because all public greens are free.[15] In other words, enter, loiter or leave your things at your own risk. Similarly, a separate legal tract demands compensation for damage by small boys in driving balls outside the appropriate green.[16] A lengthy discussion of liability for balls landing outside the green is provided. Considerations include the necessary retrieval of the ball; permission to enter private property; permission to open any fence or gap in order to retrieve the ball; and care that any such barrier is once again secured.[18]

Assemblies and fairs were also frequent settings for field games. In 'The Pursuit of Diarmaid and Grainne' a 'driving contest' is arranged at a fair convened by the king of Ireland.[18] The participating sides must have been particularly numerous as the text states no one remained sitting in the assembly except the king, Fionn and Diarmaid. Field games at fairs were most often played on the established fair green. The laws specified the fair green as an inherent right of a territory, a right that is free and due to every individual.[19] The parameters of a proper fair green are described as the four fields adjacent to the chief residence.[20] In the case of the absence of recognisable fields, the fair green is described as encompassing land as far as the sound of a bell is heard.[21]

Playing greens and fields seem to have received a fair degree of upkeep, primarily for sporting contests, which included horse-racing. Specific and meticulous maintenance of a fair green was to be undertaken 'in the time of games'.[22] An amusing insight on the measure of the trimmed grass is offered in a rather colourful description of a dwarf. The passage states, or rather seems to complain, that the cropped grass of the green was so high it reached the thick of the dwarf's thigh.[23] The description implies a well-recognised and appreciated shortness of the grass upon a green. Properly manicured public greens would provide not only an optimum playing surface, but also reduce unnecessary injury.

References for field games at fairs often suggest that spectators were present. Gender-specific areas for spectators are suggested in a poem celebrating the large annual fair at Tailtiu. Emphasising the nobility and virtue of the famous fair, the poem states that men do not enter the seating area of the women, nor women the seating area of the men.[24] Spectators were not limited to field games at fairs. In the 'Táin', Conchobor, king of Ulster, is said to divide his day into thirds, spending the first third watching the feats and the 'drivings' of the boys on the green.[25] In a later tale, a driving game is arranged and won by Aedh, son of the king of Connacht, whose parents number among those gathered to watch.[26] Ample evidence for spectators at field games is offered in the legal material, primarily concerning potential involvement and injury. A passage from a tract on liability lists circumstances in which spectators must be compensated for injuries to them while watching the play.

A final setting for field games is that of strands. Interestingly, references to field games played on strands are limited to the later medieval period, mainly the fourteenth and fifteenth centuries. One such account describes particularly skilful play upon the broad beaches of Finntragha (modern Ventry, Co. Kerry).[27] The sweeping strands in the north-west of Ireland, as well as many along the Scottish coasts, have been and continue to be the sites of formal and informal athletics contests, particularly those like hurling which require flat, expansive areas. While strands are not specifically mentioned as playing-grounds elsewhere in the sources, it must be assumed their highly suitable physical features were commonly exploited as venues for field games.

Detailed evidence for the strategy of medieval field games would be the touchstone for determining whether or not hurling has the storied past it is so often granted. The likeliest contender for a precursor to modern hurling is the 'driving game', mentioned frequently in the saga texts though not in the legal material. What is known of the actual game of 'driving' is insufficient to identify it as hurling or suggest a continuum of the game from early Ireland to the present day. The difficulty lies not with a lack of evidence for strategy consistent with hurling, but rather an excess of detail which allows the game to be identified with a variety of pursuits. Examination of the evidence reveals several different potential field games, including ones both similar and distinct from hurling.

Naturally, it is also both difficult and dangerous to attempt to interpret strategy from limited description and obvious embellishment. This said, a modicum of reality can be safely assumed. A sufficient amount of any tale or account, of any age or time, must be comprehensible to the intended audience. As such, reference to a game, its strategy and its rules must ring true, especially when the details are creative filler, as they often are, and ineffectual to the overall theme.

The most informative passage for the strategy of an early Irish field game is found in the 'Táin'. The game pits Cúchulainn against the boys of Ulster, who are gathered on the king's own playing-field. The game is termed *cluichi puill*, 'the hole game', and is identified specifically as one which is played on the green at Emain. The game resembles a mix of modern soccer and golf as much as hurling or hockey. Cúchulainn stands at one end of the field defending a hole, into which the boys of Ulster attempt to cast or strike their 'thrice-fifty' balls. Predictably, Cúchulainn defends a perfect scorecard. When it is his turn to score, he unerringly sends each of the boys' own balls into the opposing hole.[28]

The passage has been used as evidence for the Irish invention of golf.[29] Beyond this rather far-fetched possibility, the description offers valuable specifics to differentiate the 'hole game' from other field games. A goal is clearly described, in this case a hole in the ground. The hole is guarded by a defender against balls either driven or thrown.

The 'hole game', or a game like it, finds further support in an early law text, once again discussing liability for injuries incurred in play.[30] The passage is unfortunately obscured by difficult idiom. Roughly paraphrased, the description suggests that a ball is struck at a defended hole, from which a defender can strike the ball away, ideally towards a 'free' dividing line. While admittedly cryptic, the passage suggests a playing-field with particular and recognised areas. The suggested 'dividing line' is attested elsewhere in the sources as a line or area of partition. It also indicates a boundary or tactical field line, and can perhaps be understood as mid-field, etc.[31]

A slightly different version of this passage is found as a fragment in a later legal manuscript. The strategy of the fragment is somewhat clearer. According to the brief account, a hole must be defended from balls being struck at it. Participants are free from liability for any injuries they cause in driving the ball around the hole or in driving balls away from the hole.[32] The legal conditions seem to indicate that injuries sustained in play outside of the area around the hole, or outside of the area where balls are driven, are actionable by the victim. Participants or spectators injured within the proscribed areas are not entitled to legal redress.

While the legal sources provide evidence for strategy through potential infractions and sanctions, the saga literature hints at strategy through descriptions of the skills and talents of its sporting heroes. A late medieval tale details the exploits of a 'foreigner' plying his skills upon a strand. The figure dons his best clothes, picks up a stick and ball and strikes the ball from one end of the beach to the other without letting it touch the ground. The story relates that such skill had not been seen since the times of Cúchulainn himself, or indeed the equally mythical Lug. The foreigner is not however satisfied with a single display. A series of later exploits paint him as a skilled footballer as well as a potential hurler. He is described as expertly juggling the ball upon his knee up and down the strand, capping off the impressive display by bouncing the ball from one shoulder to the other in one final length of the course.[33] The most noticeable and deliberate aspect of the foreigner's strategy and skill is that the ball is never allowed to touch the ground. The style of play emphasises keeping the ball aloft, offering further support for an association with hurling, support which is also undeniably different from the various forms of hockey, which aim to limit play to the ground.

A separate and seemingly distinct field game is played when Cúchulainn first joins the boys at Emain. The hero catches the ball between his two shins and, while numerous opponents attempt to knock it free, he carries the ball away from them and scores by carrying it across the goal.[34] The passage suggests the goal was a line or border to be crossed by a player, rather than an upright structure or hole for a ball to be thrown or struck into. As the ball is carried between his shins, it was perhaps not allowed to be played or touched by the hands.

The duration or completion of a field game is never stated. A curious disparity is found in evidence relating to scoring. When Cúchulainn successfully carries the ball over the goal, the boys promptly attack him. Such a response suggests that the game concluded after the goal. Later in the same episode, Cúchulainn once again gains a win by 'taking the goal'.[35] A victor in a separate saga tale reports he has secured victory by taking seven games from his opponents by scoring seven goals, suggesting each game concluded after a single goal.[36]

Elsewhere a 'driving contest' lasts an agonising three days and nights, as neither side is able to score a single goal against the other.[37] Earlier in the same story, however, the hero Diarmaid joins a game and is described as having 'won the goal' three times that day.[38] This may be a reference to a running score of goals or perhaps a reference to victory in each of three individual matches. A tally of scores is certainly the reckoning used in a game described in a later medieval text. The young Aedh mac Muiredach, son of the king of Connacht, scores six goals in a single match, without assistance from his peers. His victory came at a cost. He is described later in the tale as nearly dying from wounds he received on the field.[39]

The question as to who participated in the field games of medieval Ireland is the easiest to answer. As expected, young men and boys comprise the largest group of participants. Young heroes such as Fionn mac Cumhaill and Cúchulainn are the archetype of the skilled and athletic youth. Cúchulainn is able to single-handedly and repeatedly defeat his 150 opponents in at least two different games on the playing-field at Emain. Often reminiscent of Cúchulainn, Fionn mac Cumhaill excels in various contests and athletic events, characteristically while heavily outnumbered by his opponents. The young and equally heroic Mael Dún is said to best his opponents in all his play, including running, wrestling, putting stones and throwing and striking balls.[40]

A requisite for heroes is of course to stand out among their peers. The saga literature describes many contests of large numbers of players. Fixed and rounded numbers such as 100 and 150 are common, suggesting sides were made up of considerable numbers, or perhaps simply as many as showed up. A reference to girls competing in field games is included in such a description. In 'The Wooing of Etain', the king watches 150 girls at their daily games.[41] Girls at play are in fact mentioned infrequently in the saga literature. A singular reference in the 'Conception of Cú Chulainn' describes a girl considered the champion of all the girls of Ireland.[42]

Evidence found in the early legal material reinforces the literary portrayal of field games as the particular pursuit of young boys. As discussed, a son must be provided with a *cammán* upon entering fosterage, suggesting that stick and ball games were a customary and expected activity of children throughout their period of fosterage, generally 7–14 years of age. This finds further support in a legal heptad listing blood shed by boys in games as one of seven types of injuries that cannot be prosecuted.[43] Its inclusion in the list, among more adult concerns such as blood shed in battle, blood shed by a physician and blood shed by a jealous wife, verifies the popularity and social currency of the games, as well as the expected violence of the activity.

Adult men of course also played field games. As discussed, games were a particular entertainment at assemblies and fairs, where they are described as being played exclusively by men. Men are also the primary concern of the medieval legal material in relation to liability in field games, liability most often concerned with injuries, their prosecution and compensation.

A final aspect of field games to be noted in relation to the sources is that they are often mentioned in religious contexts. In the 'Life of Maedoc of Ferns', a boy fresh from the playing-field, where he had been 'playing and driving', graciously opens and closes the gate for the bishop, who promptly chooses the boy as his successor.[44] This is as generous as the texts get as regards the games. In a separate, slightly alarming hagiographical episode, St Féchín of Fore is disturbed at his prayers by the noise of children 'driving' on the nearby green. Frustrated, the saint approaches the boys, telling them to go and drown themselves in the lake, whereupon their souls will be free to ascend to heaven.[45] The exchange occurs among Féchín's more saintly activities and seems to underscore a concerted and, it must be said, quite frank opinion by the clergy of such frivolity and sport.

In a later work, a fifteenth-century Irish translation of the 'Life of Gregory', the young Gregory strikes a playmate on the shin with his *cammán* while 'playing and driving'.[46] The reference is undoubtedly a deliberate substitution by the translator to add national flavour to the tale. St Columba is also remembered in connection with the sporting sphere. In his sixteenth-century Irish 'Life', the saint demands reciprocity for a boy killed in a game by a blow from a *cammán*.[47] Like the episode in the Gregory's 'Life', the event is likely included for national appeal, to enhance and authenticate the saint's 'native' connection.

There are countless remaining references to field games in Ireland's medieval sources, all attesting to the popularity and frequency of the various activities and contests. The examples discussed above are simply those which illuminate aspects helpful to a broader understanding of the games, their participants, structure and strategies. The medieval period is very well represented in terms of available sources, and field games themselves find special and repeated mention in them. A critical examination of the terms and descriptions of early field games demonstrates there is no reason or justification to limit the discussion of the games to hurling or its precursor. The fact that this has largely been the case in the established historiography is a reflection of modern sentiment rather than medieval reality.

1. This 1970 photograph shows Foireann na Gaeltachta from Conamara. The players are: *front row (left to right)* Al Ó Conghaile (An Spidéal), Tommy Keaney (Carna), Pádraic Corbett (Captaen) (Carna), Pádraic Kelly (An Cheathrú Rua), Pádraic Ó Conghaile (Leitir Mór/Naomh Anna), Máirtín Ó Flathartha (Leitir Mór/Naomh Anna), Micheál Breathnach (Leitir Mór), Micheál Tom Folan (Leitir Mór); *back row (left to right):* Christy Scanlon (Micheál Breathnach), Conor O'Malley (Leitir Mór), Frank Ned Ó Finneadh (Micheál Breathnach), Nioclás Ó Conchubhair (Leitir Mór/Naomh Anna), Joe Keane (Carna), Mícheál Tim Ó Conghaile (Micheál Breathnach), Máirtín Ó Conghaile (An Spidéal), Joe Lydon (Carna); missing from photograph: Seáinín Ó Conghaile (Leitir Mór/Naomh Anna), Patsy McDermott (Micheál Breathnach), Maitiú Ó Domhnaill (An Cheathrú Rua), Johnny Mulkerrins (Carna). The photograph and names were supplied by Máire Áine beran Uí Choirbín, Carna.

2 Riotous Proceedings and the Cricket of Savages: Football and Hurling in Early Modern Ireland

EOIN KINSELLA

The term 'Gaelic games' is generally understood to refer to those games that are unique to Irish heritage and are administered by the GAA – hurling, Gaelic football and camogie. In an early modern context, the term is somewhat anachronistic. Camogie was not established as a sport until 1904.[1] Gaelic football was not a distinctly Irish game until the structure and rules imposed on it by the GAA in the 1880s distinguished it as such. Hurling stands apart, with an Irish heritage that can be traced back to pre-Christian times. Although, as A. B. Gleason shows in Chapter 1, this is a matter of considerable complexity. Stick-and-ball games were not, of course, unique to Ireland – a stick-and-ball game was played in Greece as long ago as the fifth century BC (though we have no information as to rules or playing styles), while the earliest styles of hurling in Ireland bore a strong resemblance to the game of *camanachd* or shinty in Scotland. Under the GAA, hurling also benefited from the Victorian trend towards codifying playing rules. Unlike football, however, hurling had developed characteristics that were unique to Ireland at least as early as the seventeenth century.

Sport across Europe in early modern times tended to be the preserve of the lower classes, whereas, for obvious reasons relating to the literacy of the population, written records for the period largely focus on the upper echelons of society. As a result, sources for the history of hurling and football before the eighteenth century are generally scarce. During the sixteenth and seventeenth centuries, references to both games are sporadic at best, usually found in early statutes and Irish poetry. From the mid-eighteenth century onwards, however, an increase in sports patronage by the upper classes, a surge in printed social commentary and the proliferation of newspapers allows a clearer picture of the two games to emerge.

FOOTBALL

And now the bands in close embraces met,
Now foot to foot, now breast to breast was set;
Now all impatient grapple round the ball,
And heaps on heaps in wild disorder fall.[2]

The history of football in Ireland is difficult to trace. Its anarchic nature, along with the perception that it was a less skilful or exciting game than hurling, generally dissuaded poets and commentators alike from writing about football. It has been contended that football was introduced to Ireland sometime during the seventeenth century.[3] This assertion, however, dismisses evidence provided by a statute passed by the corporation of Galway in 1527, which outlawed hurling but allowed the playing of football to continue.[4] 'Folk' or 'traditional' football had been played in Britain since at least medieval times, and it is reasonable to assume that the game spread to Ireland long before the seventeenth century.[5] Séamas Dall Mac Cuarta's poem *Iomáin na Bóinne*, written in the late seventeeth century, recounted a match of football played on the banks of the Boyne – *iomán* is more commonly used to refer to hurling, but in this case football is the subject. John Dunton, a prominent London bookseller during the 1690s, wrote in 1699 that '[The Irish] do not play often at football, only in a small territory called Fingal near Dublin the people use it much, and trip and shoulder very handsomely. These people are reckoned the best wrestlers of the Irish.'[6] Though obviously popular, football was by no means the only sport played by the people of Fingal.[7] Dunton was wrong in his assertion that football was confined to Fingal, but it seems that it was not as widely played across the country as hurling. In the eighteenth century, football was certainly played in Dublin, Kildare, Louth and Meath. Football matches were often played 'cross country' between parishes. With the ball 'thrown in' at the boundary of both parishes, victory was claimed by the team that carried the ball all the way to the centre of the opposition's parish, presumably denoted by a church or some such landmark. Other versions of the game were similar in structure to hurling, with the object being to score a goal, usually achieved by forcing the ball through a specially constructed target, as depicted in *Iomáin na Bóinne*. Football games were physical contests, often stopped to accommodate bouts of wrestling.[8] Gaelic football shares a common ancestry with 'traditional' football, the game that spawned soccer, rugby league and rugby union. In their early format, football matches in Britain and Ireland often resembled 'rolling rucks' or melees.

One of the earliest and most comprehensive descriptions of an Irish football match is found in a poem written by Matthew Concanen, first published in 1720. Concanen was born in Ireland and later trained as a lawyer, but beyond that not much else is known of his early life. In 1722 he travelled to England where he wrote and edited poetry collections, attracting ridicule from both Alexander Pope and Jonathan Swift.[9] Following his move to London, Concanen showed very little interest in Irish affairs, so it is fortunate that one of his earliest publications sheds some light on the nature of an Irish football match. The style of *A match at football* is that of burlesque and owes a debt to the poetry of Alexander Pope.[10] It follows the tradition of Homeric epic poetry by insinuating the gods into the action at pivotal points to alter the flow of the game and decide its outcome. The match took place at Swords in north county Dublin, between the baronies of Swords and Lusk. A large crowd waited impatiently for the match to begin, while their appetites were whetted by preliminary games, including 'country lasses' dancing in competition for cakes.[11]

The playing-field is described as a 'wide extent of level ground, which spreading groves and rising hillocks bound'. The goals were a simple yet effective design: 'The goals are formed by sticking two willow twigs in the ground, at a small distance, and twisting the tops, so they seem a gate.' As for the football, it was made from three pieces of leather stuffed with hay, held together by leather thongs.[12] Concanen depicts two teams of just six players each, yet this seems to be a concession to his desire to provide a miniature biography for each of the players. It is almost certainly not reflective of the reality of football matches played at this time. Organised matches such as that described by Concanen may have limited numbers, but in general football matches appear to have been played by large numbers and with less structure. Concanen notes that each team's players were distinguished by coloured ribbons: red for Swords and blue for Lusk. Throwing of the ball was permitted, as was kicking. The tackle does not appear to have had many limitations, with pulling, pushing and tripping allowed. Tripping or 'hacking' was a prized feature of football in Ireland (as well as England) before it was outlawed in the Irish game by the GAA. One-on-one wrestling matches for possession of the ball are described. If the ball crossed either end line without passing through the goal, each team changed ends: 'This is done, to prevent the sun, or wind's, being for any time of either side.'[13] In this particular instance, the game was decided when a goal was scored by the Swords team.

The description offered by Concanen more closely resembles rugby than modern Gaelic football, particularly in the tackle. The match between Swords and Lusk was obviously played within a defined boundary. When the game was not confined to such boundaries, it proved to be a nuisance, particularly when played in urban areas.

Concanen's match of football passed off peacefully and without any outbreak of violence or faction fighting. The description he offers suggests a well-organised game, with entertainment provided for the spectators, making for a pleasant evening's diversion. Other sources, however, paint a less than flattering picture of football, suggesting an anarchic game with few rules and much bloodshed. Newspaper reports from the latter half of the eighteenth century portray a game with little cohesion, prone to the destruction of property and peppered with frequent outbreaks of violence. *Sleator's Public Gazetteer* reported that 'a riot happened near Finglas Bridge among a parcel of fellows playing football, in which one of them had his skull fractured and his nose partly cut off'.[14] In February 1789, a match was played at the foot of the Three Rock mountains (near Sandyford, south Dublin) 'between a party of mountaineers and the neighbours of the adjacent valley'. A 'degenerate quarrel' broke out among the players, leading to much 'bloodshed and battery'.[15] The word 'riot' appears in many descriptions of football matches. Accordingly, local militia or army regiments were occasionally called in to break up matches in order to preserve the peace. Members of the 55th regiment of foot soldiers were despatched to Drumcondra (Dublin) in April 1774 'to disperse a riotous mob who weekly assemble there to play football'.[16] Similar steps were necessary after the destruction of fences and hedges in the fields near the Gallows Road (present-day Baggot Street, Dublin) during a football match in 1754. 'A stop was put to their riotous proceedings by the arrival of a guard of soldiers and a posse of constables.'[17] Attempts to prevent football matches getting started could also prove troublesome:

> Yesterday evening a fellow well known in the neighbourhood of Dorset Street by the name of 'Clubby', being placed in a field near Eccles Street by Justice Graham, to prevent idle disorderly persons from playing at football, shot an innocent man, a baker from Church Street, with a blunderbuss. The delinquent was committed to Newgate [prison].[18]

There has long been a connection drawn between sporting activity and violence.[19] It may well have been the case that among the football-playing population, a level of aggression that would be distasteful to modern sensibilities was accepted and even encouraged. Such violence has been labelled 'expressive' or 'recreational' violence, lacking a specific goal or rationale, and not restricted to football.[20] The evidence provided above of the turbulence associated with football matches certainly suggests that most disorder was localised and lacking any sort of political or social agenda.

In the nineteenth century football appears to have suffered from the social devastation of the Famine to the same extent as hurling. Football does not appear to have been widespread outside of Leinster. Even so, in counties such as Westmeath, where cricket was the dominant sport by the mid-nineteenth century, football needed the intervention of the GAA to re-establish its popularity.[21]

HURLING

> The lusty youths advance in equal rows,
> Each parent's breast with blushing transport glows,
> Silk kerchiefs bind their close compacted hairs,
> Each strong nerved hand a polished hurley bears.[22]

The game of hurling in Ireland has a long history and is more richly represented in literature during the early modern period than football. The comparison is, however, relative. It is not possible to definitively trace the development of the game up to the late nineteenth century. A stick-and-ball sport, known variously as *iomáin*, hurling, 'common' (from *camán*) or 'shinny' has been present in Ireland since at least the seventh century. Mythology recounts that a form of hurling was played by the *Fir Bolg* and the *Tuatha Dé Dannan* as early as the twelfth century BC, while the legend of Cúchulainn includes mention of his prowess as a hurler.[23] Stick-and-ball games were not, however, unique to Ireland, and hurling, up until the seventeenth century, more closely resembled modern Scottish shinty than the game that is played today. It was largely a winter sport, often played around Christmas time.[24] From the seventeenth century, a summer variant developed in the south and east of the country, with broader-bossed hurleys, a lighter ball and more aerial play than was common in winter hurling.

One of the earliest written records for hurling is found in clause six of the Statutes of Kilkenny, enacted in 1366. It stated:

> Whereas a land which is at war requires that every person
> do render himself able to defend himself, it is ordained

and established that the commons of the said land of
Ireland, who are in divers marches of war, use not henceforth the games which men call hurlings with great clubs
of a ball on the ground, from which great evils and
maims have arisen.

The statute went on to insist that archery and use of the lance were
more suitable recreations, 'whereby the Irish enemies may be better
checked'. As might be gathered from the wording of the Statutes of
Kilkenny, they were not intended to apply to the Gaelic Irish population. They were, in fact, aimed at the Hiberno-Norman settlers
who had begun to adopt the customs of the native Irish. The statutes
were intended to arrest this 'decline' in the morality and homogene-
ity of the ruling class, the better to protect the integrity of the English
monarch's rule. Among the other provisions of the Statutes of
Kilkenny were those that prevented marriage with the Irish, fostering of their children or use of the Brehon laws.

A further attempt to limit the playing of hurling was made in
Galway in 1527. The corporation of Galway enacted a statute similar in tenor to the Statutes of Kilkenny:

It is ordered, enacted and statuted that whatsoever man
is found, of what degree or condition so ever he be of,
playing at quoits or stones, but only to shoot in long
bows, short crossbows and hurling of darts or spears, to
lose at every time so found in doing the same, eight
pence and also at no time to use the hurling of the little
ball with hockey sticks or staves, nor use no handball to
play without the walls, but only the great football, on
pain of the pains above limited.[25]

It is not clear what the motivation for this statute was. Possibly it was
intended to eradicate a nuisance to the corporation, as team sports were
often disruptive to daily life and to business. However, the exemption
granted to football would seem to counter such an interpretation. In
contrast to the Statutes of Kilkenny, which were enacted by parliament
to cover the whole country, the statute passed in Galway was a local
one. It is doubtful whether there was much authority to enforce the
statute outside of the confines of Galway town. The statute may well
have been successful in removing hurling from within the boundaries of
the town, but the game continued to be played in Galway county.

The vibrancy of hurling throughout Ireland was again attested to
when the Irish parliament passed legislation in 1695 seeking to outlaw
sporting activity on Sundays. The Sunday Observance Act became

law on 7 December 1695, seeking to preserve the sanctity of the Lord's Day. The act sought to prevent any form of labour or trade being undertaken on Sundays, with the exception of works of charity. In addition, certain sports were identified as 'disorders and breaches of the peace ... by reason of tumultuous and disorderly meetings, which have been, and frequently are used on the Lord's day, under pretence of hurling, commoning, football playing, cudgels, wrestling or other sports'. The penalty for failure to adhere to the new law was a fine of up to 20 shillings or a period of two hours in the stocks.[26] The year 1695 marked the beginning of a difficult time for Irish Catholics, as the Irish parliament passed the first of the penal laws. However, the Sunday Observance Act does not belong in the same category, though Catholics made up the majority of the playing population. Similar acts had previously been passed in England, while the Irish act was complemented by legislation designed to suppress 'profane cursing and swearing'.[27]

From this point, hurling escaped official censure. As the game progressed through the eighteenth and nineteenth centuries, it does not appear to have been as disruptive a game as football, thus escaping some of the criticism and repression that football was subjected to. In this respect, it was probably aided by the fact that it was generally played in rural areas, away from the centres of commerce and government, thus minimising any chance of becoming a disruptive force. The Statutes of Kilkenny, while representing an attempt to eradicate hurling among a specific section of Irish society, did not set out to wholly suppress the game. In fact, at no stage in Irish history does hurling appear to have been subjected to outright repression, as were some of the popular games of the early modern period. Unlike sports that were later outlawed, such as cock fighting and bear baiting, the only injuries that hurling inflicted were on its human participants.

Writing in 1841, Mr and Mrs S.C. Hall gave a glowing description of hurling as

> A fine, manly exercise, with sufficient danger to produce excitement; and is indeed, par excellence, *the* game of the peasantry of Ireland. To be an expert hurler, a man must possess athletic powers of no ordinary character; he must have a quick eye, a ready hand, and a strong arm; he must be a good runner, skilful wrestler, and withal patient as well as resolute.[28]

Descriptions of hurling are quite common in the literature of the early nineteenth century, though they generally tend to describe summer hurling. The seventeenth and eighteenth centuries are not so well served, with the result that it is not possible to trace how the game may have developed over the centuries. It is likely that there was very little variation in the general style of play: two teams from anywhere between 10 and sometimes as many as 100 men or more faced off against each other, with the object being to score a goal. Often, a single goal decided the outcome of a match, which could last all day. The method of scoring a goal appears to have varied between driving the ball through a specially created goal (usually the branch of a supple tree such as willow, with both ends stuck into the ground to create an archway), through a gap in a hedge or wall, or even into a ditch at either end of the field of play.[29]

The type of *sliotar* used varied between the two styles of play. Winter hurling favoured a small wooden *sliotar*, while summer hurling used a more malleable *sliotar* of animal hair, sometimes covered in leather.[30] The prevalence of winter hurling in the west and north of the country, coupled with the season in which it was played, probably made the use of a wooden and consequently drier *sliotar* preferable. Conversely, summer hurling allowed the development of a softer *sliotar*, with reduced stress on water resistance. The softer *sliotar* was also less dangerous to the health of players. An account of winter hurling in pre-Famine Leitrim, where the ball was made of bog-oak, noted that 'a stroke from [the ball] was as bad as a bullet'.[31] A number of summer hurling *sliotars* have been unearthed in Irish bogs. They consist of a core of animal hair, tightly compacted, and ringed with braided strands of horse tail or mane hair to provide a firm covering and to keep the integrity of the ball intact. These balls appear to have been particularly common in the south of the country. All of the surviving hair *sliotars* that have been found would appear to date from the mid-seventeenth century, while small wooden balls have been unearthed in Galway and Donegal.[32] John Dunton provides a description of how these *sliotars* were made: 'When their cows are casting their hair, they pull it off their backs and with their hands work it into large balls.'[33] There is also evidence for a leather-covered wooden ball in use in Wexford at the end of the nineteenth century.[34] Size and weight of course varied across the country, with the surviving hair *sliotars* ranging from 5 to 8 cm in diameter. Writing about a game of hurling in Wexford in 1817, Patrick Kennedy referred to the *sliotar* weighing three pounds.[35]

The design of hurleys also differed between the two styles of hurling. Winter hurleys were usually thin, with a narrow crooked boss, similar to modern shinty or hockey:

> Amongst [young people's] other amusements, the game
> of shinny, as it is called by some, and common by others,
> is worthy of note. Common is derived from a Celtic
> word 'com',[36] which signified 'crooked', as it is played
> with a stick bent at its lower extremity somewhat like a
> reaping hook. The ball, which is struck to and fro, in
> which the whole amusement consists, is called nag, or in
> Irish brig. It resembles the game called golf in
> Edinburgh.[37]

The Halls's description of summer hurling conveys a somewhat different game:

> The ball must not be taken from the ground by the hand;
> and the tact and skill shown by taking it on the point of
> the hurley, and running with it half the length of the
> field, and when too closely pressed, striking it towards
> the goal, is a matter of astonishment to those who are
> but slightly acquainted with the play.[38]

Summer hurling favoured the use of a hurley with a broader boss, which allowed the ball to be carried, similar to the modern game. This development appears to have occurred at some point in the seventeenth century. Dunton described hurleys as approximately three and a half feet in length, with a boss of three inches in width, while over a century and a half later John O'Hanlon noted that hurleys were 'generally made of seasoned ash, thus combining the qualities of endurance and lightness. The handle was smoothly fashioned and round; the extremity of the common was crooked and flattened on both sides.'[39] Ash was not the only wood used for hurleys; the use of furze, whitethorn, crabtree, hazel, holly, sally and bog-deal has also been recorded.[40]

Dunton also provides one of the few detailed descriptions of summer hurling from the seventeenth century. His account states that often 2,000 or more spectators were attracted to hurling matches: 'Their champions are of the younger and most active among them, and their kindred and mistresses are frequently spectators of their address.' Dunton predates the Halls by 150 years in describing the *sliotar* being carried on the hurley before being struck forward, noting that 'sometimes if he miss his blow at the ball he knocks one of the opposers down, at which no resentment is to be shown. They seldom come off without broken heads or shins, in which they glory very much.'[41] There is no doubt that the game was very physical. A nineteenth-century commentator noted that 'Hurling is the national game

2. A match between two unknown teams in Croke Park in the 1920s.

of Ireland, and is much practised in the southern and western counties ... the "melee" of a hurling match has rather the appearance of hostile encounter than rustic sport and is therefore better adapted to the rude and martial people who practise it than the more scientific but less exciting game of cricket.'[42] Patrick Kennedy wrote of the type of hurling practised in Wexford in 1817. The reader is left in no doubt as to the physicality of the game, though it was generally played in a sporting manner: 'Now and then [the hurley] comes into contact with heads reasonably hard, with shoulders, sides and legs; and if any inactive town dweller asks me why someone is not killed or disabled for life ... country boys [not having doctors and hospitals] could not afford to lie under hurts.'[43] The Halls make mention of men grappling and wrestling in an attempt to reach the ball first, 'neither victor nor vanquished waiting to take breath, but following the course of the rolling and flying prize'.[44] Due to the large numbers that were generally on the field at one time, space was at a premium. Kennedy gives us the following depiction: 'The whole field seems inextricably interwoven, and short strokes and pushes are all that can be made; and they charge with their shoulders, each against the nearest opponent.'[45]

Hurling was evidently a fast, exciting and physical game, yet it does not appear to have had anything like the same frequency of violence as football. The reasons for this can only be guessed at – perhaps the actual presence of potential weapons on the field of play encouraged restraint, or the speed of play in general prevented prolonged wrestling matches, which had potential to escalate into something more serious. Unlike football, hurling was usually played within a fixed boundary – though cross-country hurling was not unknown. Consequently, it proved the perfect sport for attracting spectators, a feature that helps explain why the eighteenth century is sometimes referred to as the 'golden age' of hurling.[46]

The patronage of the Irish gentry was a feature of hurling in the eighteenth century, though this patronage was exclusively aimed at summer hurling. It was also the century in which newspapers became a regular feature of Irish life, allowing for prior advertisements of hurling matches. Local folklore in Tipperary holds that one of the Barons Purcell, in the eighteenth century, kept a team of hurlers to challenge neighbouring parishes. One of his hurlers was famed for his ability to strike the *sliotar* over Loughmoe Castle and race around to catch the ball on the hurley before it hit the ground and return it to the other side, repeating the feat nine times in all.[47] There is ample evidence in newspapers of the eighteenth century for this type of patronage, though unfortunately we are rarely informed who the patrons were. Food and drink was regularly supplied for the refreshment of players and spectators alike. Sums of money were frequently mentioned in newspaper advertisements for the victors of games of hurling, ranging anywhere from 20 to 300 guineas. A typical advertisement is found in the *Cork Evening Post*: 'A bet of 300 guineas, and a ball at night for the ladies, to be hurled for, by 21 married men and 21 bachelors, on the Green of Ardfinnan in the county of Tipperary. None admitted to play but gentlemen of baronies of Iffa and Offa in the said county'.[48] According to Richard Holt, contests between married and unmarried men were 'a very important part of the festive life of a society'.[49] Matches between married men and bachelors were frequently organised throughout the eighteenth century, and in all probability long beforehand.

Inter-county hurling matches were also a feature of the eighteenth century, and are likely an innovation spurred by patronage. Kilkenny, Tipperary, Dublin, Meath, Kerry and Kildare are all recorded as having played matches against each other.[50] The method of selecting teams, however, is unknown, though it is likely that it was done by the patrons of the match.[51] Inter-parish or inter-barony matches were also recorded, suggesting that a solid tradition underpinned the GAA's decision to organise competitions along parochial and inter-county lines.[52] Inter-provincial matches were also not uncommon. In particular, there appears to have been a keen rivalry between Leinster and Munster from the mid-eighteenth century. Twenty men from each province played against each other at Crumlin Commons (Dublin) in May 1748, with Leinster emerging victorious. Two weeks later a return match was again staged at Crumlin (possibly with the same participants), with Leinster proving too strong for Munster for the second time.[53] One account notes that Munster 'made their utmost efforts to retrieve their honour; but all to no purpose'. The following verse appends the report:

> Munster powers, in vain, 'gainst East unite,
> The South is doomed to tread the Northern Flight,
> Gallea to Britain quits the glorious field,
> To Leinster, Munster ever forced to yield.[54]

A year later the two teams played out a stalemate, nightfall forcing the suspension of hostilities.[55] No further record of a match between the two provinces is found until 1768. *Finn's Leinster Journal* reported that 'the grandest match that ever was hurled in Ireland was played ... between the provinces of Leinster and Munster for 68 guineas ... near Urlingford.'[56] Unfortunately, the outcome is unknown. The rivalry was due to be revived again in 1792, on this occasion at the Fifteen Acres in the Phoenix Park. Munster were to be strengthened with the addition of the pick of Connacht, for the prize of 100 guineas.[57]

For all of its athleticism and crowd-pulling attractiveness, hurling could also be a hazardous game. Early Brehon laws included the right to claim compensation for injuries sustained during hurling matches, suggesting they were a common occurrence.[58] The Halls noted that '[Hurling] is often attended with dangerous, and sometimes fatal, results.'[59] Eighteenth-century newspapers bear out the truth of the Halls' assertion. Thomas and John Clarkson of Co. Laois were due to stand trial for the killing of a man during a hurling match in 1755.[60] It is not clear whether the death was a result of an accidental blow or from more sinister play. A tragic story is recounted in the *Hibernian Journal*: during a hurling match near Dundrum, Co. Tipperary, a man was instantly killed after receiving an unintentional strike from his own brother.[61] At Gowran, Co. Kilkenny, a row broke out during a hurling match in July 1768. In the ensuing melee, one Anthony Langford's skull was fractured. He was taken to hospital, 'with little hopes of his recovery'.[62]

These tragedies aside, it was not uncommon for newspaper reports to be glowing in their praise for hurling. Players were described as 'the most superior and elegant players in Europe', with one newspaper declaring: 'there is not, perhaps, a country in the world that could make a more striking display of the agility that was exhibited on this occasion'.[63] Not all, however, were enamoured with the sport. Criticism was usually based around the fact that it was played on the Sabbath, reflecting the growing move towards Sabbatarianism in the latter half of the eighteenth century.[64] Arthur Young, having encountered the game during his time in Ireland in the 1770s, dismissed hurling as 'the cricket of savages'.[65] Some early nineteenth-century commentators, while expressing grudging admiration for the game, deplored the socialising that occurred before and after hurling matches.[66]

In the nineteenth century, hurling became a symbol of Irish nationalism. Fostered by perceptions of its antiquity, the game was viewed by many as a unique and superior expression of Irish culture. At the funeral of Charles Stewart Parnell in October 1891, 2,000 men paraded with hurleys draped in black.[67] It is worth exploring the extent, if at all, to which hurling in Ireland prior to the nineteenth century was connected with popular opposition to English/British rule in Ireland.

The Statutes of Kilkenny drew an explicit correlation between incivility and hurling, yet attempted only to ban the game among the ruling class. There is no suggestion that hurling was at that time viewed as a threat to law and order. Indeed, the propensity of the Hiberno-Normans to participate in the game suggests that it represented a common ground between native and newcomer. Similarly, the Galway statute of 1527 does not suggest that hurling was associated with civil unrest or political agitation.

One of the first parallels drawn between hurling and seditious activity among the populace was made in June 1666 by Roger Boyle, earl of Orrery. Writing to an unidentified recipient, Boyle expressed his concern regarding recent large gatherings of Catholics:

> I hear out of Tipperary, that there is a view taken of Irish Papists, and several are enlisted, both horse and foot, and are buying arms and fixing old ones. Since the enlisting,

the priests have had great meetings, one at Knockgraffan of about 800 men, whereof many armed. Their pretence was for consecrating a priest. Another great meeting in Clanwilliam, on the edge of Kilnamanagh, under pretence of a match at hurling.[68]

Tensions between the Catholic and Protestant communities in Ireland rose throughout the seventeenth century, exacerbated by the Catholic-led rebellion of 1641. Allegations of horrific massacres of Protestants by Catholics during the civil war became part of the folklore of Protestant Ireland, to the extent that any gathering of large numbers of Catholics came to be viewed with suspicion. The defeat of the rebellion, followed by the Cromwellian land settlement, had secured political and land-owning dominance for Irish Protestants. As a minority of the population, Irish Protestants were uncomfortable with any assembly of Catholics, for fear that a further uprising was planned. The playing of hurling matches, attended by large crowds, evidently tapped into that fear.

Though the total conquest of Ireland was emphatically achieved with the defeat of James II's army in 1691, Irish Protestants continued to be wary of Catholic rebellion well beyond that date, retaining a watchful eye on the activity of the Catholic population.[69] Sporadic threats of invasion from France ensured that any suspicious activity was closely monitored. In 1726 concern was raised in Dublin about the possibility of Irishmen leaving to join the army of France. In giving evidence, Owen Sweeney, a native of Cork, swore that he had been present at a meeting at the house of Charles McCarthy, where men were persuaded to enlist in the French army. Sweeney also declared:

> There was a great assembly on 24 June to play at Hurley which this examinant believes was contrived on purpose to bring persons together in order to be enlisted and the rather for that there had not been any hurleying suffered by the said Charles McCarthy on his lands … since his turning or pretending to turn Protestant.[70]

Sweeney implied that Charles McCarthy was one of the leaders of this illegal recruitment. The information provided by Sweeney sheds invaluable light on some of the social conditions that faced the Catholic population. Between 1691 and 1709 a series of laws aimed at the Catholic population, commonly known as the penal laws, were enacted by the Irish and English parliaments which dramatically reduced employment opportunities for educated Catholics. Employment in civil or national government and as a lawyer was restricted to those willing to take a public oath repudiating the doctrine of transubstantiation, in addition to denying the spiritual authority of the Pope.[71] One method of circumventing these restrictions was conformity to the Church of Ireland, a step not lightly taken in the eighteenth century. Catholic converts were often regarded as opportunists, whose commitment to their new faith was less than steadfast. McCarthy had conformed in 1718, and Sweeney's information suggests that McCarthy distanced himself from hurling in an attempt to boost his Protestant credentials.[72] Later in the century, a correspondent to the *Freeman's Journal* drew a direct parallel between the playing of hurling and the Whiteboy movement – an agrarian protest that agitated for tenant farmers' rights, often using violent methods.[73] This same correspondent had some years earlier offered the following judgement on the game of hurling:

> [It is a] scene of drunkenness, blasphemy, and all kinds and manner of debauchery, and faith for my part, I could liken it to nothing else but the idea I form of the Stygian regions, where the demonic inhabitants delight in torturing and afflicting each other.[74]

The explicit connection of hurling to the Whiteboy movement was undoubtedly exaggerated, but can be seen as a further example of Protestant fears of large crowds of Irish Catholics.

It was in the nineteenth century that hurling, and specifically the hurley, became loosely associated with Catholic political agitation and support for Irish nationalism, both cultural and political. The foundation of the GAA and the efforts of Michael Cusack in particular had much to do with this in the later nineteenth century. The seeds were, however, already present. In the 1830s opposition was raised to the tradition of paying tithes to the Church of Ireland. As a part of the wider movement to secure Catholic Emancipation, opposition to the tithe was strong in many parts of the country. In Kilkenny, a large crowd of 'tithe hurlers' (protestors carrying hurleys) was observed at a political meeting near Castlecomer. Many of the meetings of protestors took place under the guise of hurling matches, a practice that was soon suppressed by the authorities.[75] Elsewhere, a Church of Ireland clergyman was prompted to write that 'a meeting of hurlers, persons unconnected with the parish, assembled at my house and I would not submit to their intimidation'.[76]

It would be inaccurate to ascribe a directly political character to the game of hurling during the early modern period. As tensions among the Catholic and Protestant communities in Ireland rose from the seventeenth century onwards, large meetings of Catholics were considered dangerous and closely monitored. It is entirely possible that hurling matches were used as a cover for political activity prior to the nineteenth century, but from the newspaper reports of the eighteenth century it is apparent that the vast majority of these games carried no political undertones. The nineteenth century saw a burgeoning popular movement for expanded political and social rights for Catholics. This occasionally spilled over into violent protest, for which hurleys probably served as a readily available and easily hidden weapon.

Hurling was a popular sport in Ireland for much of the early modern period. During the eighteenth century it attracted the patronage of wealthy nobles and gentry, reaching its pinnacle when John Fane, earl of Westmoreland and lord-lieutenant of Ireland, attended a match, accompanied by his wife, in the Phoenix Park.[77] Arguably the most important advance in the history of hurling occurred during the seventeenth century, with the evolution of summer hurling. Utilising a broader-bossed hurley, allowing the ball to be carried while a player was in motion, the modern game of hurling is directly descended from the summer game. During the nineteenth century patronage of hurling declined, reflecting a European trend as the gentry generally turned from sports patronage to more 'polite' pastimes.[78] This trend was accelerated in Ireland in the aftermath of the 1798 rebellion. Alongside summer hurling, landlord and gentry patronage of the game stands as one of the key developments in the game, prior to the foundation of the GAA. Since the institution of the All-Ireland championship, hurling has been dominated by counties south of the Dublin–Galway axis – where summer hurling developed. As a more attractive game than winter hurling, it was also a more natural focus for patronage in the eighteenth century. With regard to newspaper reports of hurling matches located to date, only one details a match held in the northern half of the country, and that only as far north as Mayo. A total of eighteen families have been identified as patrons of the game during the eighteenth century, with not one based north of Dublin–Galway.[79] Though both variants of hurling were still played in the early nineteenth century, the devastation of the Famine appears to have led to the near extinction of hurling except for a few pockets of the country, notably Galway, Wexford and Dublin. The political unrest of the nineteenth century also played a part. According to one source, hurling in Leitrim was stamped out by the local priest because of the inclination of the participants, at election time, to fight rather than to hurl.[80]

The efforts of the GAA, and particularly Michael Cusack, were crucial to the survival of hurling and football. Cusack's preference for summer hurling saw its basic tenets enshrined in the association's official playing rules, ensuring not only its widespread popularity but also establishing the basis of the game as it is played today.[81] Football in the early modern period remains a more inscrutable subject. Its evolution and development prior to 1884 cannot be traced with certainty. The introduction of standardised rules by the GAA, under the direction of Maurice Davin, formalised Gaelic football as a uniquely Irish game.[82] Without the intervention of the GAA, football in Ireland might well have adopted the rules and structures developed in England that now characterise rugby union, rugby league and soccer, to the detriment of Irish sporting life.

3. Maurice Davin, the first President of the GAA, was also the outstanding athlete of his generation. He is pictured here sporting the most important medals he won before he retired at the beginning of the 1880s.

3 Ireland and the Birth of Modern Sport

RICHARD HOLT

The Gaelic Athletic Association was founded at a critical moment in the history of world sport. Created specifically to revive and celebrate traditional forms of Irish sport, the GAA was also part of a much wider international phenomenon: the creation of modern sport. Traditional village games were in decline and a new world of modern sports with written rules and national organising bodies was coming into existence. New ball games such as association football in Britain or baseball in the United States were invented to meet the changing needs of the modern western world. Industrial towns and cities were spreading at an astonishing speed. Men now had to work in large factories or offices, standing at machines or shop counters, sitting at office desks, living their lives indoors, deprived of fresh air and exercise. Modern sports fitted into these new forms and rhythms of life, slotting neatly into the limited time and space available in new industrial towns or vast conurbations such as London. In North America, in Britain and in Europe the same changes in sport took place at broadly the same time, beginning in England and the US in mid-nineteenth century and spreading rapidly around the developed world by 1900.

These new team sports could be rough – they were meant to instil courage as well as competitiveness – but they were supposed to be less dangerous than the violent sports of the past. It was a priority to regulate team ball games such as football or rugby to reduce the risk of serious injury while encouraging the display of strength, effort and determination by the individual and the team. These sports were first and foremost designed to be played by 'amateurs' – lovers of sport – for fun. But soon the best teams began to attract spectators and to provide weekly entertainment, especially in the new industrial towns. Professional leagues were formed in the 1870s in the US for baseball and in Britain in the 1880s for association football. There was a new urban market for spectator sport to replace the folk games that had been part of a wider pattern of seasonal festivities since the Middle Ages. While these profound changes were not felt as sharply

33

in rural and Catholic Ireland as elsewhere, the spread of modern sports posed a sharp and sudden threat to the maintenance of an older way of living and playing.[1]

This new world of sport was dependent on a range of other social changes, which spread quickly around the western world. First, there was a transformation in communications with the completion of railway and tram networks. This permitted quick and easy travel to play and to watch sport within and between towns and cities. Second, there was the setting up of national systems of state education, which taught children to read and introduced them to elementary forms of exercise. This was complemented by a much expanded private school sector, which made sport a central part of the curriculum for élites of birth and wealth. Third, there was now a newly literate public seeking entertainment, who could learn about sports from books and magazines and follow their favourite games and teams through the emergence of the popular press.

Modern sport, in short, did not come 'out of the blue'. It was a logical consequence of the wider changes that were taking place in the modern world. The origins of the GAA tend to be seen in political terms, as part of a powerful movement for popular national self-expression in Ireland. Less immediately obvious but no less important is the context of unprecedented social and cultural transformation. Modern sport, in Ireland as elsewhere, was the product of 'modernisation' – in the case of the GAA both as a reaction against modernity and as a consequence of it.[2]

What forms did these new sports take? There were the winter team games such as association football, rugby football and American football, which were 'invented' in the 1860s and 1870s. Then there were summer ball games such as cricket and baseball, first played in the US in the 1840s and organised as a professional spectator sport from the 1870s. Cricket, which had been widely played in England since the eighteenth century, only took on its modern form in the third quarter of the nineteenth century. Men had been running, jumping and throwing since historical records began. But it was not until the 1880s that national governing bodies for athletics were set up in North America, Britain and France. There was a sudden rash of new organisations to regulate, codify and record competition for sports as different as tennis and rowing or hockey and swimming.

These sports were mainly run by private clubs. Clubs of all kinds had been created by eighteenth-century gentlemen with the time and money to spare on their hobbies and their sports. However, this way of organising leisure through private associations did not become widespread until the second half of the nineteenth century. Increasingly, those who had been to the same school or worked and lived in the same area would band together to form a club and rent facilities in which to play. Modern sport began as an urban phenomenon, offering not only healthy exercise but a reassuring network of friendship in the big industrial city with its daunting scale and dizzy pace. However, many of these sports soon spread to rural areas as the old world of country fairs and festivals declined and much of the traditional way of life was swept aside. For Ireland this spelt danger. The railway had opened hitherto remote areas of the country to new influences, including modern sports. The outside world was breaking in.

Hence the timing of Cusack's initiative was no accident. Nor was the broadside of Archbishop Croke against the 'ugly and irritating fact that we are daily importing from England … her games and pastimes to the utter discredit of our grand national sports'.[3] Modern sports were spreading with extraordinary rapidity around the world. International competition and the creation of representative national teams posed an acute problem for the growing number of nationalists for whom 'the nation' was a cultural as well as a political question. Who would represent the nation and how?

Ireland, as it turned out, forged her own sporting destiny. But this path was not so clear at the time. Would Ireland take up English sports and beat England at her own game as the Australians did? Perhaps she should emulate the sons of those who had emigrated after the Famine and who now played American sports? Or would she be tempted by a more European model of gymnastic exercise, which had spread from Germany and appealed strongly to those such as the Czechs who wanted to train the body in the interests of national independence? What new sports did Irishmen see when they looked across the Irish Sea and the Atlantic ocean to Britain, Europe and North America?

BRITAIN

Apart from the English language itself, sport is probably Britain's most successful cultural export. Soccer – Oxford student slang for 'association' – turned out to be more influential than Shakespeare. The rules of 'the world game' were first set down in 1863 in a London tavern by former public schoolboys who wanted to continue playing football and needed to agree on how to organise it. According to the inscription at Rugby school, William Webb Ellis, 'with a fine disregard for the rules of football as played in his time, first took the ball and ran with it, thus originating the distinctive feature of the Rugby game. AD 1823'.[4] This, in fact, is a 'myth of origin', dreamt up in the 1890s when the gentlemanly control of rugby was threatened by professional teams from the north of England. The modern form of the game was not clearly established until the setting up of the Rugby Football Union in 1871.

Rugby, in particular, embodied an attitude to sport steeped in the new élite values of the English middle and upper classes, which was famously set out in the novel written about Rugby school by a former pupil: *Tom Brown's Schooldays* by Thomas Hughes. The sixth edition, dated 1885, shows an engraving of Tom leaving Rugby in triumph, 'borne aloft by the eleven, shouting in chorus, "For he's a jolly good fellow" ... and the next morning after breakfast he squared up all the cricketing accounts ... said his hearty goodbyes, and by twelve o'clock was in the train, and away for London, no longer a schoolboy'.[5] It was the Tom Browns of London, seeking to keep their old school sports going in the metropolis, who shaped much of modern sport. The novel was very influential beyond England, making a powerful impact in North America, where it inspired a generation of Ivy League amateurs. It was also the favourite novel of a Frenchman, Baron Pierre de Coubertin, who founded the modern Olympic movement in 1894 on the principles of British amateurism.

`What were these principles and why did they have such a firm hold over the Victorians and their successors in British sport for so long? Consider the following passage by a literary contemporary of Thomas Hughes:

> It was a noble sport – a sight as only to be seen in England – some hundred young men, who might, if they had chosen, been lounging effeminately about the streets, subjecting themselves to intense exertion, for the mere pleasure of toil. The true English stuff came out there ... the stuff which had held Gibraltar and conquered Waterloo – which had created a Birmingham and a Manchester, and colonised every quarter of the globe – that grim, earnest, stubborn energy, which since the days of the old Romans the English possess of all the nations of the earth. I was as proud of these gallant young fellows as if they had been my brothers – of their courage and endurance (for one could see it was no child's play, from the pale faces, and panting lips), their strength and activity, so fierce and yet so cultivated, smooth, harmonious, as oar kept time with

oar, and every back rose and fell in concert, and felt my soul stirred to a sort of sweet madness ... My blood boiled over, and fierce tears swelled into my eyes; for I too was a man, and an Englishman.[6]

Nowhere has the role of sport as an expression of English nationalism and imperialism been better expressed than in this passage from the novel by Charles Kingsley, published in 1848 – the year of European revolutions. Kingsley tells the story of a tailor, Alton Locke, who is transformed from a political radical into an English patriot through this vision of the body in the service of the nation. What is striking here is the clarity with which the amateur ethic of effort and competition is tied to a powerful sense of national destiny. These young men were amateurs, rowing with the determination of professionals but without the taint of corruption that went with money prizes and gambling. In one sense Victorian sport offered Irishmen an attractive moral example: sport for personal improvement and for a pure national purpose. While those who formed the GAA attacked British sport for its associations with British imperialism, like the British they condemned the gambling and corruption associated with professional sport. Irish nationalists agreed with British amateurs that sport should be a form of moral education while rejecting the wider ideological agenda of British sport. Those who joined the GAA denounced the fact that England 'colonised every quarter of the globe' while acknowledging the 'grim, stubborn energy' they displayed in their sports.

In principle, the amateur did not play for profit or personal fame. Tom Brown's housemaster was particularly fond of cricket for 'the discipline and reliance on one another which it teaches ... it merges the individual into the eleven; he doesn't play that he may win but that his side may win'.[7] Kingsley spelt it out in even greater detail. 'Through sport boys acquire virtues which no books can give them; not merely daring and endurance, but better still, temper, self-restraint, fairness, honour ... and all that "give and take" of life which stand a man in good stead when he goes out into the world'.[8]

Sport was about 'building character' as well as developing muscles. Amateurism was a fusion of long-held gentlemanly ideals of honour with the new ideal of a meritocracy, of 'letting the best man win' regardless of status or wealth. Free and open competition ruled in the marketplace and on the sports field. Amateur sporting bodies established common laws where men could compete equally regardless of origin or occupation. Only the Amateur Rowing Association formally excluded 'mechanics, artisans and labourers'. In theory modern sport was open to all, though sports such as tennis or golf attracted only an élite following in England. Private sports clubs could admit or exclude whoever they wished. However, the principle itself *was* important. Modern sport was part of a new world of competition: between political parties for votes, between firms for customers and between teams for trophies.

Amateurism operated on several levels. As well as providing a new code of 'sportsmanship' and 'fair play', it was also a form of national organisation for sports, free of state control or subsidy, run by unpaid officials elected by the member clubs. The Football Association, formed in 1863, was the first such body, but was soon followed by the Rugby Football Union in 1871 and the Amateur Athletic Association in 1880. These in turn had their counterparts in the different constituent parts of the United Kingdom. In football the Scots formed their own FA in 1873, the Welsh in 1876 and the Irish in 1882. That same year the four associations formed the International Football Association Board to harmonise laws and run a British championship. Similarly, rugby spread rapidly after the setting up of the RFU in 1871 in Scotland, Wales and Ireland. The Irish Rugby Football Union was formed in 1879 and matches between the four 'home nations' became a regular event, providing the perfect platform for little Wales to beat her overbearing neighbour and discover a new national hero: Arthur 'Monkey' Gould, the brilliant centre three-quarter who engineered the first Welsh victory over England on home soil.[9]

This was a key moment. Either Ireland would adopt 'English' sports as the Welsh and Scots had done, or they would find an alternative path. What made this even more urgent was the spectre of professional sport. Sportsmen had fought or played for money from the eighteenth century. But in the 1880s a new kind of professionalism emerged in the mill towns of the north of England, where local industrialists offered jobs to bring in the best players, often from Scotland. In 1883 one hundred teams entered the FA Cup, which since its inception in 1871 had been dominated by regimental officer clubs and clubs of public school 'old boys'. Blackburn Olympic, a specially trained team supported by a local manufacturer, beat the Old Etonians in the 1883 FA Cup final. No amateur team has won it since. There were fifty-five of these imported Scottish players – the so-called 'Scotch professors' – playing in eleven clubs in Lancashire in 1884. In that year Preston were disqualified from the FA Cup for using professionals, which prompted forty clubs to meet in Manchester to explore the possibility of forming a break-away

British professional league. Enter Charles Alcock, the secretary of the FA and of Surrey County Cricket Club, a former pupil of Harrow public school and the 'fixer' of English football, who proposed that professionalism should be legalised under FA control. This led clubs such as Aston Villa and Everton – both beginning as church clubs – to join northern textile towns such as Blackburn and Preston to form the Football League in 1885. Football was split from the start – a fate the GAA always wished to avoid.[10]

The same process of regional and social segregation happened in rugby. But without the compromise brokered by Alcock rugby split into two different games in 1895: the southern-based Rugby Football Union and the Northern Union, which later became the Rugby League. Cricket had always permitted amateurs and professionals to play together providing the social distinctions between 'gentlemen' and 'players', as they were called, were respected. The 'players' called the 'gentlemen' 'Sir' or 'Mister', travelled and lodged separately and had their initials placed after their surnames on scorecards.

County cricket was beginning to become popular in England, whose new sporting hero, W.G. Grace, was a bearded country doctor. He played his first game at the age of 16 in 1864 and dominated the English game for the following forty years. To facilitate the spread of the game the Marylebone Cricket Club – the private gentleman's club which governed the game – revised the 'laws of cricket' in 1884. This was not good news for those who wished to curb the spread of English sports in Ireland. For cricket, as Tom Hunt has shown in a splendid case study of Westmeath, was already widely played in Ireland. Ireland, it seemed, was on the brink of becoming British in its sports just as the prospect of home rule and national self-determination appeared on the horizon.[11]

As this was happening in Britain, sport was also spreading fast in distant parts of the British empire. In Australia 'Melbourne Rules' football was begun, which became 'Aussie Rules' and attracted Irish emigrants, through Collingwood – a celebrated working-class Irish club. Rugby union and rugby league were both well established by the end of the century, but it was in cricket that Australia truly excelled, touring England in 1882 and beating the mother country on her own turf. *The Times* published a mock obituary of English cricket, whose ashes were to be cremated and taken back to Australia. This gave rise to the bi-annual series of matches for the 'Ashes', which quickly developed a huge following in both England and Australia. New Zealand also played cricket, but it was rugby where they made their mark. In South Africa rugby came to be dominated by the Boers, while the

Anglophones took to cricket. The Dominions soon surpassed the home nations in rugby, with both the All Blacks and Springboks proving virtually unbeatable. Canada, however, was different, developing her own national sport of ice hockey and preferring a version of American football to rugby along with a preference for baseball over cricket. Meanwhile, in the West Indies cricket was king. The pattern of diffusion was complex. The British did not impose their sports on their colonies and the colonised chose to respond in different ways in different places.

EUROPE

The Irish were not the only ones to feel the challenge from British sports. In continental Europe new sports came via British tourists or through contact with British diplomatic and business communities. As British business increasingly penetrated European markets, British sports tended to follow. 'Just fix your eyes on those robust, overgrown fellows who have been fed by *sport*', remarked a Dutchman of English visitors as early as 1866.[12] Not long after, in neighbouring Belgium, an Irish schoolboy, Morragh of Killarney, introduced football to his Belgian school friends in Ghent. One of these boys was Emile Seeldreyers, whose son later became the President of FIFA.[13] Expatriate Britons started sports clubs across Europe in the 1870s and 1880s: in Antwerp, Copenhagen, Bremen and Berlin. Switzerland was a favourite destination for the Victorians, whether for education, work or tourism. British schoolboys formed a club in Geneva as early as 1869 and the famous FC Grasshoppers were set up by British residents of Zurich in 1886. The Swiss, bitten by the football bug, took the game to southern Europe on their business travels, notably to Spain where Hans Gamper founded FC Barcelona.[14]

The spread of sport in Europe was not the result of an English campaign to convert Europeans to football or rugby. In sport as in other respects, the British held aloof in 'splendid isolation'. Rather the rapidity of diffusion revealed the receptiveness of educated European youth to sport in general and football in particular. Continental schoolboys were sometimes sent to British boarding schools and returned with boots and footballs. Walter Bensemann, the son of a German medical and banking family, studied briefly in Britain before founding clubs in Montreux, Strasbourg and Karlsruhe between 1887 and 1892. Eduardo Bosio worked in Nottingham and returned to found FC Internazionale in Turin while 'Milan' is still not 'Milano' in recognition of the early British influence in the city.

Of course, not all British sports were so successful. Rugby had little success in Europe outside of France, and cricket almost none at all. Why did Europeans love football and loathe cricket? The Nederlansche Cricket Bond was founded in 1883 by Dutch Anglophiles. But this was the exception which proved the rule. Cricket was too slow and took too long; its rules were too complex and its terminology ridiculous. It was too static. Most of the players did not do much in comparison to football, which required intense effort. Cricket was just *too* English and too traditional for Europe.

The new British sport of lawn tennis, however, spread very rapidly among the upper and upper-middle classes of Europe in the later nineteenth century. So, too, did cycling, both as a recreation and a sport. The modern bicycle was invented in Coventry in the mid-1880s but the British banned road racing in 1896 because of the risk of accidents, leaving the way clear for France to take the lead. Races on public roads radiating out from Paris to Brest, Bordeaux, Tours and Roubaix were established in the 1890s, culminating in the Tour de France in 1903 – the largest annual sporting event in the world, highly commercialised and suffused with an intense French patriotism. The British could no more understand a cycle race lasting three weeks than the French could comprehend watching a cricket match for five days.

French sport is particularly interesting for the Irish case. France emulated *both* the Germans and the British as well as reacting against both. Germany stuck to its tradition of 'turnen', or group gymnastics, which claimed to have a million followers by the late nineteenth century. In the wake of their catastrophic defeat in the Franco-Prussian War of 1870–1, the French founded a national gymnastic organisation in 1873 to promote national revival and paramilitary training on Prussian lines. These clubs, with names like 'The Revenge' or 'The Sentinel', spread rapidly in the 1880s. Hence gymnastics was popular before 'les sports Anglais' – athletics, rugby, football and rowing – were introduced.[15]

Gym clubs attracted skilled workers, clerks and shopkeepers and were supported by the medical profession, the military and the state. But repetitive group exercises did not appeal to the younger members of the French nobility and bourgeoisie, who increasingly looked across the channel for inspiration. France had endured a century of revolution since 1789, while the British had combined economic growth with good order and expanded their power across the world. Young men like the Baron Pierre de Coubertin, the future founder of the Olympic Games, thought they knew why. The British public school created a vigorous and unified élite rather than a divided and embittered one, weakened by too much academic work and not enough sport. Aged just 21, Coubertin set off for Rugby school in 1884 to worship at the shrine of Thomas Arnold. Armed with a letter of introduction from a distinguished French politician, he was even granted an audience with the prime minister, William Gladstone, who confirmed that public school sport had undoubtedly been a factor in the British success.[16]

Privileged Parisian students from the most exclusive schools set up the Racing Club de France in 1882 and the Stade Français the following year to practise '*les sports Anglais*'. Coubertin and a few other young Anglophiles such as Georges de Saint Clair, a former French consul in Edinburgh, were the moving force behind the formation of the Union des Sociétés Françaises de Sports Athlétiques (USFSA) in 1889. The USFSA, which governed most French sport until after the First World War, was firmly based upon the British amateur model, with 200 member clubs by 1900 and 1,600 by 1914. Rugby was especially successful. France joined the English, Scots, Welsh and Irish to create the 'Five Nations' tournament in 1910. This was unique in Europe. No other nation outside of the British empire had as close a sporting relationship with Britain or Ireland.[17]

However, this new passion for British sports did not go unchallenged. England was 'the old enemy' from the Hundred Years War to the battle of Waterloo, which the English boasted to have won 'on the playing-fields of Eton'. In France – just as in Ireland at the same time – there was a groundswell of opposition to copying the sports of 'perfidious Albion'. The Ligue Nationale de l'Education Physique was formed to oppose the reform of French education through British sport. Like the GAA, the *ligue* wanted sport for reasons of national revival. But they wanted it with a French sauce, favouring indigenous French sports such as '*la theque*' (kind of baseball) or '*la barette*' (a handling form of football).[18]

The man behind the ligue – the French counterpart of Michael Cusack – was Paschal Grousset, a political radical who had been in exile in London in the 1870s and was highly critical of a country with a monarchy, a powerful aristocracy and an established church. He also supported Irish independence. As a radical republican, he was interested in mass-education. He thought every primary school should have a playground and that the state should create playing-fields for French sports in every city. He also believed women had a place in sport and devised special games for them. Throughout the summer of 1888 there was a propaganda battle between Coubertin and Grousset. The future of sport in France was debated in the national press. Coubertin counted seventy-four articles on the subject between May and August 1888. Grousset collected and published his own contributions as *La Renaissance Physique* under the pseudonym Phillipe Daryl, with the simple message, '*Soyons français*' – Be French![19]

This was a decisive moment. Would the French follow the American or Irish path and create a distinctive French model of sport divorced from British practice or would they follow Coubertin and the elite Anglophiles? As it happened, Grousset was far less committed than Coubertin. He was elected to parliament and turned his attention to other issues, while Coubertin went on to found the greatest sporting event in the world. The Ligue Nationale de l'Education Physique languished. The ideal of creating a separate French sporting culture with its own sports on the lines of the GAA had disappeared.

NORTH AMERICA

When nineteenth-century Irishmen looked beyond their own shores, they turned to North America rather than to Europe. Though geographically much farther away, it was culturally much closer to home. The catastrophe of the Famine led to over one and half million emigrating from Ireland to the United States in the decade following 1845–6. Many of those who left were young men, who created a new bachelor life of drinking and sports in big cities such as Boston, New York and Philadelphia. The 'fighting Irish' were famous as boxers, from John Heenan, who fought the last bare-knuckle 'world championship' contest in England in 1861 to John L Sullivan, the great Irish-American fighter who dominated boxing in the 1880s when he successfully defended his US title several times. He 'was probably the first truly national sports hero' in the US.[20] 'When Sullivan struck me I thought that a telegraph pole had been shoved against me endways', confessed fellow Irish-American, Paddy Ryan.[21] In his pomp Sullivan offered $1,000 to any member of the public who could last four rounds with him.

Boxing was a big part of the sporting culture of the United States, but baseball was the new national sport. From the 1860s baseball carried all before it, pushing aside the British legacy of cricket as the favoured summer sport of the US. Like the Irish, the Americans wanted sports that were their own rather than taken from the British. Baseball, which was claimed to have been invented in Cooperstown,

New Jersey in 1846, spread rapidly in the 1860s in the wake of the civil war. From the beginning it had a commercial aspect with the first professional team, Cincinnati Red Stockings, formed in 1869 and a national league formed the following year. However, it was not until a shrewd sports entrepreneur, A.G. Spalding, co-founded the National League of Professional Baseball Clubs in 1876 that the sport took off as a spectator phenomenon.

The Irish were important in baseball, with Mike 'King' Kelly the first national star, transferred to Boston for $10,000 in 1887 and notorious for his drinking and gamesmanship. By the end of the century it was estimated that one-third of major league baseball players were of Irish origin. The White Sox ground was built in a strongly Irish area of Chicago and the city itself was infamous for its Irish clubs, which were linked to the notorious machine politics of the city. Successful Irish-American teams such as the Ragen Colts from the stockyards district were both sports clubs and a source of strong young 'enforcers' for the corrupt politicians who sponsored them.

This was not exactly the image which Cusack, Croke and others wanted for sports in their native Ireland. Boxing and baseball were both professional spectacles where amateurism had little or no place. While the US provided a powerful example of freedom from British influence, its commercialism and dubious morality meant that it was hardly a model for sport in Ireland. More in tune with the Irish desire for hard, clean amateur sport were the élite football games played at Harvard, Yale and Princeton. When Walter Camp formulated the 'grid iron' concept of American football at Yale in 1880, he showed how a game like rugby could be adapted to a new nation for a new purpose. American football spread rapidly across the country but remained an élite inter-collegiate activity.

Sport in the United States reflected the diverse origins of the country. Caledonian clubs put on displays of Highland Games, which included foot racing, hammer throwing and tossing the caber. These events proliferated in the 1870s, with the largest gatherings such as that hosted by the New York Caledonian club attracting up to 20,000 spectators. This in turn influenced new Irish immigrants to revive ancient Irish sports. In 1881 a Boston newspaper recorded that 'a large number of the Irish people in Boston are becoming interested in the exhibitions of the games and pastimes of their ancestors', with at least five hurling clubs formed in the 1880s.[22]

However, it was in athletics that the Irish made a particular impression. This began with the ultra-long-distance events which were a survival from earlier traditions of endurance running, where distance covered was more important than recorded times. In the founding year of the GAA in Ireland, another Irishman, Patrick Fitzgerald, performed an extraordinary feat at Madison Square Garden, running a total of 610 miles in six days to win more than $18,000.

The Irish-American tradition soon came to the fore in a new international arena. The Frenchman, Baron Pierre de Coubertin, refounded the Olympic Games in 1894, holding the first modern Olympiad in Athens in 1896. From the beginning the Americans were well represented, predictably dominating the 1904 games held at St Louis and challenging British dominance at the London games of 1908. The leader of the American delegation was an American of Irish family origin, James E. Sullivan, a journalist, who bluntly declared: 'We have come here to win the championship in field sports, and we are going to do it.'[23] The mutual antagonism of British and American delegations in the London games gave rise to a flurry of protests and recriminations ranging from complaints about the way the American flag was flown to the running of the marathon and the disqualification of an American athlete during the final of the 400 metres.[24]

This was a reminder of the subtle ways in which politics permeated sport not just in Ireland but throughout the western world. The GAA was not alone in fighting a national battle through sport. In different ways in different countries sport was modernised both in its rules and organisation but also in cultural and political terms. British sport claimed proudly to be above politics, but it was permeated with imperial values and class distinctions. French sport was based on the British model but explicitly designed to strengthen France after her defeat at the hands of Prussia in 1870. In Germany and more widely in continental Europe more attention was given to collective forms of gymnastic exercise than to modern sports. America invented a new national sport and turned it into a business.

Ireland picked its way through this maze, rejecting the monotony of mass gymnastics but also refusing to follow the dominant forms of British sport. It adopted amateur values but rejected the social distinctions that went with them. It embraced spectator sport but refused the American model of sport as commercial entertainment. In doing so Ireland created a unique blend of the traditional and the modern, which has survived and prospered for 125 years. This remarkable achievement would surely have surpassed the wildest expectations of the pioneers who looked at the state of world sport in the 1880s and decided Ireland would go her own way.

4. The Cuchulainns camogie team pictured in 1904.

4 Michael Cusack: Sportsman and Journalist

PAUL ROUSE

Michael Cusack's unique personality was both his making and his undoing. At his best, he was extraordinary and brilliant, capable of great warmth, humour and generosity. His life's work is clearly that of a man of considerable vision. But Cusack's flaws were as outlandish as his talents. He was impetuous on a cartoonish scale. He also thrived on confrontation and managed to find it in most quarters. The deed of his life for which he is best remembered is, of course, the founding of the Gaelic Athletic Association. It says much for Cusack's personality that the genius who founded the GAA in November 1884 was the same peculiar genius who managed to get himself dismissed from that thriving association in the summer of 1886.

It is an indisputable fact that, in creating the GAA, Cusack turned Irish sport on its head. He successfully subverted the world of élitist sports clubs which controlled organised sports in Ireland and which were perceived as being loyal to the British crown. The remarkable truth about Cusack, however, is that, for many years, few Irish people seemed quite so committed to playing and fostering the games of the British empire. Until the early 1880s Michael Cusack's favoured games were rugby and cricket – and he was devoted to both.

I

Michael Cusack's entry into Ireland's Anglocentric world of sport was through a means shared by many sportsmen of his generation across the British empire – the education system. Cusack had trained to be a schoolteacher and subsequently taught during the 1870s at St Colman's College in Newry, at Kilkenny College (which was for educating Protestant boys) and at the Jesuit-run colleges at Blackrock in Dublin and Clongowes Wood in Kildare. By then, cricket was the principal summer game of all the leading secondary schools in Ireland.[1] This was as true for Catholic schools such as Tullabeg College in Co. Offaly, as it was for Protestant schools such as St Columba's College in Co. Meath.[2]

The first record of Michael Cusack playing cricket was when he went to work as a teacher in the French College in Blackrock in the summer of 1874. The French College (later known simply as Blackrock College) had about 200 students at the time and Cusack was given a job teaching commercial subjects in the new department which the school was opening to prepare students for civil service and armed forces examinations. There is a record in the college accounts of Cusack buying a pair of specialised cricketing pants to play the game.[3] It is likely that he had previously played for other teams in other places, but even if not, he soon became a keen cricketer. By the time he had reached his mid-thirties, Cusack was able to recall his involvement in 'many a hard-fought match'.[4] His passion for the game was obvious. He wrote once that it would help cricketers to pass away the dark days of winter, by dreaming of the wonderful six that they had hit in mid-summer, and of feeling pride at having walked to the crease, the forlorn hope of their parish, before saving the day with a memorable performance.[5] He wrote of the advisability of setting up cricket clubs in every parish in Ireland. For Cusack this was not simply a matter of boys getting exercise to enhance their health – it was also a matter of ideology. He wrote in July 1882: 'You may be certain that the boy who can play cricket well will not, in after years, lose his head and get flurried in the face of danger.'[6]

If Cusack loved cricket in the summer, he also loved rugby in the winter. By the time he began playing rugby in the 1870s, the game had finally begun to establish itself on a solid footing in Ireland. In 1874 thirteen clubs – nine from Leinster, three from Ulster and one from Ulster – joined to form an Irish Football Union, ostensibly to pick a team to play an international match against England. Later, in 1879, the union was reorganised. Provincial branches were established in Leinster, Munster and Ulster and an enduring framework was established to manage the growth of rugby football in Ireland.

Within that framework, Michael Cusack worked to further the growth of rugby in Ireland. He did this in tandem with the school he had founded in Dublin in 1877. Throughout the 1870s Cusack had revelled in the sporting life of the various schools in which he taught, not least because this was an era where teachers took to the fields and played games with their students, rather than merely organising them. For all that he was well regarded in the schools in which he taught, his restlessness did not allow him to settle in any one of them. In October 1877, in imitation of the section of the school in which he had worked in Blackrock, he set up his own academy in Dublin to prepare students taking civil service and other public examinations. It was an immediate success. In the late 1870s and 1880s nobody in Dublin was thought to be more successful than Michael Cusack in preparing Irish boys for examinations to join the civil service which ran the British empire.[7]

Sport was an essential part of the activities at his school. For the 1879–80 season, he founded the Cusack's Academy Football Club and affiliated it to the Irish Rugby Football Union. The team played out of the Phoenix Park. Cusack was club secretary and trainer, and also played in the forwards, where he built a reputation as a powerful operator. Indeed, he seems to have acquired something of a reputation for the black arts in his play, leading one journalist later to observe darkly: 'Everybody knows what Cusack is in a scrummage.'[8] Some of Cusack's students had a limited experience of playing the game, but others were country boys whose raw strength was harnessed through a season's coaching. By the end of the season Cusack's team had won more matches than it had lost and in an article printed in R.M. Peter's *Irish Football Annual*, Cusack couldn't resist the temptation to note that two of the matches 'were both lost through the bad play of a certain back, who threw the ball wildly behind him into his own goal, possibly under the idea that he was passing it back'. Cusack concluded his review of the first season played by his academy team by predicting for it a bright future and by referring to himself as 'a sterling lover of the game'.[9]

The bright future was soon behind them. The success of his students in securing jobs in the civil service exams brought a continuous struggle to field competitive teams. By the summer of 1881 Cusack had tired of the struggle and the club folded, even though the school continued to thrive. Cusack threw in his lot with the Phoenix Rugby Club. He was a member of the Phoenix team that played Dublin University at Lansdowne Road on 10 December 1881 in the first ever match in the Leinster Senior Cup competition. One of his opponents that day was Thomas St George McCarthy – a past pupil of Cusack's Academy and a man who would later attend the founding meeting of the GAA. Phoenix lost that cup match, but Cusack played out the 1881–2 season with his new club and a picture of him posing with his teammates is one of the few of him which survive. He did not return for the following season. Having turned 35 years of age, he retired from the game.[10]

II

The nature of the Victorian sportsman was often that of the all-rounder. Cusack was the epitome of this. All the while he was playing rugby and cricket he was also engaged in other sports. Shortly after his arrival in Dublin in 1874 he competed in a handball competition which was run by the Dublin University Rowing Club. He then joined that club and rowed with them for two years. Given his sporting disposition, it was inevitable that he should turn his hands to the burgeoning athletics world in the city. Michael Cusack had emerged from the rural tradition of weight-throwing and, when he arrived in Dublin, it was a natural progression for him to join in athletic activity in the city. In May 1875 he competed in the Dublin Amateur Athletic Club sports as a representative of the French College Cricket Club. He duly won the 16 lb and 42 lb weight-throwing events and subsequently joined the Dublin Amateur Athletic Club. This was more than merely an athletics club, as it catered for a whole host of sporting activity from cricket to rugby and beyond. Cusack represented that club in two other athletics meetings in the city during that summer of 1875 and again was successful in weight-throwing events.[11]

It was not the start of a glorious athletics career, however. Over the following four years Cusack seems to have disappeared from the Dublin athletics scene. The reasons for this are several. Firstly, he spent the best part of eighteen months teaching outside the city, in Kilkenny College and in Clongowes Wood College. Secondly, by the time he had returned to Dublin, he had married Margaret Woods, a Down woman, and they quickly set about starting a family, with his daughter Claire being born in April 1877. Thirdly, if domestic responsibility left limited time for Cusack's sporting involvement, his professional engagements at his newly founded school left even less.

By the time of Cusack's return to athletics participation in 1879, the Dublin athletics world had significantly changed. The Dublin Amateur Athletics Club which he had previously represented had folded. A singular feature of clubs in many sports at this time was the manner in which they rose and fell, seemingly without trace. So it is with the Dublin Amateur Athletic Club, which disappeared from view in 1879 despite the fact that it had successfully run sports meetings in the city for several summers. It was at this very time that Michael Cusack was reappearing on the Dublin sporting scene. He was immediately offered a seat on the council of the Irish Champion Athletic Club. Cusack agreed. The reasons for asking Cusack to join the club are unclear, but no doubt relate to the fact that his school had by then become known for its embrace of sport as a central part of the curriculum and Cusack himself was becoming well known around Dublin.

The emergence of Cusack as a prominent figure in the life of Dublin city was rooted in a number of factors. The success of his school and his engagement in the sporting life of the city was a partial explanation. Cusack had already cultivated an idiosyncratic appearance that allowed him to stand out from the crowd. He walked through the city in heavy working boots, a blackthorn stick swinging from his arm, and with a heavy frieze coat covering his heavy-set, broad-shouldered frame. His full black beard was beginning to streak with grey. Overall, he was remarkably proud and self-conscious of his appearance, which seems not so much to have been a mark of eccentricity but a statement of defiance.[12] He gloried in the idea of his distinctiveness, the idea that he was a singular man, of singular beliefs. And he used the rapidly developing world of the Dublin press to broadcast these beliefs.

III

By the beginning of the 1880s Michael Cusack had embarked on a career in newspapers. For the remaining twenty-five years of his life, he contributed to Irish newspapers as a letter-writer, reporter, columnist, editor, owner and historian. It is an extraordinary body of work – a monument to Cusack's brilliance. He wrote beautifully across an extravagant range of matters. The great boon for the historian in Cusack's journalism is that you can trace the evolution in his thoughts in the early 1880s through his newspaper columns. His columns in the home rule journal, *The Shamrock*, were a case in point. That Cusack remained part of the Anglocentric world of sport in Dublin as late as 1882 is abundantly clear from his columns.[13] For example, in the autumn of 1882 Cusack was offering boys advice on how to clean a cricket bat using linseed oil and how to store it for the winter.[14] By the time that winter had passed, however, cricket was gone from Cusack's column – replaced, instead, by a plea for the revival of the game he termed Ireland's 'national pastime' – the game of hurling.[15]

The shift from cricket to hurling transformed Cusack's life – and the life of modern Ireland. Why did this transformation happen? The political and social climate was obviously influential. The tumultuous events of the land war left the scent of social revolution hanging in the air. On top of that, the gathering force of Parnellism suggested the genuine prospect of legislative independence for the first time in more than a generation. The strains in the union were becoming apparent and, in late 1882, it was entirely unclear what would next come to pass. After all, this was the year when the two most important British officials in Ireland were murdered while strolling through the Phoenix Park in Dublin.

On a personal level, there are clues in the columns which Cusack wrote over these critical months, though no conclusive answers. He was clearly influenced by two non-political and non-sporting events in 1882. One was the Industrial Exhibition of Irish-made goods in Dublin, which suggested a new economic future for Ireland; the second was the groundbreaking launch of the Irish-language publication, the *Gaelic Journal*, by the Gaelic Union, of which Cusack had become a central figure. The third event was a sporting one – the establishment in December 1882 of a hurling club in Dublin, of which Cusack was also a central figure. These three events are mentioned in Cusack's columns in February 1883 when he extols, for the first time, the virtues of reviving hurling.[16] In his book on the GAA and Irish nationalist politics, W. F. Mandle has written that these three events – in particular his part in the publication of the *Gaelic Journal* – saw Cusack undergo something of a mystical experience, which left him 'unhinged'.[17]

The merits of such psycho-analytical speculation are dubious, though it might be that the change in Cusack should not be seen as unhinging, rather as a moment of maturation when he formed a coherent set of beliefs which sustained him for the rest of his life. At the heart of Cusack's new ideology was hurling. The first meeting of the Dublin Hurling Club took place on 30 December 1882. The meeting, it was recorded in the minutes, was 'for the purpose of taking steps to re-establish the national game of hurling'.[18] Internal dissent and the inability to attract sufficient players meant that the club lasted merely for a few practice matches in January and February 1883. Cusack was undaunted. He had not been the driving force behind the Dublin Hurling Club, but he saw the potential even in its failure. Along with a few others, Cusack continued to patronise the Phoenix Park on Saturday afternoons to play hurling. By October 1883, using his students to garner sufficient numbers, he established the Cusack's Academy Hurling Club.[19] This, in turn, led to the establishment on 5 December 1883 of the Metropolitan Hurling Club. It was a momentous event. Michael Cusack was later in no doubt that this was the club 'out of which the GAA sprang'.[20] Cusack, by the way, did not merely organise the club; he also played in its matches, generally as goalkeeper.

Throughout all this, Cusack used his journalism to promote the idea of hurling. He wrote of hurling as an act of freedom, of hurling as a game which was inherited from the heroes of Irish history and which a new generation was duty-bound to revive.[21] That revival took a significant leap forwards when Cusack published a brilliant article, 'A word about Irish athletics', on 11 October 1884. This was the trumpet blast which heralded the foundation of the Gaelic Athletic Association. After the establishment of the GAA at a meeting in the billiard room of Lizzie Hayes's hotel in Thurles in November 1884, Cusack secured a weekly column in the journal, *United Ireland*. This journal was founded by William O'Brien, MP at least in part to offer a more nationalistic view of Irish life to the dominant *Freeman's Journal*. Cusack used his columns in that paper to build momentum behind the GAA, to outline the philosophy of the new association, to draw a line between the association and its opposition and, in essence, to publicise everything which the new association was trying to do. The manner in which Cusack used newspapers to build the GAA is a work of brilliance – something for which media consultants and teams of spin-doctors would later be paid ridiculous sums of money.

IV

The very fact that someone like Michael Cusack was given a regular column in a variety of newspapers was emblematic of the change in the press in the later decades of the nineteenth century. In Ireland, as in Britain, the abolition of stamp duty and enhanced printing technology facilitated the production of cheaper newspapers. Improved transport allowed for more efficient distribution, and with almost 90 per cent of the Irish population literate by the end of the nineteenth century the number of potential readers had grown significantly. Before the 1880s no daily paper in Ireland or Britain had consistently devoted significant space to sport. Exceptional occasions – boxing matches, race meetings and other such happenings – enjoyed some coverage, but there were no regular features to which the reader could turn. Often, sporting events only made it into print in the event of the courts taking an interest. The phenomenal growth in sport and the establishment of sporting organisations in the second half of the nineteenth century changed all that. That the public were interested in reading about sport quickly became clear, and daily newspapers greatly expanded their sports coverage.

Indeed, newspapers played a crucial role in the development of modern sporting organisations. They not only offered a record of what happened in various sports, but also played a significant part in the extension of sporting organisations and the establishment of a regular sporting calendar. So ideal was the union between sports and the press that it was not long before dedicated sporting papers were established. By 1884, in Britain, there were three daily papers dedicated entirely to sports reporting. The first in Ireland was the weekly *Irish Sportsman*, established in 1870 and dominated by news of hunting and other horse-related activities. It was joined in December 1880 by a new weekly newspaper, *Sport*, established by the *Freeman's Journal*. This paper was also dominated by horse-racing, though rugby, tennis and cricket were also given a decent airing. As we will see, Cusack had a tempestuous relationship with both of these papers.

Overall, it is clear that Michael Cusack was no easy man to work with – he was more properly born to serve on a one-man committee. He seemed incapable of diplomacy and was utterly devoid of perspective in personal exchanges. Cusack was one the finest exponents of the abusive one-liner. He was particularly abrasive during 1885, the first full year of the GAA. Spooked by the arrival of the organisation, existing athletics clubs established the Irish Amateur Athletic Association (IAAA). A bitter dispute ensued and Cusack was in his element. He described the IAAA as a 'ranting, impotent West British abortion'.[22] When John Dunbar, the secretary of the IAAA, wrote a conciliatory letter to Cusack in the midst of their dispute, Cusack replied to him: 'Dear Sir, I received your letter this morning and burned it.'[23]

The problem for Cusack is that he fought with his allies as freely as with his enemies. The evidence for this is everywhere – even in his relationship with the three original patrons he had convinced to support the founding of the GAA. He insulted Archbishop Croke in a letter in 1886 which led to the archbishop threatening to withdraw from the association – the outcry to this spat was critical to Cusack's loss of authority in the GAA; he then fell out bitterly with Michael Davitt in the late 1880s and they subsequently enjoyed a robust enmity. It does not seem outlandish to imagine that Cusack would have managed a similar dispute with Parnell, had the latter not died so prematurely in 1891. And then there is the fact that Cusack managed to alienate practically every section of the GAA within eighteen months of its foundation. To succeed in being ejected from a thriving organisation which you yourself have founded suggests a considerable talent for making enemies.

In the summer of 1886, after Cusack's removal as secretary of the GAA, the owner of *United Ireland* – William O'Brien – was prevailed upon by the executive of the GAA also to dispense with his services. Cusack's response was typically robust – he founded his own newspaper, the *Celtic Times*, in company with a Scottish businessman living in Dublin, Morrison Millar. This was despite the fact that Cusack was already engaged in running his academy and was still writing a column on education for *The Shamrock*. Cusack later recalled that he started the *Celtic Times* with no patronage, limited money, only the faintest idea of the management of a weekly paper and no time to devote to writing except that which others required for amusement or rest.[24] None the less, on New Year's Day 1887 the *Celtic Times* was launched on the Irish newspaper market.

The *Celtic Times* was no mere sporting paper. It was, instead, a paper of diversity and learning. When he was with *The Shamrock*, Cusack had written columns on subjects as disparate as travel, ballooning, how to make fireworks and how to perform magic tricks. The *Celtic Times* saw him write on subjects that interested him. The paper's masthead read: 'Let native industries, literature, arts and pastimes flourish.' There was a page on chess (claimed by Cusack as an old Irish pastime); there were favourable accounts of a whole variety of Irish industries; articles on trade unionism and socialism; notes on veterinary and agricultural matters; serious polemics on the importance of education, of literature and of public libraries; campaigns in support of Irish dancing and Irish music; promotion of the Irish language; and essays and poetry in Irish and English.[25] There was also great space given to women and, in particular, to women's industry. Not everything intended for women was necessarily emancipationist – Cusack, for example, wrote an article called 'A plea for homely girls', which stated that 'a homely girl, if she realises that she isn't pretty, is generally good, generous, and if she gets married she makes a good wife.' Against that he also ran a 'Lessons in Cookery' series, presumably for men, which began with a lesson on 'How to boil potatoes.'[26]

Naturally, though, the GAA was the prime focus of Cusack's passion. It would appear that on a number of occasions his work as a columnist was pulled by editors and publishers who understood the value of a controversial columnist in attracting readers, but equally understood that there was a line which simply could not be crossed. The glory of the *Celtic Times* is that it is Cusack editing himself – or, more precisely, not editing himself, and what ensued was a tribute to one man's passion. Partly, this is a reflection of the times. As already mentioned, sportswriting was a new phenomenon and sportswriters had yet to fall into their dreary rehearsal of the formulaic previews and match reports which soon became their stock- in-trade. Even in match reports, the original sportswriters spoke with a candour which is wonderful to read – and they were unafraid to offer the harshest criticism without descending into the illiterate, snide tabloid humiliation of our times. For example, when – in 1886 – Ireland lost a rugby international to England for the twelfth consecutive year, an Irish rugby journalist writing for a weekly paper had no doubt that it was the fault of the backs. 'We were playing two backs against six', he wrote. 'Greene was worse than a failure because he interfered with others. Dan Ross did not come off. Joe Ross struggled gamely but without effect. M. Johnston disgraced himself …'[27]

In the *Celtic Times* – particularly through his column 'harmonic rays' – Cusack sharpened his attacks on those whom he considered opponents of the association. These included the men who had displaced him at the head of the GAA, whom he condemned as 'a junta of knaves and fools' and 'a miserable mischievous traitorous gang'.[28] He constantly fought with his rivals in the press. He castigated the *Irish Times* as the paper 'of that most despicable of all creatures – the Orange Catholic – the slave that refuses to be emancipated – the lazy, place-hunting, unprincipled knave that would sell his soul for a penny roll, for soup and hairy bacon'.[29] His dispute with the *Freeman's Journal* and with its sister paper, *Sport*, was vicious. Cusack believed that the *Freeman's Journal* and *Sport* had offered no help to the GAA when it was trying to establish itself and that it was only when it was clear that the association was going to be a success that they opened their columns to Gaelic news. In this he was largely correct, but he returned to the subject with such regularity that it is clear he was obsessing beyond good reason on the matter. Remarkably, though, for a man who was so liberal with his published assaults on others, he actually took a libel case against the owners of the *Irish Sportsman* in June 1885 for a rather mild poem about Cusack's role as a sportsman and educator. Cusack won and received £12 in damages.[30]

The immediate opposition to the *Celtic Times*, however, was not the *Irish Sportsman*, the *Freeman's Journal* or *Sport* – it was a newspaper called *The Gael*. Cusack, himself, reported on the launch of *The Gael*, saying: 'A body professing to be the Executive of the Gaelic Athletic Association met at Nenagh on Monday, the 27th of December [1886], and called on itself to establish a paper to report its proceedings and protect its interests.'[31] *The Gael* styled itself as the official organ of the GAA. In effect, it was being run by members of the Irish Republican Brotherhood, who had moved to take control of the association and who in 1887 were beginning to exercise this control in an open manner. The paper was run by Patrick Hoctor, a member of the IRB and a vice-president of the GAA. The extent to which *The Gael* was IRB-dominated can be seen by the appointment of the veteran Fenian John O'Leary as its literary editor. Indeed, it was the literary content of *The Gael* that was its most striking aspect, publishing original works from W.B. Yeats and Douglas Hyde, among others.[32]

Cusack's reaction to this paper was to deny that it was the official organ of the GAA, writing that it was, instead, the 'organ of idiocy and illiteracy; the organ of a spurious patriotism; and the organ of all that is mean and contemptible. Away with the filthy thing!'[33] And to condemn *The Gael* and the people who ran it and the GAA in 1887, he coined a new term of abuse. To Cusack, they were 'baffety', a word that appeared time after time when he wrote about the Baffety Executive. For those readers who did not understand the term, Cusack offered an explanation. Baffety, he wrote, is 'a coarse yellow shoddy cloth of English manufacture, the dust of which, if inhaled when the rag is torn, permanently injures those who inhale it'. He added that baffety had 'grabbed the Gaelic Athletic Association and wrapped it up in its yellow folds'.[34] By Cusack's standards this was insult on a minor scale, until he decided to engage in some translation. For Irish speakers he offered the following: 'The Irish for baffety is *cac air aghaidh*', before kindly translating *cac air aghaidh* back into English: '*Cac* is dirt of the vilest description; *air* is equivalent to on; and *aghaidh* means face.'[35]

This style of writing should not be seen as confirming the portrait of a vulgar, drunken, xenophobic, anti-Semitic, boorish 'Citizen' as depicted by James Joyce in *Ulysses*. Nor does it support the vainglorious, uncouth anti-intellectual who appears in Oliver St John Gogarty's novel *Tumbling in the Hay*. Historians have argued that Joyce's 'parody was only slightly exaggerated'.[36] This is unfair. The caricatures of Joyce and Gogarty should not be seen as rounded insight into Michael Cusack. Indeed, the caricatures might tell more about the men who wrote them – and their own prejudices – than about their supposed subject.

That being said, Cusack's capacity for confrontation has already been noted. He was also clearly a heavy drinker (at least periodically) and was capable of anti-Semitic comment. In February 1887 he wrote: 'The Jews, who turned the Master's House of Prayer into a den of thieves, control the money markets and the telegraph wires of Europe; but the Irish hurling field, like the German gymnasium, can upset all their calculations.'[37] At the remove of 120 years, those words are particularly jarring. In his prejudice against Jews, he was, unfortunately, a man in step with his times. It is not to excuse Cusack to point out that looking back at them through the prism of twentieth-century history casts them in a much more sinister light than their contemporary meaning.

Cusack was not narrowly sectarian or bigoted in other ways. He played sport with men of all religions in his days on the Dublin sporting scene. He had his friend, John Stewart, a Tyrone Methodist, appointed as one of the first vice-presidents of the GAA. He wrote approvingly in support of a range of Protestant and Presbyterian initiatives in the pages of the *Celtic Times*. He also numbered many Protestants among his friends – and, being Cusack, did not discriminate against men of any religion when he made his enemies.

Alongside the capacity for harsh words and conflict was a parallel capacity for humour. He had no problem laughing at himself. In responding to suggestions that he was a rash, impulsive man, he wrote that this was far from the case and that he was, in fact, 'as cool as a New England lawyer eating a cucumber at the back of a tombstone during a blizzard'.[38] He was also a man of warmth and decency. In April 1887 Cusack learned that his one-time friend but then, almost inevitably, bitter rival, J.A.H. Christian, was emigrating to America. Christian has been a central figure in the establishment of the Irish Amateur Athletic Association and he and Cusack had had a ferocious public falling out. On hearing that Christian was emigrating, Cusack wrote a charming account of how their friendship had formed and then soured. He gently jibed at how Christian was the soul of loyalty to England and that he had established a world record in proposing toasts to the Queen. However, he ended the article by warmly acknowledging the athletic ability, courage and absolute integrity of Christian, and wrote: 'May he soon enjoy the happiness and prosperity which the great Republic of the West has bestowed on so many of his fellow-countrymen; and may he realise that, whilst we may be irreconcilable foes on National grounds, in private life we may wish one another all the blessings attached to the communion of Saints.'[39]

V

There are pages and pages of such brilliant journalism – but it was not enough to save the paper. It is thought that the circulation of the *Celtic Times* may have reached 20,000 in early summer, but by the end of 1887 – after a year in existence – the paper was in freefall. The reasons for its failure were many. Without backers the paper was constantly fighting to keep its head above water, while the constant attacks on the executive and other targets took up so much space that other matters were squeezed to the side. This was a problem which Cusack recognised, but at too late a stage to avert its impact.[40] Cusack was reputed to have pawned his watch in an attempt to get printers to publish the 21 January 1888 edition. They refused and the paper folded.

It was an ominous sign of what was to come. Michael Cusack's wife, Margaret, died from TB on 16 September 1890. By then the couple had six children (several others died in infancy), who ranged in age from 6 to 13. A month after the death of his wife, Cusack also suffered the loss of his 8t-year-old daughter, Mary, also from TB.[41] Two of his sons – John and Frank – were placed in St Vincent's orphanage in Glasnevin. A third son – Michael – most likely remained living with Cusack. His two surviving daughters – Bride and Clare – were sent to live with relatives in England.[42]

Living at various addresses across Dublin over the next sixteen years, Cusack earned a precarious living from journalism and teaching. His journalism often involved articles on the founding and early years of the GAA. One such article was written in December 1902 for the *Irish Weekly Independent and Nation*. The charming, idiosyncratic piece was accompanied by specially commissioned cartoons of the leading figures of that era, complete with a paragraph on each from Cusack by way of a short biography. Beneath his own cartoon, he wrote: 'Michael Cusack of Burren, County Clare is a queer man. I am afraid to say anything more about him. He might call me names. I think I'll take the advice of my esteemed friend, Michael Smith, Baron Moynalty – I'll leave him to his country.'[43] Cusack left his country when he died suddenly on 28 November 1906. A few months short of his sixtieth birthday, he was buried beside his wife in Glasnevin cemetery in Dublin at 9 a.m. on 2 December 1906.

5. Michael Cusack, the founder of the GAA.

5 The GAA during the Irish Revolution, 1913-23

WILLIAM MURPHY

The role of the Gaelic Athletic Association during the Irish Revolution has received more, if often fragmented, attention than most aspects of the association's history. To explore the extant literature relevant is to take a tour of many of the trends in Irish historiography over the last eighty years. In the first histories of the GAA to appear after independence, the organisation's relationship with nationalism, and consequently the revolutionary period, dominated. These studies were celebratory in tone and the authors were intent on writing the GAA into the creation story of the Irish state. Those early historians were often eye-witnesses, but their accounts underwent a mild revision during the 1980s. Marcus de Burca and W.F. Mandle did not overturn the broad conclusions of earlier generations (it could be argued that they bolstered these) but they were more subtle historians who acknowledged that the GAA's relationship with radical separatism was at times complex. The rise of social history impacted little upon the historiography of the GAA, but during the 1990s an emergent generation of cultural and sports historians challenged the prevailing narrative by asking whether it might not be wise to remember that the GAA was a sports association.

Also in the 1990s academic scholars of the revolution interrogated in greater detail the social and cultural formation of the Irish Volunteers and, as a consequence, questioned the importance of the GAA to revolutionary activists. Since the publication in 1977 of David Fitzpatrick's study of politics in Clare during the revolution, the steady production of regional or county studies of Irish nationalism in that period has indicated that the GAA's role was more varied than was previously asserted. In addition, this decade has seen the publication of a series of important biographical studies that has provided insight into the relationship between revolutionary activism and commitment to the GAA in the lives of several key figures. All the while a stream of club, county and provincial studies of the GAA have appeared. The rhetoric of many of these harks back to the tone

61

of the pre-revisionist years, but that tenor is quite often at odds with the fascinating and hard-found information contained within the books. Primarily, this chapter is an attempt to synthesise, and suggest some conclusions that might be drawn from this growing body of scholarship.

I

In 1916 T.F. O'Sullivan, a GAA official and a member of the Irish Republican Brotherhood, produced the *Story of the GAA*, which claimed to be the first history of the association. Not underestimating the importance of his subject, O'Sullivan began by informing his readers that 'From a small beginning the GAA has become the greatest athletic organisation the world has ever seen.' He then explained why it was great: 'It has helped not only to develop Irish bone and muscle, but to foster a spirit of earnest nationality in the hearts of the rising generation, and it has been a means of saving thousands of young Irishmen from becoming mere West Britons.'[1] This is a representation of the association that is typical of its early (nationalist) historians, many of them GAA insiders.[2] If the GAA's unloved father was the Victorian sporting revolution that swept Britain and Ireland, then Irish nationalism has been its doted-upon mother. The association's founders believed that it was their mission to preserve and foster pastimes which were distinctively Irish. In doing this, they believed that they contributed to a wider national movement.[3] In general, posterity has judged that they were successful on both fronts. Writing of the GAA at the end of the revolutionary period, W.F. Mandle stated that 'it is arguable that no organisation had done more for Irish nationalism than the GAA … The Gaelic Athletic Association had fulfilled its mission – to revive the native games of Ireland and to awaken the national spirit.'[4]

Almost from the moment of the GAA's establishment the Royal Irish Constabulary had, with some justification, regarded it as a semi-seditious body. There were Fenians among the men who met in Hayes's hotel in 1884, but the organisation was also sponsored by Home Rule politicians and the Catholic Church and the names adopted by early clubs confirm that the association attracted nationalists of all hues. Some names referred to Fenians or Fenianism or revolutionary nationalism. These clubs included P.W. Nally GFC, founded in Dublin in 1889 and associated with leading Fenians in the city, and Thomas Addis Emmets GFC, which existed from 1887 to 1892 in the North Strand area of Dublin. On the other hand, there were clubs with names that referred to constitutional politicians; among these T.M. Healys GFC, which was founded in Inchicore, Dublin in 1887, and William O'Briens, established in Monagea, Co. Limerick in 1896. There was even a club in Balbriggan, Co. Dublin, named Gladstonians.[5]

By 1887 the IRB had succeeded in taking over the association, but in the process almost destroyed it. The sporting and cultural euphoria which buoyed the GAA in its very early, expansionary years evaporated, while revolutionary politics acted as an emetic, flushing less radical nationalists from the association at an enfeebling rate. In January 1892, as a consequence of the Fenian takeover and the Parnell split, a mere 200 clubs remained affiliated to the GAA.[6] The association began to recover in the mid-1890s when the Fenian-controlled leadership was replaced by a new regime; a regime that prioritised sport and was sufficiently centrist in its expression of the organisation's cultural ideals to accommodate most nationalists and others who had no politics at all. In the early twentieth century the IRB moved into key positions again, but on this occasion they were careful not to repeat the mistakes of the late 1880s and did not push the policies of the association beyond positions acceptable to mainstream nationalists.[7]

II

In the decades after Irish independence, those who wrote about the GAA argued, frequently and at length, that members of the association were involved, in disproportionate numbers, in the organisations that led 'the struggle' for Irish independence in the years 1913–21. This view was expressed without ambiguity in the pages of the *Irish Independent* in January 1923:

> In 1916 when Pearse and his companions unfurled the flag of liberty, the men of the hurling and football fields rolled in from far and near, and it is no exaggeration to say that they formed the backbone of that company … When the Anglo-Irish war developed, go where you would up and down the country, it was difficult to point to even one man, other than a hurler or footballer, who took any prominent part in the fight.[8]

A cohort of Gaelic games journalists who, in W.F. Mandle's words, were 'nationalists unrepentant and unconcealed' helped to fix this image in the public mind.[9] In 1915 one of these, Séamus Dobbyn, was ejected from his post as GAA correspondent of the *Irish News*, based in Belfast, when he used the GAA notes to encourage members of the association to attend the funeral of Jeremiah O'Donovan Rossa.[10] Other unrepentant nationalist GAA journalists from this era included P.D. Mehigan (also known as 'Carbery') and P.J. Devlin; both men wrote influential histories of the games and the association in the decades after independence.[11] The link between radical separatism and the GAA was symbolically re-enforced during the fiftieth anniversary celebrations of the 1916 Rising when, according to Mary Daly, 'it is evident that the GAA tried to claim a special place, as the inspiration for the Rising and a major force in keeping the flame of republican idealism alive'.[12] This was manifest in the GAA's staging of spectacular pageants to celebrate the Rising at Croke Park in Dublin and Casement Park in Belfast, while the programme for the All-Ireland hurling final of 1966 recorded that the central council took pride 'in having as its guests today the Veterans of the 1916 Rising. Their presence symbolises the indivisibility which has always existed between this Association and the aspiration of a free and Gaelic Ireland.'[13] This is a narrative which the GAA has been reluctant to nuance: at its very fine museum at Croke Park, opened in 1998, the association presents itself as having formed an integral part of the pre-1921 independence movement.

There is no doubt that many members of the GAA were active in Sinn Féin or the Irish Volunteers during the revolutionary period. These included a significant cohort of energetic men, such as Harry Boland, J.J. Walsh, Austin Stack, Dan McCarthy and Eoin O'Duffy, who took on leading roles in both the GAA and the revolutionary movement. Writing about O'Duffy, who was secretary of the Ulster Council of the GAA before he became involved in radical politics, Fearghal McGarry has argued that

> there were certainly similarities between O'Duffy's role in the GAA and IRA, both of which involved constant travelling, organising, encouraging activity where little existed, promoting co-operation between rival parishes and mediating local disputes. It was an immense advantage to O'Duffy in his latter role that he knew, and was known to, the young Gaels of Ulster.[14]

Similarly, 'it was on the playing fields and in the committee rooms' of the GAA that Michael Collins honed his political skills.[15] These men were committed to the success of the GAA, but they also utilised the association to promote revolutionary nationalism. Just as cricket matches had facilitated Fenians in their activities in the 1860s,[16] so too the GAA provided cover for the meetings and movements of radical nationalists during the revolution: they often saved on train fares by travelling on match-day specials.[17] It provided a network of contacts, a school in the rhetoric of Irish nationalism, and a recruiting ground. Sometimes, though not often, the association was used directly as a weapon in their struggle against the British state in Ireland, as when Harry Boland persuaded the annual congress of 1919 to confirm a proposed ban on all civil servants who took the oath of allegiance from joining the GAA; he famously told the delegates that the GAA 'owed its position to the fact that it had always drawn the line between the garrison and the gael'. Historians have begun to draw more subtle conclusions. Recent scholars of the ban, for instance, point to the sizeable minority of delegates that supported an amendment proposed by Jack Shouldice, a veteran of the Easter Rising, which would have considerably circumscribed the impact of the new ban. Although congress approved a ban on all civil servants who took the oath by a clear majority (50 to 31), reports of the reactions in various counties suggest that opposition was very strong among ordinary members and that the upper echelon of the association was more radically minded than its sporting constituency.[18]

In his analysis of nationalist politics in the counties of Sligo, Leitrim, Longford, Roscommon and Westmeath in the years before the Rising, Michael Wheatley has contended that 'virtually no trace … can be seen locally' of the control which the IRB appeared to exert at national and provincial levels of the GAA. Wheatley records that the RIC county inspector for Roscommon reported in April 1913 that 'The GAA clubs are chiefly concerned with their games and do not display disloyalty, but that is not saying that they are loyal.'[19] David Fitzpatrick was surely close to the mark when he suggested:

> What the [Gaelic] League and GAA had to offer the politicians they offered indiscriminately to Sinn Féiners and Redmondites alike: zest for Ireland, tangible rather than rhetorical reminders of Irish nationality, Irish reels, sets, jigs, a few words of Irish, aggressively un-English games.[20]

For these reasons Irish party figures remained very active in the association, as they too sought to harness some to its vitality.

In late 1913 and 1914 GAA members and clubs were swept up in the initial wave of enthusiasm for volunteering. Although the association did not officially endorse the Irish Volunteers, in January 1914

James Nowlan, the president of the GAA, advised every member to join the Volunteers and 'learn to shoot straight'.[21] All over the country GAA matches facilitated Volunteer displays. On 19 April 1914 a match between Armagh and Cavan at Newbliss, Co. Monaghan was preceded by parading Volunteers, while on 5 July 1914 seven hundred members of the Volunteers marched to Tralee train station to welcome the Wexford football team who were in town to play a match.[22] In Con Short's view these displays were to the mutual benefit of the GAA and the Irish Volunteers, as they attracted new members to the Volunteers and 'did much for the GAA in Ulster in the matter of attendance and gate receipts'.[23] On the other hand, Marcus de Burca has written that in Wicklow in 1914 volunteer activity crowded out the GAA calendar[24] and, in January 1915, the Kildare County Board complained that its activities had been disrupted by the enthusiasm for volunteering.[25]

It should not be taken for granted, therefore, that the cultural and political forms of nationalism always complimented each other. In some cases active membership of the GAA militated against participation in the Irish Volunteers, as the GAA and Irish Volunteers competed for the time and commitment of potential activists. In *Towards Ireland Free*, Liam Deasy recalled that he did not join the Irish Volunteers for a considerable period because

> My activities in the GAA and the Gaelic League at the time were so absorbing as to prevent my feeling any immediate urgency about joining the new movement. Besides, I felt that by being actively engaged in the two organisations mentioned I was already serving my country in a useful manner.[26]

Gerald Doyle, a member of the Geraldines GAA Club in Dublin, did join the Volunteers at an early stage, but he did not take part in the Howth gun-running incident of 1914 'as on that day the Geraldines were playing a match against a Wexford Team at Kilkenny for the Leinster Championships'.[27] Important local and national leaders of the Irish Volunteers, including Desmond Fitzgerald and J.J. 'Ginger' O'Connell, complained that too many young men preferred to play Gaelic games when they could have been drilling.[28] In 1914 in Clare, 'the first county inspection of the Irish Volunteers had to be postponed for a week as it would have clashed with the All-Ireland hurling final', which Clare contested and won.[29]

Prior to September 1914 involvement in the GAA and the Irish Volunteers was not synonymous with radical separatism. This is illustrated by the case of Laurence Roche of Bruree, Co. Limerick. Roche had been chairman of the Limerick County Board and that county's representative at Munster Council before becoming chairman of the Volunteers in Limerick city. At the Volunteer split he remained with the Redmondite majority and later served in the Royal Munster Fusiliers during the First World War. In May 1916 Roche was commended for his bravery in leading the capture of Guillemont,[30] while Éamon de Valera, the rugby-playing 'boy from Bruree', was beginning a prison sentence for his leading role in the 1916 Rising. Roche is just one example of an unexplored phenomenon – GAA members who volunteered to fight in the Great War. In Clare, Killaloe GAA Club was 'badly hit as many of its members enlisted',[31] while in September 1915 the *Southern Star* of Skibbereen, Co. Cork carried reports of former GAA players at home on leave from the British army.[32] Peter Hart claims that 'many prominent GAA players joined the British army in 1914 and 1915.'[33] The fact that a number of counties contemplated a proposal to lift the ban on GAA members joining the army for the duration of the war tends to lend credence to this suggestion.[34] Unfortunately, a systematic study of the extent to which GAA members volunteered to fight in the Great War does not exist.

The extent to which GAA members participated in the 1916 Rising has received more detailed attention. A history of Dublin GAA, published in three volumes in 2005, contains a list of the GAA players in the county who were among the rebels. This comes to a total of 302 players from fifty-three identified clubs.[35] In the past this list would most likely have been accompanied by a ritual repetition of the conclusion that the GAA was to the forefront in providing the men and women who fought for Irish freedom. In this case such an assertion was avoided and the reasons are obvious. Although we do not know how many men and women participated in the Rising in Dublin, the accepted estimates centre on 1,500 to 1,800 men and women. This means (allowing for the participation of some GAA players from outside of Dublin) that the overwhelming majority of those who fought in 1916 were not members of the GAA. GAA players were more likely to have participated than many other sectors of Dublin society, yet rebellion remained a minority sport even for them. The figures in *The Gaelic Athletic Association in Dublin 1884–2000* indicate that seventeen of the seventy GAA clubs in Dublin did not have a single member who participated in the Rising, while the majority of remaining clubs (thirty-two) contributed three or fewer. In truth, a handful of clubs contributed the majority of

GAA-playing rebels and it has been suggested that if the rebels were inspired by cultural nationalism, then 'it was not so much membership of the GAA that motivated men and women to take up arms but membership of the Gaelic League'.[36] At the time, the authorities were inclined to suspect the GAA, prompting the internment of a slew of leading GAA figures. While acknowledging that members had participated, the GAA denied any responsibility.[37] Arthur Griffith is supposed to have courted arrest in the days after the Rising, noting that anyone who was not arrested was unlikely to have a political career in the future. There is no evidence however that non-participation in the Rising became an insurmountable obstacle to high office within the GAA. John J. Hogan, chairman of the Leinster Council, retained his post in 1917, although his candidature prompted a disgusted response from Maurice Collins in a letter to Harry Boland: 'I suppose Hogan will go forward again as Chairman. The b——y hypocrite. The scoundrel. Where was he when he was wanted? His excuses would make a dog vomit.'[38]

III

Recent historians of Sinn Féin have recognised an important overlap between membership of the post-Rising party and the GAA. In his study of politics in Clare, David Fitzpatrick acknowledged that the GAA had a role in facilitating Sinn Féin activity in the county. The Clare County Board began the process that saw de Valera nominated to contest the by-election of July 1917[39] and during its march to the All-Ireland football final of that year the Clare team entered the field, round after round, under the banner 'Up de Valera'.[40] Political chat and scheming took place amid the crowds at GAA matches in Clare as elsewhere, but, in Fitzpatrick's opinion, 'the GAA never became so subservient as the Gaelic League to the political organisation'.[41] More recently, Michael Laffan has written that 'members of Sinn Féin were characterised ... by their support for the Gaelic League, the GAA and (most decisively of all) the Irish Volunteers',[42] while Peter Hart has suggested that 'a significant correlation can be found for GAA and Sinn Féin membership as of July 1917 ... but this shrank as the party grew over subsequent months'.[43] That the GAA maintained a recognisable distance between itself and Sinn Féin, despite their shared membership, is perhaps best evidenced by the government's decision not to suppress the association in November 1919, when the Gaelic League was proscribed, along with Sinn Féin, Cumann na mBan and the Irish Volunteers.[44]

Although the first convention of the Irish Volunteers post-Rising was held at Croke Park,[45] historians of the IRA have been less than convinced of the importance of the GAA to the military wing of Irish nationalism. In major studies of Irish Volunteer activity after the Rising, both Joost Augusteijn and Peter Hart reached similar conclusions: Augusteijn wrote that 'there was no direct relationship between the local strength of the Irish-Ireland movement and violent republicanism',[46] while Hart concluded that most Volunteers did not have 'any previous contact with organised cultural revivalism'.[47] Such general statements may, of course, hide regional patterns; a point that Hart makes in his study of the IRA in Cork. Particular IRA leaders probably made extensive use of their GAA connections in their effort to recruit, including Mick Murphy on the south side of Cork city and Eoin O'Duffy in Monaghan.[48] In the summer of 1918 O'Duffy travelled to Wattlebridge to address the local GAA team and seek enrolments in the Irish Volunteers. Francis Tummon remembered:

> On this particular Sunday there were about thirty boys of all ages [playing football] but only about twenty assembled to listen to O'Duffy … His words left a lasting impression on me and, I'm sure, on all present. There were at least half a dozen who listened to O'Duffy that Sunday afternoon but never joined the Volunteers. The practice game of football from which we were summoned to listen to Gen. O'Duffy was resumed, but the foundation of a company was laid.[49]

In a recent study of the northern IRA, Robert Lynch has acknowledged that many Irish Volunteer companies were formed 'around a nucleus of Gaelic football and hurling teams' and argues that 'the democratic notion of electing leaders resulted in the rise to prominence of men with connections to the GAA', but then suggests that 'such moderate or ill-suited leadership led to often chaotic results'.[50]

A strong GAA was not a necessary prerequisite if an area was to develop into a centre of revolutionary activity. The GAA in Co. Longford was very weak in this period, yet Longford became the most violent county outside of Dublin and Munster. Indeed, as far as Seán MacEoin, the most important IRA figure in Longford, was concerned, the GAA was a disadvantage. He wrote: 'One of my early decisions as Director of Organisation was to proclaim all football and hurling matches in the area. I found that they were interfering with the efficient mobilisation and use of my men.'[51] In February 1919 Michael Brennan, a leading figure in physical force nationalism in

Clare, turned up at the GAA county convention. As the jails of Ireland filled with IRA men, Brennan listened to a meeting dominated by one issue: the dangers of 'pitch and toss'. Seemingly without irony, Fr W. O'Kennedy of St Flannan's College warned that 'In Clare it [pitch and toss] is the principal obstacle to a genuine national revival'.[52] Such incidents illustrate the importance of treating with scepticism the notion that the GAA was a politically and nationally minded body above all else. Phil O'Neill's comment that 'Our National Athletic Association nobly contributed its quota of heroic men, who left aside their camáns for more deadly weapons' should be balanced by an acknowledgement that there were countless ordinary members of the GAA, obscure men, who chose the hurley rather than the rifle.

Throughout the revolutionary period the GAA contributed to fundraising for the political prisoners and their dependents. During the nineteenth and twentieth centuries, supporting 'the prisoners' was an activity which allowed mainstream nationalists to indicate a certain degree of sympathy for radicals without becoming entirely identified with their aims; collecting for the prisoners could be presented as a philanthropic rather than a political act. In June 1915, when Seán McDermott and Stephen Jordan, a prominent figure in Galway GAA, were jailed for making statements likely to be prejudicial to recruitment, the GAA in Athenry held tournaments in their aid.[53] In the aftermath of the Rising the GAA, through the organisation of national and local tournaments, became a promising source of income for the most important prisoner support organisation, the Irish National Aid & Volunteer Dependents' Fund (INA&VDF). Mandle, relying on the GAA central council minutes, has suggested that by February 1918 the INA&VDF had received a mere £150 from the GAA. The INA&VDF's correspondence and minute books suggest that it received considerably more than that (£434.3.11 by November 1917), although less than it had hoped for. It is likely that the differing figures can be accounted for by the tens of small donations raised at local tournaments, for which central council took no responsibility, and which the INA&VDF received directly from county boards and clubs.[54] In addition to raising money for prisoners, the GAA in various counties suspended games on a number of occasions as a mark of support for striking prisoners.[55]

Inside prisons and camps Gaelic games occupied an important place. The boredom of prison life and the dearth of other distractions ensured that even former sceptics adopted Gaelic games. This activity also carried a message. The concentration on Gaelic games was intended as a symbolic statement of the prisoners' commitment to Irish nationalism and a rejection of Britain. The internees described their sporting activity in familiar ideological terms. In a manuscript account of Ballykinlar camp in 1920 and 1921, a former member of the camp's GAA board wrote that 'in working for what appeared to be our own salvation, we indirectly arrived at the old Gaelic idea of civilisation, which required a man to be trained physically as well as mentally'.[56] Some sports were banned. When athletic contests were organised in Frongoch camp, in the aftermath of 1916, and in war of independence and civil war internment camps the Irish internees' leadership tolerated one code of football, Gaelic football. This forced the soccer-playing Todd Andrews to struggle with the Gaelic code when he was a prisoner in the Curragh in 1921; he found the style of play too robust for his liking.[57]

In conventional prisons the facilities for field sports did not exist, but basic games of football were played. One former prisoner remembered the 'strenuous games of football played with a rag ball' in Belfast prison in 1918.[58] In March 1921 the governor of Mountjoy prison, C.A. Munro, reported that Eileen McGrane, the spokesperson of the untried women prisoners held there under the Restoration of Order in Ireland Act, had asked that they be allowed

> to play some game while at exercise such as Camog – which I understand is a kind of hurley for women – or football. As a matter of fact a football has been sent in for one of these prisoners, neither game seems suitable but as regards the football I gathered that all they wanted to do was to kick it about in their exercise ring.

When Munro was informed that he might permit such games if 'conducted in a nice and seemly manner', he decided that football was suitable but not camogie.[59] Handball and rounders were more suited to the confined spaces of prison exercise yards. In August 1918 Frank Fahy reported from Reading gaol that 'Handball is our chief exercise. Of course the alley is not perfect, but its erratic construction gives the game an element of the unexpected.'[60] When Peter de Loughrey contested the position of quartermaster to the prisoners in Lincoln gaol his manifesto asked: 'Have I not kept up an abundant supply of handballs with which to stir the athletic spirit of my comrades to glorious & hilarious rivalry & emulation in the Ball Alley?'[61] In Birmingham prison they preferred rounders, which afforded the twelve prisoners there 'a chance to lead active lives at the same time'.[62] The prison and camp authorities forbade hurling for the obvious reason that hurleys could be used as weapons, but they encouraged the other Gaelic sports. They viewed the games as a welcome outlet for energies and aggression that might otherwise be directed at them. In writing about his prison experiences during the civil war, Peadar O'Donnell noted that a rising tide of unrest would suddenly dissipate when 'a football match seemed to catch on, the crowd cheered, and our ridiculously small exercise ground sated the fever out of our minds'.[63]

As an organisation, the GAA's most explicit act of resistance during the revolutionary period came in August 1918. In one of the most successful examples of mass defiance witnessed during this period the GAA flouted an attempt to halt football and hurling matches instituted by the government in July 1918 as part of a clampdown on public meetings. After several weeks of localised conflict between the GAA and the RIC, the GAA decided that on Sunday 4 August, matches would be played simultaneously in as many parishes as possible all across the country.[64] In Kildare the county board warned that it would suspend any club that failed to field a team on what came to be called 'Gaelic Sunday' and, in the event, seventeen matches were held across the county.[65] It is estimated that between 50,000 and 100,000 people participated in games all over Ireland. Realising that they did not have the resources to enforce their policy in the face of such widespread and coordinated resistance, the authorities backed down.[66]

It is noteworthy that the occasion on which the association acted with greatest vigour and unity to oppose the British state occurred when that state threatened the very business of the association – its games. Even then, however, there were those who objected. In the aftermath of Gaelic Sunday, the *Dundalk Democrat*, a Redmondite newspaper, complained that local games had 'descended more and more into the troubled sea of politics until they were simply recognised as so many Sinn Féin demonstrations'.[67] In general, the association – as an association – remained wary of running ahead of the political attitudes of the majority of the nationalist public and managed to retain the loyalty of most nationalists, whether radical or constitutional. This does not mean that there were not local splits: Eoghan Corry suggests that in Monasteravan, Co. Kildare, rival Sinn Féin and Irish Parliamentary Party clubs existed and, according to the *Leinster Leader*, 'some of the best clubs' in that county were 'broken up because of politics'.[68] The danger of a national split was real, certainly between 1914 and the Irish Parliamentary Party's destruction at the general election of 1918, but the GAA was sufficiently cautious to ensure that this threat never gained destructive momentum. Between February 1916 and 1918 a secessionist organisation did exist called the National Association of Gaelic and Athletic Clubs (NAGAC). The driving force behind this organisation was the Kickham's club in Dublin, which had split from the Dublin County Board as early as 1913. Kickham's discontent had its origins in a range of issues, but in part the NAGAC proved attractive to members of the GAA in several counties, who feared that the association had become too close to radical separatist forces. One county where the initiative received notable support was Galway. There a rival county board was established by clubs wanting to distance themselves from the actions of the leading figure in the county GAA scene, Tom Kenny. Kenny was a radical's radical and, with the Volunteer split in 1914, he made it clear that he regarded Redmondites as unwelcome in the association.[69]

When the authorities looked at the GAA, men like Kenny crowded their view. The crown forces generally regarded the GAA as a nest of rebels, an image that informed the decision of those who targeted Croke Park on Sunday 20 November 1920, when they wreaked a bloody afternoon's revenge for a bloody morning's assassinations. It is the most written about day in the history of the GAA in this, or any, period and is the most extreme indication that in an era of political revolution the GAA was more impacted upon than impactful.[70] The successful completion of GAA competitions – both at local and national levels – became very difficult in the years 1918 to 1923. Jack Shouldice, secretary of the Leinster Council, remembered the effort involved in maintaining any inter-county activity in 1921:

> This was not an easy matter. Contact had to be kept up with the different Counties, meetings of the Council held, fixtures made and carried out at different points. Difficulties had to be overcome in the way of transport, suitable venues arranged, accommodation for teams etc. We managed to keep going, however, and had games played in Athy, Kilkenny, New Ross, Portlaoighise, Drogheda and other centres. Some obstruction was experienced at a few venues where we had visits from Crown Forces when searchings occurred and threats of arrests and other action were made. The attendances at the games suffered considerably but we kept on …[71]

In the same year there was no Munster senior football championship and only Limerick and Cork contested the hurling, while a mere twenty-seven delegates attended the annual congress of the GAA in Dublin.[72]

During the revolution Dublin's GAA calendar was moderately inconvenienced – the senior football championship of 1920 was completed in the summer of 1921[73] – but in several counties the games were severely restricted. In Kilkenny senior hurling championships were not organised in 1917, 1918, 1920, 1921 or 1922. An attempt was made in 1919 to hold a senior hurling championship, but this was not completed. The impact upon junior hurling, and junior and senior football championships in that county was less serious; none the less, championships in these grades were not held in 1917, 1918 or 1921.[74] As a consequence of restrictions imposed in the aftermath of the Soloheadbeg shootings in January 1919, the Tipperary football team had to prepare for the All-Ireland football final of 1918, which was fixed for 16 February 1919, in a camp in Dungarvan.[75] In Tipperary the senior hurling championships were not held in 1920 or 1921, while the senior football championship was a casualty in 1920.[76] With the truce of July 1921 such disruption ended, only to return with the outbreak of civil war on 28 June 1922.[77]

IV

When GAA insiders have come to write about the civil war they have emphasised the role of the GAA as a force for reconciliation, while the dilemmas which that bitter conflict posed for the association, the limits of the association's capacity to influence their environment, and the lingering consequences for the association have been faced less frequently. Two examples of the traditional tendency should suffice. In 1934, when the civil war was barely ten years in the past – the GAA celebrated its fiftieth anniversary in a welter of self-congratulation and newspaper supplements. The *Irish Press's* golden jubilee supplement noted with admiration:

> It is hard to conceive that the deeper wounds of the Civil War would have so greatly or so swiftly healed. Again in the playing pitches the divided brothers found an unbloody outlet for their rivalry and in that generous conflict recaptured their kinship and came to share again the great ideal.[78]

This was an interpretation that was reiterated to popular acclaim sixty-three years later in J.J. Barrett's *In the Name of the Game*, published in 1997. The book tells the story of the Kerry football team that won the All-Ireland championship of 1924, a team which included men who had defended both the Treaty and the Republic in a county where the war was fought with the greatest cruelty. For Barrett, that team is a lesson in the facility of the organisation to provide a forum in which enmities might begin to be laid aside.[79] This is a story which is very personal to Barrett, whose father, Joe Barrett, was one of the republicans who played on that team, and the story is a very attractive metaphor for the potential of the GAA to act as a neutral, healing social space.

There were, however, severe limits to the GAA's powers of healing. In December 1922 (almost certainly as a response to the assassination of Seán Hales, a pro-Treaty TD from Cork, and the retaliatory executions of four republicans, the least well-known of whom was Dick Barrett, a former inter-county footballer and hurler with Cork) Cork County Board proposed that the GAA organise a 'national convention' to promote peace. Central council considered the proposal, but soon abandoned the idea. The initiative had no chance of success and there was the evident danger that such a convention would expose, and even exacerbate, divisions among GAA members on the issue of the Treaty.[80] A month later the GAA community in Clare split as a consequence of their failure to agree a response to the execution of two republicans from the county who were leading GAA figures, including Paddy Hennessy, the county secretary. In 1924 and 1925 two rival county boards existed for over a year. The boards reunited,[81] but the bitterness lingered within Clare GAA. In *Over the Bar*, Breandán Ó hEithir recalled with glee the political invective used in a heated row he witnessed as a child, in the early 1940s, between a 'republican' and a 'Free State' band as 'to which of them would have the place of honour' in the parade which preceded a game between Kilmurry and Cooraclare.[82]

In the immediate aftermath of the civil war, the issue most likely to reveal this fault line was the association's attitude to the continued detention of republican prisoners. In November 1923 the Kilkenny County Board faced a motion calling on the board to suspend all matches until the republican prisoners were released. The proposal was rejected, the pro-Treaty Chairman, Tom Walsh, stating that

> The GAA has never allowed itself to be dragged into any political party, no matter what that party, or whether that party is in power or out of power. Our policy is broad enough for every creed and for every party. It embraces all parties, and we cannot attach ourselves to any particular one.

This prompted a walk-out by the delegates of the Clomantagh club and an announcement by the Callan club that they would take no further part in the county championships.[83] This exemplifies a conundrum which the GAA was not alone in facing. Like the official labour movement at that time, in attempting to remain officially neutral the GAA in effect took a side; to not oppose the Treaty involved an implicit acceptance of the new dispensation. The pro-Treaty forces certainly attempted to use the GAA to give its army legitimacy. On 5 June 1922 the *Freeman's Journal* announced with great fanfare a new 'Association' within the 'Irish Army' which would 'cater for all forms of Gaelic sport' and 'become part of the Gaelic Athletic Association'. Eoin O'Duffy, who chaired the meeting at which this 'Association' was announced, reported that the central council of the GAA had 'presented two cups to the Army, each value £50, one of which was to be offered as a trophy for hurling, and the other for football'.[84] When he became commissioner of the new civic guard later in the year, O'Duffy urged his men to 'play their way into the hearts of the people'.[85] Throughout the civil war period the GAA co-operated with the Free State authorities in preparing for the Tailteann festival, which has accurately been described as an exercise in state-building.[86]

Now that stories of the GAA have been told from many different perspectives – for different places, by different people, from different ideological standpoints, and with different themes in mind – has the grand narrative changed? Historians of the GAA will continue to emphasise the strength the association drew from, and the contribution it made to, Irish nationalism, but the association's vulnerability and the limits of its influence in a period when nationalism released revolutionary change is now evident. On balance, it seems that revolutionary activists and their opponents had more impact upon the GAA than the association or its members had upon the revolution: the GAA appears to have been a playground of the revolution more often than it was a player in the revolution. In 1934 the *Irish Press* supplement that celebrated the organisation's golden jubilee contained an article by P.J. Kavanagh on the contest for control of Irish athletics between the GAA and Irish Amateur Athletic Association. It ran under the title 'How GAA Won Its Independence'. Tellingly, the contents list of the supplement indicated that on page eighty-nine readers would find an article headed 'How GAA Won Independence'.[87] In 1934 the prevailing view of the GAA's history encouraged such an error. Today, it is likely that our errors are different.

6 The GAA in Ulster

DAVID HASSAN

In comparison to the rich history of indigenous games played throughout Ireland prior to the formation of the Gaelic Athletic Association in 1884, very little is known about their development within the northern province of Ulster. That said, Gallogly's seminal work on the history of the GAA in Co. Cavan contains clear reference to a form of football, possibly *Caid*, being played in counties Cavan, Monaghan and Armagh, as well as Louth throughout much of the nineteenth century and before. Indeed other texts, among them Art Ó Maolfhabhail's *Camán*, Liam P. Ó Caithnia's *Scéal na hIomána*, Marcus de Burca's *The GAA: A History* and Séamus Ó Ceallaigh's *Story of the GAA*, present further evidence of pre-codified games taking place within Ireland.[1] On the whole, though, it is difficult to suggest that these games provided the basis of what we now recognise as Gaelic sports anymore than they do any other form of football or stick-and-ball games currently in existence.

Instead, most GAA scholars take the events of 1 November 1884 in Thurles, Co. Tipperary as their starting point when examining the impact of the GAA on Irish life. The inaugural meeting of the association was largely a southern affair, presided over by Maurice Davin and Michael Cusack. However, records indicate that a Belfast man, John McKay, then on the staff of the *Cork Examiner*, was also in attendance. Indeed Cusack himself had northern connections, as he taught at St Colman's College in Newry from 1871 to 1874, and it is quite probable that it was during his tenure at the school that he was convinced of the need for action, faced with the unrelenting Anglicisation of Irish life.[2] It is significant that Cusack was working in the north of the country at this point, as it is here that a strong unionist ethos was particularly apparent among a majority population that was sympathetic to the British way of life. Indeed de Burca draws attention to the degree of unionist support the GAA received in its formative years. Ironically, much of this early backing emerged from Ulster, including from the Revd Samuel Holmes of Down, Dr Larry C. Slevin, Armagh and the brothers Frank and Robert Patterson of Newry. Sadly, as events overtook the GAA shortly after

77

its inception much of this initial backing dissipated, although this was less obvious in Ulster when compared to major urban locations such as Dublin.[3]

The early development of the GAA in Ulster was modest. It followed a clear path, initially in Co. Cavan, then through Fermanagh and the remainder of the southern part of the province. O'Sullivan notes that the Cavan club, Ballyconnell (variously referred to as the Biggar club or First Ulsters), was founded in May 1885, making it the first GAA club to be established in the province. That said, clear lines of communication had been established between the central council of the GAA and other, largely sporadic units throughout the rest of Ulster. The first official Gaelic football match in Ulster took place on Sunday 7 March 1886, also in Ballyconnell. In so doing the participants were breaking the Sunday Observance Act of 1695, which prohibited the playing of football on the Sabbath, but despite protestations from members of the local Royal Irish Constabulary (RIC), the game continued unabated.[4] No doubt inspired by the successes of their near neighbours, clubs quickly became established in Co. Fermanagh. In 1887 a certain Master Maguire oversaw the formation of Newtownbutler First Fermanaghs, which in turn allowed for the formation of clubs in Roslea, Lisnaskea, Derrylin and Kinawley.[5] By February 1887 a club had formed in Dromintee, Co. Armagh, while at the same time a group of hurlers from Stewartstown, Co. Tyrone had also expressed an interest in forming a club. Indeed it wasn't until 1887, three years after the GAA had been officially inaugurated in Thurles, that the GAA in Ulster had fully arrived. Numerous clubs affiliated to the association during this year, among them Crossmaglen Red Hands of Ulster and Carrickmacross Thomas Sextons, as the growth of the organisation became apparent throughout the north of Ireland.[6]

Although there is clear evidence of the GAA having a presence in Derry at this time, it was in Monaghan where the association again demonstrated its organisational capacity with the establishment of a county board, following a meeting on 27 December 1887. Of course 1887 also saw the first ever All-Ireland GAA championships take place, although none of the Ulster counties took part. Instead, Short reports that the football played in Ulster at this time combined elements of association football and rugby union. He contends that fielding the ball in the air was not a discernible feature of the game in the northern province until at least the 1910s. What was unique was a particular style of play in Ulster, which saw exponents bouncing the ball up and down off the open palm while moving towards

6. The great Kilkenny hurler, Lory Meagher, gives advice to a Kilkenny player during a match in Croke Park in the 1940s.

their opponents' goal. This was referred to a 'dandling' the ball and overcame some of the early rules within Gaelic football, which had proven to be restrictive to the coaching and playing of the sport.[7] Each team fielded twenty-one players and their playing attire included jockeys' caps, *geansaís* and black britches. The games were considerably more physical than their modern-day equivalents and injuries were commonplace.

Of course the GAA was still a fledging organisation during this time and therefore prone to both external pressures and internal rancour. The latter led to the dismissal of Michael Cusack from his post as secretary of the association in July 1886 and the subsequent resignation of Michael Davin as its president in April 1887. An administrative vacuum allowed for political opportunism and at the GAA's annual congress of 1887 the Irish Republican Brotherhood (IRB) seized upon the growing popularity of the association to take control of it. There were no Ulster delegates at this congress, despite the GAA having by now gained a strong foothold in the province.[8] De Burca and Purcell offer comprehensive accounts of this particular meeting, widely regarded as the most contentious, ill-tempered and occasionally riotous gathering of its type throughout the GAA's long history.[9] Within a month more than 150 clubs in Ulster had registered their objection to this turn of events and there was a real danger that the association's early appeal could be reversed due to the actions of the IRB and its supporters. Fortunately this was only a temporary setback, as an extraordinary convention in early 1888 allowed for some degree of normality to return to the GAA, a meeting, incidentally, that marked the first occasion during which Ulster was represented at an annual congress in the guise of John Trainor and Fr McCarney from the recently constituted Monaghan county board.[10]

Ulster GAA went from strength to strength in the ensuing period. In fact Short refers to 1888 as the 'golden year' of this era. Gaelic football was being played in all nine counties while hurling matches also took place in Donegal, Antrim and Derry. By this time there were over thirty clubs in Monaghan and a similar number in Cavan. Yet by the early 1890s the GAA scene in Ulster, similar to that elsewhere in Ireland, experienced a sharp decline in popularity following the Parnell split, a lingering suspicion of the association held by the Catholic clergy and the ever-present spectre of emigration, a constant scourge on the GAA in the north.[11] Bourke details at some length the opposition of the Church in Ulster to the GAA, principally the claim that it was little more than a 'flag of convenience' for 'secret societies'. Indeed he is strongly of the opinion that it was the vehement opposition to the GAA from the Catholic hierarchy, rather than the popular view concerning the Parnell split, that most accurately explains the decline in the fortunes of the association during this critical phase in its development.[12] The GAA in Ulster had become virtually extinct by this stage, with many clubs folding, a lack of any administrative base worth mentioning and a dislocation from the association at a national level combining to render the body virtually defunct. This continued to be the case until the turn of the century and further inhibited the development of the GAA in Ulster, which was already some way behind the three other provinces on the island. Indeed, Bourke is correct in his assertion that were it not for the records of GAA activity held by the RIC, very little about the early life of the association would be known.[13] This turbulent period only really drew to a close with the formation of the Ulster Council of the GAA on 22 March 1903. This is not to imply that the problems that beset the association at a national level, principally its perceived alignment with militant republicans, had been overcome entirely. None the less with a provincial body in place the GAA in Ulster could at least look to a more secure future. Its work was supplemented by two other organisations that had been formed around this time – the Pioneer Total Abstinence Association (1898) and the Gaelic League (1893). While the former helped to ensure that Ireland's youth were more inclined to engage in healthy sporting pursuits, the latter assisted the promotion of Gaelic games through their inclusion in the *Feiseanna* programmes. For instance, an active Gaelic League division in Strabane, Co. Tyrone led directly to the foundation of four GAA clubs in the town in the late nineteenth century.[14]

By 1910, after an initial spurt in Gaelic games activity throughout Ulster, there was again a declining level of interest in the association. Only four counties were represented at the 1912 Ulster convention and McCaughey reports that when Cavan played Armagh in the semi-final of the Ulster championship that year they couldn't even muster a full set of jerseys and some players took to the field in shirt and trousers.[15] By 1913 the Irish Volunteers had been formed and GAA members joined in great numbers, affecting the development of the association throughout the country. Subsequent to this the Easter Rising of 1916 was to prove the opening act in what was to be a very turbulent period in the history of the GAA, especially in Ulster. Ironically, the Ulster convention held on 17 March 1917 had a full attendance, as the significance of all things Irish became evermore apparent. It was at this meeting that the delegates heard one of the most compelling speeches from an Ulster Council president in the history of the association. Patrick Whelan, a moderate in every sense of the word, delivered a wide-ranging address but focused in particular on the impending political crisis that threatened to undermine the GAA during this period.

> While it gives me pleasure to congratulate old comrades on the success of their efforts, it is still more pleasant for me to have engraved on my mind the conviction that in the struggles that are yet before us, those comrades will, with God's help, be available to lead our movement to victory and to aid by their earnestness and courage in steering it safely over the pitfalls that hover before it. The Gaelic Athletic Association has had to face grave difficulties here in Ulster in the past. Today it appears faced with barriers, traps and misrepresentations that some years ago no sane man could conceive possible from men in authority.[16]

Whelan's protégé, Eoin O'Duffy, acted as Ulster Council secretary during this period, but was considerably more active in a political sense than Whelan. O'Duffy provided the GAA in Ulster with a more robust response to what were, during that time, consistent attempts on the part of the British to repress Gaelic games. In 1918 Tyrone was one of more than a dozen counties in which the GAA had been proclaimed by the government, which meant that a permit from the police had to be secured before matches could take place. The RIC enacted a number of offensives designed to eradicate the GAA once and for all, including attacking club property and disrupting the travel plans of members.[17] The GAA's response was to organise an event on 4 August 1918, which came to be known as 'Gaelic Sunday', during which Gaelic games were played in every parish in Ireland, with an estimated 100,000 players taking part. The ensuing years were difficult ones for the GAA in Ulster, and large parts of the province, specifically west Tyrone and north Fermanagh, had become virtually bereft of any GAA activity.

The political situation in Ireland at this time was intense. Inevitably the GAA became embroiled in this, including in Ulster where a number of incidents took place. In January 1922 the 'Monaghan senior football team' journeyed to Celtic Park, Derry ostensibly to play an Ulster senior football final against the host county. However, their travel plans were disrupted in Dromore, Co. Tyrone when the team was arrested by the B-Specials, who believed that the game constituted little more than an excuse to conduct a reconnaissance mission aimed at releasing three IRA men imprisoned in Derry gaol and scheduled to be hanged on 9 February.[18] Those arrested included senior officers of the IRA's Monaghan-based 5th Northern division, including the divisional commandant, Dan Hogan, brother of Michael Hogan who lost his life on 21 November 1920 following the infamous Bloody Sunday attack on Croke Park. Hogan was a close associate of O'Duffy, a fellow IRA man, and his arrest along with Éamon Carroll, Pat Winters, Tommy Donnelly and John McGrory, all of whom were divisional officers, had the dual effect of disrupting the IRA campaign in Ulster and further discrediting the GAA in the eyes of the security forces.

At an adjourned convention of the Ulster Council held on 17 April 1920, Eoin O'Duffy was arrested and detained by the RIC, who stormed the meeting held at the home of Mr C. O'Neill in Armagh city. During this period, Lynch argues, aside from his strong involvement in GAA affairs O'Duffy was 'arguably the most important IRA figure in Ulster'. The minutes of the gathering make for remarkable reading as they relay the exact point at which O'Duffy is forcibly removed from the meeting. Having just dealt with possible strategies to increase attendances at the convention, its business is abruptly interrupted.

> At this stage armed aliens surrounded the place of meeting and invaded the room; the secretary being taken away by the military oppressors. The Council deliberations were only suspended while members wished our secretary God speed and good wishes for a safe return. For some time the meeting was carried on under the eyes of the oppressor as an armed guard was placed in the room.[19]

Subsequent records reveal attendances at meetings of the Ulster Council to be sporadic, the secretary rarely present as he is variously detained or attempting to evade capture by the British forces.

As the War of Independence raged throughout Ireland, the following two years were to prove difficult ones for the GAA in Ulster. For one it was in the midst of a severe financial crisis and records reveal the concern of senior officers about the very future of the association. By March 1922 the British army had withdrawn from its bases in Cavan, Monaghan and Donegal, save a small number, and the RIC did likewise, eventually handing over to the Free State's new police force, *An Garda Síochána*. Almost immediately GAA activities in Northern Ireland became embroiled in controversy, mostly on account of clashes with the Royal Ulster Constabulary (RUC), the north's new police force. According to Short:

> The Border, which was to separate Monaghan, Cavan and Donegal from the rest of Ulster and which has been the cause of so much agony and misery since and has cost countless millions to maintain, became a reality. Apart from niggling restrictions on cross border traffic, the formation of the Border did not unduly interfere with GAA activity in Ulster and the Ulster Council continued to serve the nine counties as it had always done and has done since.[20]

In spite of obvious difficulties the GAA in Ulster enjoyed something of a revival in the second decade of the twentieth century. In 1923 the famous Breffni Park opened in Cavan, a stadium that has become practically synonymous with Gaelic football. Indeed the counties of south Ulster, specifically Cavan and Monaghan, dominated the provincial championship until the 1950s. Cavan won the province's first All-Ireland senior title in 1930 with its defeat of Galway, while two years earlier Monaghan suffered a heavy loss to Kerry in its only All-Ireland final appearance. However, the honour of becoming the first county in Ulster to claim an All-Ireland title belongs to Armagh when, in an All-Ireland junior championship final played on 14 August 1927 (delayed from the previous year), the Orchard county defeated Dublin on a score line of 4–11 to 0–4. Hurling was also in a relatively healthy state in the early 1920s, with seven of the nine Ulster counties promoting the game and engaging in active competition. However, then as now it seems, Antrim reflected a long-standing commitment to the *camán* game and was regarded as the leading county in the province by dominating the provincial championship.

The GAA in Ulster encountered problems again in the early 1930s as the full extent of British cultural hegemony became ever more apparent. Smith, in his studious history of television coverage in Northern Ireland, highlights the particular difficulty the association experienced in connecting with its followers. Under law the Government of Northern Ireland had the right to block transmissions if it believed this to be in the public interest. Understandably wary of internal dissention and keen to distinguish itself from the Free State, 'all events south of the Border were studiously ignored; even the results of matches played by the Gaelic Athletic Association were refused air time.'[21] Of course this was an approach that continued for some time; Dublin radio stations did exercise a policy of not broadcasting the results of association football matches during the same period but it is unclear if this was in direct response to the actions of BE2 in the north. Ó hAnnracháin, in his recently published paper entitled 'The heroic importance of sport: The GAA in the 1930s', argues that, far from viewing the GAA as the antithesis of how the British understood the cultural role of sport in society, 'many of the attitudes evinced by the GAA actually derived from nineteenth-century and contemporary British notions of team games and athletic competitions'.[22] It is an argument that has similarly been advanced by others, among them Cronin.[23] Ó hAnnracháin's period of study coincides with an era when the GAA was in the ascendancy and even led to certain administrators invoking the association with religious zeal, paralleling its role in Ireland to that of organised religion. Indeed at the GAA congress held on 5 April 1931 the Antrim delegate announced, to thunderous applause: 'we would have no Free State if it had not been for the GAA'.[24] Of course not only is this an entirely overstated view of the GAA's actual impact, but such a claim ran counter to one of the guiding aims of the association – to work diligently towards the achievement of a sovereign and independent 32-county Ireland. The fact that it was an Antrim representative, presumably all too familiar with the difficulties faced by the GAA in the north, who made such a pronouncement is even more remarkable. Sadly, in advancing what is on the whole a well-substantiated argument, Ó hAnnracháin chooses to say very little about the situation in Northern Ireland where, quite clearly, an entirely different interpretation of the relationship between Britain and Ireland, not least through the medium of sport, remained.

In 1934, to mark the fiftieth anniversary of the GAA, the Ulster Council held a special jubilee tournament, which Fermanagh won, defeating Armagh by 1–5 to 0–6 at Coalisland in March 1935. Indeed Fermanagh, somewhat regrettably the only county side never to have won the Ulster championship, also qualified for the Ulster championship final in 1935 only to suffer defeat to Cavan, who then went on to win its second All-Ireland title in five years.[25] The work of P.J. Devlin, whose book *Our Native Games* was published in 1934, began a process of accentuating the GAA's historical mythology and placed the actions of the British in direct contrast to the aims of the association and like-minded nationalists. Devlin's work is also significant as it was published during a time when wider debates about the status of the newly constituted north and its relationship with the Free State were unfolding. Devlin was adamant that the integrity of the Irish nation could only be secured when this issue was satisfactorily resolved and he believed that the GAA had a significant part to play in this process.[26] Cronin conducts a critical assessment of this and other similar works on the GAA in an article in which he claims that too great an emphasis has been placed on the politics of the association – its location at the core of the nationalist struggle – to the detriment of alternative, cultural and sporting, explanations for its successful emergence and longevity.[27] It is a reasoned and sound argument, countered only by Bourke who, in responding to those who would suggest that the GAA had become overly politicised, argues that the only reason why the association was founded and became as popular as it did was precisely because of the political situation in Ireland at the close of the nineteenth century, i.e., it was a product borne out of necessity.[28] Cronin does make a salient observation about the way that those sympathetic to the GAA wrote about it from the early part of the 1960s onwards. In his view two main issues defined a clear shift in emphasis and both reinforced a traditionalist link between the association and Irish nationalism. The first was the debate surrounding the GAA's ban on so-called 'foreign games', which many, including key GAA traditionalists, believed helped to secure its unique standing in Ireland.[29] 'The second factor in changing the debate was the start of the modern troubles in Northern Ireland. As the GAA had always been committed to a thirty-two-county Ireland its sympathies naturally lay with the cause of the nationalist population.'[30] Throughout the early 1960s a significant minority of nationalists, and some unionists, were engaged in a campaign of agitation designed to secure equality on civil and religious liberties in Northern Ireland for the minority population, a campaign that was often met with entrenched opposition from elements within the unionist-controlled hierarchy. At the same time the GAA, conscious of its responsibilities to Ulster, lent its support to a protest from the Ulster Council against plans on behalf of the new nationalist broadcaster in the Republic of Ireland, *Telefís Éireann*, to restrict its coverage to the twenty-six counties. It gave rise to one of the most resolute proposals from the Ulster Council in the body's long history, as the minutes of the council's annual convention held on 4 March 1961 confirm.

> We of the GAA in the nine counties of Ulster, who have the strongest claim to speak for the Gaelic-minded and nationally conscious people of the six sundered counties, make the strongest possible protest against the fact that no provision is being made to bring the Six Counties within the range of the proposed new Television service.

> Customs barriers and map lines have made no difference
> to our allegiance to the Irish nation in the past, and we
> are entitled to demand now that no cultural barrier be
> erected between us and the rest of our country.[31]

This declaration was symptomatic of two issues that were beginning to emerge in Ulster at this time. On the one hand was a genuine concern on the part of GAA followers in the province that they may be jettisoned, metaphorically and in actuality, from the Irish nation and this would have clear implications for their future relationships with the south. On the other, much more sinisterly, the GAA in Northern Ireland was becoming embroiled in a wider political and cultural struggle surrounding the sovereignty of the north. In practice it could not avoid becoming involved in an ethno-sectarian conflict that was to dominate national and international affairs for the latter part of the twentieth century in Northern Ireland. The GAA was a self-proclaimed 32-county Irish nationalist organisation, one that emerged and prospered in a context remarkably similar to that which existed in the north during the latter part of the 1960s. More to the point, its members were also actively engaged in both the civil rights campaign and the spiralling problems that engulfed the region at this time, often resulting in disputes with the Protestant majority, injury or death. Ó Maolfabhail's seminal work on the history of hurling emerged shortly after the commencement of the 'Troubles' in Northern Ireland and draws parallels between those heroic Irish Gaels, including Cusack, Davin and Croke and followers in the north, who had drawn on the symbolic power of the *camán* to confirm their sense of Irish nationalism.[32] At this time one of the province's foremost stadiums, Casement Park in west Belfast, was under the control of the British army, a development that gave rise to the now famous declaration from the then president of the GAA, Pat Fanning: 'The GAA position is clear. Its historical role is not a myth. Our charter proclaims the determination of the GAA to work for a thirty-two-county Ireland … The allegiance of the GAA is to Ireland.'[33]

Nevertheless the reality was that the GAA in the north came to fulfil a range of functions for the people on the ground during these difficult times. Firstly, GAA clubs existed as a repository of meaning for those interested in Gaelic games and keen to promote a sense of Irish nationalism. In a state where the very idea of exercising an Irish identity was problematic for some, the GAA club provided a relatively safe haven around which like-minded nationalists could cohere. Secondly, in developing this theme, it is clear that the GAA was first and foremost an important, possibly *the* most important, cultural outlet for the nationalist community in Northern Ireland. While it was undoubtedly political when it needed to be, for the most part it was – and still is – an organisation that affords considerable pleasure, pride and identity with all things Irish for its patrons. While it promotes a range of sporting activities, the GAA club also caters for those who may not be inclined to engage physically but who nevertheless wish to be part of an established community-based organisation. Thirdly, when northern nationalists wished to reconcile their everyday experiences living in a divided Northern Ireland with an aspiration of a united and sovereign Irish state, they were able to refer to the GAA. It was a tangible and very real link with the rest of Ireland and – at least in the minds of those who wished to see it as such – constituted an untainted and pure sense of Irish identity. Ultimately the GAA in Northern Ireland fulfilled an important counter-hegemonic function for northern nationalists in the absence of any alternative outlet for them to protest against their long-standing subjugation. Ironically, in successfully positioning itself as such, the GAA has received significant financial support from the British government through Sport Northern Ireland, the government body with responsibility for sport in the north. While some may interpret this as a process of acquiescence on the part of the state towards a potentially troublesome element, in reality it has allowed GAA grounds in Northern Ireland to develop at such a rate that they have become the envy of others throughout the rest of Ireland. Coupled with generous financial backing from Croke Park, the GAA in Ulster now has an array of sporting facilities that compare favourably with the other main team sports in Northern Ireland – association football and rugby union.

None the less, it is regrettable that, from the late 1960s onwards, there is no denying the reality that the GAA in Ulster, especially its units based in Northern Ireland, was subject to attack from loyalist paramilitaries and elements within the British state. Des Fahy's *How the GAA Survived the Troubles* is a reflective account of some of the worst atrocities suffered by members of the association during this time.[34] Periodically facilities vested in the GAA would be subject to arson or vandalism at the hands of those opposed to the association and its ethos. One of the earliest examples of this was the arson attack on Ballycran GAA clubhouse in 1974, when the building was razed to the ground. The club, situated on the Ards peninsula, was typical of those that suffered attack; not only was it located in a remote, rural outpost, but it was the only public amenity in the region and thus an attack of this nature had a much wider resonance for the people who lived in the area. However, much more traumatic was the murder of key GAA figures by loyalist paramilitary groups who often had an ill-informed understanding of the association's *raison d'être*. To this end St Enda's GAC, Glengormley, situated on the outskirts of north Belfast, suffered the most horrendous attacks from loyalist paramilitaries, who also claimed the lives of members Seán Fox in 1993 and Gerry Devlin in 1997. This was also the year that the chairman of Wolfe Tones GAC in Bellaghy, Seán Browne, was murdered, having been abducted at the gates of the club as he locked the premises following a Gaelic football match. His death came at a time of heightened political tensions in mid-Ulster and some people interpreted the murder as an attempt to strike fear into the nationalist people of the region. Mr Browne's death was all the more futile as his community activism extended well beyond his engagement with the GAA into areas of social life designed to bring communities together. It is a reminder, if one was needed, that although some academics and commentators have sought to describe the significance of the GAA in purely political terms, the association and those that serve it interpret their involvement in much broader ways. Few GAA personnel in Ulster have been left unaffected by the difficulties experienced by the association during the last forty years. The murder of Aidan McAnespie in 1983, shot dead at the hands of a British army soldier at a checkpoint in Aughnacloy, Co. Tyrone, has been subject to much public comment because of the controversial nature of his death. The McAnespie family has consistently argued in favour of a prosecution against the soldier concerned, claiming murder, while the British state has supported its original contention that this was a tragic accident in which one man sadly lost his life.

Of course the events associated with one club embody much of the problems that affected the GAA in Ulster in the latter part of the twentieth century – the controversy surrounding the occupation of Crossmaglen GAC grounds, in south Armagh, by the British army. This was a recurring concern of the GAA's central operation and condemnation of this sequestration was a regular aspect of its annual congress. The minutes of its meeting held on 24 March 1979, for example, refer to the situation in 'the six counties' more broadly and conclude with the view: 'It is regrettable that solutions have not been found or do not appear to be on the horizon which will enable the people of this whole island to live in unity and peace with justice. This is a genuine aspiration and desire of our Association.'[35] The annual congress held on 28 March 1981 also contained two separate motions specific to the Crossmaglen issue, including one from Co. Armagh demanding the 'implementation of the guarantee given in the British House of Commons in July 1980 viz. that the land taken from the Crossmaglen GAA Club in 1974 would be restored in full'.[36] That said, it was not until April 1999 that this became a reality and the local GAA club received compensation from the British government for the inconvenience caused over the preceding twenty-five years. Of course aside from the difficulties associated with this incident, Crossmaglen, along with a number of other GAA clubs throughout the north, was subject to what appeared to be a calculated policy on the part of the security forces to again disrupt GAA activities. Routinely this would include stop-and-search tactics, delaying teams travelling to games, detaining GAA personnel for questioning and, in some case, landing helicopters on GAA grounds. Sugden and Bairner's seminal text, *Sport, Sectarianism and Society in a Divided Ireland* contains much background information on the plight of the GAA in Northern Ireland and is essential reading for those who wish to learn more about the role of the association in the north of Ireland during the 'Troubles'.[37]

In the latter part of the twentieth century the situation in Northern Ireland was transformed beyond recognition with the signing of the Belfast/Good Friday Agreement in April 1998 and the establishment of a devolved power-sharing executive sitting at Stormont. The GAA, as a major part of civic life in the north, felt inclined to play its part in the evolving peace process and, under a certain amount of political pressure, moved to delete Rule 21 from its statute book. Rule 21 prevented serving members of the police force in Northern Ireland and British security personnel from joining the association. Under a new dispensation, with young nationalists being encouraged to join the police service, it was incumbent on the GAA to play its part in ensuring no barriers remained to those members of its association considering a career in the security forces. When the decision was finally made at the association's annual congress in 2001, opposition still remained from five of the six Northern Ireland counties, with some delegates arguing that the move was premature and others unlikely to sanction such a concession under any circumstances. In any event, in a post-Rule 21 era, while the landscape in which the GAA in Ulster operates may have changed, the association remains as relevant today for northern nationalists as it always has done. The organisational infrastructure governing Gaelic games in the province has evolved considerably and become a very professional, dynamic and profitable sports body, with full-time employees based at its headquarters in Armagh city and coaching officers and administrators throughout Ulster. Ulster teams now compete very successfully at All-Ireland level in Gaelic football while, in comparison, hurling continues to struggle to make inroads in what remains a region in which the appeal of the big ball game appears pre-eminent.

In conclusion, the GAA effectively arrived in Ulster in 1887. Its development there was initially slow, interrupted by sporadic bursts in which organised units throughout the southern part of the province took hold. The last decade of the nineteenth century was particularly difficult for the organisation, with the opposition of the Catholic Church and severe financial shortcomings pushing the GAA in Ulster to the point of extinction. Amid this, however, a revival emerged and by 1903 the Ulster Council had been conceived and began to exercise its influence. However, the GAA still encountered problems and its appeal waxed and waned up to and including the period spanning the Easter Rising and the partition of Ireland. Inevitably the GAA, as a major nationalist organisation in Ireland at that time, became embroiled in activities that, with the benefit of hindsight, did little to embellish its appeal to the unionist majority in the north. Indeed the dual themes of struggle and resistance best define the GAA in Ulster for much of the twentieth century. Over the period of ethno-sectarian conflict in Northern Ireland, from 1969 to 1998, the GAA suffered disproportionately, with the murders of some its most valued members, the deliberate damage to its property and a difficult relationship with the British security forces. Given all that has taken place, and the inevitable concentration on political matters, it is easy to overlook the fact that for the majority of northern Gaels the GAA is an invaluable community resource, a source of physical activity for some and a touchstone of parochial identity for many more. The GAA in Ulster has come some considerable way from its early difficulties and has evolved into a sporting body arguably unparalleled in the north of Ireland.

7. This picture of the Thurles team which won the first All-Ireland hurling championship in 1887 was taken at least twenty years after the match was played.

7 The Camera and the Gael: The Early Photography of the GAA, 1884–1914

MARK DUNCAN

Historians of sport are not alone in their general neglect of photographs as source materials. Across the vast field of social history, photographic images have been exploited more for their decorative value than their interpretative potential. Cormac Ó Gráda, in remarking upon the reluctant embrace of illustrative material by Irish historians and social scientists, has observed that despite the 'ready market for books of old photographs … monographs on historical topics where the accompanying photographs inform rather than dominate the text are still relatively rare'.[1]

The growing library of books on GAA history provides excellent cases in point. Most are filled with pages of old photographs, but rarely are these used to better explain the association, its membership or its place in Irish life.[2] What these publications do succeed in demonstrating, however, is the changing character of GAA photography over time. From the static player portrait to the action shot of on-field play, the development of early GAA photography was shaped by a combination of class, commerce and technological innovation. These factors not only influenced the scope of the photography; they also determined who took the photographs, where they were displayed and how they were consumed.

The GAA and photography share their origins in the nineteenth century, and this chapter examines their overlapping fortunes through the prism of a number of key holdings: the collections of the National Photographic Archive, published GAA photographs and early newspaper photography. What emerges is, at one level, a story of absence: for reasons of class and commerce, many of the largest photographic collections for the period shun Gaelic sports, preferring instead the more sedate pastimes of the landed elite and the suburban middle classes. Elsewhere, though, the GAA was well served. Photographs of teams and players were plentiful and these, together with the development of press photography, effectively map the emergence of the GAA as a popular sporting organisation and an essential part of the mainstream of Irish social life.

I

The visual heritage of Gaelic sports predates both the birth of photography and the foundation of the GAA. As Eoin Kinsella has pointed out elsewhere in this volume, descriptions of the game of hurling were a regular feature of literary output in the early nineteenth century; but it is important to stress that what writers attempted to do in words, artists also attempted to do with paint and hand-drawn sketches. The pen-and-ink drawing of a hurling scene from 1805, by Charles MacKenzie, a Dublin-based landscape painter, is typical of this artistic endeavour.[3] MacKenzie's scene appears to depict a break in play as some players, their hurling sticks still in hand, lie on the ground, seemingly taking their rest. In showing a game played by a large group in open country, the scene is nevertheless consistent with descriptions of hurling provided later in the century by such writers as Mr and Mrs S.C. Hall.[4] A more idealised image of hurling was provided by John Fogarty, whose coloured aquatint of 1831 offers a general impression of life on the Derrynane estate of Daniel O'Connell, the champion of Catholic Emancipation. The hurling occurs in the corner of the composition and is played on open ground, without goalposts or markings. Fogarty's is clearly a work of fantasy, yet it is one which roots hurling within the rhythms of Irish rural life, a pastime the same as dancing, fishing, hunting and shooting.[5]

What is important about these portrayals – and others like them – is that they help inform popular understanding of the character and evolution of sports and pastimes in Ireland. Their difficulty, however, is that they remain just that: mere depictions, visual interpretations of people, events and scenes. They stand as creative works, born of the imagination of the artist and therefore open to rebuttal on grounds of historical accuracy. Photography was different. The invention of Frenchman Louis Daguerre in 1839, photographic images profoundly altered the way that people saw themselves and the world about them. For the first time, it was possible to freeze a moment and create, in visual form, an exact likeness. This was revolutionary. Where paintings and drawings could give an artist's perspective on, or interpretation of, a particular event or scene, photography captured the reality of it. As Susan Sontag, the American writer, would later observe, photographed images did not 'seem to be statements about the world so much as pieces of it, miniatures of reality'.[6]

The truth of Sontag's observation lay at the core of photography's appeal from the very beginning. Early photography was, therefore, less about art than imitation and the Irish took to it with enthusiasm. Or rather, a particular class of Irish did. The time and expense involved in making pictures meant that those who fuelled its initial popularity, whether as producers or consumers of images, were drawn exclusively from the privileged élite. This was hardly surprising: by the mid-nineteenth century, even as photographs had begun to cheapen somewhat, the cost of a normal-sized portrait was still £2, more than double the weekly wage of the average working man.[7] Among the wealthy gentry, however, cost was no concern and photography flourished as a hobby, aided by the invention of the wet collodion process in 1851. Patent-free, this process reduced exposure times to a matter of seconds and enabled multiple prints to be made from glass-plate negatives.[8] This development only added to the attraction of photography among propertied amateurs. Two of the most prolific of these were Gerald Dillon, Lord Clonbrock, and his wife, Augusta, whose estate ran over almost 27,000 acres of east Galway. Married in April 1867, the couple shared a fascination for photography, going so far as to build a glass-roof studio and dark room beside their Galway home.[9] Over the course of their lifetime, the Dillons built up a wonderful collection of still images, which survives as a remarkable visual record of the big house experience in late nineteenth- and early twentieth-century Ireland.

Sport was central to this experience and it was enjoyed by men and women. One of the earliest Clonbrock pictures, taken in the 1860s, shows members of the Dillon family – women and children – playing croquet on the manicured lawn of their large estate.[10] The scene is at once genteel and grand. It is also private. This is clearly a game played for recreational enjoyment rather than the entertainment of others, and it is typical of much of the collection's sporting content. In many ways, the leisure interests of the Dillons speak eloquently of the sporting preferences of their class. So while the foundation of the GAA in 1884 brought with it the revival of hurling and the introduction of an Irish variant of the sport of football, these games never intrude on the family's social world.

Nor, indeed, were they expected to. Gentry support for GAA

events were the exception rather than the rule. In March 1887 the *Celtic Times*, a newspaper launched by Michael Cusack three months before, lauded the action of Lord Ffrench in making available his land at Elm Park for a tournament organised by the Dublin Committee of the GAA. The newspaper remarked that, with one exception, this was the 'first instance when a {member} of our Irish aristocracy has, so to speak, come forward ... with the people in the promotion of an object calculated to tend to their elevation both morally and physically'.[11] The only precedent for Lord Ffrench's gesture had occurred eighteen months before, when the earl of Fingal 'placed his grounds in the vicinity of the historic Tara's Hill at the disposal of the GAA'. The whole-hearted wish of the *Celtic Times* had been that the example set by Ffrench and Fingal would help soothe class tensions and point the way to a more united national effort. 'Let us hope', the newspaper declared, that these events 'will mark a new epoch in our affairs on this island, and that it will be but a prelude to that happy period when all will join hands together, irrespective of rank and class, to advance the interests of our common country.'[12]

Such hope was misplaced. Cusack's newspaper was unlikely reading material on the big landed estates of Ireland, and this call to common purpose met with a muted response. On the Clonbrock estate at least, the photographic evidence suggests that leisure patterns were undisturbed by any sporting developments beyond. All across the south and east Galway region, hurling thrived as a popular pastime, but none of this appears to have made any impression upon the Dillon family on whose estate archery, horse-riding, croquet, cricket and tennis remained unchallenged as the sports of choice.[13]

The rise of amateur photography, as practised by Gerald and Augusta Dillon, was matched by that of the commercial practitioner. As portrait-taking and stereoscopic views became increasingly popular among the middle, as well as the upper, classes, commercial studios emerged to satisfy the growing market demand. One of these, opened on Sackville (now O'Connell) Street in 1865, was owned by the entrepreneur, William Lawrence. It was a booming business, helped by Lawrence's response to technological change. From 1880, photography was transformed with the development of the dry plate process and this greatly enhanced the possibilities for outdoor work by unburdening photographers from the need to carry awkward and weighty equipment. Now, armed with more portable cameras and a stock of glass plates, photographers could travel more freely and broaden the scope of their work. And this is exactly what they did. None more so than Robert French, William Lawrence's chief photographer. French used the railways to travel throughout the country documenting cities, towns and villages and gathering pictures of scenic views and tourist attractions. Prolific in output, French is responsible for many of the 40,000 images that make up the Lawrence collection, now held by the National Photographic Archive.[14] It is an extraordinary resource and the single largest stock of photographic information on late nineteenth- and early twentieth-century Irish life. And yet, for all that, the collection is remarkable as much for what is missing as for what it contains.

The example of sport bears this out. Robert French travelled through an Ireland that was in the midst of a sporting revolution. He used the same railway system that, in bringing teams and spectators to organised events, was driving the development of competitive modern sport. Yet little of this informed his work. Despite the widespread popularity of Gaelic games, for instance, they were completely ignored by French. So too were soccer and rugby, neither of which appear within his vast album. These omissions, remarkable for a collection of such breadth and quality, reveal less about the place of these sports within Irish society at the time than they do about the commercial imperatives that influenced the photographer's choice of subject matter. The success of the Lawrence studio was, after all, built on servicing a growing tourist industry, mostly with pictures of scenic views and tourist attractions. However, this was an ostensibly middle-class market and any sporting images they were fed appear calculated to appeal to the aspirations of this social catchment. Instead of Gaelic games, Robert French was consequently drawn to such polite pastimes as golf, hunting, polo, tennis and sailing and it is these that make up the sporting content of the Lawrence collection.[15]

II

The absence of GAA images from large collections like the Clonbrock and Lawrence was not a deliberate act of omission. These anthologies merely reflected the particular class and commercial interests of their producers – as all anthologies do. In their coverage of sport and their neglect of Gaelic games, however, Clonbrock and Lawrence are unfortunately typical of most large holdings for this period. The extensive collections of Robert J. Welch and Alexander Hogg, held by the Ulster Museum, stand similarly silent on the GAA. Indeed, judged by these key national repositories alone, the only conclusion to draw would be that hurling and Gaelic football, and those involved with them, existed beyond the reach of photography.

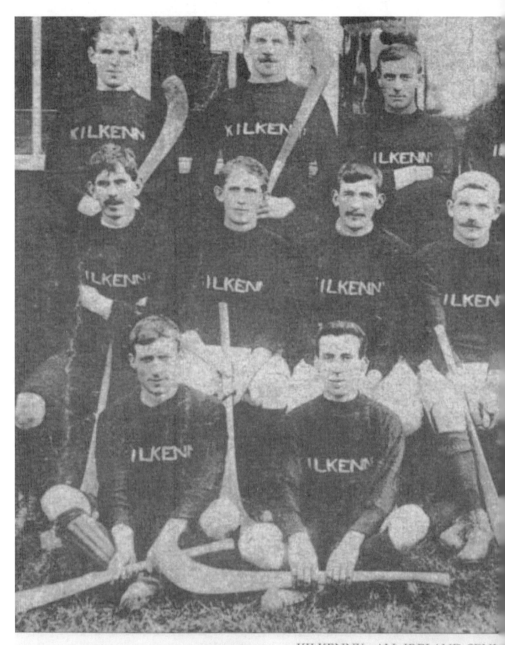

KILKENNY - ALL-IRELAND SENI◆
Back Row: (L/R) Dr. Pierce Grace, John T. Power, Dick "Drug" Walsh, Jack Rochfor◆
Jack Keoghan, Sim Walton, Paddy "Icy" Lanigan, Jimmy Keely, Pat Clohosey,
* Denny Brennan and Pat Clo◆

8. The Kilkenny team that won the All-Ireland hurling championship in 1911.

URLING CHAMPIONS, 1911 - 1912.
iy Brennan, Dr. J.J. Brennan, Matt Gargan. Middle Row: Dick Grace, Dick Doherty,
ennedy. Front Row: Dick Doyle, Mick Doyle, Eddie Doyle, Tom McCormack.
lid not play in the final. (F2-7)

The reality, of course, was otherwise. The GAA and photography were joined at an early stage but many of the pictures that survive to the present day came originally to light through local and family networks. Amateur enthusiasts would certainly have taken some, but it appears more likely, from the staged poses and compositional styles of the images, that most were the work of local professional studios. An adherence to the conventions of classic studio portraiture in much of this early GAA-related work was perhaps inevitable given the constraints of technology. By the late nineteenth century cameras were cheaper and lighter to carry, but they allowed for little by way of experimentation. Moving subjects remained difficult to capture and this meant that it was not until the early years of the twentieth century that photographers were able to convey anything of the excitement, vitality and sheer physical exuberance of the sports they observed.[16]

In the absence of action, the early photography of the GAA was dominated by static team shots and player portraits. The tradition of the triumphant team photograph was not long in the making, but it didn't come soon enough for the first All-Ireland hurling final, played out between Thurles and Meelick in Birr on 1 April 1888. No contemporaneous photograph exists of either of these two teams and even if the oversight was in keeping with the shambolic conduct of that entire championship, there was no rush to correct the error.[17] Thurles won the game, but they would wait twenty-two years before their photograph would join those of the champion teams who followed in their wake. The decision to reunite the Thurles team came as the GAA, by then well established and confident of its future, committed to a drive to shore up its historical record. In the field of athletics, Frank Dineen, best remembered for the support he later provided for the purchase of Croke Park, led the way in producing the *Irish Athletic Record* in 1907, a valuable chronicle of all Irish athletic championship results up to that point.[18] Nothing like this existed for Gaelic football and hurling, and, within GAA circles, the absence of a systematic record of competition winners became an increasing source of frustration. As always, the national press bore the brunt of the blame. Newspapers were accused of neglecting the GAA and, where not, of misrepresenting it 'in every detail and on every occasion'. In a rare gesture of humility, the GAA also accepted some responsibility, attributing gaps in record-keeping to its own 'remissness', as well as to changes in officialdom.[19] It was against this backdrop that the first *Gaelic Athletic Annual and County Directory*, also launched in 1907, begged the assistance of readers in helping to correct any factual mistakes and asked their support in giving the GAA a 'worthy chronicle' that would help 'preserve its old time champion combinations from undeserved oblivion'.[20]

Plugging holes in the record books was one way of rescuing GAA heroes from such a fate. The use of photography was another. Reuniting the first All-Ireland winning team in June 1910 amounted to recognition of the importance of photographs as historical documents and their role in the transmission of sporting achievement from one generation to the next. But the idea was not without its problems. For a start, all the Thurles players were long past their athletic prime. They were now middle-aged or older and, for most, there was no disguising the ravages of time – the greying beards and bald heads bore witness to the passage of two decades. This may not have mattered had the picture taken the form of a group reunion, but the anonymous photographer chose instead to recast the men in the role of the champion hurlers they once were. Most were pictured with hurling sticks clasped to their chests and jerseys pulled tight over collared shirts and ties. Incongruous as they appeared, the *Gaelic Athletic Annual* still contended that the picture offered 'a unique testimony to the physique of the men and the merits of our national game'.[21]

As an act of historical reconstruction, however, the exercise was not without its flaws. The photograph that would eventually pass for the first All-Ireland winning team was something of a distortion of history. Only twenty hurlers featured in the photograph (teams at the time were comprised of twenty-one players) and while all of these would have played at some point during the championship, quite a few would not have been involved on the day of the final match in Birr.[22] The confusion was understandable: on the eve of the game, a row over expenses in the Thurles camp led to the defection of several regular players, including Long Dinny Maher, the then team captain. Maher played no part in the final, but he figured in the team photograph when it was taken in 1910.[23] In truth, given the lapse of time, it would have been remarkable had the entire All-Ireland final winning team presented for the photograph. When, for example, the Limerick Commercials team that won the first All-Ireland football championship, completed within a month of the Birr final, were reunited by their county board for a special medal presentation in 1912, only ten were still resident in Limerick. Five of the players had by then died and three had emigrated – two to the United States and one to Australia. A further two had migrated to Dublin, with another one to Galway.[24] The players involved on the losing team in that football final, Dundalk Young Irelands, were also well dispersed.

Although eleven of them still lived in Dundalk town in 1912, seven had emigrated to England and America, while the remaining three had settled in other parts of Ireland.[25]

In the time that passed between the playing of the first All-Ireland hurling final and the taking of the victorious team's photograph, the line-up of players was not the only thing that had changed. The jerseys were different too. In April 1888 the Thurles team had taken the Birr field attired in a set of green jerseys emblazoned with a constellation of stars;[26] but when they reconvened twenty-two years on they were fitted with different-styled jerseys, identical to those worn by their successors on the All-Ireland winning Thurles teams of 1906 and 1908.[27]

The evolution of sporting dress is one of the most striking features of early GAA photography. In the immediate wake of the GAA's foundation, games were played where coloured caps were used to distinguish players on opposing sides, although the wearing of jerseys soon became the standard practice.[28] In choosing their team colours and design, however, clubs and their players were also expected to function as patrons of Irish industry. In his letter to Michael Cusack accepting an offer to become patron of the GAA in December 1884, Archbishop Croke had expressed concern at the Irish preference for foreign fashions and he drew a clear link between his support for national games and a wider project of de-Anglicisation and national revival.[29] In making this connection, Croke was certainly not alone. In May 1887, Annie Butler from Rathmines wrote to the *Celtic Times* to request that GAA sportswear be used to promote the skilled labour of Irish women, by having the names of clubs embroidered across the body of team jerseys. 'The knights of old went forth to conquest, wearing their ladies' colours and scarfs ornamented by them', she wrote. 'Why not, then, our young knights of the present day follow such a good example, and go forth to their invigorating sports clad in "jerseys" embroidered by deft female fingers? Such a work is much wanted, and will, if carried out, prove not only profitable to the worker, but useful to the wearer, and to everyone interested in the progress of fine art embroidery in this country.'[30] The evidence of photography is that the embroidering of place names on jerseys became commonplace without being universal.[31]

This practice was none the less important in cementing links between club and place, and later between county teams and their larger community. Photographs of All-Ireland winning teams alone point to the slow, but gradual adoption of county jerseys, and this was significant in helping to build a wider base of support for county teams.[32] Throughout the opening decade of the twentieth century, counties competing in provincial and All-Ireland championships dressed in the colours of their leading club, which was not only entrusted with the selection of the county team but invariably dominated it. The problem with this, the *Gaelic Athlete* argued in February 1912, was that it discriminated against players from other clubs and disinclined them from believing that they were representing a broader county interest.[33] The only way to address the situation, the paper maintained, was for individual county boards to decide on the patterns of their jerseys and to care for them between games.[34]

Available photographs suggest that some county boards were quicker to absorb these lessons than others. Among the first, it seems, were Kilkenny, winners of seven All-Ireland hurling titles between 1904 and 1913. Photographs show that the first four of these were won in the colours of clubs, though not without some resentment being caused. Writing of the 1907 final, Tom Ryall, a historian of Kilkenny GAA, referred to the fact that the team lined out for the game in Tullaroan jerseys because Mooncoin had supplied the captain in Dick 'Drug' Walsh. This occurred, Ryall says, in order to 'preserve unity'.[35] However, the photograph that survives of that team, taken a fortnight after the final, shows them wearing the Mooncoin jerseys, the name of club and village embroidered in Irish across the players' chests. The decision to change was taken as a gesture to J.B. Dollard, a cleric home on holiday from the United States who was seated in the front row of the photograph. The last All-Ireland winning Kilkenny team to be photographed in club strip was that of 1909 and when the Mooncoin and Tullaroan clubs returned to win a further three All-Ireland titles in a row between 1911 and 1913 they did so as a united county team, the Kilkenny name sewn across each player's jersey.[36] By documenting this supplanting of club with county colours, photography combined with hurling in the cultivation of a popular county identity.

Other counties gradually followed a similar course, urged on by the *Gaelic Athlete*, which in May 1912 repeated its plea for all counties to fall into line on the issue:

> We have already enumerated the many advantages of this course, its greater convenience to the outside public, who would always know with certainty which was which, as well as its greater acceptability to the players who do not belong to the county champion club. We shall await with interest the advent of the next county to move in the matter.[37]

There is, however, something deeply ironic about the *Gaelic Athlete*'s championing of the standardisation of county team clothing. The paper's support for such a move arose principally from a desire to encourage a closer identification among players and supporters with the county team; yet at the very same time it was advocating the dismantling of the county structure upon which the entire GAA was organised. In May 1912, convinced that the adherence to established county boundaries was acting as a brake on the progress of the association, the *Gaelic Athlete* editorialised on the need to redistribute districts under the control of various county committees. Readers were reminded that the existing county structure was a contrivance of English government in Ireland, which divided the country into administrative units of 'varied sizes and most irregular and absurd shapes'. In the circumstances, there was absolutely 'no sentimental reason why Gaels should not, if conscience and commonsense determined it, break away from the present county system'.[38] The development of a national railway system served only to reinforce this argument for change, and examples were cited of how GAA activity could be improved by adjusting administrative units to take account of new transport routes. Leitrim provided one such example: since the two ends of the county were served by different railway systems, the obvious solution was to split it along north–south lines. Offaly was in a similar position: the townlands of Birr and Shinrone may have been geographically positioned within the Offaly boundary, but the railway had forced them into a closer relationship with north Tipperary than with the rest of their own county. On grounds of pragmatism alone, the *Gaelic Athlete* maintained that such realities necessitated the complete redrawing of the GAA administrative and competitive map.[39]

In the end, no radical revision was countenanced. The boundaries of Irish counties may have been of artificial design and lacking in any geographical or administrative coherence, but it was the very upsurge in the GAA's fortunes that made them more secure. The photographing of teams in newly designed county colours or with county names sewn on jerseys pointed, for instance, to a hardening of county identities, not the reverse. But this construction of county consciousness was not the only thing revealed in the team photography of the early GAA.[40] As the dominant GAA image to emerge in the late nineteenth and early twentieth centuries, the static team photograph provides a rich source of information for historians working across a broad spectrum of subject matter, including class, clothes, crowds, gender and body language. Player portraits, another popular photographic form, yield similar evidence and, taken together, these images come loaded with a wider cultural purpose. Writing of the British context, the historian Richard Holt has identified the importance of photography in propagating the 'amateur cult of the active body'. According to Holt, photography

> posed the athlete in the manner of classical portraiture, confident, calm and authoritative, the cricketer holding a bat as a general might rest his hand upon a sword. The heroic tradition of representing the male body was reinvented in sporting iconography just as it was disappearing from fine art. Sport allowed the male body to be openly and beautifully displayed without ambiguous moral connotations. So taking photographs of players coming out to bat or in a commanding pose with a football or an athletic trophy was a feature of the iconography of amateurism.[41]

As it was for cricket and football in Victorian Britain, so too it was for Gaelic sport in Ireland. Champion athletes, hurlers and footballers were regularly photographed in heroic guise. They would appear, for the most part, in their sporting dress, standing upright, medals pinned to their chest or a trophy at their side.[42] These images not only emphasised the nobility of the Gaelic sportsman, they also informed a wider argument around the importance of the GAA to the formation of Irish manhood. Across Europe and the United States, sport played a vital role in the construction of a masculine identity, and the GAA fully understood that it was involved in a similar project.[43] The physical and moral stature of GAA players was a theme to which contemporary writers frequently warmed and many were keen to propagate a myth of Gaelic exceptionalism. By way of example, the ideal Gael, as envisaged by the *Gaelic Annual*, cut an extraordinary figure; he was, the journal insisted, 'a matchless athlete, sober, pure in mind, speech and deed, self-possessed, self-reliant, self-respecting, loving his religion and his country with a deep and restless love, earnest in thought and effective in action'.[44]

For the purity of the vision and the sheer extravagance of the racial claim, this has been a favoured passage of historians; yet it was entirely in keeping with much of the writing on Gaelic games at the time. Throughout this period of GAA history, newspapers and journals were suffused with equally confident assertions of the physical improvements that Gaelic games could bring to young Irish men. Or, for that matter, what they had already brought: in 1908, for example, the journalist P. J. Devlin, writing under the pseudonym 'Celt' declared that you could not 'walk the streets of our metropolis without meeting a specimen of what hurling has made, developed or maintained'.[45] Photography cultivated a particular image of Gaelic manhood and pictures of teams and players testified to the physical benefits that accrued from participation in Gaelic sports. However, even a cursory comparison with the photography of other sports was sufficient to demolish any notion of Gaelic superiority.[46] Pictures attest more to the similarity than the difference between sportsmen as, in both style and content, the early photography of the GAA is largely indistinguishable from that of the rival codes it set itself so fervently against.

III

Until the end of the nineteenth century, the range and reach of GAA photography was limited by the constraints of technology. A paucity of action shots ensured that the visual focus narrowed on players and teams to the exclusion of the sporting spectacle in which they were involved. At the same time, the diffusion of these images was curtailed by the inability of many newspapers to reproduce them in print. Initially at least, their absence damaged neither the newspapers nor the sport. On the contrary, from the 1880s onwards, sport and media in Ireland were drawn into an ever closer relationship and the courtship worked spectacularly to their mutual benefit. Helped by improved literacy rates, enhanced printing technology and better distribution networks, newspapers developed a far wider readership and this determined the expansion of their coverage of sports. In doing so, they held a mirror to a growing social phenomenon and reinforced its place within the popular culture.

By the time the GAA was founded in the mid-1880s, the Irish newspaper market was sufficiently large to support two dedicated weekly sporting papers: the *Irish Sportsman and Farmer* and *Sport*.[47] The first effectively functioned as an organ of the rural leisured class and was dominated by news of hunting and related activities, while the latter, as part of the *Freeman's Journal* stable of newspapers, was more populist in appeal, reflecting more fully the diversity of Irish sporting interests.[48] By 1887, a mere three years after its foundation, the GAA had given rise to two further sporting titles. The *Celtic Times*, launched by GAA founder Michael Cusack, was the first newspaper to cater exclusively to Gaelic games, although it was primarily used as a vehicle for the views of Cusack, which were freely given, and often in the most robust terms. Cusack was particularly given to excoriating the executive of the GAA, from which he had been removed in 1886, and it was largely in response to these criticisms that *The Gael*, edited by IRB man and executive member, Patrick Hoctor, was launched in April 1887. The two papers were ostensibly borne of a divided GAA, but they were united in their failure. The *Celtic Times* was only a year old when falling circulation plunged it into financial crisis, forcing its closure;[49] and soon after, denied its *raison d'être*, *The Gael* went the same way.[50]

Almost a decade passed before the GAA re-entered the newspaper market. Exasperated by their treatment at the hands of a national press that was viewed as being 'openly hostile or secretly indifferent' to their aims and general welfare, they launched the *Gaelic News* in July 1897.[51] Edited by Dick Blake, then secretary of the association, this was very much an official GAA publication, but in terms of layout and design it sought to learn from past experience by making 'its bow to the public in a somewhat different guise'.[52] The *Gaelic News* was a monthly tabloid whose major claim to originality lay in its use of photographs. Trumpeting its own uniqueness, it claimed – justifiably – to be the first newspaper to provide 'high-class illustrations and exclusive reports' on Gaelic matters and for this reason alone, it believed that it 'ought to command the hearty support of every Gael'.[53] The emphasis on strong visual content was obvious from the front page of the first issue, which was dominated by a large picture of the Dr Croke Challenge Cup, a newly instituted inter-county competition to mark the silver jubilee of the archbishop's episcopal appointment. Inside, a glossy supplement carried additional photographs of the Arravale Rovers (Tipperary) and Young Ireland (Dublin) teams which contested the final of that competition.

The first issue ran to a total of eight pages and though it contained news of GAA events at home and abroad, the Dr Croke Cup final stood as the centrepiece of its coverage, with the illustrations complemented by a lengthy report on the game itself. This was a format which Blake, as editor, was clearly intent on developing in further issues; by way of advance publicity, for instance, readers were advised that the next instalment of the paper would include a much larger selection of illustrations. As well as photographs of the Lee (Cork) and Commercials (Limerick) football teams, portraits were promised of champion GAA athletes such as John Flanagan, who had enjoyed success at the previous year's English Championships in Northampton.[54] That promise was never realised. The GAA had hoped that the *Gaelic News* would eventually evolve into a weekly GAA newspaper, yet it didn't survive beyond that first issue.[55] For all its innovation and visual appeal, the paper effectively crashed before take-off.

If the demise of the *Gaelic News* was entirely in keeping with the

GAA's abysmal record in such ventures, the choice of the illustrated format was at least indicative of a willingness to try something new. The marriage of photography and type had been made possible with the introduction of the half-tone printing process, but this was not fully adopted by Irish newspapers until the early twentieth century.[56] Once it was, the impact on the appearance of newspapers was transformative: the regular inclusion of photographic images enabled newspapers and magazines to shed their dull, type-driven look, while also offering an exciting vehicle for photographers to display their work. The *Cork Weekly Examiner* was among the first to include regular photographs, but the real impetus in this direction came with the launch of a new-style *Irish Independent* in 1905. This paper typically dedicated a page to publishing images on different subjects, grouping them together under such broad headings as: 'Illustrated News'; 'Pictures of the Day'; 'Topical Photographs'; 'News from the Camera' and 'Pictures of Interest'.[57] The format worked. Within three years the *Irish Independent* boasted sales of 40,000 copies daily and this, it has been claimed, had 'a devastating effect on the rest of the newspaper industry'.[58]

With the Irish media landscape in the process of being redrawn, the GAA looked on askance. Although the early years of the new century had seen the newspaper publication of the first action images of Gaelic games, the association continued to nurture a grievance at the quality of coverage it was receiving in the national press.[59] True to form, the response was to establish a new GAA paper to fill the perceived vacuum. Launched in January 1912, the *Gaelic Athlete* was an unofficial organ, but it represented the views of the broad membership, including leading officials, on whom it relied for copy to fill its pages. The *Gaelic Athlete* made little use of photographs and it was not unusual for a run of issues to contain none at all. However, in terms of the visual record of Gaelic games, the paper was significant less for what it produced itself than for the reaction it drew. Six months after it was set up, when the *Gaelic Athlete* took stock, it reflected with pride on the impact it had made to the general media coverage of Gaelic sports. Forsaking any pretence of modesty, the paper claimed to have

> very seriously revolutionised the attitude of the so-called National Press towards matters Gaelic. Prior to our advent a few lines were considered by most journals to be quite sufficient to devote to a Gaelic match, and even those papers that were somewhat more generous, and gave a quarter or half column report, did so in a slap-dash, care-

less fashion that plainly proclaimed the contempt in which the proprietors held the National pastimes. All this is now changed. Our intelligently-written descriptive reports of matches have set the fashion in sporting journalism, and other papers are now making strenuous efforts to copy our style and method.[60]

Although the *Gaelic Athlete*'s reading of the national press was largely correct, the biggest change in GAA coverage was not so much the increased column inches but the expansion of newspaper photography. When the All-Ireland football and hurling finals were played in November 1912, for instance, the most striking feature of the media treatment was the sheer volume and variety of images used across all the main titles. These photographs underscored the reality that finals were as much social, cultural and commercial events as sporting fixtures. On-field action shots were coupled with images of the pageantry and social activity around the game, with marching bands, pressmen and important dignitaries sharing the limelight with the players and officials.[61] The crowd was pictured too. On 18 November 1912, for example, the *Cork Examiner* ran a photographic feature under the heading 'All-Ireland Hurling Final: Snaps at Dublin Yesterday'.[62] Included was a photograph of the Cork hurlers and their supporters outside Wynn's hotel, from where they set off for the game at Jones's Road. Once inside the ground, however, these supporters found themselves part of a crowd too big for the facilities at the ground to cope with. A photograph which appeared in the *Cork Examiner* the following day (the photographic coverage ran over two days) highlighted the inadequacy of spectator accommodation at Jones's Road – it showed a large crowd of men spilling from the terraces onto the goal line, a situation which, the caption explained, got progressively worse as the match wore on; by the start of the second half, the crowd on the pitch had swelled to the point that the 'angles of the field [were] converted into perfect curves'.[63]

IV

This type of photographic coverage was unprecedented, but it established a standard which would be maintained and built upon in subsequent years. Photographs now became as integral as written reports to the newspaper coverage of major games and this, in turn, revolutionised the visual experience of readers.[64] None of this could have happened without the dual drivers of new technology and industry competition, and the combined effect was to generate more work for photographers and more publicity for the GAA. Growing media coverage not only helped to transform the general appreciation of Gaelic games, it equally facilitated the emergence of a culture of celebrity around those who played it. Prominent hurlers and footballers were no longer known by name alone. Their faces filled the popular press and they became recognisable beyond their places of home and work. Through the mediums of newspapers and photography in particular, the celebrity of players like Kerry football captain Dick Fitzgerald transferred from the local to the national stage. Fitzgerald was the best-known footballer of his age and he used his fame to publish the GAA's first ever coaching manual, *How to Play Gaelic Football*, in 1914.[65] The book was remarkable not simply for the quality of Fitzgerald's analysis of the 'scientific' character of the Gaelic code that had evolved; it was ground-breaking for the use of photographs to impart advice on the essential skills of catching and kicking.[66] A portrait of an upright Fitzgerald dressed in the playing gear of Kerry, holding a ball and standing beside a table supporting the Dr Croke Cup was also included, and this was the image most widely used in the advertising that accompanied the book.[67] Implicit in this was the recognition that celebrity sells – by promoting the image of Fitzgerald, the book itself was promoted.

In many ways, Dick Fitzgerald was the embodiment of Irish sporting celebrity; however, the construction of that celebrity owed much to the growing influence of photography on the media coverage of Gaelic games. The increased use of photographs to illustrate newspaper stories changed radically the visual representation of the GAA and placed it at the core of a new, media-driven Irish photographic tradition. By the early twentieth century that tradition was established as the primary means of visual communication, though competition had already begun to emerge in the form of the motion picture. As early as 1914, indeed, it is clear that cinematographers had joined photographers in their attendance at All-Ireland finals.[68] The age of film had arrived, but it was too late to document the first and most important phase of modern sporting development in Ireland. That responsibility had fallen to photography and the result is a rich stock of images that inform as well as illustrate the GAA's past.

8 Gaelic Games and 'the Movies'[1]

SEÁN CROSSON

9. *The Wind that Shakes the Barley* (Ken Loach, 2006).

From the earliest days of the cinema, sport was one of the most popular subjects of representation. Indeed, the first successful attempts to capture motion in photography, in the work of Eadweard Muybridge in the early 1870s, were focused on sport, from a horse galloping to 'how pitchers throw the baseball, how batters hit it, and how athletes move their bodies in record-breaking contests'.[2] As film developed as an enterprise, 'the first flickering, commercial motion picture' was the depiction of a prize fight between 'Battling Barnet' and 'Young Griffo', a four-minute film shot by Woodville Latham and his two sons and shown to an audience in 1895.[3] This was preceded the year before by Thomas Edison's filming of a boxing exhibition match between Mike Leonard and Jack Cushing, fought in Edison's Black Maria, the first recorded motion picture use of 'actors'.[4]

Unsurprisingly, when film arrived in Ireland, Irish sport, including Gaelic games, would soon feature. The earliest record we have of the

111

filming of a Gaelic game – a clip that does not survive, unfortunately – is a 1901 Cullen's Challenge Cup hurling game between 'Rovers' and 'Grocers' played at Jones's Road – now Croke Park – on 8 December 1901. The Irish Animated Photo Company (an early Irish actualities company) film was shown as part of a 'Grand Gaelic Night' at the Rotunda the following Wednesday.[5] Gaelic games would continue to feature in both actualities and newsreel, even if many of these, particularly between the wars, would emerge from foreign companies, often with a strong British bias.[6]

As the twentieth century developed, sport and the media became increasingly interconnected. As Raymond Boyle and Richard Haynes have noted, 'Sport and the media ... are now integral components of what we often called the entertainment or cultural industries'.[7] However, while sport has been a recurring presence throughout film history, sports fiction films – the primary focus of this chapter – have played a relatively small role in the pantheon of cinema history, such that there is considerable difficulty in defining what exactly a 'sports film' is.[8] As J.H. Wallenfeldt observes in *Sports Movies*, though the sports film is 'among the most engaging the cinema has to offer and one of Hollywood's specialties ... it isn't easy to define the difference between a sports film and a film with sports in it'.[9] Wallenfeldt's comments are particularly relevant in the Irish context, where it is difficult to definitively identify a distinct genre of Irish sports film *per se* – outside of documentary – and indeed few fiction films that feature sport at all, and still less that feature Gaelic games.

However, Gaelic games have had a place in film, and arguably a role that outweighs the actual minutes of screen time such games occupy. In particular, I want to explore how representations of Gaelic games have related to two major forces in twentieth- and indeed twenty-first-century Ireland – nationalism and tourism. Both of these issues are important to any understanding of the role and significance of representations of Gaelic games in film and, indeed, sometimes intersect in the context of individual films.

Mike Cronin has argued in *Sport and Irish Nationalism* that

> As sport is so popular and has such a long history in Ireland it is the ideal vehicle to use to establish an understanding and appreciation of how Irish nationalism has been formed and has functioned over the last century or so. While the political and literary versions of nationalism are élitist, the nationalism that is propagated by sport is not. While literature is high culture and the preserve of the few, sport is low culture and the passion of the many.[10]

However, cinema, similarly, has a place in society comparable to sport in that it too appeals across all sections and is arguably embraced even more by the lower classes than those who occupy the upper echelons. Indeed, in the early decades of the twentieth century cinema acquired a huge following among the working classes that would be sustained throughout the century, at least until the advent of television. While precise attendance figures are difficult to find, the number of venues showing films and the sheer speed with which they emerged is indicative of a considerable following. As Irish film historian Kevin Rockett has recorded: 'By 1916, 149 cinemas and halls were listed as showing motion pictures and, by the end of the silent period, 1930, there were 265 cinemas and halls throughout the island as a whole.'[11]

In her contemporary study of 'Cinema Statistics in Saorstát Éire-ann', Thekla J. Beere found that by 1935 there was one cinema for every 16,000 people in the Free State, and one cinema seat for every twenty-seven persons. The vast majority of these cinemas had show-ings at least five days per week.[12] Beere estimated 18.25 million admissions per year to cinemas in the state – an average of over 350,000 people, of a population of nearly three million, attending each week – with most in Dublin and urban Ireland. While this is far from the highest figure per capita in Europe in this period, Beere's description of the rise of cinema 'from a little-known new invention to one of the greatest social institutions the world had ever known' is certainly appropriate to Ireland.[13]

The popularity of cinema among the Irish people is apparent both in its influence and use in the milieu of rising nationalism and the attempts made firstly by the British administration (concerned about film's contribution to nationalist sentiment)[14] and subsequently by middle-class Catholic Ireland (more worried about film's impact on the moral fabric of Irish society) to control its influence, culminating in one of the first pieces of legislation, the Censorship of Films Act, passed by the new Irish Free State in 1923. Cinema's importance in communicating to nationalist Ireland the tumultuous events of 1921 was signalled by Ken Loach in an important scene in *The Wind that Shakes the Barley* (2006), where we witness the ordinary foot soldiers of the IRA acquire their information on developments post the Anglo-Irish treaty in the picture house.

Loach is actually closer to the truth in this scene than some view-ers may have realised. As Rockett has noted, the most important indigenous film company in Ireland prior to independence, the Film Company of Ireland (established in 1916), 'made a short film for the Republican Loan Bonds campaign which featured Michael Collins,

Arthur Griffith and other prominent nationalists'.[15] Indeed, it was Collins himself, who has been described as 'one of the first Republicans to realise the propaganda value of the new medium of film',[16] and who arranged for this and several other republican films to be made. As Rockett also notes, 'In Ireland the [Republican Loan Bonds] film had unorthodox exhibition when Volunteers entered cinema projection rooms, ordered the projectionist at gun point to remove the film being shown to put on the Republican Loan film instead.'[17]

Loach's *The Wind that Shakes the Barley* (illus. 9) also features an opening scene depicting the playing of hurling – prohibited during the war of independence – which results in the interrogation of the participants by the black and tans and the eventual killing of one because of a refusal to give his name in English. Loach is alive to the political significance of the game of hurling and cinema-goers in Ireland in 1918 would have been still more so, when one of the most important films made by the Film Company of Ireland, *Knocknagow*,[18] was released. Indeed, the political resonances of this work could not have been lost on contemporary audiences, based as it was on the hugely popular book of the same name by the prominent Fenian, Charles

10. *Knocknagow* (Film Company of Ireland, 1918).

Kickham. While much of the novel is taken up with a succession of drawn-out love stories, in the film, no doubt to accentuate the political resonances of the work, it is relationships to the land that are to the fore.[19] To further connect with recent tumultuous events, the film had its first public showing on the second anniversary of the 1916 Rising, on 22 April 1918, in the Empire theatre in Dublin.[20]

But the film has a further significance in terms of representations of Gaelic games, as it contains one of the first depictions of hurling on film – when the central protagonist, Mat Donovan, leads his local team in a game (illus. 10). This depiction could only have further encouraged its political connotations for contemporary spectators, given the British government's imprisoning of many GAA members after 1916, including the association's president, James Nowlan.[21] Furthermore, hurling sticks were used by republican volunteers for both training and drilling sessions, in the absence of sufficient arms, throughout the 1910s, as depicted in several recent films including *The Wind that Shakes the Barley* and Neil Jordan's *Michael Collins* (1996).[22]

While *Knocknagow* was a major production of the Film Company of Ireland and showed great promise for the nascent Irish film industry, the following four decades would see relatively little fiction film-making in Ireland, let alone films that had Gaelic games as their subject. Important newsreel and documentary work was done by the National Film Institute of Ireland from 1948 onwards (and latterly Gael Linn) to film successive All-Ireland finals (and sometimes semi-finals) before the advent of television. While not wishing to downplay the significance of these films and their important contribution as among the first detailed indigenous depictions of Gaelic games, it is worth noting their relationship with the nationalist and traditionalist ethos of the new state. As Mairéad Pratschke has noted of Gael Linn's Amharc Éireann series in particular:

> The meaning of Irishness is the underlying theme of the entire Amharc Éireann series. The films are pointedly in Irish, and nowhere in the series is it more clear what Irishness entails than in the films that deal specifically with traditional Irish culture … The extensive coverage of such Irish sports as hurling and Gaelic football, and the exclusion of English soccer, also underlines the role of these games in traditional Irish identity.[23]

In terms of fiction filmmaking, however, it would be primarily left to filmmakers outside of Ireland to depict the country and its pastimes in film, some examples of which we will return to shortly.

However much Gaelic games were part of the construction of Irish identity before and immediately after independence, the depiction of these games in Irish films when a critically engaged indigenous cinema finally began to emerge in the late 1960s would also be part of the deconstruction of such an identity and critique of the failures of the state. Indeed, one of the first major works that would anticipate the emergence of an indigenous cinema of national questioning in the 1970s included a segment focused on revealing the continuing anachronisms of the GAA, in particular the ongoing imposition of a ban on players from watching or participating in English games. Peter Lennon's *Rocky Road to Dublin* (1968), while a documentary work, none the less in its highly critical approach to the Irish state on the cusp of huge change in the late 1960s anticipated the work of fiction filmmakers such as Bob Quinn, Joe Comerford, Cathal Black and Fergus Tighe in the 1970s and 1980s.[24]

If there is one indigenous narrative film that deserves the title of GAA 'sports film' it is Tighe's partly autobiographical début work filmed in his home town of Fermoy, Co. Cork in August 1986. The film was over four years in production and shot on a shoestring budget of £112,000 – funded by RTÉ, the Arts Council and Bord Scannán na hÉireann/ Irish Film Board. Indeed, *Clash of the Ash* was one of the final films to receive funding from the board before it was deconstituted in the round of cutbacks that followed the return of Fianna Fáil to government in February 1987. Furthermore, the film became the subject of the debate that followed the board's demise in the Seanad where Senator David Norris called on the government to reverse its decision in the interests of the Irish film industry. Norris picked out *Clash of the Ash* in particular as an example of the finest work funded by the board and drew attention to a letter from Tighe published in the *Irish Press* on 3 July 1987 where the director remarked that the film was only made 'because the crew worked for nothing, the equipment was mostly borrowed and I went into debt of £700'.[25]

Clash of the Ash has been described as 'one of the key Irish films of the 1980s'.[26] 'This 50-minute drama', the *Irish Times* reviewer continued, 'offers a portrait of a still largely uncharted part of contemporary Irish society – small town life and the struggle of the young to resist its stifling conformity.'[27] The film was well received on release and won several awards, including the Starting Out category award at the Eighth Celtic Film and Television Festival, the fiction prize at the Interceltic Festival[28] in 1987 and the Gus Healy Award for Best Irish Short at the Cork Film Festival in the same year.

Described by Éamon Sweeney as one of the few films with a 'real feel for the GAA',[29] it is not so surprising when one considers Tighe's own background as a hurler, winning an All-Ireland senior colleges hurling medal with St Colman's in Fermoy. Indeed, the violent climax to the film's final hurling game re-enacts an event Tighe has recalled from his own playing days.[30] As Lennon did in *Rocky Road to Dublin*, Tighe used his depiction of Gaelic games to draw attention to his own concerns regarding the state of the nation in the mid-1980s. Phil Kelly is the star player with the Fermoy hurling team and is tipped to make the county minors, but his application leaves something to be desired, at least in the eyes of the team's foul-mouthed and two-faced trainer, Mick Barry. His mother meanwhile is more concerned with Kelly's lack of application to his Leaving Certificate studies, but Kelly's interests lie further afield than the modest plans his parents have for him in the local garage, particularly after he meets the glamorous Mary, returned from London. While the GAA had promoted for much of the century an ideal notion of Ireland as Irish – Irish-speaking if possible –and celebrated the bravery, nationality, masculinity and high ideals of its members, Tighe's film reveals its central protagonist, Phil Kelly, the star of the local team, to be a poor student, temperamental, violent and prone to binge drinking and drug abuse. This includes a scene of Kelly and Mary smoking a joint brazenly in the local coffee shop, where Kelly boasts of smoking joints 'all the time'.

Indeed, such is its depiction of Ireland in the mid-1980s that the film was lucky to be made at all, especially when the local bishop got his hands on the script. Advised by the president of St Colman's college, where Tighe had hoped to make the film, the script was condemned as blasphemous and resulted in a call to the local GAA club in Fermoy by the bishop asking that they would have nothing to do with the production.[31] In a sign of changing times in Ireland, the local club declined the bishop's advice and continued to facilitate the production while the local technical school provided teams and permitted Tighe to use its grounds for the film. Colman's president and the local bishop may have been partly concerned for the reputation of a school, whose first president was Archbishop Croke, first patron of the GAA and a cleric with a particular concern for Irish culture and its representation.[32] The bishop's ire was no doubt further inflamed by aspects of the script which may have offended religious sensibilities but which are absent from the finished film, including a shot early on, shot 17, described as 'THE FACE OF CHRIST, crucified on a hilltop shrine, the RAIN TEEMING down as a DROP OF BIRDSHIT splatters on his forehead'[33] and a scene,

11. *Clash of the Ash* (Fergus Tighe, 1987).

also left out, of the young protagonist playacting outside a church and choosing to head for a pint rather than go to mass.[34]

Overall, in both script and film, we are presented with a town characterised by unemployment, drug abuse and emigration, where hurling offers one of the few outlets for youths to unleash the frustrations and disappointments of their everyday life. Unsurprisingly, these frustrations spill over into violence on the field of play, in the film's climactic encounter in the county final between Fermoy and Mitchelstown. When Kelly is hit over the head with a hurley by an opposing player, he retaliates in a similar fashion, and runs from the pitch with his trainer's shouts of 'there'll be no job in the bank for you' ringing in his ears (illus. 11).

The Irish Film Board was re-established on 30 March 1993, the morning after Neil Jordan won an Oscar for his screenplay for *The Crying Game* (1992). Though not depicted, Gaelic games (in particular hurling) is mentioned in Jordan's film, providing an opportunity for the IRA man Fergus to bond with his British soldier prisoner, Jody, as they compare the Irish game ('that game where a bunch of Paddies whack sticks at each other?' as Jody calls it) with cricket. Jordan's most famous depiction of Gaelic games is found in his later film *Michael Collins* (1996). Jordan's biopic, however, proved controversial when released in Ireland on 8 November 1996, not least because of the manner in which it portrayed the events surrounding 21 November 1920, 'Bloody Sunday', when British forces opened fire on a Gaelic football match between Tipperary and Dublin in Croke Park. Interestingly, in light of its popularity in other international productions, in the original script it is hurling, not football, that Collins describes as being played, with the unfortunate player killed on that day – Tipperary midfielder Michael Hogan – taunting the British armoured car with a hurling stick before being shot dead.[35] *Michael Collins* was funded largely by the Hollywood studio Warner Brothers to the tune of $28m and, conscious of the need to provide epic cinema for an international audience, Jordan chose spectacle over substance in his re-enaction, shot at the Carlisle soccer ground in Bray. As the film's producer, Stephen Wooley, has admitted, speaking of the attempt to raise funding from the studio, 'The reality is to make this story … you have to make it an epic picture'.[36] Presumably Jordan at first thought hurling would provide the greater spectacle, but thought better of it in the final production. It is a fact that on 'Bloody Sunday' British armoured cars did not invade Croke Park;[37] this was how Neil Jordan depicted events, however (illus. 12).

Jordan has defended his use of armoured cars as he wanted this 'scene to last more than 30 seconds',[38] yet his choice of spectacle over

12. *Michael Collins* (Neil Jordan, 1996).

fact is also apparent elsewhere in the film, including a scene which depicts the IRA's use of a car bomb, a weapon that wouldn't appear in the Irish conflict until the 1960s.

But spectacle is central to another related activity that has had a considerable influence on the depiction of Ireland and Gaelic games in film: tourism. Solange Davin's remarks about television in *The Media and the Tourist Imagination* are equally, if not more, applicable to film: 'The hallmark of television and of tourism is, first and foremost, spectacle.'[39]

Those international productions that have featured Gaelic games have often been influenced, or concerned with, a force termed by John Urry as 'the tourist gaze'. In referring to the 'tourist gaze' in his 1990 book of the same name, Urry was drawing on Michel Foucault's ideas of the medical gaze or the surveillance gaze of the Panopticon[40] to describe a culturally constructed manner of perceiving a place which informs tourist expectations. For Urry the tourist gaze was 'constructed through difference' and 'in relationship to its opposite, to non-tourist forms of social experience and consciousness'.[41] Furthermore, whereas in commercial cinema, stereotypes play a central role, providing 'characters with an almost instant knowability'[42] by 'reducing other landscapes, other peoples, and other values ... to a normative paradigm',[43] the tourist gaze is similarly, Urry argues, 'constructed through signs, and tourism involves the collection of signs'.[44] 'The tourist', Jonathan Culler has also observed, 'is interested in everything as a sign of itself ... All over the world the unsung armies of semioticians, the tourists, are fanning out in search of the signs of Frenchness, typical Italian behaviour, exemplary Oriental scenes, typical American thruways, traditional English pubs'[45] or, indeed, typical Irish pastimes, such as Gaelic games. Urry's work has been criticised for allowing too much agency to the tourist in the construction of the gaze, and indeed failing to 'acknowledge that tourists are equally vulnerable to the gaze of others', with So-Min Cheong and Marc L. Miller arguing for what they call a 'touristic gaze' for which professionals within the tourism industry, from guides to tourist agencies, who select particular aspects of a place to focus upon, are chiefly responsible.[46] Apart from such professionals, film, and particularly since the second half of the twentieth century popular media such as television, have also had a significant role to play in influencing tourist preconceptions, while also working from their own particular presumptions regarding tourist expectations in constructing representations of places and cultural practices. With regard to perspectives on indigenous sports, Gaelic games are by no means unique in this respect and John Arundel and Maurice Roche's 1998 study of the relationship between British rugby league and Sky television found similarly that

> [A]s with the tourism industry, the media sport industry, in general ... tends to promote local identities in a way which transforms them from the unreflected 'ways of life' and traditions of local people, into reflexive and organised cultural productions and stagings for outsiders, whether tourists or TV viewers. [Where] this process does not threaten the very existence of cultural forms and ways of life, it certainly raises the problem of their 'authenticity' in their new touristic or mediated guise.[47]

Ironically, as Gerry Smyth has noted, the search for the 'authentic' has none the less been an important determinant of tourism in Ireland, though one 'with a long and troubled career in Irish cultural history'.[48] Hurling in particular, by far the most common sport portrayed, or alluded to, in international productions, would seem to have provided an authentic and 'primitive' contrast to the modernity of American sports such as American football, while also apparently containing the violence so often associated with the Irish. As Rockett, Gibbons and Hill in their influential study *Cinema and Ireland* have noted, in terms comparable to Urry's description of the tourist gaze, 'Whether it be rural backwardness or a marked proclivity for violence, the film-producing nations of the metropolitan centre have been able to find in Ireland a set of characteristics which stand in contrast to the assumed virtues of their own particular culture.'[49] Hurling's setting in rural Ireland, and the apparent violence of the game, seemed to encapsulate both of these elements, and it is these traits that are often to the fore in depictions, descriptions and references to the sport in American productions.

The tourist gaze, while greatly influenced by brokers within the tourist industry, from tourist agencies to guides and local beneficiaries, is also subject to engrained or established prejudices and preconceptions. By 1952 and the release of *The Quiet Man* (arguably the single most important text in framing both a tourist imagery and influencing preconceptions of Ireland) and the establishment of Bord Fáilte, particular emphases were already apparent in representations of hurling in American cinema. Indeed, in the first American productions to focus on hurling in the 1930s we find a recurring emphasis on the alleged violence associated with the game. The GAA organised

13. A promotional poster and advertising material for David Miller's *Hurling* (MGM, 1936).

annual tours to the US in the 1920s, 1930s and 1940s by the All-Ireland winners in both hurling and Gaelic football to promote the games stateside. These visits would seem to have inspired some American producers to consider hurling in particular as a subject for their work. While both Pathé and Fox Movietone newsreels covered several of the games during these visits,[50] hurling would also appear in a number of short films released in cinemas in the early 1930s including two segments of sports series narrated by seminal American broadcaster Ted Husing, 'Ted Husing's Sports Slants' and 'Sports Thrills', made by the Vitaphone Corporation for Warner Brothers, in 1931 and 1932 respectively, and most controversially, the MGM-produced Pete Smith Specialty *Hurling*, made and released in the US in 1936, a film that resulted in a deputation from the GAA visiting the Irish film censor to demand that objectionable images be removed.[51] In all of these depictions, it is the potential for injury in the game of hurling that is to the fore in the minds of the producers, as evidenced in the promotional posters and advertising materials (illus. 13) used to promote *Hurling* (1936).

Irish-America provided both the participants and no doubt a large segment of the hoped-for audience for films such as *Hurling*. The presence of this huge ethnic community in the United States was an important factor in the popularity of Irish-themed subject matter in American productions. As Martin McLoone has noted, Irish American filmmakers such as John Ford were also engaged in a project of exploiting the performative potential of Irish stereotypes in film while contributing to the assimilation of Irish-America into mainstream American life.[52] However, as the reactions of the GAA would suggest, the performative dimension of films such as Ford's *The Quiet Man* and particularly *The Rising of the Moon* was not always recognised by audiences in Ireland. As Arjun Appadurai has noted in his discussion of the increasing 'deterritorialization'[53] of the planet (the process through which such diasporic communities have emerged), while such

> deterritorialization creates new markets for film compa-
> nies ... the homeland is partly invented, existing only in
> the imagination of the deterritorialized groups, and it
> can sometimes become so fantastic and one-sided that it
> provides the fuel for new ethnic conflicts.[54]

This 'fantastic and one-sided' perspective might be compared to certain preconceptions regarding the tourist gaze, both in its distance from life or culture in Ireland and its concern with contrasting presumptions regarding American culture with the exaggerated depictions of Ireland found in some American films. While one is hesitant to compare the work of a filmmaker of the stature of John Ford with a film such as *Hurling*, none the less it is notable that where referred

14. *The Quiet Man* (Republic Pictures, 1952).

to in Ford's films, hurling also seems inevitably to precede or suggest an occasion of violence, though the game of hurling itself is never depicted.[55] With regard to the tourist gaze, Ford's own comments indicate at least an awareness of the contribution of his work to tourism in Ireland,[56] while, as Luke Gibbons has noted, Ford's most popular Irish-themed film, *The Quiet Man*, provided a template for Bord Fáilte's promotion of Ireland from its establishment in 1952, the year of *The Quiet Man*'s release, apparent in such subsequent travelogue films as *The Spell of Ireland* produced two years later and particularly *O'Hara's Holiday* made in the late 1950s.[57] While we do not actually witness a game of hurling in *The Quiet Man*, significantly the mere mention of the game, during a dispute between the engine driver, Costello (Eric Gorman), the train guard, Molouney (Joseph O'Dea), and the stationmaster, Hugh Bailey (Web Overlander), seems to inspire violence in those discussing it (illus. 14).

A common motif in representations of Ireland is its positioning as a primitive traditional society. As Gerry Smyth has observed:

> One of the discursive mechanisms through which this effect is realised is the 'chronotope', described by Joep Leerssen (after Bakhtin) as 'a place with an uneven distribution of time-passage, where time is apt to slow down and come to a standstill at the periphery ...' What Leerssen is referring to here is the impression that not only is the island physically removed from 'real' life, but also that time functions differently there.[58]

For Ford's next Irish-themed film, *The Rising of the Moon*, time did indeed appear to function quite differently in Ireland, not just through the film's depiction of the country as a traditional society, emphasised in the characters and stories chosen for this three-part work called *Three Leaves of a Shamrock* during production and on release in the United States, but equally in the difficulty this society appears to have in adapting to modernity. This includes, in the central segment – 'A Minute's Wait', based on a one-act Abbey play by Michael J. McHugh – the Irish approach to time-keeping, whereby in rural Ireland time, here represented by the Ballyscran to Dunfaill train, could wait for everything from prize goats to bishops' dinners, and, in one of the film's most infamous sequences, the local victorious hurling team with its piper's band, both additions by screenwriter Frank S. Nugent to the original play. Though a commercial failure on release in 1957, *The Rising of the Moon* was important as part of Ford's ongoing attempts to promote the establishment of an Irish film industry that would partly encourage others to set up

Ireland's first designated film studios at Ardmore the following year. In terms of representations of hurling, however, the film included a controversial depiction that resulted in considerable press coverage during the film's production and a staunch defence of the film and Ford's work by *Irish Times* columnist Myles na Gopaleen.

'A Minute's Wait' was shot in Kilkee, Co. Clare. As Joseph McBride has observed, the segment

> reinforces the insidious notion of Ireland as a backward island filled with lovable incompetents who haven't yet made it into the twentieth century. Ford's use of an old-fashioned train with an engine built in 1886 was deliberately anachronistic, provoking a complaint from the director of the West Cork Railway who could not understand why Ford refused a modern train with a diesel engine. 'He'll find out when the tourists come over next summer,' Ford grumbled in what [Frank S.] Nugent [the film's scriptwriter] took as an allusion to the tourist craze for jaunting carts provoked by *The Quiet Man*.[59]

Myles na Gopaleen – probably better known today as Flann O'Brien, the acclaimed author of the novels *At Swim Two Birds* (1939) and *The Third Policeman* (1967) – was an occasional commentator on cinema and was particularly upset by reactions to *The Rising of the Moon* among members of the GAA, even before the shooting of the film was complete. On Tuesday 1 May 1956, both the *Irish Press* and *Irish Independent* reported the shooting of a scene of hurlers returning victorious from a game, with some 'on stretchers' after 'an encounter' which, the *Independent* correspondent related, 'from the appearance of the players, must have been bloody and very rough, and hardly played according to the rules of the Gaelic Athletic Association'.[60]

Unsurprisingly, the GAA responded with some alarm to the reports the following day with a statement, published in both papers, from the General Secretary, Pádraig Ó Caoimh, declaring that he was 'deeply concerned lest there should be any substance in this report'. The statement went on to note that Ó Caoimh had been 'in touch with Lord Killanin, one of the directors of Four Provinces Productions, the production company behind the film. 'He has assured me that the report referred to is exaggerated and completely out of context; that there are no stretcher-carrying scenes, and that in fact there is nothing offensive to our national tradition in this film.'[61] The controversy rumbled on none the less, and by Friday of that week it was on the front page of the *Irish Times*, where it was announced that the shooting of the scenes 'resulted in an official deputation (consisting of Rev. John Corry, CC, chairman and Mr Seán O'Connor, treasurer) from the Clare County Board of the GAA making a strong protest yesterday in Kilkee to Lord Killanin'. A statement was issued by the board which said it was a matter of 'grave concern to the GAA that the national game of hurling should, or would appear to be held up to ridicule … the matter of 15 players returning home all suffering injuries would be calculated to give the impression that instead of a national sporting game that they were casualties returning to a clearing station at a battlefield'. While noting that such violent incidents and injuries were extremely rare in GAA games, 'Father Corry pointed out that the scene as depicted was completely derogatory to the Gaels of Ireland and to the hurlers in particular. The scene if placed on the screen as filmed would bring the association into disrepute and would be calculated to hold up the national game to ridicule both at home and abroad.'[62]

These final remarks were quoted at length by Myles na Gopaleen some weeks later while referring to what he called the 'farcical drool emitted by the GAA'. Na Gopaleen, apparently at that time a regular reader of the provincial papers, 'the only true mirrors' he observed 'of Ireland as she is', was quoting the Clare County Board's statement not from the *Irish Times* but from the *Clare Champion*. He went on to note a report on the same page of the *Champion* of a local hurling game between Ruan and St Josephs where the game was described as 'probably one of the worst exhibitions of bad sportsmanship ever seen on a Gaelic field'. There was 'literally a procession to the Co. hospital from the match', the report continued, while 'One, a spectator from Ennis, had survived the war in Korea but he almost met his Waterloo in Cusack Park.'[63] Na Gopaleen was dismissive of the GAA's criticisms of the film and while extolling the virtues of Ford (apparently a close friend, the article suggests), remarked that

> To many people, the possibility of vital injury is part of the attraction of hard games … The non-belligerent spectators regard absence of such occurrences as an attempt to defraud them. They have paid their two bobs to see melia murdher. Failure to present it is, they feel, low trickery.[64]

It would appear that na Gopaleen, a commentator whose own contributions to the *Irish Times* were often *tour de force* performances in themselves, including his celebrated moniker,[65] admired the

15. *The Rising of the Moon* (Four Provinces Pictures, 1957).

performative elements within Ford's work while also being highly critical of the hypocrisy he sensed in the reactions of the GAA. Indeed, na Gopaleen may also have recognised the 'self-interrogation' Luke Gibbons has identified in Ford's *The Quiet Man*,[66] in *The Rising of the Moon*, which seems as much concerned with ridiculing the reactions, and lack of familiarity, of tourists to Ireland (in this case the holidaying English couple depicted on the train as the injured players pass by on stretchers) to a sport such as hurling as it does with any particular critique of the potential for violence in hurling itself. As the lady asks, 'Charles, is it another of their rebellions?' Charles replies, 'I gather it's the local cricket team' (illus. 15).

Ultimately, it seems the reactions of the GAA were not taken seriously among those involved in the production. Records of correspondences with Lord Killanin held in the Lord Killanin collection in the Irish Film Institute reveal that the film's producers collected correspondences and newspaper clippings both for and against the depiction, and would appear to have been amused more than alarmed by the response (illus. 16).

Anita Sharp Bolster, who played the part of the recently wed English woman in 'A Minute's Wait', recalled, in an article published after the film's production, the arrival at the film's wrap party of

" *Go easy with the skullduggery, lads—Ford and Killanin may be on the sideline!* "

16. Cartoon from *Dublin Opinion* (1956) .[67]

'John Ford [and] [Lord] Killanin … doing a very funny turn in the hurley boys' jerseys'. Furthermore, Ford appeared in a small part in an Abbey theatre Irish-language play shortly after the film's production in which a 'short passage of Gaelic dialogue was improvised for him'. When asked if 'he was going back to Spiddal' (the birthplace of his parents) he said he was not as he was 'afraid of the GAA'.[68]

While *The Rising of the Moon* was on release in Ireland, another foreign film, a British adaptation of Catherine Cookson's novel *Rooney* directed by George Pollock – in which hurling would have an important role – was in production. Pollock, according to Sandra Brennan in the *All Movie Guide*, is 'best remembered for directing films in the 1960s Miss Marple series'.[69] The film was produced by George H. Brown, who had enjoyed a minor success two years previously with another Catherine Cookson adaptation, *Jacqueline*, a film that also saw the transfer of a Cookson story from its original English setting to an Irish locale, if in the north rather than the south of Ireland. Brown, incidentally, has a rather intriguing connection with Irish cinema, including *The Quiet Man*. He was the first husband of Maureen O'Hara, who, though not at all interested in Brown, married him, her autobiography suggests, to stop him hassling her to do so, a rather novel approach to rejecting a potential suitor. The marriage was

17. *Rooney* (Rank Film Productions, 1958).

never consummated and was quickly annulled when O'Hara's mother got wind of it.[70]

Though not a Hollywood production, produced as it was by the British Rank Film Company, in its style, content and humour *Rooney* is clearly influenced by previous Hollywood depictions of Ireland. While set in Dublin, the original Catherine Cookson novel of the same name was set in the English coastal town of South Shields, the town in which Cookson was born and where much of her work is set. Indeed, an important aspect of her work was her ability to capture the distinctive accent of the north-east of England, and her contribution to the representation of the region and its people was recognised in later life when she was awarded the Freedom of the Borough of South Tyneside (known today as Catherine Cookson country). However, in its tranference to the Dublin milieu considerations of accent were far from the producer's mind, reflected in the choice of non-Irish actors (such as Liverpool-born John Gregson as the eponymous Dublin binman James Ignatius Rooney) for most of the leading roles, who make little attempt to approximate an Irish, never mind Dublin, accent in the film. The production of *Rooney* was motivated not so much by a concern with authenticity of voice or place but rather by the expectation of cashing in on the success of *The Quiet Man* with international audiences earlier in the decade.

Described by Éamon Sweeney as maybe 'the most stage-Irish film of all time ... [making] *Darby O'Gill and the Little People* look like a documentary',[71] the rudiments of stage Irishry are apparent in *Rooney* right from the opening shots of the Guinness brewery, which we are told is 'essential to the life of a great city'. From early on faces familiar from *The Quiet Man* appear, including Barry Fitzgerald as the querulous grandfather in Rooney's rented accommodation, and Jack MacGowran, who plays one of Rooney's closest friends and co-worker, Joe O'Connor. *Rooney* also takes from *The Quiet Man* not just the whimsical depictions but also the almost musical quality of the film; in this case workers without notice break into song, particularly the risible theme tune 'Rooney-Oh' (illus. 17).

It is in this context that Rooney includes hurling as a significant part of the narrative, with the central protagonist, James Ignatius Rooney, a Dublin dustbin man whose real talents (apart from being much sought after by a succession of landladies) are on show with his local hurling club – the fictitious Sons of Erin. The club depicted in the scenes of Rooney playing early on in the film was actually St Vincent's and their star player, and dual county star and twice All-Ireland medal winner in football in 1958 and 1963, Dessie 'Snitchy'

Ferguson, attempted valiantly, with little success, to educate Gregson in his use of the *camán*.[72] Rooney is eventually spotted by a county selector, leading to a place in the Dublin county team that reaches the All-Ireland final. His hurling exploits are also paralleled by his developing relationship with the much put upon Máire (played by English actress Muriel Pavlow), the niece of the lady who runs his rented accommodation.

The film's distance from reality is also apparent in its depiction of a Dublin team wearing the black and amber of Kilkenny – required because Kilkenny had played in, and won, the 1957 hurling final which was used for the scenes in Croke Park in which our hero is depicted. Kilkenny's opposition in that game, Waterford, were offered first option of having Gregson togged out in one of their jerseys for the parade. However, 'conscious perhaps that this was the Déise's first final appearance since their victory over Dublin in '48 – and not wishing to add to the team's nervousness – the Waterford mentors refused permission.'[73]

The captain of the 1957 Kilkenny team, Michael Kelly, has recalled the All-Ireland and Gregson's involvement:

> He stepped into the pre-match parade, tucked in behind Seán Clohessy, the left full-forward. A lot of people, especially Waterford people, wondered at the time who was Kilkenny's extra man! The scenes from play that feature in the movie were filmed afterwards. We went back up to Dublin the following Saturday – both teams – and filmed those scenes in Croke Park.[74]

The première of *Rooney* was a major event for Dublin city, including in the audience the president of Ireland Seán T. O'Kelly and receiving considerable coverage throughout the press the following day. Critical reaction to the film was also generally positive, regarding it, surprisingly, as a film eschewing stage-Irishness.[75] However, the one recurring criticism of the film in the press was of its suggestion of violence (yet again) in association with hurling. As the *Irish Independent* critic remarked: 'Why Pollock wanted to introduce a bit of Donnybrook Fair stuff at another hurling game is his own affair, but he could have left it out.'[76] Benedict Kiely's review in the *Irish Press* was particularly critical. 'Mr Gregson is not … Christy Ring', Kiely reminded readers (in case there was any doubt) and 'The Croke Park scenes … I found embarrassing. The preliminary hurling game, with Noel Purcell *et cie* in grips on the green sward, I found offensive.' Kiely also recalled in his review angry reactions to the depiction of battered and bruised hurlers returning from a game in *The Rising of the Moon*.

Furthermore, he makes the astute observation that we have in *Rooney* a depiction of a national sport unlikely to be found in films concerning English national pastimes. 'Nor do I recollect', he declares,

> any occasion on which a Wembley Cup Final, or say, Twickenham, on the day of a Wales–England game (or Lords on the day of a Test match) was used thus as a stage-setting for mediocre comedy. Here was one excellent case for the application of the ban. Keep the mummers off the green ground of Croke Park. It was meant for higher things.[77]

Whether, as John Ford seemed to suggest, film had a significant impact on tourist numbers coming to Ireland in the 1950s is hard to quantify precisely. What is clear is that the numbers did increase as the decade developed and four days before the Irish première of the final film I want to discuss, the Justin Herman-directed *Three Kisses* (1955) at the Capitol theatre in Dublin on 18 July 1956, the *Irish Times* carried a front-page headline declaring 'Tourist industry has prospects of record year'. 'Since the beginning of the summer', the report continued, '[Aer lingus, British railways, and the British and Irish Steam Packet Co.] have been transporting the biggest number of holiday-makers to this country in their history'.[78]

The Oscar-nominated *Three Kisses*, like the Pete Smith Specialty *Hurling*, was released – along with a further Paramount short on the Irish bloodstock industry, *Champion Irish Thoroughbreds* (1955) – as an opener for a main feature, this time as part of the Paramount Topper series,[79] running for two weeks in Ireland as support for the Alvin Ganzer-directed *The Leather Saint* (1955). *Three Kisses* features a young hurler, Colm Gallagher, narrator of the film, who progresses from playing with his local team in the fictional rural Cork village of Ballykilly to training with the senior Cork team and eventually playing in the Munster championship final. Gallagher's sporting prowess is partly motivated, the film suggests, by his quest for three kisses from the girl he loves, thus giving the film its title, each a reward for his improving fortunes on the playing-field.

While *Three Kisses* is unquestionably quite a patronising and problematic depiction of Ireland, it is a considerably more interesting work than this description might suggest, not least because, though written and directed by an American filmmaker, it is one of the first examples of the Gaelic Athletic Association and Bord Fáilte together informing and facilitating a major American studio to produce a fictional work[80] (though one billed as 'documentary') on Gaelic games primarily for international consumption. In terms of the GAA's involvement, as well as featuring several scenes from hurling games in the Munster championship, including the 1955 Munster semi-final between Cork and Clare, the film also includes appearances by the legendary Cork manager, Jim 'Tough' Barry[81] (illus. 18), most of the great all-Ireland winning Cork team of the 1950s in training (including Vincy Toomey, Paddy Barry, Seánie O'Brien, John Lyons, Joe Hartnet, Mick Cashman, Christy O'Shea and Jimmy Brohan (to whom I am grateful for his assistance in identifying those mentioned here)), the GAA general secretary Pádraig Ó Caoimh in attendance at an under-age hurling game in Ferranferris and several other prominent hurling figures from Cork in the 1950s.[82] With regard to Bord Fáilte's involvement, newspaper reports of the Irish première of *Three Kisses* – which was also the Irish première of *Champion Irish Thoroughbreds* – describe the film as having been made with the co-operation of the board and give considerable space to the comments of its then director-general, T.J. O'Driscoll, who introduced the film to audiences on the night. According to the *Irish Times*, O'Driscoll 'welcomed the growing interest among foreign

18. *Three Kisses* (Paramount Pictures, 1955).

film companies in making films in Ireland', pointing out that 'film-making was a costly business which the board could not attempt on its slender budget, in the ordinary course of events. For that reason it was more than grateful to Paramount for making these films and distributing them throughout the world.'[83] In the *Irish Independent*, under the headline 'Film and the Irish tourist industry', the paper's film correspondent also quoted O'Driscoll's remark that 'Films are one of the best methods of publicising the tourist industry of this country.'[84]

Film reviews also recognised the tourist potential of the work. Benedict Kiely in the *Irish Press*, under a headline 'The tourists and the screen' remarked of *Three Kisses* and *Champion Irish Thoroughbreds* that

> Even with their defects from our point of view, they could get people interested in Ireland ... we should always remember that films like these documentaries and *The Quiet Man* are meant not for us but for an American public. *The Quiet Man* I'm told was a great help to the tourist trade; and why not indeed. Who wouldn't like to spend a holiday in a land of green fields, sunshine, horse-racing, singing, fighting, boozing and romance?[85]

Given the differing concerns of each of the organisations involved, however, it is not surprising that the finished film is one more remarkable for the tensions it reveals between an attempt to depict indigenous culture authentically and engage a diverse international audience (with preconceived notions of Ireland and the sport of hurling) than for the quality of either the sport depicted or film produced. The film, none the less, features an intriguing encounter between the traditional and the modern – young Gallagher's village of Ballykilly, for example, is depicted as an idyllic pastoral and pre-modern space, complete with familiar horse and cart in the background and village pump for running water. However, Gallagher's – who seems remarkably young for the honour – elevation to the senior Cork team is described as being picked to represent the 'city' rather than the county, and the city itself is depicted as 'the mighty metropolis ... with its busy vehicular traffic and its fine buildings of stone and brick'. However, there is in all of this quite a patronising tone apparent, including in the film's representation of women and the women's sport of camogie, and where the mere mention of some-one having been to the US is considered a remarkable achievement by the narrator, ostensibly young Gallagher himself. Indeed, the film is narrated in an extraordinary accent, which suggests the tension between a wish to present an authentic Irish voice but also one that remains accessible to an American audience. And it is an American audience that is the primary concern here, for all involved in the production. A recurring feature of representations of hurling, as apparent in the films I have mentioned, is the bewilderment of those who encounter it from afar at the apparent irrationality of the sport and its potential for violence. A strong focus is placed in *Three Kisses*, therefore, on illustrating the rationale behind the game, emphasising its rules and downplaying the potential for injury. However, it is a less than convincing riposte to previous representations. As the cinema correspondent of the *Irish Times* remarked: 'The soundtrack informs us that "though you may suffer a fracture of a leg or a concussion of the brain … [hurling] is not considered a rough sport – at least, not by us Irish."' 'This', the indignant correspondent continues, 'is certainly nice to know!'[86]

To conclude, in line with the depiction of sport in cinema generally, Gaelic games is not the most popular motif associated with Ireland in film. However, it does none the less occupy a significant role. In particular, the forces of both nationalism and tourism have influenced how Gaelic games have been depicted, with the latter principally influential in fiction filmaking given that most fiction films featuring Gaelic games have emerged from outside Ireland. The focus of filmmakers such as Miller, Ford, Pollack and Herman on audiences in America, influenced by preconceptions regarding the tourist gaze, has had considerable consequences for the portrayal of a Gaelic sport such as hurling. Indeed, hurling would seem to have provided a useful motif for filmmakers outside of Ireland encapsulating prevailing stereotypes regarding the Irish, including their alleged proclivity for violence. While a filmmaker such as John Ford may provide his own internal interrogation of this phenomenon within a film such as *The Rising of the Moon*, ultimately the images of badly injured players returning from a game on stretchers may contribute to the perpetuation of such stereotypes. For what is remarkable for those who follow the sport of hurling is not so much the potential for injury but rather the sophistication and skill levels involved in a game in which injuries are no more common than many other field sports, aspects almost entirely absent from these foreign depictions. Even in a film such as *Three Kisses*, which appears at least partly an attempt to correct these perceptions, the complicated address involved in such a project ultimately compromises the veracity of its portrayal. Colm Gallagher is clearly the local guide who is bringing the uninitiated into the world of hurling, remarking along the way on the perceived incorrect preconceptions regarding the sport. However, all of this is very much framed within a context understandable to the would-be tourist, a fact commented on by local observers of the film. In this respect, a film such as *Three Kisses* anticipates Dean MacCannell's observation in the late 1970s that the 'structural development of industrial society is marked by the appearance everywhere of touristic space'. Indeed, *Three Kisses* might be regarded, following again from MacCannell's seminal essay, as an example of 'staged authenticity', lending the film, adapting MacCannell's words again, an 'aura of superficiality, albeit a superficiality that is not always perceived as such by the tourist, who is usually forgiving about these matters'.[87] Local commentators tend however to be less forgiving. As the *Cork Examiner* reviewer remarked on the film's release in Ireland, while drawing comparisons between the film and other depictions of hurling, including that found in *The Rising of the Moon*:

> That more Americans are likely to come here looking for the 'traditional' Ireland is evident from [the] film … It is in line with other productions of the type … *Three Kisses* … accurately describes the game itself, but the film company have gone to a great deal of trouble with the insertion of the 'Blarney'. Result: the picture becomes a farce and hardly a true representation of the Irish scene.[88]

9 The GAA and the Irish Language

BRIAN Ó CONCHUBHAIR

> The GAA has no desire to take sole possession of the language as an organisation. We would like to lend strong support to others' work on the ground and give tangible recognition to organisations engaged in promoting the language.[1]

Edwin Poots, former Democratic Unionist minister for culture, arts and leisure in the Northern Ireland Assembly, created history by attending and addressing the 2007 annual Ulster Council of Cumann Lúthchleas Gael (CLG)/Gaelic Athletic Association. Prior to the event Poots, despite intense pressure from Sinn Féin, the SDLP and various language groups, ruled out an Irish Language Act for Northern Ireland, thus adding additional resonance to the occassion. He availed of this opportunity to address that controversy, stating: 'I know the Irish language is very important to the Gaelic Athletic Association – can I say this – I will be doing nothing that would inhibit you from enjoying your Irish culture and language.'[2] Addressing the proposed bill at this gathering reveals not only the historic and symbiotic links between the GAA and the language movement, but underscores the association's broad cultural agenda and also recognises its important role in promoting Irish. For Poots as government official, and by extension the wider unionist community, it is the GAA, rather than POBAL, Glór na nGael, ULTACH Trust/Iontaobhas Ultach, Conradh na Gaeilge/Gaelic League that represents the Irish language. The GAA is the primary popular organisation through which to address those interested and supportive of Irish language and culture.

The shared bonds between the GAA and the Irish-language movement derive from the Revival period and Michael Cusack in particular.[3] A native speaker of Irish for whom 'English was with him an acquired language',[4] Cusack joined the Society for the Preservation of the Irish Language in 1882 and became honorary treasurer of Aontacht na Gaedhilge/Gaelic Union on 9 August that year.[5] He regularly hosted meetings at his Dublin residence – 4 Gardiner Place – the same address from which he dispatched letters in 1884 inviting interested parties to a meeting in Hayes's hotel, Thurles which led to the GAA's foundation. The historian W.F. Mandle suggests Cusack, when establishing the GAA, attempted to replicate the Gaelic Union's success in crossing political and sectarian boundaries and consequently sought advice from Douglas Hyde and Maxwell Close.[6] When the Gaelic League was founded in 1893, Cusack was again a key member and regular contributor at meetings. The *Irish Independent* describes an 1893 Gaelic League meeting where 'Mr Michael Cusack related in Irish some interesting experiences in the west of Ireland.'[7] The following month the *Freeman's Journal* reported a meeting where 'the Chair was taken by Mr Michael Cusack. The Chairman read a humorous Gaelic poem sent him by Father O'Leary, PP, Castlelyons and translated it into English.'[8] The same paper reports in January 1894 that 'A discussion of the movement in general followed, in which Messers T. O'Neill Russell, David Fagan and Michael Cusack took part, the last named gentleman speaking in Irish.'[9] Cusack's links with these three language organisations not only established a pattern of overlapping membership, but reveals a commonality of purpose that moulded the GAA and the language movement. This common purpose manifests itself again in Douglas Hyde's reference to the 'brave and patriotic men who started the Gaelic Athletic Association' in his 1892 lecture 'The necessity for de-Anglicising Ireland':

> I confess that the instantaneous and extraordinary success which attended their efforts when working upon national lines has filled me with more hope for the future of Ireland than everything else put together. I consider the work of the Association in reviving our ancient national game of *camán*, or hurling, and Gaelic football, has done more for Ireland than all the speeches of politicians for the last five years. And it is not alone that the splendid Association revived for a time with vigour our national sports, but it revived also our national recollections, and the names of the various clubs through the country have perpetuated the memory of the great and good men and martyrs of Ireland.[10]

Despite this admiration, Hyde, according to Mandle, 'more than once regretted the fact that the links between the Gaelic League and the Association were not closer, although there is some evidence of overlap in membership'.[11] These overlaps have continued ever since. In the early 1930s both bodies co-published a newspaper entitled *An Camán* despite disagreements over 'the ban'.[12] Pádraig Ó Caoimh, general secretary (1929–64), was an avid advocate of Irish.[13] Seán Ó Síocháin, director-general (1964–79), served as a trustee of Gael Linn and his successor, Liam Mulvihill, (director-general 1979–2008), became chairman of Foras na Gaeilge in 2008. Peter Quinn, president (1991–4), was appointed chairman of TG4 in 2007. Seosamh Mac Donnacha, president (1997–2000), served as chief executive officer of Foras na Gaeilge (2002–6) and TG4 (2000–4). The first public camogie match on 17 July 1904 featured the ladies of two Gaelic League branches, Craobh an Chéithnigh and Craobh Chú Chulainn, and Foras na Gaeilge has sponsored the camogie championship in recent years. Oireachtas na Gaeilge features an annual inter-county hurling competition and TG4 sponsors the Ladies football championship. Historians and GAA members will forever be in debt to Br Liam P. Ó Caithnia 'for his three magisterial works on the true history and origins of hurling and Gaelic football and his biography of the key founder'[14] – all written in Irish.

Such links stem from a shared origin during the Irish Revival. R.F. Foster writes the notion that the GAA, the Gaelic League and the Celtic Literary Society in unison formed a trinity, responsible for a 'cultural revolution',[15] and F.S.L. Lyons argues that the GAA provided each individual with a channel for 'local pride in his county, and also national pride in his country' but attributes the Revival's 'intellectual basis' to the Gaelic League as 'revolutions are made with ideas, not hurley sticks'.[16] If their common origins are clear, accounting for their subsequent divergent fortunes is less so. At the end of the nineteenth century the GAA was in decline while the Gaelic League was thriving. Yet the reverse would soon be the case. The GAA's decline necessitated a radical overhaul and consequently, according to Diarmuid Ferriter, it 'matured administratively' and 'became so tightly controlled and ultimately the great success story of twentieth-century Irish sport ... From 1900 on its regional and national administration was overhauled and the entire infrastructure radically altered ... with ever-increasing attendance and renewed clerical support'.[17] J.J. Lee attributes its success to a 'cooption of intense loyal loyalties into a wider sense of national identity, reflected a capacity for organization and a sense of communal coherence'.[18] The Gaelic League, in contrast, 'activated a relatively small minority of the population' and Ferriter cites Paul Dubois's assessment that the League's contribution was psychological and most keenly felt in the educational sector.[19]

The League declined after the civil war. Many of its most competent members became politicians and civil servants and it effectively ceded responsibility for the language revival to the Free State with the acceptance of Coimisiún na Bealtaine in 1926.[20] The GAA's success, on the other hand, Ferriter writes, illustrated the Irish public 'embracing the British model of sport codification and mirroring the European, African and Asian trend of ball games becoming an important part of the social fabric'.[21] Fintan O'Toole correctly informed readers of the *London Review of Books* that 'Of all the institutions that emerged from the Irish nationalist cultural revival of the nineteenth century, it [the GAA] is the only one still unequivocally in rude good health. It embodies a sense of Irish identity that is tangible, local and pleasurable.'[22]

The GAA, loyal to its roots, has long preserved its efforts to promote Irish. The nature and success of such efforts, however, have varied. Mandle claims that Irish was 'fostered, at least, in theory' and describes how 'there was even a move to penalise the use of English on the playing field, and in 1912 it was ruled that from 1917 onwards all annual convention proceedings should be conducted in Irish.'[23] Similarly the 1928 Ulster Council urged closer co-operation with the Gaelic League. The 1942 Ulster Council passed a motion that their business be conducted through Irish and in 1960 it initiated an Irish-language course in Ros Goill, Donegal.[24] For many the GAA's promotion of Irish is encapsulated in the winning captain's speech and the words 'Is mór an onóir dom an corn seo a ghlacadh ar son … / Tá an-athás orm an corn seo a ghlacadh...' Prior to TG4, Irish was, and remained for many, a classroom language rarely heard in emotional, joyous or authentic situations, the singular exception, perhaps, being the opening line of this acceptance speech. While easily dismissed as trite symbolism or empty ritual, the utterance was for many the sole Irish expression to be greeted ecstatically and inserted the language in a communal and national occasion that was both joyous and prestigious. This phrase, practised and modelled voluntarily and happily by children the length and breadth of the island, remains an important tradition that survives despite the modernisation of the presentation ceremony. The Irish-language speeches of Joe Connolly (1980), Páidí Ó Sé (1985) Dara Ó Cinnéide (2004) and Seán Óg Ó hAilpín (2005) hold a special resonance and symbolic significance for admirers and speakers of Irish. But there is more to the GAA's language advocacy than the acceptance speech.

Among the association's additional aims are the following: that it 'shall actively support the Irish language, traditional Irish dancing, music, song, and other aspects of Irish culture. It shall foster an awareness and love of the national ideals in the people of Ireland, and assist in promoting a community spirit through its clubs.'[25] The 2008 *Official Guide*'s preamble explains that those 'who play its games, those who organise its activities and those who control its destinies see in the GAA a means of consolidating our Irish identity … and the promotion of native pastimes becomes a part of the full national ideal, which envisages the speaking of our own language, music and dances'.[26] Additional references pertaining to Irish include the submission of a list in Irish of all full and youth members (18 a & b); a club must bear a name in the Irish language (25 a); the annual county convention shall elect … an officer for Irish language and culture, if desired (50 a); a county committee shall appoint the county cultural committee – which shall be responsible for (a) the Irish language (b) scór and (c) other cultural activities (60 vi). Rule 154 (f) states: 'In the Gaeltacht, or where Bye-Laws stipulate, Objections and Counter-Objections shall be written, and where feasible, or where stipulated in Bye-Laws, discussed, in the Irish language.' And 154 (g) states: 'In the Gaeltacht, or where Bye-Laws stipulate, Appeals shall be written, and where feasible, or where stipulated in Bye-Laws, discussed, in the Irish language.' Part II of the *Official Guide* requires that 'Before all official games, the referee shall be given a list of players, in duplicate and in Irish (except as provided for in Rule 10, Part 1), giving full Christian names' and among a referee's duties are to 'receive lists of players, sign them in Irish, and give a copy to the opposing team before the game'. The oft-cited Rule 10 relates to exceptions to the Irish rule official documents and correspondence and occurs

> In the cases of unusual surnames or where there is more than one form of a surname in Irish, the English form of the surname may be added for the purpose of identification. In cases where there is no Irish form of a name, names mentioned in Referees' Reports may be in English.

Coiste Cultúr agus Teanga directs the GAA's cultural aims. Chief among their successes is Scór – Scór na nÓg and Scór Sinsir – a competition initiated in 1969 for dance, song, music, recitation and acting, commencing at club level and proceeding to national level. More recent initiatives include a booklet of Irish terms produced by Jarlath Burns, chairman of Coiste Cultúr agus Teanga, and designed for officials, players and supporters. In 2004, as part of its contribution to

Conradh na Gaeilge's Seachtain na Gaeilge, Coiste na Gaeilge launched a nationwide Irish-language quiz.[27] Collaboration with Foras na Gaeilge in 2005 produced a bilingual version of 'Gaelic Games: Football' and 'Gaelic Games: Hurling', a Playstation 2 game with Irish and English user options. 2008 saw the launch of *Céim ar Aghaidh (Step Ahead)*, a cross-curricular educational resource for primary schools with the dual-language *The World of Gaelic Games* text that narrates the experience of 'newcomer children and diaspora children'. Several county boards, such as Mayo, have long provided scholarships for teenage members to attend language summer camps. The most important administrative intervention, however, is the 2001 *Plean Gaeilge na Mílaoise (Plan for the Irish Language in the New Millennium)*, described as a blueprint for promoting Irish in co-operation with Glór na nGael, the Irish government and the political structures in Northern Ireland.[28]

The challenges involved in implementing such aspirations are not insignificant. In 2007 a Longford player received a two-month suspension for verbally abusing a referee. Despite unsuccessful appeals at lower levels, the Disputes Resolution Authority (DRA) quashed the punishment as the referee had listed the player's name in English rather than Irish. Eugene McGee questioned the policy's logic as follows:

> Had the player in question broken an opponent's jaw deliberately with a box the DRA would have let him off scot-free just because the Irish version of his name was not used. What sort of world do GAA legislators actually live in? Are they seriously saying that it is more important to use two words of Irish than to enforce discipline in the GAA? … I have often written that the GAA's attitude to the Irish language in relation to the rule book simply brings Irish into disrepute and heaps derision on the language and this latest development proves the point. Team lists for all GAA games must be in Irish, otherwise a team automatically forfeits the match. This in effect is a form of compulsory Irish and is a totally negative approach to the Irish language which even the State has long since abandoned. Nowadays in every county there are dozens of foreign nationals playing GAA games with names that are impossible to translate into Irish, therefore the rule should be scrapped. There are many other ways for the GAA to promote Irish and many clubs and officials do so very well.[29]

Such, argues Nioclás Ó Braonáin, is neither the fault of the language nor the association, but indicative of a 'growing culture of disrespect for our rules, regulations and match officials'. Rather than rewriting the rules, he suggests:

> Changing the culture of individuals, although equally challenging, is far more important. Without a seismic culture change towards greater respect for our rules, regulations and match officials, I remain unconvinced that even a newly written Rule Book would adequately address some of the issues we encounter right now.[30]

If implementation of official rules incensed McGee, contempt for Irish-speakers dismayed Seán Bán Breathnach, 'probably the best commentator in the country'.[31] He described 'several incidents in which Irish-speaking players had been on the receiving end for not speaking in English. And it was not just opposing players and mentors who were guilty; the problem extended even to referees':

> 'I remember one occasion when a young player came over to me in tears and told me that the referee had asked him for his proper name after he had given it to him in Irish,' said Seán Bán. 'That to me is racism. We have about ten clubs in Co. Galway that conduct their business in Irish and it is the first language of the players and officials. But there is an increasing level of abuse being directed towards them and I am very concerned about what will now happen when the GAA integrates people from other origins into the organisation.'[32]

Such treatment echoes Marcus Ó Buachalla's complaint in the *Irish Times* regarding Tipperary County Board's efforts to Anglicise Coláiste Eoin players' names prior to the 1999 All-Ireland senior colleges 'A' football semi-final in Semple Stadium: 'Shortly before the match the school was contacted by the Tipperary GAA Board's PRO, Liz Howard, requesting that we send the English translation of our names to accommodate the "wider English-speaking community" at the match. I and my team-mates, as young members of the GAA and as Irish speakers, were disgusted.'[33]

As an amateur sporting organisation promoting Gaelic football among men and women in Ireland and the Irish diaspora, the GAA is an undeniable success. As a promoter of hurling, camogie, rounders and handball, it is considerably less successful despite 'verifiable statistics that show that the game [of hurling] is being played by more people now than ever before and in areas of the country where it was never played'.[34] Frequently criticised for its perceived lack of enthusiasm and success in promoting both hurling and Irish, comparisons between the popularity of hurling and Irish are common,[35] but Marcus de Búrca cautions that

> Critics of the GAA who argue that it merely pays lip-service to the language overlook the fact that there is a limit to the contribution which a sports body can make to a cause such as the revival movement. They also ignore the very substantial material assistance that has been provided for many years by the Association to the language bodies, including in particular the proceeds from the annual Oireachtas hurling competition and the provision of Gaeltacht scholarships.[36]

Breandán Ó hEithir's critique of the GAA's bilingual members not withstanding, an assessment of the association's shortcomings regarding Irish suggests that many of the complaints are technology related and result from the high standards and expectations set for the GAA.[37] Ciarán Dunbarrach argues that the lack of Irish on the official website http://www.gaa.ie illustrates the 'breathtaking hypocrisy of the Irish establishment towards the Gaelic language' and maintains that it 'sends a clear message to the young people of the Gaeltacht and Gaelscoileanna, "No Gaelic here" ... While the GAA is not covered under the Official Languages Act, despite being happy to receive government funding, one would imagine that they would pay some attention to section 4 (a) of their own constitution. Not available in Irish, by the way.'[38] The unrelenting use of 'Gaelic Athletic Association' rather than Cumann Lúthchleas Gael irks Gearóid Ó Colmáin, who considers 'the persistent use of the English acronym for a Gaelic association' to be 'a terrible pity' that 'reflects the all-pervasive linguistic myopia of this country'.[39] The website is again a source of frustration: 'If you look at the CLG website, you will see GAA with Cumann Lúthchleas Gael underneath. Slightly confusing, don't you think? There is also no Irish language option on the site; if it is really a "Gaelic" Athletic Association, then the Irish language should have a primary role – in matters of cultural regeneration, everything is significant and important.'[40] Bilingual announcements at Croke Park are praiseworthy, as are the practicable and achievable suggestions in *Gaeilge sa Club*, but as in the case of almost everything relating to language policy, it is inevitably subject to the social attitudes of individual members. The Irish-language cover of the clár

(programme) and the generous use of Irish in headings in programmes are well received; but could be supplemented by articles in
Irish (and indeed Polish and Chinese), not only in the All-Ireland
publications but in county and club programmes.

Such criticisms are easily addressed at little cost and minimum
effort. More problematic are grievances relating to TG4's inability to
broadcast senior championship games. In 2001 Mark Gallagher
reported that TG4 'after providing GAA die-hards with Gaelic
throughout the winter months', 'the Gaeilge channel will feel
aggrieved if they are left with summer scraps. Of course, there is one
loophole. Raidió na Gaeltachta has been covering the GAA championship since 1972.'[41] Despite the excellent coverage provided by
Raidió na Gaeltachta (RnaG), Concubhar Ó Liatháin bemoans the
lack of live Irish-language television coverage of the All-Ireland football and hurling championships due to what he describes as 'the failure of the cash-hungry GAA to see beyond the big-money deals
offered by the likes of RTÉ, TV3 or Setanta. TG4 cannot hope to
compete with any of these broadcasters in terms of acquisition budg-
ets or audience share.' He continues:

> It is extremely ironic that TG4 can broadcast live the All
> England Lawn Tennis Championships from Wimbledon
> and the Tour de France, both great sporting events from
> foreign shores, but is prohibited from providing similarly
> excellent coverage of the major native sporting events of
> the Irish summer. All the more so, given the commitment
> in the GAA constitution to promote the Irish language.
> TG4 can afford to broadcast these events as the owners
> of the rights weigh the station's audience share in Ireland
> as they determine the level of payments due. I have no
> doubt the GAA could accommodate TG4 at no cost to
> the organisation if it wanted to. It could, for instance,
> offer a specific package – the rights to broadcast all its
> games *as Gaeilge* – in addition to the other packages it
> offered to broadcasters earlier this year. Given the failure
> of the national broadcaster, RTÉ, to live up to its statu-
> tory obligation to the Irish language with respect to
> sporting events, and TV3's non-existent interest in Irish-
> language programming, I suspect that this package could
> be secured by TG4 at a fraction of the cost of the
> English-language equivalent.[42]

Such criticism, however, cuts both ways, as is evident in Liz Howard's allegedly 'stinging broadside' against TG4 at the 2007 congress. While sponsoring women's Gaelic football, the station failed to cover camogie, 'a skilful, attractive game that is indigenous to Ireland and that caters for over 100,000 members'.[43] For Howard, TG4's exclusion of camogie, while 'it shows horse racing from Dubai, greyhound racing, sends Hector to Newcastle and Sydney',[44] is unacceptable. Yet the GAA have long insisted that minor championship games be broadcast in Irish, and when the 2001 minor hurling championship game was unexpectedly broadcast in English, promptly informed RTÉ 'that it wishes to continue its traditional policy of applying Irish commentaries in its live television transmission of the All-Ireland minor hurling and football championships'.[45]

Despite the efforts of officials, administrators and Coiste na Gaeilge in particular, much of the aforementioned criticism appears to collaborate the statement attributed to Peter Quinn when speaking at the Merriman Summer School in 2002 that 'the GAA had never realised its potential … in relation to the Irish language'.[46] Trenchant critics, however, tend to forget that the association has remained steadfast in its commitment to its wider cultural agenda despite the inevitable criticism this entails, particularly in Ulster.[47] For Brian Walker, the accommodation of rugby and soccer at Croke Park, while welcome, fails to convince. He wrote in 2008:

> There are still barriers for people like myself which need to be dealt with: the promotion of the Irish language, the sectarian position given to the Catholic church in throwing in the ball and in patronage of the GAA, and – one of the most hurtful – the naming of grounds after Irish patriots, priests and, more recently, terrorists. The GAA is primarily a sporting organisation and needs to abandon the above to attract more people like myself to its games.[48]

Reducing 'the force of Irish nationalism … to the status of the ninety minute patriot'[49] and abandoning Irish would, in the eyes of some, make the GAA more politically palatable. But, as Gearóid Ó Tuathaigh noted in 1991, it 'is neither anti-modern nor Anglophobic nor perverse to advocate that the cultivation of the Irish language should be undertaken and supported with purpose and pleasure by all those who value cultural diversity and cultural continuity on this island'.[50] Indeed Darragh McManus believes that the GAA language policy 'has been vindicated now, with the acceptance of Irish as an official EU language'.[51] Regardless of such criticism and pressure, the

2002 Strategic Review Committee – commissioned by Seán McCague and chaired by Peter Quinn – as a follow-up to the bilingual 1971 *McNamee Commission Report* 'strongly endorses the use of the Irish language and Irish culture in everything the GAA does'.[52] Nevertheless critics cite a Danny Lynch interview in which he allegedly suggested the 125th anniversary should mark a change of policy:

> I think for the 125th anniversary the GAA should refocus, and concentrate on promotion of the main games. Coming from a quasi-Gaeltacht area I have a huge interest in the Irish language, my kids are involved in it, but there are a multiplicity of highly-funded State agencies dealing with the Irish language, and I don't think we should be taking on the amount of responsibility in that regard that we do.[53]

For critics, this indicates an alarming withdrawal from the established policy.[54] There are several, possibly too many, Irish-language organisations, but none of the stature or command of the GAA. None have the popularity, reach, resources, command or profile of the association, nor is any language group, semi-state or voluntary, embedded in Gaeltacht life in the manner of the GAA. No language group rivals it in terms of membership, resources, infrastructure, contacts or capital. The GAA provides Irish with a prestige, visibility and status via programmes, jerseys, speeches, announcements and signage that would otherwise be unattainable. For many in the diaspora, the language component of All-Ireland final day is their sole exposure to the language. The association's various efforts and initiatives – Scór and Seachtain na Gaeilge – entice people to experience Irish and expose them to the language throughout the island and reach areas and enclaves unknown to language organisations.

This is where the GAA finds itself in the first decade of the twenty-first century; labelled with sectarianism and bigotry for promoting Irish on the one hand, accused of hypocrisy for its failure to promote Irish (and hurling and rounders) as successfully as football on the other, yet ever conscious of the *tsunami* of globalised mass culture looming on the horizon. No more than with disciplinary rules and the promotion of hurling, the difficulty lies with social attitudes and behaviour, as Paul Rouse attests:

> the true place of the Irish language within the GAA reflects the position of the language in wider life: official window-dressing, popular disinterest, sporadic enthusiasm …

There are those within the GAA whose love of Irish is as central to their lives as their love of hurling and football. However, the sincerity of their pro-language initiatives is smothered by the disinterest in the wider membership which sees the GAA only as a sporting body.[55]

'The annual GAA spectaculars at Croke Park are less important', argues John A. Murphy 'than the association's socially regenerative work throughout the parishes of Ireland.'[56] This is certainly true of the association's impact in Gaeltacht areas, where it provides a focus for all ages and an expression of community identity. Any effort to describe the role of the Irish language within the GAA would be remiss if failing to address the synergy of Comórtas Peile na Gaeltachta:

> one of the finest spectacles this country has to offer. There are top senior teams like An Ghaeltacht, An Cheathrú Rua from Galway and Naomh Abán from Baile Bhúirne itself, and there are small junior teams who've had to battle through qualifying sections to get there and for whom participation is the real triumph. Last year, there was even a team of Connemara men based in London.[57]

Held at a different location every year over the June bank holiday weekend and broadcast live on TG4 and RnaG, Comórtas Peile na Gaeltachta is a social and sporting highlight for Irish speakers and 'one of the GAA's most innovative club competitions'.[58] Eamonn Sweeney describes the spectacle of

> people playing the game of Gaelic football shouting at each other in Irish, complaining to the referee in Irish while small kids sell programmes written in Irish and ask if you've got any smaller change in Irish while an Irish radio station does commentaries in Irish. The managers discuss tactics with the mentors in Irish and the pubs nearby are full of people asking for drink in Irish.[59]

Martán Ó Ciardha, writing in *Foinse*, captured the amateur spirit, community effort and local pride witnessed in abundance at the 2008 finals in Gleann Cholm Cille: 'Cruthúnas eile ar an gcaoi a bhfuil an spórt in ann mórtas agus bród an phobail a thabhairt le chéile agus stáitse a thabhairt dó faoinar féidir é a léiriú.'[60] The competition, however, is not without its controversies. The growing use of English as well as the debatable status of some 'Gaeltacht' clubs are persistent concerns. While *Gaeilge sa Club*, available at www.gaa.ie, exhorts all clubs to 'set the club's entry in Comórtas Peile na Gaeltachta as a long-term objective/bíodh ballraíocht i gComórtas Peile na Gaeltachta mar sprioc fadréimhseach ag an gClub',[61] some recent efforts to include Irish-speaking teams from Dublin (Peileadóirí Dhuibh Linne) and Mayo have met with disappointment. Piaras Ó Raghallaigh, Mayo's Oifigeach na Gaeilge agus Cultúrtha argues that participation of non-Gaeltacht Irish-speaking teams would offer 'such players a reward for their promotion of the language and encourage more players to speak our native tongue'.[62] Laochra Loch Laoi, a junior team comprised of Irish-speakers from Belfast's An Cheathrú Ghaeltachta, however, competed in 2007,[63] as did Móindearg in 2006 – a London team, founded in 1973, Foireann na Mílaoise, comprised largely of Conamara exiles.[64] In addition to the men's senior and junior competition, it also features a ladies' football competition in addition to An Cailín Gaelach pageant, with finalists also having qualified through a series of local competitions. In 2000 Comórtas Peile na Gaeltachta in conjunction with RTÉ Raidió na Gaeltachta selected their 'Team of the Millennium' (Table 1.1).

TABLE 1.1
FOIREANN NA MÍLAOISE, COMÓRTAS PEILE NA GAELTACHTA

	(1) Micheál Ó Críodáin (Naomh Abán)	
(2) Páidí Ó Sé (An Ghaeltacht)	(3) Seán Seosamh Ó Dochartaigh (Naomh Columba)	(4) Micheál Ó Scanaill (Naomh Abán)
(5) Antóin Ó Cearúil (Gaoth Dobhair)	(6) Micheál Ó Sé (An Ghaeltacht)	(7) Seán Óg de Paor (An Cheathrú Rua)
	(8) Diarmuid Ó Loinsigh (Naomh Abán) — (9) Liam Seosamh Mac Pháidín (Béal an Mhuirthid)	
(10) Dara Ó Cinnéide (An Ghaeltacht)	(11) Máirtín Beag Mac Aodha (Cill Chártha)	(12) Aoidh Mac Laifeartaigh (Na Dúnaibh)
(13) Stiofán Seoige (Naomh Pádraig, An Fhairche)	(14) Seán Ó Drisceoil (Béal Átha an Ghaorthaidh)	(15) Neillí Ó Gallachóir (Gaoth Dobhair)

COMÓRTAS PEILE NA GAELTACHTA

Bliain/Year	Ionad/Venue	Sinsir/Senior		Sóisir/Junior	
		Buaiteoirí / Champions	Tánaistí / Finalists	Buaiteoirí / Champions	Tánaistí / Finalists
1969	Gaoth Dobhair	Gaoth Dobhair	Corca Dhuibhne	-	-
1970	Gaoth Dobhair	Conamara	Baile Bhúirne	-	-
1971	Baile Bhúirne	Maigh Cuilinn	Baile Bhúirne	-	-
1972	An Daingean	Na hAghasaigh	Baile Bhúirne	-	-
1973	An Cheathrú Rua	Maigh Eo	Gaoth Dobhair	-	-
1974	Baile Bhúirne	Na hAghasaigh	Naomh Conall	-	-
1975	Gaoth Dobhair	Baile Bhúirne	Leitir Móir	-	-
1976	An Cheathrú Rua	Gaoth Dobhair	Baile Bhúirne	An Fhairche	C.L. Bréanann
1977	An Daingean	Na hAghasaigh	Baile Bhúirne	Carna	Naomh Micheál
1978	Gleann Chom Cille	Gleann Cholm Cille	An Fhairche	Naomh Micheál (Baile na Sceilg)	Gleann Fhinne
1979	Baile Bhúirne	Baile Bhúirne	Corca Dhuibhne	Naomh Micheál (Baile na Sceilg)	Túr Mhic Éadaigh
1980	An Fhairche	Baile Bhúirne	An Fhairche	Na Dúnaibh	Naomh Micheál (Tír Chonaill)
1981	Indreabhán	Baile Bhúirne	Naomh Ciarán		
1982	Gaoth Dobhair	Baile Bhúirne	Béal an Mhuirthid	Na Dúnaibh	Cloich Cheannfhaola
1983	Gaoth Dobhair	Na Dúnaibh	Béal an Mhuirthid	Túr Mhic Éadaigh	An Cheathrú Rua
1984	Rinn Ua gCuanach	Béal an Mhuirthid	Ard an Rátha	Béal Átha an Ghaorthaidh	Clann Choláiste Mhuire
1985	Gallarus	Béal an Mhuirthid	Corca Dhuibhne	Naomh Micheál (Baile na Sceilg)	Béal Átha an Ghaorthaidh
1986	Na Dúnaibh	Gleann Cholm Cille	An Fhairche	An Clochán Liath	Rath Cairn
1987	Béal an Mhuirthid	Cill Chárthaigh	An Fhairche	Leitir Móir	Gaoth Dobhair
1988	An Cheathrú Rua	Múscraí	Cill Chárthaigh	Rath Cairn	Túr Mhic Éadaigh
1989	Gleann Cholm Cille	Cill Chárthaigh	Naomh Columba	Cill Chárthaigh	Na Piarsaigh
1990	Gallarus	Cill Chárthaigh	Corca Dhuibhne	Corca Dhuibhne	Piarsaigh na Dromada
1991	Béal Átha an Ghaorthaidh	Cill Chárthaigh	Maigh Cuilinn	Béal Átha an Ghaorthaidh	Clann Choláiste Mhuire
1992	Indreabhán	Cloich Cheannfhaola	An Cheathrú Rua	Béal Átha an Ghaorthaidh	Acaill
1993	Rath Cairn	Cloich Cheannfhaola	Leitir Móir	Rath Cairn	Rinn Ua gCuanach
1994	Gaoth Dobhair	Gaoth Dobhair	An Cheathrú Rua	Piarsaigh na Dromada	Naomh Muire
1995	An Fhairche	Corca Dhuibhne	An Fhairche	Béal Átha an Ghaorthaidh	Carna Caiseal
1996	Baile Bhúirne	Corca Dhuibhne	Baile Bhúirne	Micheál Breathnach	Naomh Micheál (Tír Conaill)

COMÓRTAS PEILE NA GAELTACHTA cont

Bliain/Year	Ionad/Venue	Sinsir/Senior		Sóisir/Junior	
		Buaiteoirí / Champions	Tánaistí / Finalists	Buaiteoirí / Champions	Tánaistí / Finalists
1997	An Cheathrú Rua	An Cheathrú Rua	Corca Dhuibhne	Piarsaigh na Dromada	Naomh Columba B
1998	Cloich Cheannfhaola	Ard an Rátha	Cloich Cheannfhaola	Piarsaigh na Dromada	Béal Átha an Ghaorthaidh
1999	Rinn Ua gCuanach	An Ghaeltacht	Baile Bhúirne	Lios Póil	Béal Átha an Ghaorthaidh
2000	Cill tSéadhna	Baile Bhúirne	Cill Chárthaigh	Micheál Breathnach	Túr Mhic Éadaigh
2001	Piarsaigh na Dromada	Clochán Liath	Baile Bhúirne	Piarsaigh na Dromada	Túr Mhic Éadaigh
2002	Leitir Mór	Gaoth Dobhair	Baile Bhúirne	Béal Átha an Ghaorthaidh	Rinn Ua gCuanach
2003	Baile Bhúirne	Baile Bhúirne	An Cheathrú Rua	Lios Póil	Béal an Mhuirthid
2004	Cill Chártha	Gaoth Dobhair	Cill tSéadhna	Béal an Mhuirthid	Na Dúnaibh
2005	Cill na Martra	Baile Bhúirne	Gaoth Dobhair	Lios Póil	Cill Chomáin
2006	An Spidéal	Béal an Mhuirthid	Micheál Breathnach	Na Breathnaigh	Gaeil Fhanaid
2007	Béal Átha an Ghaorthaidh	Naomh Abán	Gaoth Dobhair	Naomh Muire	Acaill
2008	Gleann Cholm Cille	Cill Chárthaigh	Naomh Columba	Rinn Ua gCuanach	Piarsaigh na Dromaide

The GAA's contribution to sustaining the language in Gaeltacht areas is obvious when one envisions the potential linguistic impact of an English-language-orientated association over the course of the twentieth century. The GAA not only facilitates but promotes trans-generational transmission in Gaeltacht areas and is key to successful future language maintenance. Language attitudes are interconnected with cultural values and governed by an individual's interaction with institutional practice and communicative expectation. In many Gaeltachtaí the GAA is the sole organisation to provide the community-based, linguistic environment essential for successful transmission of Irish from one generation to the next. The language culture at the U-12s practice may be a far more reliable barometer of linguistic viability and sustainability than multiple census returns. The GAA offers a social outlet and sporting interest to Irish speakers with a natural and accessible vocabulary and it is no coincidence that newspapers such as *Foinse* and *Lá Nua* and websites such as An Fear Rua (www.anfearrua.com)[65] and Beo! (www.beo.ie)[66] contain articles in Irish on GAA matters. Writing in 2007 of strategies to develop innovation and rural knowledge communities, Finbarr Bradley argues:

> Creative individual activity, such as searching for new ways to improve a community, organising people and resources, within a supportive and challenging context, is the key to a vital, thriving local economy. Communities place themselves in a much better position to improve individual lives by re-establishing the importance of community itself, emphasising values and appreciating how a limited contribution the commercial sector of the local economy makes to overall well-bring and prosperity.[67]

The establishment of a knowledge-based Irish society, as desired by the government, requires, he argues, 'a true innovation culture' that 'must be primarily founded on a spirit of self-reliance, relationships of community and trust, a sense of place, tradition and civic engagement'.[68] He concludes: 'Surviving and prospering in a multicultural world requires individuals to understand and appreciate their own cultural values. Moreover, being able to place one's own roots in a cultural, historical and social context is necessary to appreciate the values and traditions of others.'[69] In post-Celtic Tiger, post-Lisbon Ireland as global economic markets crash and the Irish 'economic zone' goes into recession, is any organisation on the island better positioned to provide such leadership?

Many of the criticisms regarding Irish are easily addressed. Yet Ó hEithir's caution that 'There is a limit to what any government and education system policy can do to revive Irish. In the end it is up to those who do not wish it to die to see that it survives through another generation at least'[70] is still valid. And it is here that the GAA may have its greatest potential, 'as the outstanding community-based organisation on this island, giving identity and pride to their birthplace'.[71] Clubs are in an ideal position to offer 'local, community-based language planning activities [which] would be more effective than a regional, macro approach to intervention in the field'.[72] The future of Irish, a communal language, depends, writes Pádraig Ó Riagáin, 'on the stability of the social networks of users, that is, on the series of interlinked social relationships that may grow out of contacts in an institutional setting, but whose survival depends on the achievement of some degree of friendship, intimacy and interpersonal knowledge among participants'.[73] It is the GAA that provides such a network in the Gaeltacht, not only for native speakers but for neo-native speakers, returned immigrants and 'the new Irish'. The abandonment by the GAA of the promotion and cultivation of Irish would deprive it of a historic link, undervalue its cultural agenda and pose similar questions for the future of camogie, and even hurling in the weaker counties. As the 2008 championship slogan proclaims, 'the height you attain depends on the depth of your roots'. There is little profit for the GAA in promoting Irish, but what profit accrues from promoting hurling in Sligo, football in Kilkenny, camogie in Donegal, handball on Toraigh, anti-racism, sportsmanship or tolerance, or making Croke Park carbon neutral? The association differs from the FAI and IRFU in that it is rooted in the revival and preservation of Irish culture. As Nioclás Ó Braonáin, president of the GAA, declared in 2008, the GAA is about the identity of the people:

> It's about pride of place. It's a national sport not dominated by world events. It gives us something different to hold on to as we become more Europeanised. As the country becomes richer, it gives us something to hold on to that is bigger than material wealth. It is encouraging that these values continue to inspire people in our Association, particularly our younger members. Let them be our inspiration also as we head towards our 125th anniversary.[74]

No more than in the case of the promotion of hurling, camogie, rounders and handball, 'Perhaps Michael Cusack's great revival project was only ever half accomplished. The new frontier lies not abroad but at home.'[75]

In 1999 Colm Keys commented on the lack of fluent speakers playing Gaelic football: 'It's only when you go to count them that you realise how few fluent Irish speakers there are playing inter-county football.'[76] As 2009 celebrates 125 years of the GAA, it is fitting to concentrate on the association's many positive contributions to the language movement and the social infrastructure of Ireland's Gaeltachtaí in that period. Numerous Irish speakers have played, and currently play, Gaelic games with distinction and honour, including notables such as Mick O'Connell (Kerry), Brian Mullins (Dublin), Mickey Ned O'Sullivan (Kerry), Jarleth Burns (Armagh), Charlie Vernon (Armagh), David Henry (Dublin), Adrian Morrissey (Wexford) and Andriú Mac Lochlainn (Kildare). Tables 9.2 and 9.3 are an acknowledgment of some Gaeltacht players who have graced the game at inter-county level.[77]

TABLE 9.2
ALL-TIME GAELTACHT SELECTION

1
Séamus Mac Gearailt
(Ciarraí)

2	3	4
Páidí Ó Sé	Jack Cosgrove	Marc Ó Sé
(Ciarraí)	(Gaillimh)	(Ciarraí)

5	6	7
Tomás Ó Sé	Anthony Lynch	Seán Óg de Paor
(Ciarraí)	(Corcaigh)	(Gaillimh)

8	9
Darragh Ó Sé	Máirtín Beag
(Ciarraí)	(Mac Aodha)

10	11	12
Seán Ó Domhnaill	Dan Larry Ó Caomhán	Michael Ó Cróinin
(Gaillimh)	(Ciarraí/Gaillimh)	(Corcaigh)

13	14	15
Brendan Devaney	Dara Ó Cinnéide	Seán Ó Drisceoil
(Dún na nGall)	(Ciarraí)	(Corcaigh)

TABLE 9.3
CONTEMPORARY GAELTACHT SELECTION

1
Pádraig Lally
(Gaillimh)

2	3	4
Tomás Ó Sé	Marc Ó Sé	Niall McGee
(Ciarraí)	(Ciarraí)	(Dún na nGall)

5	6	7
Éamon McGee	Anthony Lynch	Rónán Ó Flatharta
(Dún na nGall)	(Corcaigh)	(Ciarraí)

8	9
Darragh Ó Sé	Noel Ó Laoire
(Ciarraí)	(Corcaigh)

10	11	12
Paul Clancy	Kevin Cassidy	Michéal Ó Cróinín
(Gaillimh)	(Dún na nGall)	(Corcaigh)

13	14	15
Fiachra Breathnach	Stephen Cassidy	Liam Ó Lonnáin
(Gaillimh)	(Dún na nGall)	(Port Láirge)

19. Eamon de Valera throws in the ball to start a match in Croke Park.

10 'The Greatest Amateur Association in the World'? The GAA and Amateurism

DÓNAL McANALLEN

That the GAA is the 'the greatest amateur sporting body in the world' has been, in various forms,[1] among the proudest boasts of its officials, members and admirers over the last century. The claim derives from the high levels of application displayed by many of its players, sometimes before large crowds, without pecuniary gain; and by its legions of voluntary officials and helpers, serving it often at considerable personal cost. Such dedicated amateurism has been heralded as unparalleled in any comparable sports. Yet the GAA always had a keen commercial acumen; indeed, its critics labelled it the 'Grab All Association'. This chapter will examine the origins and development of the association's amateur status, particularly what it meant for players and officials in terms of effort, commitment and constraints. It will further assess how much this amateur ethos was observed and enforced. Attention will also be paid to the GAA's financial activity and attitudes towards commercialism. The focus will be confined to the main GAA sports, hurling and Gaelic football; the many issues of amateurism in handball and athletics require separate treatment elsewhere. From this analysis it is hoped to determine the overall strength and substance of the GAA's amateurism over its history.

GAELIC TEAM SPORTS AND THE GAA'S AMATEUR ETHOS, 1889–1912

By the time hurling and Gaelic football competitions were proceeding in earnest, the GAA had already reached its own rational compromise on amateurism for athletics. Its first set of rules for athletics, in 1885, allowed only amateurs who had 'never competed for a money prize, or staked, bet on (with or against) a professional, for a prize, or ... taught, pursued, or assisted in the practice of athletic exercises as a means of obtaining a livelihood',[2] but did let amateur athletes compete for money prizes of limited value, to offset their travelling expenses. The rationale, as espoused by GAA founder Michael Cusack, was that instead of typical amateur athletic prizes like fish knives and butter coolers, it was more useful for 'a poor Irish youth to accept his travelling expenses and a sovereign or two to get the fish or the butter'.[3] This was notably different from the elitist 'gentleman amateur' ethos of Victorian English sporting bodies, like the Amateur Athletic Association, which only allowed reimbursement for travelling expenses from 1899.[4]

The GAA's early rule books did not specify that its two main team sports, hurling and Gaelic football, were amateur sports; only its rules for athletics and later for cycling specified an amateur status.[5] That the team games were amateur was understood, though. Playing Gaelic games for local pride was a tradition with the GAA from birth. The 1873 novel *Knocknagow*, immortalising the cry of the heroic farm labourer, Mat the Thrasher – 'For the credit of the little village!'[6] – encapsulated a real feeling among Irish peasant sportsmen. An 1882 press report referred to a living Cushendall (Co. Antrim) man who had starred 'in innumerable hurling matches where the reputation of a whole parish was at stake'.[7] A similar inter-parish rivalry fuelled the explosion of Gaelic games under the GAA's auspices from 1884. One simply could not demand a fee if playing for local pride. Elitism was anathema. No one would be let make a living from playing. Hurlers and footballers seldom 'trained' for games, except big finals; even 'practice' was irregular.[8] Sheer physicality was the most extolled virtue in early players. 'Specialisation' was neither common nor encouraged; a player who used a body swerve to avoid tackles was ridiculed.[9]

GAA structures ensured that the games developed along amateur lines. There was no money-based transfer system. Residence qualifications, stipulating playing adherence to one's parish club (the 'parish rule') and county, kept centralisation and free-market capitalism at bay.[10] The playing rules equally exuded amateurism. The natural freedom of movement allowed to players was inherently amateur, argued an early champion; other codes, with artificial restrictions like offside, required players to 'devote practically all their time to learn how to play'.[11] The ban on members playing soccer, introduced in 1886,[12] effectively blocked the entry of professional players and payments into Gaelic games. An amateur ethos was also implicit in the determination to make Gaelic games as widely accessible as possible. Virtually all matches were held on Sunday, the day of rest, so that men could play or watch without missing work;[13] and club membership and entrance fees were only fractions of those for other field sports in Ireland.[14]

Open amateurism was quite a democratic principle,[15] and the GAA's administration was itself both democratic and amateur.[16] Its

democratic legislative process may account for why the amateur status of its team games was not defined in rule. From 1889 until 1997,
rule changes could only occur via motions from club units; they often
did so, but with a lack of proper management or overarching coherent view of the legislation.[17] Officials operated in a voluntary capacity, some incurring substantial financial loss. Only the athletics hand-
icapper and the national secretaries were paid travelling expenses in
the early years, mainly due to the GAA's meagre income. Cusack's
workload as the first national secretary cost him a lot of time and
expense, and the neglect of his (formerly thriving) private business.
Generally, senior officials seemed to accept their loss as a contribution to the national movement, but at times the pressures proved too
much. Personal financial concerns played a part in Maurice Davin's
resignation as president in 1889.[18]

The GAA's amateurism was conditioned from the off by commercial fundraising activity. Admission fees for spectators were the norm.
Advertisements, such as one for sewing machines on the cover of the
1889 rule book,[19] abounded in GAA publications. An industry sprang
up around the sale of Gaelic sports equipment.[20] Vendors, hawkers,
shopkeepers and taxi-men profited from big games. Some of those,
such as publicans and bookmakers, who set up shop around match
venues, were opposed and confronted by GAA officials.[21] The custom
of playing for wagers survived into the GAA's early days. In Galway,
for example, between 1884 and 1886 several hurling games were
played for sums of up to £10 a side.[22] Similar wagers are reported for
club games in Kildare[23] and Dublin in the mid-1890s, and probably
increased the propensity of games to end in disputes.[24] But even as
these age-old wagers disappeared, the conduct of early players and
supporters regularly conflicted with the stylised Corinthian amateur
fair-play ethic; the pursuit of victory too often produced rowdy GAA
games in the early years and later.[25] Commercial sponsorship, albeit
limited, made inroads through businesses donating trophies for competition.[26]

County champion teams playing in the inter-county championships
from 1887 had to travel further, at greater expense. The All-Ireland-
winning Limerick (Commercials) football team of 1887 paid their own
way to Dublin, and did not receive medals until over twenty years
later.[27] But players began to demand recompense. Seven of the
Thurles team for the first national hurling final (in 1888) did not travel due to a row over expenses.[28] Soon most teams in inter-county
games had their expenses defrayed. This reflected Cusack's belief that
working men, many barely scraping by, should not suffer financially

for playing their national sport. Often teams would only travel to play if reimbursement was guaranteed in advance.[29] Yet Gaelic team sports stayed immune to the professionalisation of Irish soccer (1894) and similar trends in other sports. The GAA simply did not have the potential income to accommodate semi-professional games. The Irish population and economy were too small. Efforts to diffuse Gaelic games abroad, beyond Irish communities, failed. Most teams were ephemeral 'combinations', coming and going almost in an instant, rather than from properly organised clubs. The heavy voluntary administrative burden would smother many teams or clubs in future years also.[30] Money matters caused plenty of controversy, however. Accusations or insinuations about misappropriation of funds were frequently made against senior officials or gatemen then (and indeed intermittently for some time thereafter).[31] 'What becomes of all the money collected at GAA gates?' many asked, but few bothered to check its audited accounts.[32]

In the 1900s, on the crest of a cultural nationalist wave, the GAA enjoyed a national renaissance, and a new breed of idealistic members sought to promote 'contests in pure athletics'.[33] The GAA itself was reconceptualised as a 'voluntary school of physical training for Irish youth'.[34] A new emphasis was placed on players' conduct. They were expected to be role models, to set a good example; to be 'men of discipline, or self-control and self-respect, men of sober habits'. 'On their shoulders especially rests the reputation of the Gael.'[35] Drinking and gambling were discouraged among members.[36] Writers such as Fr James Dollard portrayed young men forming teams 'to do or die for the "honour of the little villages"';[37] 'one grand day' at Gaelic sport gave 'pure enjoyment and more genuine satisfaction than a thousand years in America or other foreign lands'.[38] The idea of playing for the pride of one's county developed also. The Cork hurling team of 1903 bonded 'as one man, one brother … all in it together for the honour of the county'.[39] Whereas for the 1900 All-Ireland football final only half of the Galway (Tuam) team trained at all (and even then just a few days before the game),[40] both Kerry and Kildare trained regularly for the 1903 final, with the latter peaking at three collective sessions a week.[41] Economic reasons also underlay the improved preparations. More players could now afford football boots, proper playing attire and the time and expense of playing, although these were still beyond the means of many at club level.[42]

Many players accepted and relished their amateur status as an automatic corollary of the GAA's patriotic ideals. The famous Kerry player, Dick Fitzgerald, cherished 'playing the game for its own sake, because it is OUR OWN GAME'.[43] Some players were praised for paying their own travelling expenses for games near and far.[44] The Antrim (Seaghan's) football team that won six successive Ulster titles (1908–13) played all but one game away, at distant venues, so that the destitute Ulster Council could get better 'gates', and also passed up its claim to medals.[45] GAA officials lauded the sacrifices of their 'pure athletes of a thorough Irish cast',[46] yet they did not define the games as 'amateur'; the term was still equated with English snobbery and élitism.[47] An outside admirer of the GAA's playing ethos was the mayor of Kilkenny, the Hon. Otway Cuffe. In presenting All-Ireland medals to Kilkenny hurlers in 1908, Cuffe celebrated their distinctness from the professionalism and commercialism that ruined sportsmanship in other codes.

> It was not as if they had gone elsewhere and hired so many players at so much a head to come and play the games ... they should have their own Kilkennymen, Corkmen or Limerickmen ... upholding the honour of their own counties and their own homes ... Let them try to have sport for sport's sake ...[48]

Gaelic games ideologues in the nationalist press denounced professional sport more explicitly, as the epitome of English iniquity. While the Gael had 'ideals higher than cash', claimed one, 'Mammonism is the archpriest of British sport'.[49] Sport became business due to the fixation of the 'nation of shopkeepers' with profit-making, said another.[50] The financial incentive, explained an Ulster observer, bred in players a 'secret ambition ... to become – not a clean athlete – but ... to receive the plaudits of the mob who have paid'.[51] The alleged degeneration of 'the mob' exacerbated GAA members' anti-professionalism. Echoing a contemporary British belief that poor national fitness – seen as a cause of defeat in the Boer War – owed in part to the mania of professionalism turning sportsmen into spectators, GAA writers deplored how a crowd would 'watch a number of trained and paid performers take part in a game in which they themselves are too emasculated to participate'.[52] Journalist and GAA official, 'Vigilant' (Séamus Upton), lampooned the cult of the professional star:

> In England it is the players who are popular. Here it is the game. There it is the credit of little Teddy Bulletscull from Rochdale that is at issue, for his professional keep ... depends on his out-manoeuvring Alf Smithers of the Bolton Blues.[53]

The *Gaelic Athlete*, edited by Upton and the official GAA organ, went further. 'Professional players are the very vagabonds and out-laws of the sporting fraternity.'[54] Inspired by a book (of 1910) which described how professional sport had corrupted heroic ancient Greek athletics and society,[55] Upton argued that Ireland of the Tailteann Games 'first gave the lead to humanity in the art and sci-ence of athletics', before the Greeks and before Saxon influence tainted it.[56]

Nationalists also distrusted professional sport due to the percep-tion that it was a northern Protestant/unionist activity, emanating as it did mainly from Belfast.[57] Contempt for professionalism and mone-tarism in sport was possibly strongest among the GAA members clos-est to it, in Ulster. An article in the official GAA annual depicted how Ulster did not indulge in athletics 'for pure love of them' as the rest of Ireland. Industrial Belfast, having forsaken 'manly games', 'prefers to take exercise by deputy', and 'like the large cities of England and Scotland, has in athletics become simply spectatorial'.[58] Professional soccer's Irish League, claimed a *Derry People* column, was 'merely an organisation for money-making purposes', only admitting Catholics to be 'used as money-making tools'.[59] It suited GAA officials to depict soccer as unethical and corrupt, as the Irish Football Association was then subsidising the game's promotion in some areas. GAA officials lambasted the 'soccer soupers'[60] for trying to 'bribe' nationalists in Fermanagh and Sligo with 'thirty pieces of silver' to convert to the English game, and, by extension, to sell their nationality for the British way of life.[61] A few years later an Ulster GAA secretary lam-basted the 'West Britishers' of soccer who offered money, silver cups, free outfits and 'high class cuisine' to GAA members in counties Donegal and Monaghan, to change sport; such efforts were made, he asserted, to prepare Ulster culturally for partition.[62]

The notion of playing for one's parish was not universal to all players. In large urban centres, where clubs were numerous, more resources were available and parish boundaries were blurred, big clubs were prone to poach talented players from other clubs. Illicit payments and other offers were made. Some 'prosperous combina-tions' would 'even go beyond the limits of their county to strength-en their reserve',[63] offering jobs to players to sign them up. Dublin County Board tightened its transfer byelaws to stop 'the gentry who manage to move around half-a-dozen clubs in the course of a year',[64] but the practice carried on.

Material reward in silverware also motivated GAA players to compete. If no trophy was on offer, teams might not enter an event.

Many early players wore their medals pinned to their clothes.[65] Sometimes local heroes were feted more liberally. Supporters presented silver watches to the 1900 All-Ireland-winning Tipperary team,[66] and a cheque for £100 to Limerick hurler 'Tyler' Mackey, on his retirement as team captain in 1913.[67] These un-amateur gifts were akin to (but smaller than) those in Welsh club rugby, where small payments were largely ignored by the sport's authorities, apart from sporadic clean-ups; in both cases, the games were too tied up with national sentiment to enforce a high moral line on the odd present.[68]

Playing for one's county was not always viewed as a privilege either. As inter-county competitions became more regular in the 1900s, and travelling expenses and hotel bills increased, teams sought greater reimbursement. Central Council and provincial councils began to pay travelling expenses to inter-county teams,[69] at rates specified in rule,[70] but expenses rows persevered. The Clonmel Shamrock club even took a court decree against Central Council in 1903, to obtain extra payment (of £10) for its travel to Dublin for an All-Ireland football final; the club was duly expelled from the GAA.[71] Occasionally, selected players did not show. For some, going to distant venues was a turn off, if it meant being away from dawn until after midnight.[72] Many cared little for the county team; county identity was still nascent, and the champion club selected the team, so players from other clubs might opt out, especially if they disliked that club or area of the county, or the selection.[73] A rule was introduced to suspend (for six months) any player who refused to play for his county,[74] however it conflicted with the element of voluntary participation in amateur sport. The expense of treatment or loss of income due to injury also caused discontent. Players injured in inter-county games were regularly reimbursed in part, but they resented officials' scrutiny of their claims.[75] An aggrieved Cork hurler bemoaned in 1908 how 'players draw the crowds, make the money and lose their sweat at many a hard hour's game, while those gentlemen at the head of affairs take charge of the bag and jump in their cars again before the match is over – off to their hotel to count.' The administration, he argued, was 'captured by non-players'; the players made the games but had no direct representation.[76] A Cork official replied that the same player had demanded payment of expenses to play in a local benefit game.[77] Officials saw good reason for close scrutiny. A few players fiddled their payment of expenses claims or other matters. Three Kildare players were found to have 'sold' a challenge game to Dublin in 1906 for ten shillings, funded by sums gambled.[78]

From an early stage the GAA paid a handful of high-ranking officials more than ordinary expenses, on account of their increasing
workload and responsibility. From 1891 the national secretary was
paid a percentage commission of gross receipts: 5 per cent initially,[79]
and 15 per cent from 1896.[80] From the early 1900s provincial council secretaries[81] and a few county secretaries[82] also received honoraria or stipends. Such payments caused grumblings here and there.
Why did some officials deserve payment and others not; and how
much was appropriate? Committee delegates were now refunded for
travel and meal expenses. Referees were not given a formal fee,[83] but
occasionally got paid slightly more than their actual expense. The
GAA hierarchy did not expect to get manual labour *gratis*; in 1905
congress decided to pay men for all contract work at 'the current rate
of wages in the district'.[84] The association was not investing much
money. Largely as a result, it owned not a single ground after one
quarter-century.[85]

Further afield, in American cities, where Gaelic games were mainly
autonomous from the GAA, the amateur status was habitually
infringed. Some early games were played for stakes, such as a hurling game between clubs from New York and Philadelphia in 1891,
for $60 and the championship of America.[86] From the 1900s, the
proprietors of Celtic Park, New York's main Gaelic venue, split the
gate receipts with the 'big four' teams in the city, the biggest crowd-
pullers. Some of the profit was given to players. American club mag-
nates induced players to come over from Ireland; three Kerry players were invited over on an all-expenses-paid trip to assist a New
York team for two months in 1906.[87] There were calls for the suspension of American Gaelic clubs for such 'unsportsmanlike' practices,
but none ensued.[88] In 1914 the formation of the 'Gaelic Athletic
Association of the United States' by the smaller 'county' clubs limited clubs to $50 from gate receipts to cover their expenses – a reduc-
tion of some $1,500 for the 'big four'. After a temporary stand-off,
the 'big four' relented and joined the GAA board.[89]

But the American scene never truly conformed to the amateur
ideal. Players continued to be induced over from Ireland, chiefly with
job offers.[90] The extent of the 'pull' of inducements is hard to quantify; some of these players might have pursued the American dream
anyway, given the 'push' of economic gloom in Ireland. Irish GAA
officials criticised the 'professionalism' of the games in America.[91]
From the late 1940s the New York scene became further commercialised, prospering as a 'semi-independent republic' of the GAA.
John 'Kerry' O'Donnell, the city board's mogul, owned the lease on

its Gaelic Park headquarters and controlled income from games. Teams were handed some of the big gate receipts. It was doubly troubling to Croke Park officials that the games had commercial sponsors, including an alcoholic drink.[92]

THE INTER-COUNTY SCENE, 1913–54

From 1913 the inter-county Gaelic games scene came into its own. Levels of preparation for inter-county teams were revolutionised in that year, when teams in major national finals began to go on collective training camps. Louth footballers hired professional coaches and paid the players' wages for two weeks' training, in preparation for the Croke Cup final replay; opponents Kerry also trained in camp.[93] After initial anxiety that this fad might work in a 'direction contrary to the purely amateur status of the Association',[94] in 1914 the GAA's official journal hailed scientific training for All-Ireland players towards 'Gaelic physical perfection' as 'a harbinger of progress', beneficial to the entire organisation.[95] There was a desire to provide entertainment to attract crowds to fund the modernisation of the GAA. Yet Kerry's All-Ireland-winning captain of 1914, Dick Fitzgerald, in his pioneering coaching manual of that year, decried the 'tendency towards professionalism' in players being unfairly 'forced to go into special training for some weeks'. Most players could not afford the time or the expense to do so, nor could many supporters afford the subscriptions asked of them to defray the expense.[96] He advised that the game should 'ever be developing on the scientific side', but 'never become the possession of the professional player'.[97] None the less, pre-final training camps of a fortnight or longer became ritual. To assuage players' reluctance to set aside work for training – one player was apparently 'more interested in farming than hurling' for Laois in the 1914 All-Ireland final[98] – county boards paid them the equivalent of their wages, or 'replacement money' to those who worked in their place. Central Council and provincial councils gave special grants – which rapidly increased – to All-Ireland final teams to reduce their training costs,[99] but did not audit how they were spent.

The training revolution from 1913 instigated much administrative change as well. The record profits of that year's Croke Cup final enabled the GAA to buy its first permanent ground, Croke Park. A new workload resulted. Ard-Rúnaí Luke O'Toole was appointed manager of the grounds at a salary of £75, with a residence there at nominal rent;[100] prior attempts to pay him a £100 bonus for his extra toil sparked uproar over the 'excessive sum'.[101] In the provinces and counties too, some secretaries were paid (relatively smaller) sums, usually by commission, in proportion to increasing duties. The merits of such stipends provoked intermittent debates.[102] Yet more numerous were accounts of officials paying bills and players' expenses from their own pockets,[103] or making astonishing unreimbursable efforts, like cycling the breadth of a province for a meeting.[104] Some declined to claim even for travelling expenses to national meetings.[105] While the Croke Park purchase marked the GAA's arrival as a commercial organisation[106] – it duly became a limited company[107] – it retained a conscience about financial activity.

Gaelic games expanded rapidly in popularity, to become mass-spectator sports. All-Ireland final crowds increased from 17,000 in 1913 to 37,500 in 1926 and to 68,950 in 1938. The pressures and profile of inter-county players rose accordingly. From the early 1920s county boards took complete control of selecting inter-county teams, thus extending players' expected obligations to, and average playing career for, the county. Players who ignored the county's call were sometimes suspended.[108] A series of new competitions from the mid-1920s, principally the National Leagues, multiplied the frequency and distances of travel to inter-county games. Some players, like gardaí, had to sacrifice days of annual leave to make the long trips.[109] A policy of 'speeding up the game' to please spectators took root.[110] The level of personal fitness required to play inter-county games escalated. Some players adopted serious, systematic personal regimes. Tommy Doyle, a Tipperary hurler from 1937 to 1953, got up each day at 7 a.m. and did sprinting; spent at least an hour each evening on 'ball-punching, skipping and physical drill'; ate a diet of raw eggs; and went to bed at 10 p.m.[111] Christy Ring, a Cork hurling icon from 1937 to 1966, had a spartan philosophy of 'hard work' rather than practice, repeating tedious ball drills for long hours daily.[112] Ring, like many players, did not drink alcohol. Those who drank before a game might be castigated for letting the county down.[113]

The GAA's ability to manage the boom in top-level games and retain a general amateur ethos owed largely to the prevailing national mood. The mission, to which the GAA was pledged, to turn the Free State into an all-Ireland Catholic and Gaelic republic or even a corporatist state[114] reinforced opinion to the defence of Irish amateur sport against the advance of the evils of professionalism. Modesty, manliness and voluntarism were central themes of Catholic Ireland. Sacrificing the body for the greater good, a theme of Catholic teaching – symbolised by the omnipresent crucifix – was elevated by the popular memory of republican martyrs such as Patrick Pearse and

Terence MacSwiney.[115] The GAA could have asked the government to give financial recognition to excellence in Gaelic games, but thought better of the amateur status. The 1923 GAA congress rejected a proposal to lobby the minister of education for a scholarship scheme for university and school hurling and football champion teams, similar to Irish-language educational scholarships.[116] From the 1920s the association's general financial policy had the semblance of a 'national co-operative entity',[117] redistributing its new-found wealth so as to provide a modern ground in each county[118] and to ensure that counties could compete on a relatively equal footing.[119]

Many sections of society backed the GAA's amateur ideal. The National Athletic and Cycling Association (NACA), which the GAA helped to set up in 1922, stood firm against betting, a stance which led some Belfast clubs to secede from it in 1925.[120] In 1928 the Catholic bishop of Ossory (Dr Collier) spoke of his hope that the 'clean, manly, Irish games' would always resist 'commercialism and professionalism'.[121] It was widely believed that for nation-building purposes, popular participation in sport should be prioritised over the glorification of individuals. Better that great numbers play at a mediocre level than thirty excel.[122] This resonated with contemporary concerns around Europe about national degeneracy, which prompted greater interest in physical fitness, to the point of promotion by the state. Garda Commissioner Eoin O'Duffy preached a 'gospel of national virility', and as NACA president, 1931–3, he tried (with some success) to shift the focus from national and international contests to inter-parish and inter-provincial athletics, and to discourage professional tendencies.[123] The fact that Catholic teachers (and clerics) held many of the GAA's key offices in this period consolidated its voluntary ethos.

Several nationalist writers warned against professionalism in the GAA. Arch-GAA essayist, P.J. Devlin saw 'no room for gladiatorial shows or subsidised competitors';[124] exultation of sheer physical strength was 'fundamentally pagan, basically carnal and foreign'.[125] The GAA upheld the 'higher ideals' of classical Irish manhood.[126] Civil servant and author, Joseph Hanly contrasted the 'Christian Gaelic' legacy of 'education by athletics' with how professional sport degraded ancient Greece.[127] In a new GAA journal, Séamus Upton likened 'hired footballers' to the 'paid acrobats in a circus who change their masters every year' for the biggest fee.[128] Seán McKeown, a journalist, Antrim hurler and ex-Belfast Celtic soccer player, put a motion to 1931 congress, 'That the GAA use its power to ban professionalism in sport'; that is, to lobby the government for such a ban, and to educate public opinion on the issue. Citing the

British government's recent problems in finding fit army recruits, he argued that professional soccer was 'the greatest enemy we have in Ireland', as it gave people 'their games by deputy' and would 'undermine the manhood of the State'; 'professionalism will gain such a hold on our people ... that the time will come when, whatever government is in power ... will not have Irish ideals'. Delegates rejected the motion as impractical.[129] McKeown and others also defended the GAA's ban on members playing soccer, as professional soccer players were barred from Gaelic games, lest they be injured. The GAA, it was posited, should not 'rear and train players for professional soccer teams'.[130]

Inter-county GAA players remained largely unaffected by the growth of professional sport elsewhere. Their playing careers were not like those of professionals, except during brief training camps. Inter-county teams rarely held collective training outside of championship season, which, as a straight knockout, lasted less than a couple of months for most. For the rest of the year training or practice was left to players' own devices. The entertainment provided by players catalysed the growth of the games, but probably less so than in other codes. GAA heroes' appeal remained predominantly local. Their names became nationally famous, but not their faces; few were physically recognised outside their own and adjacent counties.[131] They were not seen on television, and only rarely in the newspapers. Press and radio journalists tended to avoid idolatry or controversy about players; those sent off were not reported by name.[132] Cigarette card profiles of GAA players were launched once in the late 1920s but did not catch on as they did in soccer and baseball. Not half a dozen games per year attracted crowds of over 40,000; even then, many came simply to follow their county jersey (whoever was wearing it) or for the sense of national occasion in Croke Park rather than to see the *best* players.[133] The pressure on top players was hardly stifling; some could be seen laughing and waving to the crowd before 1930s All-Ireland finals,[134] in a way that would be frowned upon decades later. They could remain dedicated to their jobs even on the days of their greatest glory: an All-Ireland-winning Dublin hurler in 1917 hurried to work the rest of the day in a bar,[135] and the victorious Kildare captain of 1928 reputedly milked fourteen cows that night![136]

Gambling was very popular in Ireland, and proved difficult to remove from Gaelic games. GAA officials believed, like one journalist in 1920, that 'the presence of bookmakers wipes out the element of sport and is calculated to introduce corruption and discord into the ranks of players as it has on the other side of the channel.'[137] A lot of money was placed on big games, and bookmakers' presence in some places fed (usually uncorroborated) rumours of players 'not trying' due to collusion in bets. Star player Larry Stanley was suspended for allegedly doing so in a benefit game in 1920, soon after helping Kildare to win the All-Ireland title.[138] Rumours of players 'selling a match' circulated after most Kildare football defeats in this era, especially the shock by Monaghan in the 1930 All-Ireland semi-final.[139] Betting on games endured in other places too.[140] In the 1940s it was reportedly increasing in Ulster.[141] However, the few players who bet on games they played in would not bet to lose.[142]

The GAA at various levels compromised slightly to keep the most successful inter-county players content, by granting them certain perks. The greatest of these were the annual tours to America for All-Ireland final teams from the 1920s. Some of the trips lasted up to three months, so players were remunerated for time off work and given spending money. This was not a secret. Central Council's audited accounts disclosed details of these 'personal allowances'.[143] The Cavan players each received £8 from Central Council before leaving for the 1947 football final in New York, and another $32 per week over there.[144] Irish-American well-wishers also donated handsomely. A Wexford hurler returned from a team trip with 'a lot more money than I had brought with me', due to people shoving cash in his pockets.[145] These payments, however un-amateur, caused little rancour. The GAA hierarchy was happy to have ambassadors to promote its games internationally; players enjoyed all-expenses-paid trips of a lifetime; and clubs were proud of their representatives on the world stage (and were wont to present them with 'wallets of notes' on their return).[146] Croke Park also presented gold watches to the Cork and Kilkenny teams of 1931, after their three-game final saga lifted hurling to a new level of popularity. Most inter-county players got no perks beyond travelling expenses and occasional hotel stays with their teams, and expected no more. If, however, they felt that county officials were mean to them, some would make a stand. Even the Cork minor hurlers of 1941 threatened a mini-strike before their final at Croke Park, in order to get to stay that night in Dublin; they got their way.[147]

The injury compensation problem was gradually tackled. Following recurrent debate (and dispute) at GAA conventions, in 1929 Central Council set up an insurance scheme, to cater only for cases of serious accidents and prolonged disability, with a limited grant (not for total remittance of lost earnings).[148] Camogie players, by contrast, had no such support structure. Even inter-county camogie teams could expect to bear their own expenses; for Cork players to play in Dublin might cost them several times their average wages, but they did it for the sport, excitement, and the honour of playing for their county.[149]

Training camps, and payments surrounding them, represented the biggest threat to the amateur status. The issue surfaced in 1926, when a fixture delay prolonged the Kilkenny hurlers' training camp. The team reportedly insisted on a cash payment of £10 per man to play in the final. It was, claimed the Gaelic games writer of *An Phoblacht*,

> the most mercenary action we have ever heard of in con-
> nection with native games, and must have humiliated
> every sincere Gael in the country. The adhesion of such
> men to the GAA is worthless. They would play any other
> game for ten guineas each. They have brazenly declared
> themselves professional 'Gaels' ...[150]

The Kilkenny board received £360 in grants to offset training costs, and paid £327 to players for 'replacement'.[151] Seeing that they were effectively bankrolling 'broken-time' payment and tending towards professionalism, more officials opposed the grants.[152] The 1927 con- gress passed an Antrim motion declaring them 'antagonistic to the spirit of the GAA and ... tending to give a monopoly of champi- onships to strong counties'.[153] 'When people get half-a-loaf they will soon want the whole loaf', said future president Pádraig McNamee.[154] Yet Central Council continued to award grants to final- ists, albeit in more modest sums.[155] 'The public expected it of them' to have players well trained, said another future president, Bob O'Keeffe.[156] The more time players spent in the custody of county boards, the more grew the idea that such boards had a duty to 'look after' their ordinary welfare. This could mean funding them through injury, helping them to get jobs, defraying the loss of personal items[157] or donating a sum to those emigrating.[158] Two Dublin-based Kerry players demanded £10 up front, ostensibly for expenses, before the 1938 All-Ireland football final replay, but their county board refused and they withdrew from the panel.[159]

From the 1940s collective training became lengthier, more wide- spread and more contentious. Some camps stretched out from a fort- night to six weeks or more; to provincial games as well as the All- Ireland series; and spread to junior and minor final teams also.[160] In football especially, rural counties whose players lived in disparate areas or outside the county (due to work) believed such training necessary

to enable them to compete at the highest level. But players were financially compensated for missing work to train ('broken-time' payments); indeed some got more than their normal wages.[161] County
boards might pay the equivalent wage of the highest-earning players,
or an average of their wages, to those off work. Mid-1940s Cavan
players got £4 a week each during camps;[162] Roscommon players in
1946, over £10 a week;[163] and Armagh players in 1953, £20 each.[164]
Players who did not miss work – teachers on vacation, undergradu-
ates[165] and even school pupils in county minor training[166] – got small
amounts too. Some officials, notably Pádraig Ó Caoimh, deplored this
pattern and called for an end to training camps.[167] A Leitrim motion
to restrict them to All-Ireland finalists was rejected at 1947 congress,
but prohibitionists grew in number. They argued that camps overem-
phasised winning; gave players 'swelled heads';[168] over-trained and
over-hyped teams;[169] and killed the GAA's unique ideals of 'splendid
selfless service'.[170] They also abhorred asking fans to subscribe to
training funds without declaring that players would be paid.
Moreover, as players in camp quibbled over expenses payments, it
was feared that the 'lure of money [was] getting a grip on a lot of people', breeding greed, jealousy and obstreperousness – a 'spirit of shon-
eenism'.[171] References abounded to the 'greasy slope of professionalism'[172] and the masked onset of 'shamateurism' in other codes.[173]

In April 1953 Central Council set up a special committee to examine the issue. The committee reported that full-time training was
'inconsistent with the amateur status', because it involved payments in
cash or kind to players.[174] There was a fierce reaction to the proposal.
Kerry, Cavan, Roscommon and Mayo, the dominant counties in football over the previous decade, opposed it, arguing that without full-
time training they could not compete.[175] Their officials portrayed it as
an attempt by the stronger, more urban counties, chiefly Dublin and
Cork – where evening-time training was more feasible – to thwart the
more rural counties.[176] Some Kerry people saw it as a jealous effort to
halt their success; 'collective training was our thing', said one of the
players.[177] Some officials insisted that as the players did not make their
living from their sport, it did not involve professionalism.[178] Others
claimed that the standards of play would be lowered, resulting in a
loss of spectator appeal and less finance for the association.[179] With
final crowds now exceeding the 80,000 mark, there was a lot at stake.
'You are killing the goose that lays the golden eggs', asserted a
Roscommon delegate.[180] None the less, 1954 congress took the bold
decision to abolish training camps. 'Full-time training is inconsistent
with the amateur status of members of the Gaelic Athletic Association'

stated the new rule. It was the first time 'the amateur status' of Gaelic team sports was referred to in rule. How this status was defined, or breaches to be punished, was not specified.[181]

The development of county GAA grounds from the 1920s raised new issues for the voluntary ethos. These premises, of which almost every county board had one by the 1930s, were business concerns, housing the crowds which funded the GAA's expansion. In Belfast, the labour was reportedly 'purely voluntary',[182] but this was not always so. To construct the Mullingar park in the early 1930s, Westmeath County Board paid over £1,600 in fees, mostly to the contractor, who in turn paid standard wages to twelve workers; their demands for a pay rise led to an industrial dispute.[183] Groundsmen were employed or given honoraria for maintaining the facilities. In time though, and especially in Ulster, voluntarism drove capital development projects. Local communities were tapped for subscriptions or donations,[184] while voluntary labour undertook the huge task of converting a rugged field into a mini-stadium.[185] Some men devoted 'practically all their leisure hours' to such work,[186] during times of economic hardship. So GAA grounds cost much less to develop than those of other sports. Not everyone thought the system fair, however. Volunteer road workers at Breifne Park, Cavan, in 1933, were 'victimised', claimed an observer; many had to walk up to eight miles without 'a single copper of compensation' before being given 'peremptory' orders. Such treatment, he suggested, gave rise to communism.[187]

THE CLUB SCENE, 1913–54

Gaelic games at club level remained essentially amateur. It was only from the 1920s onwards, as life in Ireland became more stabilised, that most clubs became truly durable, to the extent that one could play for and serve the same club for life. More and more rural club catchment areas became configured with parish boundaries. Service to a club became stylised as a duty to the parish. Clubs were also limited in potential growth since they could no longer contest inter-county competitions; now they could only aspire to internal county titles or the occasional outside tournament, and had not the means to endanger the overall amateur status of the games – unlike some other field sports, in which big clubs rivalled their governing bodies in terms of profile or financial resources.

Club training was quite basic in nature. A lack of local physical education techniques and adequate training facilities, and the availability of only one ball for training, dictated as much. It usually consisted of running a few laps of the field, a few sprints, and a haphazard puck- or kick-about between two bunches of players.[188] Most teams did not really train much outside of county championship season; weaker sides might not train at all. Players improved their game mostly through unstructured practice, at their own leisure. Long working hours and the lack of club facilities obviated against team training. Besides, it was widely accepted that many players, doing manual labour by day and travelling mainly by foot and bicycle, were fit enough anyway. Even the top players remained primarily club players, practising or training mostly with their local club, with inter-county duties as mere brief interruptions.[189] Travelling expenses were only paid to players who made long journeys to play, in the few clubs where funds permitted.[190] Many clubs did, however, buy (and keep) football boots,[191] because only some players could afford their own.

Some activity was less amateur. The Garda GAA Club loomed large in Dublin in the 1920s, through its superior (occupational) fitness training, resources and recruitment policies. Its amateur status was questioned in the press,[192] and opposing crowds jeered 'Come on the professionals'.[193] Player inducements spread elsewhere too. In Louth, there were motions as early as 1915 seeking a ban on clubs offering 'any inducement in any shape or form' to secure a transfer.[194] Byelaws or none, dubious transfers persisted in urban centres. As a Dundalk reporter explained in 1927, 'a club which is doing well or which can use the necessary blandishments will always attract those who are not comfortable'.[195] Many transfers involved no financial incentive, though; talented players at junior clubs regularly joined nearby senior clubs in the pursuit of victory or places on the county team. This was accepted as normal but resented.[196] Even in rural areas, a player might feel compelled to transfer if, for example, his employer was from a nearby club, and asked him to.[197]

Occasionally, illicit payments were made to players at club level. In 1927 a Louth Gaelic footballer, who also played semi-professional soccer, stated in court that a town club (through its secretary) paid him to play Gaelic; 'a good many of them' got such payments in the GAA, he claimed.[198] Talented players could easily play as 'dark horses' in other counties; their legality was rarely challenged as opponents tended to include illegal players too. Among others, Nick Rackard (Wexford hurler) and 'Mixie' Palmer (Kerry footballer), while study-ing in Dublin and Cork respectively in the 1940s, played illegally for many clubs (the latter for as many as fifteen) and were paid liberally for doing so. Both men got as much as £5 per game – roughly half a week's wages then – for these star turns. Even junior clubs in rural west Cork would pay outside players, to win bets on games.[199] The payments were probably made under the guise of travelling expenses. Despite a 1915 congress resolution 'that no money prizes whatever be given in connection with hurling, football, or athletic sports meetings in future',[200] prizes in cash or in kind featured in club tournaments from the 1930s. By the early 1940s prizes of 5 shillings a man were common; by the early 1950s prizes of £5, suit lengths or gold watches a man were on offer. The valuable prizes ensured keen contests between top teams, and so as to evade penalty host clubs advertised them under the guise of parish or carnival committees.[201]

Notwithstanding these occasional abuses, the vast majority of club players were pure amateurs. They relished the excitement of the games, the trips to strange places and the camaraderie forged along the way, as a break from the daily monotony.[202] They played in often primitive playing conditions, and expected nothing better. Even a star like Nick Rackard, having played elsewhere briefly, treasured his home turf as a veteran player. As he reportedly explained in the 1950s,

> There is always a particular thrill in playing for your own county and for your own people, and it's the same at club level. You play for the sake of the little village, and no man is greater than the club. Each one of us is a cog in the wheel …[203]

Rackard also acclaimed the GAA's club workers:

> the 'nameless men' … who through love of the games and the Association keep the small clubs going, come what may – these are the backbone of the GAA … the salt of the earth, deserving of more credit for too often unrecorded efforts than all the stars who achieve glory.[204]

The fact that a player could become nationally famous and still be ensconced in the local club which nurtured him was, in the eyes of many members, a special, even unique, quality of the GAA, and one which safeguarded its amateur status.

THE INTER-COUNTY SCENE, 1955–90

With the end of training camps in 1954, there was no issue over illicit payments at inter-county level for a generation, and forecasts of reduced crowds were confounded. There was concern, though, that some inter-county players had 'now reached breaking point', due to myriad local tournaments crowding the schedule of games.[205] 'We must not forget that our players are amateurs', Ard-Rúnaí Pádraig Ó Caoimh reiterated in 1959. 'Sometimes they are expected to act as if they were professional whole-time players.'[206] To protect them, Central Council brought in regulations for tournaments in the early 1960s.[207] But inter-county teams were training more often anyway. The wider accessibility of cars now enabled players to assemble for evening sessions. The Dublin football team introduced pre-season training, with twice-weekly sessions from October 1957.[208] Less well disposed counties were slower to follow, but by the 1960s most trained at least once a week from January.[209] Leading university teams added to the spiral of training. With higher education becoming more openly accessible, they could field entire teams of inter-county stars, and they trained hard through the winter.[210] By the late 1960s one team trained thrice weekly at 7 a.m. for ten weeks.[211] The overlapping inter-varsity and inter-county seasons, and the creation of under-21 competitions from 1964, kept a profusion of young players training almost all year round. With so many demands on their time and services, it was occasionally said that they got 'no rest at all'.[212] Some players brought increased demands on themselves. From 1959 Mick O'Connell of Kerry had a career-long 'obsession' for rigorous personal daily training,[213] even declining university education and overtime work in order to train.[214] Others chose their jobs over Croke Park glory.[215] But all accepted, without public complaint, that these were the choices that surrounded their inter-county participation.

The new training system was not universally welcomed by county officials. Some lobbied for a return to training camps. Dr Éamon O'Sullivan, the famed Kerry trainer, argued that part-time training could 'only lead to fitness of a restricted, partial type and is, consequently, an unsatisfactory substitute'.[216] Some counties had material reasons to feel aggrieved. Roscommon, Cavan and Mayo, having between them won the bulk of All-Ireland football titles between 1943 and 1954, did not even reach the final for decades thereafter. As late as 1980 Roscommon proposed (unsuccessfully) to relegalise training camps.[217] For some county boards, regular short sessions imposed new budgetary pressures, which led to occasional friction with players over expenses.

Senior GAA officials remained very protective of the amateur ethos. They abhorred a more player-centred approach in media coverage – since the advent of Irish television in the early 1960s and more diverse press features (such as players writing columns) – creating a personality cult for top players.[218] Yet such players generally declined lucrative offers for celebrity endorsements or interviews, out of sheer modesty.[219] Many were even shy about signing an auto-graph in public.[220] The advent of specialist coaching to the GAA, through newly qualified physical education teachers, became a major battleground. In 1964, Joe Lennon, a recent All-Ireland-winning Down player and a PE teacher, launched a book on coaching and the first national coaching course for Gaelic football, but senior GAA officials viewed it as an élitist 'campaign by some to intensify the training of players', classifying them in a way that would discourage the majority.[221] Such courses, it was projected, would yield a raft of specialist coaches, charging high prices for their services. Alf Murray, GAA president, 1964–7, labelled it as a 'new cult' of 'professionalism of the worst kind'.[222] Players, he said, 'should know why they play Gaelic games rather than merely seek to excel in playing them'.[223] Yet Croke Park organised and endorsed other large coaching courses at this time (mainly in hurling). The ire towards Lennon may have owed to an innate suspicion by GAA officials of players taking bold independent initiatives. His role in starting a players' association for his county team,[224] and the commercial interest and élitist title of his book (*for Champions*)[225] were possibly factors also.

The landscape for amateurism changed again in 1971, on foot of two events. The first was the removal of the GAA's ban on members playing soccer. Many members feared that the GAA might now be exposed to erstwhile professionals coming into its playing ranks, demanding wages to play.[226] A special committee, appointed by Central Council, to write a new GAA charter duly drafted a proper definition of amateurism. The amended rule, as passed at a special congress, stated that the GAA was 'an Amateur Association', and pro-hibited 'Payment or other material reward ... for participation in games and pastimes'.[227] The year also saw the GAA accept commer-cial sponsorship on a limited basis. In came sponsored (seven-a-side and inter-varsity) competitions, advertising hoarding at major venues and sponsored annual All-Stars player awards. The rationale was that sponsorship would boost the GAA's public profile in an increasingly competitive leisure market and help to fund ordinary activities, to the benefit of spectators. Without sponsorship, advised a review group, 'it may find itself at a serious disadvantage' to other sports bodies.[228]

Annual All-Stars team trips to America and the development of compromise games between Irish GAA and Australian Rules teams from the late 1960s[229] brought more exotic holidays, and perhaps a 'junket' culture, onto the horizon. This contented most leading play-ers, though it did create occasional friction about how much spending money they got or who could travel.[230] Many leading GAA players also profited from playing in America. American GAA clubs, having fewer Irish immigrant players after the 1965 Immigration Act, availed of the revolution in trans-Atlantic air travel to lure leading players over from Ireland for the summer or for a weekend game.[231] The usual suspects were students, teachers and those whose teams lost in the inter-county championships early in the summer. The match fee in New York for top players in the early 1970s was about $200 plus airfare;[232] by the late 1980s it was $500.[233] They could also get non-strenuous work and be well paid for it.[234] GAA leaders in Ireland, ever uneasy about the American black market, occasionally threatened action, but felt powerless to go beyond monitoring the legality of transfers. So it continued.[235]

In the 1970s the public profile of inter-county Gaelic games was magnified and the amateur status came under new stress, due to a combination of more active media reporting and marketing of the games, advancing commercial activity in the GAA and developments in how the games were played. The excellent Kerry and Dublin football teams of the period raised the bar for fitness, beating opponents with ease. They attracted a new type of publicity and hype to the game. Commentators hailed their approach as 'truly professional'[236] – i.e. meticulous – while 'amateurish' became a synonym for inept.[237] The Kerry team that won a record eight All-Ireland titles between 1975 and 1986 exploited commercial openings to a new level. It organised fundraising games for foreign holidays, pocketing some of the gate money. It took inducements from sportswear firms to wear gear,[238] and advertised commercial products (notoriously, an electrical appliance in 1985).[239] By the late 1980s hurlers had a niche market in endorsing agricultural wares. Prominent Kerry personalities began to call for inter-county players to be paid.[240]

Leading GAA players came under increasing demand as ambassadors, to make guest appearances and present medals or make a speech at club functions, often outside their own county and far away. Club and county officials saw such cameos as providing powerful publicity for the GAA against rival sports. Many players were paid their actual expenses or perhaps more, while others got just a memento of crystal or a plaque. Some players, however, especially at the top level, would simply name a price and usually got it.[241]

The GAA hierarchy made warning sounds about suspected transgressions, and in 1985 a special congress tightened the definition of amateur status, on the proposal of a rules revision committee, to bring it 'more in line with recent developments'.[242] This was only the second amendment to the amateur rule since 1954, and by far the most ambitious. There were three new principles: that no one could receive a payment 'in connection with his membership' of the GAA; that expenses payments would be confined to a ceiling rate, laid down by Central Council; and that breaches would be stiffly punished (with a minimum six months' suspension). The first proved hard to police, and disciplinary action was not attempted. The rule also seemed slightly contradictory: it stated that someone could not receive cash for being a GAA member, yet could receive wages as a GAA employee.[243] The increase in full-time staff at Croke Park, from a handful to over twenty in a short period, caused some disquiet; why, some asked, were so many professional staff needed to run an amateur body?[244] Croke Park was at a crossroads over money matters in the mid-1980s. It accepted sponsorship for the National Leagues, but not the major championships. Decisions to host pop music concerts at GAA stadia[245] and to allow alcoholic drinks sponsorship[246] further indicated how financial pragmatism was eclipsing long-standing ideology.

By the late 1980s counties were training harder to keep up with their rivals. Whereas Kerry had sixty-one collective training sessions before the 1981 All-Ireland final, by now final teams reportedly had over a hundred between February and September, with many players doing extra training on their own.[247] Inter-county players began to complain publicly about their treatment: of being expected to prepare and think like professionals; of supporters not realising their sacrifices and often subjecting them to verbal abuse and wild rumour (about their social lives);[248] of getting unfair expenses payments and frequently only one free ticket for games in which they played, regardless of their families.[249] Exacerbating the pressures was the decade's recession and high unemployment. Yet leading players seldom struggled to find a job; their high profile often landed them jobs as sales representatives or in banks.[250] A 'Gaelic Players' Association' was formed in 1981 to represent inter-county players (on matters such as insurance, rules and fixtures),[251] but fell through due to players' general apathy and time constraints. Most inter-county players remained amateurs, accepting their playing conditions, for good or bad. There was still no defined county squad outside championship season; players joined and left teams without ceremony.

The first review of all aspects of the amateur status was conducted by Central Council in the late 1980s. Its report was positive, but weak, finding little evidence of illicit payments – despite one player's open admission that he and others collected almost £4,000 'as a result of one year's football', through various perks[252] – and it recommended strict application of the existing rules. Most tellingly, it stated that 'players were not adequately treated' by several county boards. From here onwards Central Council appealed for the provision of meals after training, free playing gear and adequate travelling expenses,[253] so that players would happily remain amateur in a more prosperous GAA as long as they received the basics. Accordingly, the association's accelerated commercialisation from 1991 led to increased demands on, and material concessions to, leading players, akin to incremental professionalisation in other sports.[254]

THE CLUB SCENE, 1954–90

In the post-training-camp era more attention was paid to voluntarism and capital development at club level. A greater slice of income was allocated to the provision of permanent club facilities. By 1955 the GAA could boast 'a practically endless chain of playing fields from Doire to Daingean'[255] – over a hundred in total – but its leading officials called for every parish in Ireland to have a GAA ground.[256] Answering the call, scores of 'jacketless men with upturned sleeves' took up spades, shovels, picks and rakes, and 'laboured voluntarily night and day to make the ideal a reality'.[257] Each time a ground or hall was vested in the GAA, a branch took on a long-term commitment to its upkeep and development. A solid administrative support structure was required to raise funds, line pitches, man turnstiles, sweep dressing-rooms, etc. The national Ard-Rúnaí highlighted the 'well-fenced, well-drained grounds with embankments, terracing and stands' as 'the product of enthusiasm, not of money; voluntary workers made them and … maintain them'.[258] These grounds offered 'a challenge to the spirit of materialism which would deny the spiritual values for which individual members of the Association have always stood; those values which are not of the market-place but of the soul'.[259] In due course, many GAA halls became *de facto* multi-purpose community centres. The prototype was the Clann Éireann GAA and youth club hall in Lurgan, Co. Armagh, completed in 1954 by 160 volunteers – including 66 labouring, 23 joining and 16 plumbing – who were paid merely in tea and buns.[260] Making the tea and washing team jerseys were among many thankless tasks that women did for the GAA. A yet more crucial (and rarely acknowledged) supportive role was played by the 'GAA widow', who dutifully attended to domestic chores and family needs while her husband indulged in matches and meetings.[261] The rule book also reflected the new focus on voluntarism. From the 1960s on its preface outlined how, inspired by the GAA's promotion of Irish identity, 'legions of voluntary workers willingly make sacrifices to promote its ideals and carry its daily burdens'.[262] This was equally true outside Ireland. In Britain, players, officials and referees made huge sacrifices to sustain Gaelic games, with no hope of recouping their expenses.[263] Sporting voluntarism was not merely an Irish thing. Voluntary clubs were the 'life blood' of sports provision in Britain, and a large part of the general social fabric.[264] Yet the GAA's voluntarism involved much more capital development, as municipal councils in Ireland rarely provided playing-fields.

The club game became more serious, however. Even with more young men in higher education in Irish cities and in Britain, from the 1950s strong clubs were prepared to pay their travelling expenses to play in crunch games.[265] Unofficial tournaments with cash prizes (which had climbed as high as £300 in 1964)[266] were prohibited from 1965[267] and mostly eradicated.[268] A more regular, competitive series of games came with the introduction of all-county leagues and provincial club championships. Many senior club teams stepped up training; by the mid-1970s twice-weekly regimens, from February until autumn, were common. Intermediate and junior clubs were slower to follow suit, but by the late 1970s most had at least one session a week. Unlike inter-county players, however, the intensification of training brought no financial dividends for ordinary club players, and only greater sacrifices.

There were some concerns that the intensified inter-county scene was driving a wedge between inter-county players and their clubs. Club games were frequently postponed to avoid clashes with inter-county players' busy schedules, causing prolonged inactivity for ordinary club players.[269] The stars stayed involved with their clubs, but the seeds were sown for greater bifurcation of the club and inter-county games in future.

A flurry of illegally paid coaches and managers also intensified training schedules. It suited those who charged per session to make them more frequent. By the late 1980s payments to club managers were identified by a Central Council report as one of the most serious breaches of the amateur status.[270] Yet in many clubs most if not all coaching personnel – who multiplied in number with the initiation of under-16, under-14 and under-12 competitions – did the role on a voluntary basis, for the love of it.[271]

CONCLUSION

The amateur status of Gaelic games was not a relic of the English Victorian sporting revolution, but rather a financially pragmatic policy and an expression of Irish Catholic/Christian communalism and fraternal solidarity. Gaelic games were plebeian in nature, and their amateurism democratic and spartan, quite the opposite to the élitist, Corinthian 'gentleman amateur'. The GAA championed the playing of its games as a moral duty to Irish nationality, parish and manly Christianity. This helps to explain why it gave priority to team games over individual codes. The idea of playing sport for monetary reward was discountenanced because it was perceived as English, mercenary and debasing – both spiritually and physically – and on a practical level the GAA simply could not afford it. To pay players to play would undercut and cheapen the values of the GAA for the vast majority of its playing and administrative volunteers. Their belief in the amateur and voluntary ethos informed their sacrifices and work for the GAA, principally in the development and upkeep of club facilities since the mid-twentieth century. As these club structures expanded into wider functions for local communities, so the centrality of voluntarism to the GAA and Irish community life was reinforced.

Like in any popular spectator sport, the amateur status of Gaelic games was never unanimously upheld. At first it was most commonly breached by urban clubs, but with the gradual growth of the inter-county Gaelic games scene it was challenged primarily by the intensification of training schedules, increases in teams' travelling and encroaching commercialism. The more developments tended to consume the time and energies of players, the more players were inclined to want recompense. Many of the challenges to amateurism in the GAA as it entered its second century were residual, but magnified by changes in Irish society and in the association. As the GAA reached its 125th anniversary, a drift towards élitism accentuated the pressures and priorities placed on leading players and opened up divisions in the association's social order.

[Established over a Century.]

The Commercial and Family Hotel,

AND POSTING ESTABLISHMENT,

THURLES.

LIZZIE J. HAYES, Proprietress.

20. Hayes' hotel, where the GAA was founded on 1 November 1884.

11 The GAA: Social Structure and Associated Clubs[1]

TOM HUNT

Michael Cusack writing in the *United Irishman* in 1898 suggested that in its formative years the Gaelic Athletic Association had 'swept the country like a prairie fire'.[2] Cusack was a gifted propagandist and as a piece of spin-doctoring this was a classic statement: memorable and partly true. The initial expansion of the GAA was rapid and far more effective than any of the other organisations achieved at the time; however, there were also large areas of the country that remained untouched by Cusack's prairie fire.[3] Cusack was writing in terms of geographical spread, but if one was to apply his prairie fire image to the diffusion of the GAA among the different social and occupational classes of the time what findings would emerge? An enormous amount has been written about the GAA but very little about the people who became members. Very little research has been carried out on the occupations of the early players and their social standing in the community. Closely associated with this issue is the nature of early GAA clubs and the community networks that facilitated their formation. These issues will be the focus of this chapter.

A database of 500 players involved in hurling (276) and football (224) between 1886 and 1905 was constructed. This was compiled from a variety of sources including team lists published in newspaper reports. Players' names, occupations and places of residence obtained from club histories and commemorative booklets were also used in constructing the database. Where possible and when necessary the names were then matched with data extracted from the manuscript census returns of 1901 or 1911. The amount of land held by farm families and its valuation was identified from the records available at the Valuation Office. The sample study includes players from Kilkenny (90), Tipperary (76), Waterford (46), Clare (23), Galway (37), Kerry (27), Dublin (42), Meath (18), Longford (29), Westmeath (97) and Wexford (15). Thirty clubs were represented.[4] The published volumes of the 1901 Census of Ireland classified the occupations the people into six different categories. Class I comprised of professionals and Class II was made up of those engaged in domestic offices and services. Those employed in commercial activities formed Class III while Class IV consisted of those engaged in agriculture. Class V categorised those employees engaged in a variety of industrial employment.[5] The census also included an unclassified group of individuals that was largely composed of children under 15 years of age and women who worked in the home (Class VI). A similar system was used to classify the GAA players identified in this study

TABLE 11.1
NUMBERS AND CATEGORIES OF EMPLOYEES AS RETURNED IN 1901 CENSUS

Category	Number employed	% of Total
Category I: Professional class	98,361	6.95
Category II: Domestic class	26,087	1.85
Category III: Commercial class	92,863	6.57
Category IV: Agricultural class	790,475	55.90
Category V: Industrial class	406,157	28.73
Total	1,413,943	100

In 1901 a total of 1,413,943 economically active males were divided into one of the above five categories and the numbers of people employed within the different categories is illustrated in Table 11.1. As can be seen, almost 85 per cent of the workforce was either engaged in agriculture or industrial employment. The industrial employees were a disparate group and included artisans and general labourers as well as those who were factory employees. The agricultural category was also an extensive one and included graziers, farmers and their sons and other family members, as well as agricultural labourers and farm servants.

In the initial analysis, a similar system was used to classify the GAA players identified in this study, with one exception. The unclassified category was ignored as the numbers of early GAA players in this category was minimal. On the rare occasions where a student was also an early GAA player he was assigned to the same category as the head of household. The results of the classification of the 500 hurlers and footballers whose occupations were identified are shown in Table 11.2.

TABLE 11.2
CATEGORIES OF OCCUPATIONS OF HURLERS AND FOOTBALLERS 1886–1905

Category	Number of players	% of Total
Category I: Professional class	11	2.2
Category II: Domestic class	0	0
Category III: Commercial class	106	21.2
Category IV: Agricultural class	309	61.8
Category V: Industrial class	74	14.8
Total	500	100

Three points are particularly noteworthy from this basic analysis. The GAA playing population was chiefly composed of those classified as belonging to the agricultural class, with those belonging to the commercial class next in importance. Both categories significantly exceeded the national average for these occupations in their representation. The agricultural class consisted of farmers and their sons as well as farm labourers; the commercial class was a more diverse constituency but was mainly composed of retail assistants and commercial clerks. The agricultural class was slightly more involved in the GAA world than their overall representation in society at large. However, members of the commercial class were over three times more likely to be found in a GAA club than their overall participation in the labour force might indicate. The third major feature evident was the extent to which the industrial class was under-represented.

The divisions used by the census authorities were very general and as presented in the above tables were suitable for only the most cursory analysis of the early players' social and economic circumstances. The occupations of the players were further subdivided as presented in Table 11.3 and this analysis provides a more comprehensive insight into the occupational characteristics of early hurlers and footballers.[6]

TABLE 11.3 OCCUPATIONS OF PLAYERS, 1886–1905

Occupation		Total	%
Farmer/son	267	53.4	
Farm labourer	24	4.8	
Un/semi-skilled	38	7.6	
Skilled	67	13.4	
Shop asst/clerk	81	16.2	
Professional	11	2.2	
Merchant/son	12	2.4	
Total	500	100	

The professional classes who became members of the GAA were members of the lower middle classes. They were mainly teachers but also included one member of the medical profession, rugby international Dr William O'Sullivan of the Dr Croke's club in Killarney.[7] Sports such as tennis, golf and the other football codes were more popular with higher status professionals.[8] Merchants and their sons were mainly of the shopkeeper/rural publican variety and included the O'Keeffe's, public house, grocery and provision merchants in Horse and Jockey; Charlie Maher, who carried on a licensed and grocery trade at Two Mile Borris and Dick Fitzgerald, a member of a Killarney merchant family who were proprietors of a successful egg, poultry and butter exporting business.[9] Skilled workers at 13.4 per cent formed a significant proportion of the players. These were mainly tradesmen and many were an integral part of the rural economic system with strong links to the farming community. Blacksmiths, carpenters, boot makers, tailors, boilermakers and painters were well established in the GAA community.

Second in importance to the farmer in the GAA community were shop assistants and clerks. This was the group that formed the majority of the commercial class as defined by the criteria used in the 1901 census, when that class formed 6.57 per cent of the male national workforce. However, 21.2 per cent of early GAA players belonged to this class, while shop assistants and clerks in particular formed 16 per cent of the playing population of the period of study. Shop assistants and clerks were therefore twice as prevalent among the GAA playing population when compared to the general population. These were the young men that had in the words of Peter Harte exchanged 'the artisan's cloth cap and apron' for 'the collar and tie of the shop boy, the draper's assistant, and the junior clerk'.[10] Their background was a farming one and at the time the retail assistant or clerk represented a popular career choice for younger farmers' sons, the eldest son normally inheriting the family farm. The shop assistant was generally recruited from the national school by a store proprietor. These were the bright young boys that obtained employment on the recommendation of the national school principal and had distinguished themselves in literacy and numeracy. The requirement that the potential recruit be a member of a good and respected family in the locality ensured that recruitment was almost always made from a farm family. The larger Dublin shops usually recruited young assistants from the country and trained them over a seven-year period. Parents paid Dublin employers between £40 and £50 to indenture their child and teach him the skills of the shop assistant trade. The qualified Dublin-based assistant could expect to earn between £40 and £50 annually in the early 1900s.[11] The top employee in Eason's was earning £9 weekly and the head of one of the firm's retail departments earned £4. 10s. weekly.[12] Despite the relatively poor remuneration, assistants generally felt socially superior to craft and general workers. Assistants did not form a cohesive body of workers and the various categories of assistants were wont to cast a somewhat jaundiced eye at their fellow 'black-coated' worker. They were ambitious and status conscious and were habitual joiners of clubs, and membership of a GAA club provided an opportunity for physical recreation and socialisation. Many of those involved in GAA clubs were the leaders of their particular community. Many were important enough in their place of employment to represent their firm at formal occasions such as funerals. It was a time when young men working in white-collar occupations were becoming increasingly organised into social organisations that reflected the Victorian desire for self-improvement.[13]

The dominance of farmers and their sons might be expected but the virtual exclusion of farm labourers from those forming the database on which this analysis is based is extraordinary. Nationally, in 1901, 543,114 people were classified as farmers and there were 135,349 agricultural labourers, which amounted to a ratio of farmer to farm labourer slightly in excess of 4:1. The ratio of these occupations represented in the GAA is close to 11:1. Based on this analysis, the early GAA failed to fulfil one of the intentions of Maurice Davin, who was convinced of the need for games, 'especially for the humble and the hard-working who seem now to be born into no other inheritance than an everlasting round of labour'.[14] It has been suggested that the coalition of interests represented in the rural parish-based club was instrumental in reducing a potential source of tension between 'the rising class of prosperous small farmers and the continually depressed class of farm labourers'. Their weekly contacts in committee rooms and on the playing field supposedly went a long way to reduce friction between the two classes.[15] The rural GAA club represented no such coalition and instead was composed essentially of the sons of the farm families in the locality and some skilled craftsmen. This farmer dominance of the club is encapsulated in the constitution of the Tipperary All-Ireland title winning team of 1887. It was made up of eleven farmers; six players were engaged in business-related activities and the team also included two tradesmen and two labourers.[16] It was possible to identify the occupations of fifty-one of the players who won All-Ireland medals with Tubberadora, the Horse and Jockey and Two Mile Borris in the period between 1895 and 1900.[17] The list was dominted by forty-two farmers while only five farm labourers were involved. This level of under-representation is found in Tipperary, a county that had, in 1901, 21,254 farmers and 6,832 farm labourers or a ratio of farmer to farm labourer of 3.1:1.[18]

The status and position of GAA families within the farming community was established by examining data on both the size and value of the family farm. The size of 170 family farms and the valuation of 160 holdings was identified. The valuation measure was a reflection of the quality of the land and this was far more important than farm size in determining farm income, status and quality of life. Farm land that was valued in excess of 15 s. an acre was high quality productive land. The national position relating to farm size and land valuation is shown in Table 11.4.[19]

TABLE 11.4
AVERAGE FARM SIZE AND LAND VALUATION IN IRELAND, 1901

Farm size	%	Valuation (£)	%
<10 acres	31.5	<£10	56.2
11–15	12.5	£11–£20	19.8
16–20	11.0	£21–30	8.4
21–30	13.2	£31–£40	4.5
31–50	13.7	£41–£50	2.8
51–100	11.1	£50–£100	5.2
101–200	4.7	£101–£200	2.1
<201+	2.3	>£200	1.0

The Irish land-holding structure in 1901 was dominated by small farms, with almost one-third of the holdings less than 10 acres in size and a further 12.5 per cent ranged between 10 and 15 acres. These farmers had some difficulty in becoming involved in the GAA and as can be seen from Table 11.5 they formed only 10 per cent of the identified players. A total of 55 per cent of Irish farms in 1901 were under 20 acres, but only 21.5 per cent of the GAA playing population in this database originated on such holdings.

TABLE 11.5
SIZE OF FARMS OCCUPIED BY HURLING AND FOOTBALL-PLAYING FARM FAMILIES,
1886–1905

Farm size	Total	%	Hurlers	%	Footballers	%
Under 10 acres	17	10.0	10	9.2	7	11.5
11–15	9	5.3	5	4.6	4	6.6
16–20	14	8.2	7	6.4	7	11.5
21–30	27	15.9	17	15.6	10	16.4
31–50	45	26.5	32	29.4	13	21.3
51–100	27	15.9	19	17.4	8	13.1
101–200	21	12.3	13	11.9	8	13.1
201 +	10	5.9	6	5.5	4	6.5
Total	170	100	109	100	61	100

The majority of players were associated with farms that ranged from between 20 and 100 acres. This constituency provided 58.3 per cent of the players while nationally this category accounted for 38 per cent of all holdings. Slightly over one-quarter of all players earned their living and their disposable income on farms that ranged from between 31 and 50 acres. The differences evident between the farming backgrounds of hurlers and footballers is partly a product of the geography of the sample, as the hurlers sampled are drawn in particular from the south-eastern counties where more substantial holdings were the norm.

TABLE 11.6
VALUE OF FAMILY FARMS OF HURLERS AND FOOTBALLERS 1886–1905

Valuation (£)	Hurlers and Footballers %
<£5	10.6
£5-£10	13.7
£11–£20	26.7
£21–£30	9.3
£31–£40	9.9
£41–£50	4.3
£51–£100	18.6
£101–£200	6.3
>£201+	0.6

The evidence from these valuation figures supports to an extent the evidence relating to farm size, suggesting that smallholders had difficulty participating in the GAA. Just over half (56.2 per cent) of the landholdings in the country were valued at £10 or less, but only 25 per cent (24.3) of the players identified came from this category of holding. However, some of the less wealthy farmers succeeded in involving themselves in hurling and football. The best-represented group of farmers were those who held land in the £10–£20 valuation category. This group occupied 20 per cent of the country's farms but formed one-quarter of the GAA playing population of this survey. A similar position is evident in the other categories up to farm values of £200. The numbers of hurlers and footballers emerging from these farms was greater than what might be expected from their presence in general society. It is also worthy of note that almost 7 per cent of those identified were substantial farmers with holdings valued at over £100. These included some very well-known names in GAA history, such as the Walsh family from Tubberadora, Pierce Grace and Henry J. Meagher from Tullaroan, father of Lory and one of the legendary figures of Kilkenny hurling.

Involvement in organised sport required some investment of time and money by participants. This applied to the young man playing hurling and football just as much as it did to the golfers, cyclists and tennis players of the 1890s. The cost factor had some impact in limiting those from the farm labour and small farmer classes in the GAA. Individual members were required to pay subscriptions to cover their club's expenses. A membership fee of 1s. was introduced for the Mullingar Football Club formed in 1891 and in addition a weekly levy of 2d. was required.[20] This club was successful in winning the Westmeath football championship in 1892 and a week later the members formed the Mullingar Cricket Club to continue their recreational and social activity over the summer months. Membership of this club was set at an entrance fee of 1s. followed by a subscription of 6d. for the first week and 3d. weekly thereafter. Members were responsible for their own travel expenses.[21] These we may presume were standard membership fees at the time, although the Turnpike Hurling Club placed a levy of 6d. monthly on its members when it was founded in 1886.[22] The hurlers of Ballyduff and Kilmoyley, Co. Kerry travelled by train to Dublin to play in the 1891 All-Ireland hurling final and were required to pay their own train fare of 16s. each.[23] This was at a time when a resident farm labourer in the Kenmare district of Kerry earned between £8 and £12 annually and when labourers working without food earned 9–10s. weekly.[24] A row over expenses deprived seven players, including the captain, Denis Maher, of their place on the first All-Ireland winning hurling team. These were from the Killinane area of Thurles and they requested the committee of the Thurles club to pay their travel expenses to Birr for the final as the players had already travelled against Clare and Kilkenny 'at a good deal of expense'. The committee refused the players' request and, 'owing to some misleading rumours', hurlers from Gortnahoe, Drombane and Moyne were called in, 'their expenses paid and seven of the old hurlers were left standing on the platform'.[25] An expenses-related dispute arising from the 1900 All-Ireland senior football final between Clonmel Shamrocks and London played on 26 October 1902 caused serious difficulties for the association. Clonmel Shamrocks contacted Luke O'Toole, general secretary of the GAA, prior to the game and requested an extra £10 expenses to cover the cost of an overnight stay for the team in Clonmel prior to departing for Dublin. His mind focused by an implied threat to withdraw if the expenses were not covered, O'Toole informed the Clonmel club that rail expenses had been paid and any extra expenses, would be paid after the match. Only the cost of the rail fares were regarded as legitimate expenses, but because of the need to accommodate the non-Clonmel players in the town prior to departure the Clonmel club claimed the extra expenses. Three months later the annual convention refused the demand. Shamrocks initiated court proceedings against O'Toole, got a court decree for £7. 10s. and had O'Toole's personal property seized in lieu of the amount. Central council decided by five votes to three with several abstentions to impose a contentious lifetime suspension on Shamrocks. This was eventually lifted in January 1905.[26]

The well-organised clubs had a comprehensive match programme, while transport expenses could be quite significant and were normally funded by the players themselves. Tubberadora played twenty-three hurling matches between 11 August 1895 and 25 March 1900 and twelve of these involved journeys outside of Tipperary. Between

January 1897 and February 1899 the Kickham's club played twenty-seven times. The Dungarvan-based Shandon Rovers club played twelve football matches during the 1897/8 season, travelling to Thurles, Clonmel, Waterford, Ballyporeen and Lismore.[27] Apart from transport costs there was a range of additional expenses that members were required to pay and these would have excluded many from the lower classes from participation. Some equipment had to be purchased and there was a very strong social scene, both formal and informal, associated with the early GAA that would have added to the cost of participation. Clubs did not just concentrate on the playing of sport. Annual dinners, farewell parties to honour departing members, pre- and post-game entertainment were part of the social curriculum of the well-organised club.[28] These were occasions of speeches, conviviality, cheers, songs and toasts. They were time-honoured rituals that helped to assert team spirit, together with establishing a sense of a club's importance and uniqueness.[29]

The agricultural labourer and farmer's son were members of very different economic gene pools and certainly inhabited very different cultural landscapes. Whether the farm labourer inhabited any cultural landscape at this time is debatable. There is evidence from Westmeath to suggest that cricket was an important recreational outlet for the labourer in the 1890s and early 1900s.[30] Social ostracisation was an important factor promoting exclusion. One historian has suggested that 'the widest gap in rural Ireland was that between the farmer and the landless labourer'.[31] The men who never dined at the farmer's table in the parlour were likely to have been reluctant participants in a recreational activity dominated by those who implemented a type of social apartheid. The farm labourers who participated in hurling and football in the time span of this study were either live-in labourers on a farm with family involvement in the games or near neighbours or employees of farmers involved. Their inclusion owed much to the sympathetic and supportive farmer who was appreciative of the skill levels that their employee had developed with stick and ball or football. There were also practical considerations that militated against farm labourer involvement. The farmer and his sons were independent enough to manage their own work schedules and as hirers of labour were in a position to organise their own free time. The farm employee enjoyed no such luxury and if the farmer's son was absent from work due to recreational activities someone had to substitute for him.

The ages of the players active in the period between 1886 and 1905 is illustrated in Table 11.7. It was possible, using manuscript census returns and other sources such as club histories, to establish the ages of 332 of the players that formed the database.[32] The average age of players involved at this time was 23.2. More than half of the players were aged 23 or under while more than three-quarters were 26 years of age or under (Table 11.7). The age of player ranged between 14 and 40. The Blackwater selection that played in the 1900 All-Ireland hurling final apparently included two 40-year-old players. Another player who had a particularly long playing career was Tom Healy, who was 39 years of age when he played for Two Mile Borris in the 1900 All-Ireland hurling final on 26 October 1902. Tom Healy occupies a unique place in GAA history as he was the man that scored the only goal in the first All-Ireland hurling final played at Birr on 1 August 1888.[33]

TABLE 11.7
AGES OF PLAYERS PARTICIPATING IN HURLING AND FOOTBALL, 1886–1905

Age	Total	%	Hurlers	%	Footballers	%
15 and under	5	1.5	1	0.5	4	3.3
16–20	99	29.8	65	30.7	34	28.3
21–25	138	41.6	84	39.6	54	45.0
26–30	69	20.8	46	21.7	23	19.2
31–35	15	4.5	10	4.7	5	4.2
36–40	6	1.8	6	2.8	0	0
Total	332	100	212	100	120	100

There was no significant difference between the average age of a footballer (22.66) or a hurler (23.45); the most important difference in the age structure for the two codes is that footballers tended to retire at an earlier age from the game. In the period covered by this study the rules of football were still in the process of evolution, the game was still a rough and rugged affair and its attritional impact was far greater than that of hurling. This may have encouraged earlier retirement.

The players involved were almost totally single and Catholic.[34] The unmarried status of the players was a product of the age profile of the participants. Delayed marriage characterised the demographics of nineteenth-century rural Ireland.[35] Single status was the norm for young Irishmen of the era. Only 2.5 per cent of the male population aged between 15 and 25 were married in 1901, although 31.5 per cent of those between 25 and 35 were married.[36] Sport was overwhelmingly the preserve of the single man in the lower- and middle-class sections of society. Marriage brought responsibilities and new financial obligations to a group with limited disposable income, and lifestyle decisions were made that excluded physical recreation.

The construction of a socio-economic profile of early GAA players also requires some analysis of the clubs with which these men were associated, and this exercise provides valuable insights into the nature of early GAA clubs. The Catholic parish unit has been regarded as one of the organisational strengths of the association, with the principle of one club to a parish paramount. The evidence presented here suggests that when territorial units formed the focus about which a club was organised smaller units than the parish were more important. Rural society in the late nineteenth century functioned not on a parish basis but on the more informal alliances that evolved among members of the farming community. It was common practice for farmers to pool their resources at busy times in the farming season to complete essential work. Such alliances of neighbours provided the network that enabled rural society to function efficiently and effectively. The operation of these community networks provides the key to the understanding of the origins of many of the early GAA clubs. The townland lay at the centre of rural communities. A townland or contiguous townlands provided the nucleus from which some clubs emerged, built around a clutch of sporting and athletic neighbours. The Suir View Rangers team that contested the Tipperary hurling championship between 1895 and 1898 provide a fine example of the nature of compact, territorial-based networks and their effectiveness in establishing club structures. The club played in three consecutive Tipperary hurling finals, winning the 1897 title in the boardroom and only losing matches to Tubberadora and Cork during the period of the club's existence.[37] The majority of the club players lived in two adjoining townlands, Bawnmore and Longfield, in the parish of Boherlahan-Dualla where three teams from the parish – Ballydine, Boherlahan and Suir View – competed in the 1897 Tipperary championship. The Suir View team developed without any links with the traditional focal points of church, shop, public house or village hall. Instead it was the forge owned by the Morrissey family of Ballyroe that provided a gathering place for the young men of the area. A field on the Fogarty family farm in Bawnmore provided the training venue. Many of the young men who played for Suir View first became acquainted with each other when they attended the national school at Ardmayle and in the period between 1875 and 1883 sixteen of those who would later form the core of the team began their schooling at the Ardmayle school. Twelve of these came from the townlands of Longfield, Ballyroe and the northern section of Bawnmore and all lived within a quarter-mile of each other. The Mahers, O'Dwyers and Fogartys came from Bawnmore and the O'Heney and Morrisey brothers from Longfield.[38] The strong family connections associated with the Suir View club illustrate another of the bonding agents of the early rural club. The Maher and Gleeson brothers and cousins were central to the Tipperary hurling success of the 1890s. The Doyle brothers of Mooncoin went on to win eighteen All-Ireland senior hurling medals between them. The list is almost endless. The pattern of family involvement was repeated in practically every rural club examined for this survey and formed a central part of the community network.

Suir View's neighbours and rivals Tubberadora provide another classic example of a club based on the small territorial unit of a townland located at the time in the Moycarkey parish. It was a team based on the 'close-knit farming community' of the area drawn mainly from Tubberadora and Nodstown and in its years of championship activity between 1895 and 1898 won the All-Ireland senior hurling titles of 1895, 1896 and 1898. As a result twenty-eight All-Ireland senior hurling medals were brought home to five houses in Tubberadora. One of the greatest of the early hurling combinations, from the first match on 11 August 1895 to the twenty-third and last match on 25 March 1900 (in the 1898 All-Ireland senior hurling final), the club scored 97–186 and conceded 23–63.[39] The team was made up of

> Big men of the land – many of them over 6 feet – with a fierce dedication and surging sweeping style that took the ball ahead of them through any opposition, their power, their fitness, their irresistible strength and their noted late rally was what made them immortal.[40]

Tubberadora Mill, the property of Thomas Leahy, was the focal point of social and economic activity for the farmers of the Tubberadora hinterland. This was the mill where farmers and others had their corn crushed to make animal feed and occasionally flour for domestic use.[41] Thomas Leahy, mill proprietor in the 1890s, was the principal power broker in the local community and he provided much of the motivational impetus that inspired the Tubberadora club. A member of the Cashel Board of Guardians and later of the Cashel Rural and District Council, he was president of the Tubberadora team and presided over it with the 'watchfulness and benignity of a father'.[42] Leahy was the founder of the club, having been impressed by the wealth of young hurling talent that gathered regularly in Walshes' kiln field for practice.[43] It was also Leahy who encouraged the hurlers to take part in the 1898 championship as a gesture of commemoration of the 1798 rebellion.

Leahy's off-field influence was matched by the inspiring captaincy of Big Mikey Maher. At a time when captaincy meant organising a team, arranging games, making sure of travel arrangements and providing leadership on the field of play, 'Big Mikey did it all and had it all' and in the locality reputedly 'carried more weight than the Parish Priest'. Maher captained Tubberadora to their three All-Ireland titles and when the club disbanded he collected two more All-Ireland titles in 1899 and 1900 with Horse and Jockey and Two Mile Borris selections respectively.[44] Suir View and Tubberadora provide clear examples of the building blocks of a successful GAA club in the early decades of the association: a strong neighbourhood network supported by inspired leadership and underpinned by family involvement. The Clonea Hurling Club, Co. Waterford senior hurling champions of 1903, provides another example of a similar organisational framework. The playing core of this team was drawn from two adjoining townlands, Ballydurn and Kilcanavee, located at the southeastern edge of the Clonea-Power parish. These key players were the sons of substantial landowners. Five were from families that farmed over 100 acres of land. Members of the Kirwan family, one of Waterford's most famous sporting families, provided the necessary leadership. James Kirwan founded the Clonea Hurling Club and captained the team on this occasion. The team also included his brother Percy, who later won three British Amateur Athletic Association (AAA) long jump titles between 1909 and 1911 as well as several Irish Amateur Athletic Association and GAA national championships. A third brother, Rody, missed Clonea's title but received some compensation in 1903 and 1904 when as a Castleisland-based bank clerk he was a member of the Kerry All-Ireland title-winning football teams.[45]

In Tullaroan, Co. Kilkenny community bonding was a result of Land League activity and cricket-playing. The club was the most successful of the early Kilkenny clubs and had won eight Kilkenny hurling titles by 1904. The area had experienced considerable Land League activity in the early 1880s and as result of this activity a community in apparent decline rallied to 'take a leading role in the land movement in County Kilkenny'. In the process the community became highly politicised.[46] Some of those involved in the Land League and the Irish National League were instrumental in the establishment of a hurling club in Tullaroan. One of these activists, Henry J. Meagher, reputedly attended the meeting in Thurles at which the

GAA was established.[47] This political activity took place at the same time as cricket-playing provided a recreational outlet for the young men of the district. Familiarity with a stick-and-ball game may have helped to lay some of the foundation for their early hurling success. This success coincided with a time when hurlers were also active cricket players. These included Meagher, James Grace, Pierce Grace, Lar Coogan and John Morris. Three cricket clubs were active in the Tullaroan area in the 1880s and 1890s when the hurling club also experienced its most successful era.[48]

Mooncoin's particular rural settlement pattern provided a different focus of community identity and network within the parish system. In the periods 1886–8 and 1897–1901, seventy-seven different players who played senior hurling for the club, and their place of residence, have been identified.[49] These hurlers emerged mainly from the farm villages that were especially concentrated in the parish of Mooncoin in south Kilkenny. The village's survival was a product of the political, social and economic stability of the south Kilkenny region since medieval times and from their location 'outside the reconstructed worlds of gentry living'. Twenty-three of these villages and townlands were represented on Mooncoin hurling selections at this time. The villages 'nurtured a society of wealth, comfort and permanence untypical of Ireland as a whole'.[50] Many of these villages were centrally located in the townland to the exclusion of all other dwellings.[51] This type of village was the place of residence of the majority of Mooncoin hurlers identified in this study; 30 per cent were from the farm villages of Doornane, Portnahully, Portnascully, Licketstown and Grange. The farm villages were not homogenous classless clusters of poor farmers of the 'clachan' model, but were socially varied and economically prosperous. They were peopled by a variety of occupational groups such as weavers, tailors, fishermen, blacksmiths and millers, as well as agricultural labourers and live-in servants.[52] Socially conservative, monolithically Catholic, Irish was still the vernacular language of the post-Famine generation and the game of hurling was firmly embedded in the psyche of the village inhabitants. In Michael O'Dwyer's forensic examination of Kilkenny cricket there is no documentation of cricket-playing in either Mooncoin or any of its surrounding villages. Some element of social segregation existed between the villages. Farm labourers occupied old Luffany while farmers inhabited New Luffany; each district produced two Mooncoin hurlers prior to 1901. Mooncoin, the chapel village of the parish, was essentially a village of landless labourers.[53] In the period between 1886 and 1901 nine residents of this village lined out for the club.[54]

In urban areas, the key socio-economic network of functioning hurling and football clubs was embedded in the retail trade and included shopkeepers, shop assistants, clerks and sales personnel. As stated earlier, this socio-economic group was significantly over-represented in the GAA. Ironically, one of the restrictive practices that operated against employees within the retail trade proved to be advantageous when it came to organising hurling and football teams. In Dublin and larger urban centres it was common for staff to be pro-vided with accommodation. It was often a condition of employment that staff members lived over the workplace in accommodation sup-plied by management or in specially rented houses. This meant that staff were under constant supervision and subjected to the discipline of their employers for practically twenty-four hours a day. Census records show that over a hundred employees of Clerys slept over the premises in 1901.[55] The opportunity to participate in a GAA-related activity provided a welcome opportunity to escape from this employer surveillance. This working environment allowed for ease of organisa-tion from a GAA club perspective. Working in offices and shops, and often sharing accommodation, meant constant contact with fellow workers, customers and neighbours. As a result, and particularly in Dublin

> Young men of fine physique from all parts of the country were thrown together having few outlets for their ener-gies but with a common bond, the same trade and corre-sponding aspirations.[56]

Migrants to urban areas and in particular to Dublin were a most sig-nificant influence on the development of the GAA. The Power Cup final of 1890, a Dublin inter-firms competition, featured Clerys and Arnotts and all thirty-seven players involved came from outside the county.[57] The Liberties-based Young Ireland club was a club 'of tall powerful men, up from the country, employed in St James's brewery to do the heavy work'. The Faughs club drew its membership pre-dominantly from Tipperary and in particular 'from a little north of the mid-Tipperary hurling stronghold of Tubberadora, Two Mile Borris, Horse and Jockey. Clusters of players came from Templederry and Drombane, and further north in the countryside around Nenagh.' Migrants used well-established economic and social frame-works to form a base in the unfamiliar metropolitan territory and in 1900 the Faughs county hurling title-winning team included fourteen

Tipperary players.[58] In Cork city, over a seventeen-year period only one player from the city lined out for the Lees club.[59] These club members were continuing with their familiar rural pastimes within the urban setting but this was not always the case. Some were using their new-found freedom from parental control to participate in football for the first time. Tomsie Walsh from Dungarvan, Co. Waterford was a member of the Dublin team that won All-Ireland titles in 1906, 1907 and 1908. He never played football until he left Dungarvan as parental permission was not forthcoming. Incredibly he played his first game of senior football for his club (Kickham's) in the 1904 All-Ireland final.[60]

Working conditions for drapers and other retail assistants were difficult and in the period covered by this study no uniform hours of closing had been agreed with employers. Dublin-based men were often required to work for up to eighty hours weekly.[61] Denny Curran was one of Kerry's players against Kildare in the 1903 All-Ireland home final series of games. As a young man Denny was apprenticed to the grocery trade and as an employee had to live-in at Bailys in the Mall in Tralee. His hours of work stretched from 9 a.m. to 11 p.m. and in summer when preparing for an important match he trained privately at the Tralee Sportsfield at 7 a.m.[62] Despite the long hours of work the critical factor was that assistants were free of Sunday labour and this free time provided the opportunity to engage in recreational activities.

It is difficult to overestimate the importance of this socio-economic group to the wellbeing of the early GAA in urban areas. In towns across the country shop assistants of various categories formed the core group of the most successful clubs. Teams associated with the grocery and bar trade dominated the early years of the GAA in Dublin. After the success of Cusack's student-dominated Metropolitan club in 1887, clubs strongly identified with the retail trade won the next twelve Dublin senior hurling titles. The Charles Kickham club, champions in 1889 and 1890, drew their players mainly from the drapery trade and the Raparees club, champions of 1891 and 1894, was composed mainly of barmen, as was the Michael Davitt club that won the 1893 title. The Rapparees headquarters was at the public house of John Connell at Cork Street, one of the club's leading players.[63] The Kickham club was centred on the drapers' stores of Henry Street and the name choice was an indication of the strong Tipperary influence among the early membership. The 1889 county title-winning side progressed to win the All-Ireland senior hurling title with a team that included ten Tipperary men.[64] In the late 1890s football became more important in the club and the rural dominance began to decline somewhat. In February 1899 the club won its first All-Ireland senior football title. The team included thirteen drapers' assistants; seven were employed by Clerys, four by Arnotts and one each by the Henry Street Warehouse and Todds. Seven counties, led by Dublin with five players, formed the team that contested the final.[65] The Commercial club of employees of the grocery trade won four hurling titles between 1895 and 1898,while the Faughs, with its strong links with the bar trade, was successful in 1892 and 1900. The 1899 senior hurling championship was won by the Grocer GAC, a club founded in February 1886 by a number of grocers' assistants, again with a strong Tipperary connection. This pattern of dominance continued well into the twentieth century.[66] In Limerick, the Commercials club won eleven senior football titles between 1888 and 1905 and the All-Ireland senior titles of 1887 and 1896.[67] In Cork city, the Lees club was the club of the employees of the business houses of the city. The club's founding father was J. Coilins, a draper's assistant at the firm of Queen's Old Castle in the city. He invited a number of fellow drapers' assistants from Cashs, the Munster Arcade, Grants and the Queen's to his home and a club confined to the assistants of the drapery firms of Cork city was formed in October 1882. The Lees club switched to Gaelic football in 1887 and won the inaugural Cork championship and were successful again in 1896. The 1896 team included twelve drapers' assistants with the remainder working in the grocery trade with Liptons and the London & Newcastle company. Such was the dominance of drapers in the team that they were often referred to as 'the collars and cuffs'.[68] In Dunmore, Co. Galway many of the members of the MacHales club worked as shop assistants in the premises of Martin McDonnell, the most successful businessman in the town; the McDonnell business empire dominated the centre of Dunmore. In the 1880s McDonnell employed over thirty men, including club secretary John Martyn, and in the late 1890s the great J.J. Nestor began his business career there. The firm maintained four houses in Dunmore that were used as living quarters for the employees and the McDonnell staff made up the nucleus of the Dunmore team between 1890 and 1910.[69]

Pre-existing sports clubs sometimes provided the nucleus from which hurling or football clubs emerged. This chapter has been focused on what was essentially a ban-free time zone and as such there was considerable movement between sports and interchangeability was an important characteristic. The experience of the Nil

Desperandum club in Cork provides an appropriate example of this process. The club began life as a rugby team known as Berwick Rangers and were based at the Grand Parade in the city. Demoralised by their lack of success, the members disbanded the club but later reconsidered and decided to reform in 1887 and attempt the newly designed Gaelic football code. Conscious of their previous 'success' rate, the members christened the reconstituted club Nil Desperandum. In 1894 the club won the Cork football championship and followed with the Munster title before losing the All-Ireland replayed final in dubious circumstances. Nils held a two-point lead minutes from the end when their Dublin opponents walked off the pitch claiming that one of their players had been assaulted. Nils refused to replay the game and had to be satisfied with a set of medals presented to them by the Cork County Board inscribed: Nils, All-Ireland football champions 1894. The club was also beaten in the 1899 and 1901 All-Ireland finals.[70] Laune Rangers Gaelic Football Club was initially founded as a rugby club and changed codes when two teachers arrived in the town and introduced Gaelic football to the members.[71]

Finally, in the period covered by this chapter Gaelic League clubs provided an important nucleus for club formation. In the late 1890s there was a significant increase in enthusiasm for nationalist causes. This was a product in particular of the 1898 centenary celebrations of the 1798 rebellion and a general growth in anti-imperialism inspired by the Boer War.[72] A growth in cultural nationalism was an inevitable by-product of this development and in the early 1900s the Gaelic League in particular expanded.[73] The organisation had expanded moderately between 1893 and 1899 when there were only eighty branches. The league quintupled in numbers by 1902 and continued to grow although at a slower pace between 1903 and 1908.[74] The mythology associated with hurling established a status for the sport as the most Irish of games and made it an ideal vehicle for promotion by Gaelic League activists. As Frank Doran, a Foxford Gaelic League activist, pointed out to Conall Gulban, the Irish-Ireland columnist of the *Roscommon Herald*:

> I would suggest that you start a hurling club in Longford. There is no game so attractive, and people who would get tired of football are sure to take a great interest in this. It is far before football, and as a game, more manly and more Irish.[75]

A hurling club, Leo Casey's, was started in Longford associated with the town's branch of the Gaelic League and during 1903 and 1904 hurling had a far greater impact in the town than Gaelic football. In Mullingar, the Mullingar Shamrocks Hurling Club, with strong Gaelic League associations, was a stable institution and outlasted its football equivalent, the Young Ireland club, by several years.[76] The pattern repeated itself nationwide and was particularly important in Dublin. The immediate impact on the GAA was a sharp increase in the number of affiliated clubs. Total club numbers increased from forty-six in 1900 to around eighty in 1904, and many of these new clubs had strong Gaelic League connections.[77] The Keatings GAC was established in 1901 by the Keatings branch of the Gaelic League; composed mainly of Munster men, the club became Dublin senior football champions in 1903. The Archbishop Croke club was founded in April 1904 from members of the Craobhin branch of the Gaelic League and members of the Cúchulainn GAA Club. Other clubs with very strong Gaelic League associations included the Confederates Hurling Club and the Laurence O'Toole club.[78] The Saint Laurence O'Toole branch of the Gaelic League was founded on 8 February 1901 and in October a hurling club was formed among its members. The class structure of the club is suggested by the inclusion in its ranks of 'a pioneer of the Abbey theatre, a sculptor member of the Royal Hibernian Academy, a number of teachers, a sailing enthusiast, a ship's engineer and a builder.[79] A similar phenomenon has been documented in Derry and in Fermanagh; the Ballinaleck GAA Club in Fermanagh was formed by members of the local Gaelic League Irish-language classes.[80] This had an impact on the class structure of the GAA and the language movement became the source of a whole new class of largely non-manual employees such as teachers, local officials and civil servants.[81]

This examination of the GAA as it operated at the grassroots level provides a very different perspective to the one that finds the IRB lurking around the corner of every GAA field. The socio-economic profile of the players suggests an organisation dominated by the lower middle classes, if we dare to assign social classes on the basis of paid employment. It was an organisation heavily influenced by rural Ireland as its membership was dominated by those from the farming communities, either involved in the association as farmers in rural areas or as retail assistants in urban areas whose background was a farming one. Community networks, whether in a rural or urban setting, were the critical catalyst in encouraging club development. A historian of Victorian sport has pointed out that up to 1901 sport was largely an urban phenomenon.[82] The formation of the GAA in 1884 changed that situation and extended the opportunity for rural dwellers to participate in sport. The GAA at this time achieved a level of inclusiveness that was unequalled by any other sporting organisation, although (based on a relatively small survey that is geographically limited) some social groups remained relatively untouched by Cusack's prairie fire.

12 Gaelic Games and the Irish Diaspora in the United States

PAUL DARBY

In announcing a partnership agreement between the Gaelic Athletic Association and the Irish government's Department of Foreign Affairs (DFA) in June 2008 to promote Gaelic games abroad, the minister for foreign affairs, Micheál Martin suggested that 'The GAA plays a key role in the social and cultural life of Irish communities abroad. The Association underpins and promotes Irish heritage and identity across the globe and is a major contributor to Irish community networks and outreach.'[1] This chapter assesses the accuracy of Martin's contentions with specific reference to the GAA in the United States. It does so by charting the history of Gaelic games on American shores, analysing the role that they have played in allowing the Irish émigré to adjust to life there and assessing the ways in which the association has helped those so inclined to maintain and express varying senses of Irishness. The arguments presented here are rooted in empirical evidence collected as part of a broader study examining the development of Gaelic games in four of the key focal points of Irish immigration and main centres of the GAA in the US, namely Boston, New York, Chicago and San Francisco.[2] Before turning to Gaelic games in these cities it is useful to comment briefly on the arrival and early experiences of the Irish in America.

Sustained Irish emigration to America has a history that stretches back long before the American Revolution to the beginning of the seventeenth century. Initially, the émigré were made up predominantly of Irish Catholics but during the late 1600s they were replaced by Protestants of Scottish and English descent as the largest grouping of Irish immigrants in the New World. This remained the case up until the end of the eighteenth century, but the early decades of the nineteenth century saw a resurgence in the numbers of Irish Catholics emigrating to America. With the end of the Napoleonic Wars and a subsequent drop in demand for Irish agricultural products, the period

1815–45 saw around a million Irish immigrants, twice as many as in the previous two centuries combined, disembarking on American shores.[3] Although it would be an oversimplification to view Irish emigration to the New World as simply a reactive or enforced process, the Great Famine (1845–50) was undoubtedly the most significant factor in the massive exodus of the Irish from their homeland. The impact of the Famine on Irish emigration was such that by the early 1870s the numbers of Irish-born people who had left Ireland had reached 3 million with over half of them settling in America.[4]

The vast majority of Famine immigrants on America's north-eastern seaboard and in the mid-west lived in impoverished conditions. They were employed on the bottom rung of the ladder as low-paid, unskilled labourers and they lived in poor, ethnic neighbourhoods characterised by inadequate housing, overcrowding, poor sanitation, disease, crime and poverty. The lives of the Irish Catholic working class in the second half of the nineteenth century were not helped by Anglo-Protestant, nativist prejudice. The Anglo-Protestant communities in Boston, New York and Chicago distanced themselves from the Irish and leading figures in this community actively discriminated against them. Evidence of the way that Irish Catholics were viewed was apparent in a particularly blunt editorial of the *Chicago Tribune*, then published by Joseph Medill, the son of Ulster Presbyterian parents, on the 'problem' of large numbers of Irish Catholics resident in the city: 'Who does not know that the most depraved, debased, worthless and irredeemable drunkards and sots which curse the community are Irish Catholics?'[5] While these sorts of anti-Irish attitudes reached their height in the 1850s with the electoral successes of the American Nativist Party throughout America's main industrial metropolises, they persisted until the close of the nineteenth century. The experiences of the Irish émigré in San Francisco were in many senses unique compared to those of their counterparts elsewhere in the New World. For example, the majority of those Irish who settled in San Francisco in the years after the Gold Rush did not arrive directly from Ireland. Initially they came from already established Irish communities in Australasia and America's eastern seaboard and thus had experience of adjusting to foreign climes and consequently were more confident about what life in the city might have in store for them and how best to avail of the opportunities on offer. Irish settlement patterns in San Francisco also differed from those found in other centres of Irish immigration and there were not the sorts of ethnic slums in the city that existed elsewhere. The socio-economic and political environment that the Irish experienced on arrival in San

Francisco also differed markedly from that found further east. While Irish progress elsewhere in the country was undermined by anti-Catholic and anti-Irish prejudice, American nativism was much less of a force in San Francisco. Their numerical strength as a proportion of the population was also important in helping the Irish to establish themselves in San Franciscan society, not least because it made them an important electoral grouping and one whose aspirations and sensibilities needed to be indulged by those seeking political office. While sections of the city's Irish community experienced the same sorts of problems of adjustment that were to be found on the east coast, they were not the destitute, diseased and dishevelled Famine immigrants that poured into New York and Boston and consequently perceptions of the rapid influx of Irish immigrants were characterised by greater tolerance.[6]

Although Anglo-Protestant intolerance of those Irish Catholics in their midst further east held sections of the Irish in America back, it also helped galvanise a strong ethnic consciousness. The Irish across America in this period were also sustained by a range of institutions including the Catholic Church and a whole host of social, political and benevolent organisations and societies, and these further allowed them to articulate senses of communal identity. The abilities and electoral successes of a range of Irish politicians increasingly provided the Irish community with a voice with which to challenge the established Protestant hegemony and gradually redress the discrimination that emanated from it. This allowed the Irish to earn a degree of acceptance in America from the 1860s onwards and helped to facilitate varying levels of social mobility. Thus, with improving opportunities, prospects and standards of living, the America that welcomed Irish immigrants in the second half of the nineteenth and early years of the twentieth centuries was considerably more hospitable than that encountered by those who had arrived earlier. As this chapter shows, the emergence of fledgling GAA clubs and organisational units in the US from the late 1870s onwards contributed much to this state of affairs.

Uncodified versions of Gaelic football and hurling were played in America long before the establishment of the GAA in Dublin in 1884. For example, Abbott and McGinn provide details of documentary evidence of the existence of rudimentary forms of hurling in New York as early as the 1780s.[7] The emergence of GAA clubs there, though, had to wait until the 1850s with the establishment of the Irish Hurling and Football Club in 1857.[8] Early versions of Gaelic football and hurling were also played on the Pacific coast at this time with *Alta California*, one of the city's earliest newspapers, reporting in May 1853 on the establishment of San Francisco's first hurling club.[ix] By the late 1870s and early 1880s Gaelic games were also being played on a relatively regular basis in Boston and Chicago,[10] but it was not until the mid-1880s, following the inception of the GAA in Ireland, that codified, organised versions of football and hurling began to be played on American shores. Beyond the inauguration of clubs and the efforts of some notable individuals, the most significant development in the emergence of Gaelic games in America was the 'Gaelic invasion' of 1888, which saw over fifty Irish athletes tour the country's north-eastern seaboard as part of an initiative aimed at helping to revive the Tailteann games, an athletic and cultural festival which had last taken place in Ireland in the twelfth century.

While the diffusion and development of the GAA in Boston, New York, Chicago and San Francisco may not have matched the pace and pervasiveness of the growth of Gaelic games in Ireland, the GAA quickly established itself as an important sporting, cultural and socioeconomic resource for those Irish immigrants who had journeyed to the New World in the latter decades of the nineteenth century. As in Ireland, the association there possessed influential and tireless patrons. Men such as John Boyle O'Reilly, Joseph P. Kennedy, William Prendergast, John F. Finerty, William Stokes and Father Peter C. Yorke did more than most to promote and popularise Gaelic games, not least because they had the profile and platform to endorse Gaelic sports in a very public way.[11] Those who worked selflessly and less publicly behind the scenes though were also crucial to the ability of the association to progress in America. Just as Gaelic games in Ireland relied on volunteers, the GAA in America was ultimately dependent on those who took on organisational, fundraising, playing and officiating roles or merely patronised the games through their attendance at matches and field days. The motivation of such individuals to give of their time so freely was undoubtedly rooted in the fact that their involvement in these games allowed them to experience excitement, pleasure and fun in what could otherwise be a drab and difficult existence. High skill levels as a player or organisational abilities as an administrator were likely to have conferred a degree of kudos on individuals and it may have been this that encouraged some to take part. For others, simply being outdoors and engaging in or watching robust physical endeavour may explain the appeal of hurling and Gaelic football in this period. The fact that Gaelic games were so intimately connected to and resonant of 'home' also undoubtedly piqued a primordial passion in enthusiasts and, as will be revealed later, this was particularly important in cementing the place of the GAA among sections of the Irish diaspora in America.

By the close of the nineteenth century, Gaelic games were well established in Irish America. Clubs were competing for regular championship honours and games were attracting attendances of up to 10,000. In the opening decades of the new century, the GAA experienced varying levels of growth. The inauguration of a number of governing bodies and a co-ordinated approach to the promotion of Gaelic games was hugely influential in this regard. The significance of the inception of the 'Gaelic Athletic Association of the United States' in New York in 1914, for example, was noted by Byrne, who commented that this development 'was to New York what the Thurles meeting was to Ireland'.[12] While the progress of Gaelic games in this period was rooted in these sorts of internal initiatives, the health of the association became increasingly susceptible to external influences, particularly fluctuations in levels of Irish immigration into the US. Thus, the outbreak of the Great War, America's decision to enter hostilities in 1917 and a subsequent decline in rates of Irish immigration saw the complement of GAA clubs in the US dip considerably.

The conclusion of the war did much to revive levels of immigration and replenish depleted GAA stocks. Buoyed by this revival, organisational bodies began to form elsewhere, most notably in Boston where the Massachusetts Gaelic Athletic Association was instituted in 1923. The GAA's Dublin-based administration looked favourably on these developments and in 1926 they sanctioned regular tours of the US by All-Ireland-winning inter-county teams in both hurling and football, a move which did much to further embed these sports in the consciousness of the Irish émigré. However, the Wall Street crash in 1929 and a resultant global depression heralded a period of stagnation and decline in the GAA's fortunes on American shores. The Great Depression, keenly felt as it was in areas of heavy industrialisation, had a devastating impact on America's Irish community, most of which depended for their livelihood on unskilled labour and as such were victims of the worst economic ravages of the era. In such a difficult environment identifying ways of alleviating socio-economic hardship as opposed to seeking to preserve the sports and games of the 'old country' became the priority for many. Dramatically reduced levels of immigration also fed into this decline. Some units of the association were better prepared for the challenges of depression-era America than others, though. For example, while the GAA in New York and San Francisco were progressive enough to initiate what became very successful youth programmes among an American-born pool of talent, the failure to do the same in Boston and Chicago quickly saw Gaelic games there go into free-fall. However, the creation of a youthful, locally based grass-roots that had been developed in New York and San Francisco could do little to prevent the virtual disappearance of Gaelic games across America once the US government took the decision to enter the Second World War. It became clear to those with aspirations to rebuild the GAA in post-war America that its revival would have to be organised around an event of considerable import.

While there were palpable signs of recovery in the immediate aftermath of the war, the historic decision by the GAA's annual congress in 1947 to grant New York the right to host the All-Ireland Gaelic football final was undoubtedly the cornerstone of the association's renewal.[13] Despite the months of meticulous planning and promotion that went into the event, heavy rain on the evening before the final between Cavan and Kerry convinced many New York Irish to stay away and the actual attendance fell almost 20,000 short of the 54,000 capacity of the Polo Grounds, the venue selected for the match.[14] Although the turnout was disappointing, the event provided a massive boost for Gaelic games throughout America. Of particular significance was the fact that the 1947 final did much to improve the relationship between the GAA in America and their counterparts in Ireland. Tangible evidence of this was quickly evident in the following year when the association's Central Council agreed to set aside an 'international fund' of £2,000 to facilitate closer relations with the New York GAA and institute more regular playing contact.[15] This level of support for 'international' fixtures was matched across the Atlantic and just three years later New York was taking part in the finals of the GAA's National League competitions.

A resumption of healthy levels of immigration during the 1950s rapidly refilled GAA clubs and new ones were established to cope with the increased demand for Gaelic games. This growth encouraged America's Gaels to turn their attentions to the establishment of a nationwide governing body to oversee the development of Gaelic games and provide opportunities for inter-city competition. Discussions involving Michael Kehoe, the association's president, and officials from the major US GAA centres led to the establishment of the National Council of the GAA. This new organisation divided the administration of Gaelic games into three 'zones', comprising New York, which contained thirty-six teams, the mid-west, involving sixteen football and eight hurling club teams across seven cities, and New England, which had thirteen football and three in hurling.[16] While San Francisco and the broader Pacific region was not explicitly incorporated into this fledgling body, officials of the association there reported to Central Council in late 1952 that they considered themselves to be under the jurisdiction of the National Council.[17] Inter-zonal contests for the title of US champions were a feature of this new administrative set-up and this competition initially proved attractive to America's GAA supporters.[18] However, despite early enthusiasm, it became clear that the plan was overly ambitious. Crucially, because it felt less reliant on other GAA units, New York soon grew disenchanted by the whole idea with its attitude towards the new body being described as 'aloof ... hesitant ... cold and detached'.[19] By 1956, New York took the decision to withdraw from the National Council, a move that effectively sounded the death knell on this body.

Despite the position of the New York GAA on the principle of a national council, a number of stalwarts of the association elsewhere in the country still believed in the need for a nationwide governing body.[20] Thus, in 1958, following a series of meetings, Cleveland's Henry Cavanagh published a document entitled 'The American County Board Plan', which was effectively a blueprint for a new organisational structure. Armed with this plan, Cavanagh and his colleagues began to lobby the clubs and seek their approval for a new divisional set-up based around the main centres of Gaelic games in the country. As John Hehir, a key figure in the inception of the new body and a subsequent president, suggested, this was not an easy process: 'This plan was difficult to sell to the different cities but we were successful in doing it and eventually they came around and accepted the principle.'[21] Thus, at a meeting in Philadelphia in 1959, the previous 'zonal' structure was effectively abolished and a new body, the North American County Board (NACB), initially comprised of six divisions (Central, Mid-West, Western, New England, Philadelphia and Northern/Canada), was formed. In a statement of intent, the NACB almost immediately sought county board status within the GAA's Central Council and congress and this was achieved when it formally affiliated to the parent body shortly after its inception.[22] In keeping with its earlier approach to national governance, New York continued with a policy of separatism, and jurisdiction over the New York and New Jersey region remained, as it does to this day, outside the remit of the NACB.

The establishment of the NACB along with continued healthy

rates of Irish immigration into the US in light of economic stagnation in Ireland did much to ensure that Gaelic games enthusiasts entered the 1960s with considerable optimism. However, what could not have been foreseen was the introduction of a piece of legislation in 1965 that was to seriously curtail Irish immigration to the US and in doing so seriously limit the development of the GAA. The Immigration Act of 1965, passed through Congress with little opposition, abolished the national quota system which had operated in the country since 1921.[23] This system prioritised immigration from northern and western Europe and while Ireland saw its annual quota increase by 3,000 to a total of 20,000, the regulations for securing entry altered. Under the new provisions preference was given to those potential immigrants with skill sets required in the US economy and those with close family ties to US citizens.[24] As a consequence of these tighter regulations Irish immigration slumped. Developments in Ireland's economy also contributed to this state of affairs. The appointment of Seán Lemass as taoiseach in 1959 and his role in Ireland's economic recovery, one built on expansionist policies and membership of the European Economic Community, also fed into the sharp reduction in Irish migration.[25] By 1969 the effects of these developments on US units of the GAA were being felt and Gaelic games once again began to struggle.

With increasing numbers of clubs folding, some within the NACB and the New York board began to feel that youth programmes, targeted at American-born children with Irish lineage, would help preserve Gaelic games and hence a number of divisional boards began to invest more time in nurturing young talent. Before this work could come to fruition, though, rising levels of unemployment in Ireland following an economic downturn in the late 1970s and 1980s revived the flow of Irish migrants seeking opportunities in the US. This did much to regenerate the association in this period and most senior clubs, eager for championship honours, had little space for American-born players. In such circumstances, youth player development and the building of a talent pool to sustain Gaelic games for the longer term was increasingly neglected. With the granting of Donnelly and Morrison visas in 1986 and 1990 respectively and a continued rise in the numbers of undocumented Irish in the US in the early 1990s, the GAA returned to a healthy position. However, with the Celtic Tiger persuading more young Irish people to remain at home as the 1990s progressed, anxieties about the preservation of Gaelic football, hurling and camogie on American soil began to resurface. The NACB's clubs were able to play down their concerns and veil the impact of slowing immigration by continuing to import high-profile players from Ireland for at least part of the regular season and the play-off stages of their competitions. From around the mid-1990s some began to question whether this strategy was likely to bring long-term benefits for Gaelic games in North America. Following an increase in complaints from Ireland and abuses of the sanction system by clubs that were desperate to stay competitive, the association in Ireland got involved in this debate and in 1998 they tightened the regulations governing player transfers to the US.[26] Although there continued to be opposition within some of the NACB's divisions,[27] following the terrorist attacks in America on 11 September 2001 and the tightening of the arrangements governing immigration, many clubs continued to recruit openly and widely in Ireland and sometimes in contravention of agreed rules. By 2002 this had created what was described in the *Irish Times* as an 'exodus' of Gaelic sporting talent from Irish shores to the US.[28] Complaints from clubs and county boards to Croke Park reached unprecedented levels and the GAA's Management Committee in Dublin took the decision to temporarily suspend all sanctions to the US. This suspension was quickly lifted, but the fact that it was imposed in the first place focused the minds of those with responsibility for the continued promotion of Gaelic games in America. Since then, some clubs have continued to call for a liberalisation of the rules governing trans-Atlantic transfer and an increase in the number of sanction players while others feel that the future of Gaelic games will be best sustained by nurturing an American-born grassroots.

While fluctuations in immigration flows have clearly had a significant impact on the fortunes of Gaelic games in the US in the latter decades of the twentieth century and opening years of the twenty-first, it would be wrong to suggest that the GAA in Boston, Chicago, New York and San Francisco sat idly by or watched passively while fluxes in immigration either replenished or depleted their stocks. Those who were committed to the sustainability of the GAA in each city were proactive in their pursuit of a sustainable and vibrant culture of Gaelic games. This was perhaps best exemplified in the establishment of permanent home venues for the GAA in Chicago and Boston in 1984 and 1999 respectively. While it has only just aquired its own premises, the association in San Francisco demonstrated its foresight and commitment in other ways, not least through the establishment of the Bay Area Irish Football Youth League (IFYL) in 1994, which has since developed into one of the largest and most successful GAA youth programmes in the US. New York also made good strides in promoting the games among young players but its focus was very much on the senior ranks, a fact evidenced by the city's return to the GAA's National League in 1989 and its entry into All-Ireland competition ten years later. Without the enthusiasm, commitment, generosity and ability of those who made these sorts of developments possible and who championed the association in America in other ways, it is unlikely that Gaelic games would have survived into the new millennium, irrespective of the numbers emigrating from Ireland.

Beyond levels of immigration and the efforts of a whole host of GAA officials, adherents and benefactors, the presence of organised versions of Gaelic games in America from the mid-1880s through to the current day has also been dependent on their ability to satisfy a number of crucial socio-economic, cultural and psychological functions for the Irish émigré. For those of a sporting disposition, the significance of the Gaelic football or hurling club in smoothing their transition from rural Ireland to sprawling, noisome and inhospitable urban centres cannot be overstated. Put simply, the GAA in the US provided a comforting 'home away from home' for thousands of Irish immigrants. It allowed them the opportunity to associate with like-minded individuals and in doing so helped to alleviate the feelings of alienation and dislocation that the Irish émigré often felt. Involvement with a GAA club or attendance at a match or function also provided entrance into the social networks that enabled newly arrived immigrants to find work, accommodation, make friends and, of course, experience the excitement of competitive sports. The functioning of the GAA in these respects has been evident in the US since the 1880s and it is these same forces and dynamics that have done so much to sustain Gaelic games there right through to the current day.

The GAA, then, has been an important sporting, social, economic and psychological resource for the Irish diaspora in America. The association has also served as a conduit through which Irish immigrants and their offspring have been able to express themselves culturally and politically and mark themselves out as ethnically distinct. As this chapter now goes on to demonstrate, since their inception in America, Gaelic games have been important practices that have allowed those who felt so inclined to retain and articulate senses of Irishness, ones that have at times been relatively benign, culturally focused, and at others much more belligerent, politicised and ethnic. While the role of the GAA in this regard helped to sustain Gaelic games in America at various points during the late nineteenth and twentieth centuries, this chapter closes by suggesting that their survival of Gaelic games in twenty-first-century America might be partially dependent on eschewing the narrow, ethnic version of Irishness typically associated with the GAA.

Before dealing specifically with these issues it is important to remind ourselves of the close linkages between the GAA and Irish nationalism in Ireland. These linkages have been the subject of much academic analysis, and while it is not necessary to revisit old ground here it is important to reiterate the point that the GAA in Ireland was established in 1884 as part of a broader Irish cultural revival aimed at resisting the Anglicisation of Ireland and building popular support for Irish independence.[29] From its formation, then, the GAA was an intensely nationalist organisation. Its remit was to foster and promote exclusively Irish sporting and cultural traditions and its patrons and founders were involved in different ways in the political and military campaign for Irish independence. The extent to which the GAA in Ireland has been used since as a medium for the construction and expression of Irish nationalism has fluctuated and varied according to circumstances in Ireland. This same trend has been very much in evidence in the history of the GAA in the US.

In much the same way that the inception of the GAA in Ireland in 1884 was rooted in an Irish nationalist agenda, the emergence of Gaelic football and hurling clubs in a range of American cities was also tied in to the development of nationalist politics there. Although Irish nationalism as a significant expression of Irish Catholic identity in America emerged in the first half of the nineteenth century, it was the Great Famine that did much to shape its appearance and expression. The Famine immigrants that poured into America developed an identity that was intensely ethnic and primordial and was underpinned by what the great Irish poet William Butler Yeats described as a 'fanatical heart'. This latter element of Irish diasporic identity was rooted in the fact that the post-Famine émigré adopted the motif of exile and saw Britain as responsible both for their poverty and starvation in Ireland and for their exodus to what was for many of them an existence characterised by disease, destitution and hostility from America's Anglo-Protestant establishment. This type of existence did much to strengthen their desire to see Ireland free of British influence. Indeed, the émigré of the second half of the nineteenth century believed that their progress, acceptance and recognition in the New World could only be won through the achievement of emancipation in Ireland.

So how did the disapora give vent to and express these elements of their Irishness? They joined revolutionary organisations, donated their dollars to parliamentary nationalism, attended political meetings, patronised Irish clubs and societies and voted for Irish politicians. All of this certainly bolstered support for politicised nationalism. However, taking their lead from Irish nationalist thinking in Ireland around the importance of a cultural revival, Irish-American nationalists soon recognised that any contribution to separatist aspirations, politically, financially and militarily, would be much stronger and more coherent if it were built on a strong sense of cultural Irishness amongst the diaspora. Thus, as occurred in Ireland, Irish cultural forms, Irish literature and the Irish language were promoted in America as a way of achieving this end. Gaelic games featured prominently in this regard and their emergence in the late 1870s and 1880s was clearly linked to this broader groundswell of support for Irish nationalism.

This linkage manifested itself in a number of ways. The pioneering figures behind the inception of the GAA in America were mostly staunch nationalists who saw in the Gaelic games an opportunity to not only get involved in and promote healthy, physical activity among the Irish diaspora but also perceived it as a vehicle for building the vibrant Gaelic culture in America upon which support for the political objectives of Irish nationalism might be built. John Boyle O'Reilly, a former member of the IRB and a key figure in the early promotion of Gaelic games in Boston, certainly saw the GAA in this way, as did John F. Finerty, the firebrand Irish nationalist newspaper publisher who played a major role in helping to popularise hurling and football in Chicago and Father Peter Yorke, one of Irish America's leading churchmen and a committed nationalist who did likewise in San Francisco.[30] Beyond these individuals, the founders of America's earliest Gaelic football and hurling clubs also sought to align their activities to the cause of Irish independence and they did this most visibly by following the trend evident in Ireland of naming their clubs after historical and popular nationalist personalities and organisations.[31] Thus, appellations such as Emmetts, Redmonds, Parnells, Wolfe Tones, Young Ireland, Davitts, O'Connells, Emeralds and Shamrocks were adopted by clubs across America.

The place of the GAA in the psyche of Irish nationalists in America at this time was also cemented and broadened with a range of nationalist organisations, of both the physical force and parliamentary kind, who turned to Gaelic games as a way of attracting adherents and promoting their cultural and political agenda. In New York, Boston and Chicago, for example, organisations such as the Irish National League, the Hibernian Rifles, the Advanced Irish

Nationalists and Clan na Gael harnessed the mobilising power of Gaelic games to recruit members, fundraise and encourage the Irish immigrant population to view and express themselves as Irish nationalists. This pattern was repeated on America's Pacific coast where groups such as the Knights of the Red Branch (KRB), the Gaelic League and the Ancient Order of Hibernians (AOH) all ardently got behind Gaelic games and were more than happy to be closely associated with the GAA. The ties between Gaelic games and Irish nationalism were also reinforced among the broader Irish community through evocative, rousing and intensely nationalistic reporting on GAA activities in the Irish-American press. For example, the *Irish Echo's* and *The Gael's* accounts of GAA field days in Boston in the early 1880s routinely described them as 'patriotic', imbued with the 'spirit of freedom' and part of a practical drive for 'Irish emancipation'.[32]

The portrayal of Gaelic games as emblematic of Irish identity and aspirations for independence did much to bolster the strength of the GAA in the late nineteenth century. Those who took up the baton of progressing these sports in America at the outset of the twentieth century were well aware of their significance as important markers of Irish ethnic identity. However, the extent to which they specifically sought to link their activities to overtly politicised expressions of Irish nationalism became largely dependent on the ebb and flow of the nationalist struggle in Ireland. Thus, as hopes for Irish independence grew around the beginning of the 1910s, there was less evidence in the Irish-American press of Gaelic games being used specifically to further the agenda of Irish nationalism. Instead, sporting rivalries and a desire to preserve what was on the whole a benign sense of cultural Irishness replaced more militant expressions of nationalism as the key driving forces behind the GAA's growth in America. By 1913, though, the association between the GAA in America and a more hostile, belligerent Irish nationalism once again began to gather strength. Again, this was rooted in events in Ireland where the slow progress of parliamentary nationalism and agitation for home rule increased support for militant separatism and led to plans for a military rising against the British presence in Ireland. These developments reinvigorated the desire of GAA members in the US to demonstrate their patriotism by backing the Irish nationalist cause in very tangible ways. This was done most specifically through fundraising activities in Boston, Chicago, San Francisco and particularly New York aimed at arming the Irish National Volunteers. The Irish-American press did much to ensure a healthy turnout at fundraising matches, field days and social events organised by the GAA, not least by using evocative, rousing and intensely nationalistic language. One editorial in the New York Irish paper, *The Advocate*, was typical:

> The Gaelic athlete here never forgets his national hon-
> our. Today Ireland is undergoing a trying ordeal.
> Thousands of Irishmen have volunteered to defend
> IRELAND FOR IRELAND, and in this way they must
> be armed. The Irishmen of Greater New York can show
> their appreciation of Ireland's National Volunteers by
> turning out in their thousands at Celtic Park on Labor
> Day … It's an occasion that the Gael should make the
> most of and show the hated Saxon that at least there
> are a few Irishmen in New York who are not willing to
> 'hold Ireland for England'.[33]

In the aftermath of the failed Rising in 1916, the GAA in America continued to promote a virulent, revolutionary Irish nationalism. For example, during the war of independence between 1919 and 1921, fundraising and expressions of support for the IRA were common-place at GAA events. However, from the mid-to late 1920s this trend began to decline, largely as a consequence of broader transforma-tions in the identities of Irish Americans.

For a short while, the partition of Ireland in 1921 into the Northern Ireland state and the Irish Free State and a resultant civil war served to harden the nationalist visage of some US branches of the GAA, particularly in New York, not least because many of those Irish republicans who had fought on the anti-partition side in the civil war sought refuge there following their defeat by pro-treaty forces. However, for the majority, partition had effectively resolved Ireland's relationship with Britain. Many were bemused by the civil war and felt increasingly alienated by some dimensions of post-partition Irish nationalism, particularly its isolationist Gaelic and socialist leanings. While there remained some support for complete reunification, greater levels of social mobility and cultural assimilation into American society led to less of a preoccupation with the affairs of the 'old country' and hence a more general decline in Irish nationalism as an expression of Irish Catholic identity. McCaffrey succinctly and simply summarised this development: 'As the Irish achieved success and respectability in the United States, they became more American and less Irish.'[34] As a corollary to this, sporting and cultural forms that had previously been so closely linked to Irishness and the Irish nationalist cause experienced a decline in adherents, investment and interest. As noted earlier, while the Great Depression, a sharp fall in levels of Irish immigration and the onset of the Second World War were important in this regard, it is feasible that the broader decline in support for Irish nationalism among the American diaspora was crucial in the virtual cessation of organised GAA activity by the 1940s.

The hosting of the All-Ireland football final in New York in 1947, the first and only time that this event has been staged outside the island of Ireland, did much to revive the popularity of Gaelic games in America in the post-war era. While involvement in Gaelic football and hurling in this period continued to allow individuals to mark themselves out as ethnically Irish, there was less of an inclination on the part of the GAA fraternity to link its activities specifically to a political agenda. The onset of the 'troubles' in Northern Ireland in the late 1960s changed this and the GAA once again took on an overtly nationalist visage as immigrants drew on their membership of the association as an affirmation of their nationalist credentials. This trend manifested itself in numerous ways from the onset of the 'troubles' right through to the late 1990s. In the early 1970s, for example, a close association developed between Irish Northern Aid (Noraid) and the GAA, particularly in New York.[35] That such an association developed is hardly surprising, given that the men who were instrumental in setting up Noraid – Michael Flannery, Matthew Higgins, Jack McCarthy and John McGowan – were all influential figures in the Gaelic games fraternity.[36] As the 'troubles' began to unfold in Northern Ireland, these key figures ensured that the GAA and its headquarters at Gaelic Park in the Bronx were at the forefront of Noraid activities. For example, a matter of months after the killing of thirteen civilians by the British army during a peaceful civil rights march in Derry, the New York GAA began sponsoring a series of field days in support of Noraid which ran throughout the year.[37]

Beyond New York, there were other highly visible examples of the close relationship between belligerent irredentism and American-based GAA clubs. Indeed, in some cases a desire to promote an Irish republican agenda was central to the inception of some clubs. There are two notable examples in this regard. The first can be found in the establishment of the Ulster Gaelic Football Club (GFC) in San Francisco. This club was founded in 1986 at a time when the inflow of new Irish immigrants to San Francisco convinced some members of the McDermott's club that there was scope to break away and establish another team. However, the rationale behind this decision extended beyond sporting concerns. The majority of those behind the founding of the club hailed originally from Northern Ireland and were republican in their political outlook, and they strove to ensure that the Ulster GFC reflected their political orientation. This was done through the club's constitution, Article 2 of which states that

> The objectives of the club shall be to preserve and defend democratic principles enshrined in the Declaration of Independence, and the Proclamation of the Irish Republic, declared on Easter Week 1916.[38]

This inherently political stance was further amplified by the fact that of the five key aims of the club, four dealt specifically with its commitment to remembering, celebrating and supporting those who were involved in the movement for a united Ireland and those who had suffered hardship as part of this movement. Indeed, it was only the club's fifth aim that specifically mentioned the promotion of Gaelic games and the culture of the Irish people. The club strove to meet its objectives and satisfy its overtly political agenda in a number of ways. For example, a Political Wing Committee (PWC) was established to oversee and promote its republican underpinnings. The club also closely aligned itself with the activities of Noraid in San Francisco and there was significant cross-membership between both entities.[39] Club members also demonstrated their political orientation by organising remembrance masses for IRA volunteers killed in the conflict in Northern Ireland and perhaps most notably through the annual Easter Brunch, organised to commemorate and celebrate those who took part on the 1916 Easter Rising. In conducting itself in this manner, the club and its members represented perhaps the clearest example in the late 1980s and early 1990s of GAA members not only accommodating a political component within their broader promotion of Irish cultural pastimes, but actually proactively using Gaelic games as a medium through which to promote republicanism in the US. These San Francisco Gaels were not alone in this regard, though, and while the rationale underpinning the establishment of the McAnespie's club 3,000 miles away in Boston was not as overtly political, this club did function as a channel for the expression of similar versions of Irishness.

The McAnespie's GFC was established in 1993 in memory of Aidan McAnespie, a GAA member from Co. Tyrone who was shot dead by a British soldier in February 1988 as he crossed the Irish border on his way to a Gaelic football match. McAnespie's murder was viewed by many within the association as a clear manifestation of what they believed to be an organised and concerted campaign of violence, intimidation and harassment perpetrated by the British crown forces and loyalist paramilitary groups against GAA members in the north of Ireland. The fact that the case of the soldier who had fired the shot did not go to trial due to 'lack of evidence' served to intensify this belief and hardened the attitudes of sections of the GAA towards the British authorities and Ulster loyalism. McAnespie's murder served to solidify the links between the association and Irish nationalism, particularly among hardliners in the north of Ireland.[40] The repercussions of McAnespie's death were also felt in GAA circles across the Atlantic. Driven by a desire to express solidarity with the McAnespie family, a number of individuals involved in Gaelic games in Boston decided that a new club would be a fitting and lasting tribute. Although their motives may have been first and foremost a gesture of sympathy and remembrance, membership of and support for the club also provided Irish Catholics living in the Boston area with a vehicle for expressing a more politicised and belligerent Irish nationalism. This point is made explicit by John Hehir, a Boston GAA stalwart, who commented that 'the formation of the McAnespie's club was about the promotion of Irish nationalism'.[41] The fact that the founders also intended using the profile of the club to 'highlight political injustice in Northern Ireland' (North American County Board, 1998) reinforced the extent to which sections of the Boston GAA could draw on their games to demonstrate their solidarity with the aspirations of northern nationalists in Ireland.[42]

As noted earlier, the intensity and visibility of the GAA's nationalist persona in the US was often determined by events in Ireland, particularly in the North. Recent developments linked to the peace process which culminated in a statement by the Provisional IRA in 2005 that the 'war was over' were key in this regard and reflected a shift towards a commitment to constitutional, non-violent republicanism in Ireland. This trend also manifested itself in the US, where the majority of those with republican sympathies either followed the official line of Sinn Féin and committed themselves to a peaceful, constitutional campaign for a united Ireland or simply allowed the more belligerent elements of their Irishness to slowly subside. The terrorist attacks on 9/11 have also hastened this process in a number of important respects. The security climate that emerged in the aftermath of 9/11, particularly the rigorous enforcement of the visa waiver system and the passing of the Patriot Act, have significantly dented the inclination of Irish immigrants, particularly those in America illegally, to express political views or support organisations that might bring them under the radar of branches of the Immigration and Naturalization Service (INS) and lead to deportation. While some immigrants remain publicly opposed to the peace process in Northern Ireland and are more militant in their agitation for a united Ireland, the vast majority have either softened their position or have become increasingly circumspect about publicly expressing a form of nationalism that might be construed as being supportive of terrorism.

On an ideological level, this trend has been evident within GAA circles and fewer have felt inclined to use the association as a vehicle for exhibiting any leanings towards physical-force republicanism. There have been other, more pragmatic reasons for this, though. The restrictions on immigration imposed in the aftermath of 9/11 have dramatically reduced the numbers of immigrants, and hence fresh playing talent, making the journey across the Atlantic. Thus, many feel that the future of the GAA in the US will be predicated on reaching out to young people, not necessarily of Irish descent, born in America. As a consequence, considerable energies are being invested in youth programmes and competitions aimed at building a sound grassroots for both football and hurling. For those involved in this process, selling the ludic and aesthetic qualities of Gaelic football and hurling to a broader constituency rather than packaging or promoting them as a resource for the expression of Irish national identity, as was the case in the past, is key to the maintenance of a strong GAA in America. This philosophy is particularly marked in San Francisco, as outlined by Éamon Gormley, a former public relations officer of the Western Division board:

> our plan in San Francisco is about how to generate growth ... and how to evangelise and say there's a new game in town, to say what are the benefits for them, not necessarily 'take up this game because it's Irish' ... We need to talk about the inherent qualities of the games, the fact that it's faster, it's higher scoring, it's better to watch, there's more skill and it has the benefits of almost every other sport combined.[43]

Thus, whereas in the past the strength of the GAA in America has been built in part on its close association with Irish nationalism, the future of Gaelic games there might be partially dependent on eschewing the narrow, ethnic version of Irishness previously associated with the GAA.

13 More Than Just Hurling and Football: The GAA and its Other Activities

MIKE CRONIN

A leading supporter of the Gaelic revival in the late nineteenth century noted how Irish popular culture was dominated by the

> inanities of the English concert room and the vulgarities and veiled indecencies of the London music hall. Similarly the most vapid specimens of English and foreign music had displaced our lovely old melodies; and the banjo, concertina and melodeon were heard instead of the old-time harp, bagpipes and fiddle. The old athletic games of hurling, leaping and putting weights, etc. have given way to cricket, tennis, golf, etc.[1]

Such comments about the speed with which English culture was replacing an indigenous Irish one were a common feature of cultural commentary in the last two decades of the nineteenth century. One of the key moments in such a rejection of English culture, and a call to arms to arrest its spread, was made by Douglas Hyde on 25 November 1892, in a lecture before the Irish National Literary Society. Primarily concerned with supporting the Irish language, Hyde was well aware of the widespread consumption of English culture within Ireland. He stated:

> We must set our face sternly against penny dreadfuls, shilling shockers, and still more, the garbage of vulgar English weeklies like *Bow Bells* and the *Police Intelligence* ... On racial lines, then, we shall best develop, following the bent of our own natures; and, in order to do this, we must create a strong feeling against West-Britonism, for it – if we give it the least chance, or show it the smallest quarter – will overwhelm us like a flood, and we shall

find ourselves toiling painfully behind the English at each step following the same fashions, only six months behind the English ones; reading the same books, only months behind them; taking up the same fads, after they have become stale there, following them in our dress, literature, music, games and ideas, only a long time after them and a vast way behind.[2]

The main issue, at the heart of the debate advanced by Hyde and others, was that Ireland could not begin working towards some ideal of political home rule if culturally it had ceased to be Irish. By reading the papers, playing the games and wearing the fashions of England, the Irish were failing to be their own people. Without a cultural conception of what it meant to be Irish (and the historical cultures that underpinned such), then home rule, should it come, would be a meaningless achievement. Unless Irish culture – in all its forms – was preserved and fostered, then any moves to political independence would most likely fail. To become an independent nation, even to aspire to being one, would require all Irish men and women to think hard about how their daily choices in consumerism, reading material, the arts and on the playing-field spoke to their sense of identity. Much has been written about the impact of the cultural revival on literature and drama, and the complexities associated with a movement that was predominantly driven by a coterie of élite Anglo-Irish writers.[3] Another main issue, the place of the Irish language in society, was largely the concern of the Gaelic League, and has been discussed in this book, in the context of the GAA, in the chapter by Brian Ó Conchubhair.[4] What lies at the heart of this chapter is the GAA's embrace of a broad cultural revivalist message that stretched beyond the reinvigoration of hurling and football. The GAA, from its point of origin as the Gaelic Athletic Association for the Preservation and Cultivation of National Pastimes, looked to the creation of a whole body of activity that would preserve, support and encourage Irish culture. It is important to recognise that this mission, despite the common contemporary perception of the GAA being dominated by its two main games, has meant that the association has acted as an umbrella for a wide range of cultural and sporting activities over its lifetime. As such, this chapter will explore those activities that have been supported by, and associated with, the GAA over its 125-year history. These include sports such as athletics, handball and rounders, women's sports such as ladies football and camogie, international variants of the GAA's games and the cultural competition, Scór.

The current rule book of the GAA is highly instructive in understanding the unique place of the association in Irish society, and the breadth of its vision beyond the organisation of its own games. It states:

> Those who play its games, those who organise its activities and those who control its destinies see in the GAA a means of consolidating our Irish identity. The games to them are more than games – they have a national significance – and the promotion of native pastimes becomes a part of the full national ideal, which envisages the speaking of our own language, music and dances. The primary purpose of the GAA is the organisation of native pastimes and the promotion of athletic fitness as a means to create a disciplined, self-reliant, national-minded manhood. The overall result is the expression of a people's preference for native ways as opposed to imported ones.

Such a remit is unique in the world of sport. It places the GAA in a position where it is not simply a sporting body, but rather a conduit for the creation and promotion of a national ideal. The significant issue here is that the GAA was never conceived by Cusack, Davin or any of the other founders or early activists as a straightforward sporting body that would bring hurling and Gaelic football back to life as Irish pastimes. The founders conceived the organisation as one that would underpin parallel efforts elsewhere to create an Irish culture, and neither would it restrict itself to specific sporting activities. The association, from the time of its foundation, had a large-scale agenda which sought to promote a series of different sports (but with associated specific Irish, moral and philosophical values), as well as elements of non-sporting culture which would bring communities together in a common celebration of Irishness. The GAA began life with a macro-approach to the promotion of sport and culture, and in its early years neither hurling nor football were promoted as being the cornerstone of the association or were they the most popular of its activities. While that position has clearly changed, the GAA is still a broad church of activities and its reach stretches far beyond the players and supporters of the two main sports. While often overlooked by the media and in the public mind, the full spectrum of activities that the GAA promotes still serves to promote a national ideal and brings the widest possible cross-section of people into clubs to take part in a range of different events.

As well as hurling and football, the GAA currently hosts two other sports: handball and rounders. Handball, which was a favourite game of Archbishop Croke, had a long history and was listed as one of the banned pastimes for the Irish under the Statutes of Galway in 1527. It was an ideal game for the founders of the GAA to support. The facilities required, namely a wall, were cheap and easily accessed and, apart from the ball itself, no specialised equipment was required. Handball was included in the original GAA charter as one of the sports it would support. There was, however, a tension. Handball, as it had been played up to that time, was a sport that was about, at the élite level at least, money. For example, David Browning of Limerick, reputedly the top player of the 1880s, was defeated in a challenge match by the American-born John Lawlor, who claimed then to have established himself as the world champion. Lawlor was subsequently challenged and beaten by Phil Casey of New York. In a series of matches played between Cork and New York Casey triumphed and took home the prize of $1,000. For the GAA, with its core principle of amateurism, such prize money was anathema to the spirit of the sporting and cultural revival. Despite the problems of professionalism that were associated with handball, the game spread rapidly across the country and alleys became a common architectural feature in towns and villages.

The appeal of the game was obvious. One observer describing the handball alley wrote: 'The setting, too, was simple, with little to distract the eye from "the stage". A sloping hillside where spectators sat, a clay or flagged floor, a front wall with or without side walls or wing walls as they were sometimes called.'[5] Building on the success of the game, listed by the School's Inspectorate in 1910 as the most frequent form of recreation for children, the GAA stamped its authority on handball in 1923. In preparation for Aonach Tailteann, discussed below, the GAA organised a national handball championship as a means of selecting an Irish team, and in 1924 it established the Irish Handball Council. This was followed swiftly, and in line with the standard GAA sporting model of organisation, by the establishment in 1925 of the first All-Ireland championships. The competing Irish Handball Union, which allowed its players to compete for cash prizes, opposed the Irish Handball Council and ran its own events until 1936, when the council came to dominate. Under the auspices of the GAA, handball has functioned as one of the truly international sports of the association, with players being drawn from the United States, Canada, Australia and the United Kingdom.

The fortunes of handball have undoubtedly declined during the twentieth and into the twenty-first centuries. While popular among players, the game has never received a great deal of media coverage – although RTÉ did screen a handball 'top ace' competition during the

1970s and 1980s – and has struggled in comparison to the popularity of hurling and football. One key move in the 1960s was the construction of indoor courts, and the concomitant shift of the game from open spaces, walls and courts into a more controlled setting. Despite the construction of 152 indoor courts between 1973 and 1980, and the establishment of Comhairle Liathróid Láimhe na mBan in 1971, which brought women into handball under a formal structure, many outdoor handball alleys fell into disrepair or were demolished.[6]

The game of rounders was part of the GAA's original mission in 1884, and built on a long-standing tradition of the game which was identified by the folklorist Alice Gomme in 1898.[7] In many ways it is the least known of the GAA's activities, although the game does draw on solid support around the country from both sexes. More closely associated with baseball than the English game of rounders, the GAA version is seen as important to the organisation as it offers it a mass-participation, cross-gender game in a way that neither hurling nor football do. This has been likened to the recent phenomenon of tag rugby, which has been one of the most successful mass-participation leisure sports of recent years.

Organised athletics first came to Ireland in February 1857 when foot races were arranged by the Dublin University Football Club in College Park. Such was the popularity of the event, and an avowedly Anglo-Irish one at that, that it was restaged a month later and eventually the Foot Races Committee evolved into the University Athletic Club in 1872. The 1870s saw a burgeoning interest in athletics across Ireland. Although it began behind university walls, athletics spread quickly, with clubs being formed in all the main towns and cities. The Irish Champion Athletics Club (ICAC) was formed in 1873 and leased grounds beside Lansdowne Road as a home for its contests. In 1877, Michael Cusack joined the ICAC council. A former weight-throwing champion, he had long been a supporter of athletics and was a regular judge for events around the country. Cusack had one major problem with the ICAC; while he believed in athletic contest, he argued that the sport was dominated by a thin strand of Irish life and spoke to the well-to-do and the Anglo-Irish rather than the populace at large. Cusack resigned from the ICAC and cited a whole series of abuses – money prizes, gambling and the control of entry to events along socially exclusive lines – that he believed were corrupting athletics in the country. For Cusack athletics had to be open to all – including artisans and rural and manual workers – and the abuses had to be cleaned up. To his mind athletics should be free of gambling, financial reward, drink and élitism.

It can be argued that it was a desire to promote athletics, rather than Gaelic games, that really drove Cusack to bring together the inaugural meeting of the GAA in 1884. In response to the arrival of the GAA on the sporting scene, various athletics bodies came together the following year to form the rival Irish Amateur Athletics Association (IAAA). Put simply the two were at loggerheads. The IAAA would not accept anyone into its fold who refused to sign up to the rules of the English Amateur Athletics Association, and conversely the GAA banned all athletes who had competed under IAAA rules. While the ban was lifted under pressure from Archbishop Croke, the two organisations could find no common ground. The battle between the two was one of hearts and minds, and driven by the success (or otherwise) of events organised across the country. The pattern became familiar. The IAAA would schedule an event, for example in Tralee in mid-June 1885, and the GAA would set about organising a competing athletics schedule in the locale. With support from local clergy and nationalists the GAA event in Tralee was a success and attracted 10,000 spectators; the IAAA event, on the other hand, was deserted.[8] The growth of athletics as part of the GAA agenda in the 1880s was evidenced by the large number of meetings organised each summer, amounting to upwards of forty athletics events in 1887. It is likely that Cusack's departure and Davin's waning influence did much to dent support for athletics within the GAA, and by the second decade of the GAA's life athletics was becoming a secondary concern.

In the 1890s the GAA concentrated its efforts on football and hurling, at the expense of athletics, which had also been damaged by the effects of the Parnell split and the internal battle for control of the association between the Irish Republican Brotherhood and the Catholic Church. Effectively the GAA and the IAAA agreed to live and let live, and with the GAA's efforts focused on native games the IAAA made significant strides in gathering support across the country. Although the GAA revived its interest in athletics in 1906, in the process denting support for the IAAA, the association remained focused on the success of hurling and football. Indeed, the running of athletics was left in the hands of an Athletics Council within the GAA under the leadership of J.J. Keane.

Athletics had a specific problem that was not shared by hurling and football: it was an international sport. While the GAA may have wished to organise and control athletics in Ireland, the sport was an international concern and as such had come under the control of the International Amateur Athletics Federation (IAAF) in 1913. The IAAF was not concerned with the intricacies of Irish politics, issues of class or any nascent nationalism but it expected a single body with control of athletics in any given country to be that nation's representative. In 1914 the IAAA acknowledged that the IAAF wished to see a single organising body for Britain and Ireland, and it allowed the AAA to take control. Such centralised control created problems for the GAA, which was in competition with the IAAA, but importantly, after independence in 1922, it also created opportunities.

In May 1922, following Irish independence, the GAA agreed to dispense with its involvement in athletics and supported J.J. Keane's creation of the National Athletic and Cycling Association (NACA). The NACA was strengthened at the time of its formation by the decision of the IAAA to dissolve itself and join the NACA. This meant that the Free State had a single organising body for the new nation, and as such was recognised by the IAAF. The result was that in 1924 the Irish Free State took its place on the athletics field at that year's Paris Olympics. That the NACA would become locked into a long-standing argument with the IAAF and Northern sporting bodies over its all-Ireland policy is not a concern here, but suffice to say the split in athletics in the 1930s was long and damaging. Formally resolved in 1967, the division in athletics harmed the sport in Ireland, slowed the provision of facilities and left athletes poorly supported. Given Cusack's original support for athletics and the importance of such meetings in the early years of the GAA, the failure to nurture track and field beyond the first decade of the association's history is one arena in which the original aims of the founders were lost.[9]

At the moment of foundation the GAA was conceived, in common with most Victorian sporting bodies, as an organisation specifically for men. However, the combination of a community-based sport that provided entertainment and which was linked with the prevailing national mood meant that women were attracted to the association as spectators. Inevitably, and in line with developments elsewhere in the world, women wanted their own space in sport. In the early twentieth century certain women, Catholics of middle-class standing, were finding their way into universities, teacher training colleges and the ranks of the civil service in administrative roles. Such women, freed as they were from work on farms or in family homes, had a degree of independence that had never been witnessed before. It was these women who spearheaded the move into the world of Gaelic games.

Initially, such women were more at home in the learned and socially acceptable world of the Gaelic League than among the masculine physicality of the GAA. Indeed, it was from the Dublin-based Keating branch of the Gaelic League that camogie first emerged. In

1903, Màire Ní Chinnéide, Seán O Ceallaigh, Tadgh O'Donoghue and Séamas Ó Braonáin came together and adapted hurling into a game for women; the first practice sessions and games were held in Drumcondra Park and later the Phoenix Park. Slowly, other clubs emerged in Dublin and in Newry, and in 1904 the first public challenge match was played between Keatings and Cúchulainns during the Gaelic League Aeridheacht at the Meath agricultural grounds in Navan. By the end of summer 1904 five teams from Dublin had taken part in a league competition and camogie was established as the women's game.

The game grew steadily in popularity, although not across the whole country, and such was the number of clubs that in April 1911 the national Camógaíocht Association was founded. A sense of the class difference between the men's and women's codes was evidenced by the first president of the association: Eleanor, Dowager Countess of Fingal. The establishment of a national body and the steady awareness, given the suffrage movement of the time, of the rights of women economically and socially meant that the game prospered. The first inter-county game took place in 1912 and the Ashbourne Cup, the inter-varsity competition, was established in 1913.

In the years following the revolution a central council for camogie was established, and by 1932 a special convention brought the All-Ireland championship to life and could, by the presence of over sixty delegates from across the country, talk of the game being truly national. The years after independence were also important for the grass-roots of the game as the new state's education system for girls embraced, where facilities allowed, camogie as the game for young women.

Once established on a national footing camogie existed as the single most important game for women until the advent of ladies football. Full-time officers were appointed for the first time in 1978, and television coverage, particularly on TG4, has cemented the game as one with a solid and popular following. The relationship between the women of camogie and the GAA, like that of ladies football, has always been complex. Camogie is allied to the GAA and has offices in Croke Park, but is not a sport governed by the association. Predominantly the view has been that while the GAA supports the games of women and recognises them as an important part of the cultural and sporting identity of the island, self-management by the women officers of camogie is preferential to being 'taken over' by the GAA.

Given that camogie was an adaptation of hurling, it is perhaps surprising that a women's version of football took so long to emerge. There had been the suggestion of a parish competition for a women's version in 1926 from Tom Garry of Clonreddin, but after a couple of seasons enthusiasm fizzled out. It would take until the 1960s before regular fixtures for a women's game were staged for teams from Galway and Offaly in sevens tournaments, and in June 1968 a women's tournament was organised as part of the Dungarvan Festival. The social make-up of the teams was not as rarified as the pioneers of camogie, but one of the first major challenge matches did speak volumes about the social and economic place of young, active women in the 1960s. The match for the Dungarvan Festival, in aid of the Biafra Relief Fund, was played between teams from the post office and the county council, the very kinds of jobs that single women in their twenties, earning a living but still living at home, would have been doing. Football, like camogie before it, was not a game of the urban working classes but one for a social group that had completed their schooling and worked behind a desk. These were the women who had the free time and the means to take part in sport.

In the first years of the 1970s football teams sprung up across the country and challenge games and mini-tournaments became a common feature of the sporting summer. In 1973 and 1974 several county boards were established to oversee the women's game, and on 18 July 1974, at Hayes's hotel ninety years after the GAA had been founded, the Ladies Gaelic Football Association was established. A sign of progress was immediate as, on 13 October 1974, the first Ladies All-Ireland final took place at Durrow, Co. Laois, between Offaly and Tipperary, the eventual winners.

Ladies football was regularly cited through the 1980s and 1990s as the fastest-growing participation game in Ireland. Support for the game in schools was strong and a developing scheme of university scholarships in the 1990s and into the 2000s did much to keep key players involved while constantly improving their skills and the spectacle of the game. As with camogie, support from TG4 in television coverage and the GAA in terms of opening Croke Park for major games has been vital in spreading the sport to an ever-wider audience and giving it a seal of approval. While it is clear that football has overtaken camogie in terms of player numbers and spectator interest, both games flourish. They reflect the growing importance of sport for women and the delivery of the spirit of Cusack (although he would never have envisaged women athletes) and his Irish games for an Irish people to the non-male half of the population.

One of the realities of Irish life until the mid-1990s was emigration. Although numbers fluctuated over the decades, the routes to the UK, the US, Australia and elsewhere that were so well trodden during the Famine years became familiar to successive generations of the Irish. Paul Darby outlined the links between the GAA and the Irish diaspora in his chapter in this book, and the ongoing promotion of the association's games on foreign fields will be an important issue in an age characterised by global capital, economic migration and the relative ease of air travel. The nineteenth-century Irish emigrant bound for Boston by ship may have been replaced by highly educated graduates working in the financial markets of the Middle or Far East, but the role of the GAA in supporting links with home, providing a common social and sporting outlet and sustaining a sense of Irishness are little changed. One way of promoting the games of the GAA overseas has been the international tour, and in its most modern guise – the Compromise Rules tests against the players of the Australian Football League – the association has found a regular international outlet. Tours by clubs have also been an important part of club culture, both as a means of celebrating the end of the season and linking with emigrants from the home place living overseas. They play an important role in team bonding and socialisation and, at the élite county level, are increasingly used as a means to access warmer climates for training. If the idea of the overseas tour is now so recognisable, how did it come into being, and how has its purpose changed?

The first GAA tour took place only four years after the foundation of the association. Led by Maurice Davin, a team of fifty athletes and hurlers travelled to the United States for a tour of the major cities of the north-eastern seaboard. In line with the sporting diversity of the GAA in its early years, track-and-ield athletes were the most important component of the tour, as they would be competing in challenge events against their American counterparts. The hurlers who travelled were to play purely exhibition games against their own number as a means of showcasing the games of the association. The major aim of the tour was to raise £5,000 so that the ancient Irish Olympiad, Aonach Tailteann, could be brought back to life in 1890. In addition, the journey afforded Davin and the others entry into the Irish-American community so that they could spread the word about events in Ireland and showcase the cultural lead that the GAA was taking at home. In the event the tour was a disaster. It incurred heavy financial loses, seventeen of the fifty tourists chose to stay in the US rather than return home, and it did not ignite an enthusiasm for the GAA in those towns and cities visited. It is doubtful that the GAA has ever attempted anything on the scale of the 1888 'invasion' since, and it is clear that the failures of that tour made many a committee wary of such

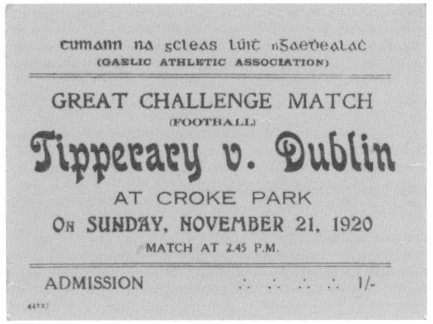

21. A match ticket from Bloody Sunday, 1920.

grandiose undertakings. In the twentieth century a mixed policy of tours and one-off matches became the norm. Most famous was the 1947 All-Ireland final played in New York and broadcast to eager listeners back home. The Cavan–Kerry game at the Polo Grounds, the top-level county game played as the finale of the season in response to a specific invitation from New York, was a one-off experience never to be repeated. While club and county tours to the US have remained popular, and talented players have gone there as individuals during the summer to work and play, it is Australia that has become the key focus for the GAA in terms of élite-level touring and attempts to internationalise the games.

The similarities between Australian Rules football and its Gaelic counterpart have long been noted, and both have existed in relative isolation as they are indigenous games. The main mover in the first joining of the codes was the Australian businessman, Harry Beitzel. In 1967 he organised for a select Australian team to play in Ireland. The arrival of a foreign team to play Gaelic football (only one rule change was introduced in 1967) brought a crowd of 23,000 to Croke Park, who watched on as the Australians heavily defeated the reigning All-Ireland champions, Meath. In response to the success of the games, and stung by their loss, Meath agreed to play in Australia the following year. The tour was a success both on and off the field, and there were high hopes that 1968 marked the beginning of regular interaction between the two codes.[10] Unfortunately this was not the case. Kerry toured Australia in 1970 and again in 1981, but contact became infrequent and the benefits accrued by such matches unclear. In 1982 moves were made to revive contacts, and a committee put in place to draw up an agreed set of compromise rules. In 1984, during the GAA's centenary year, the rules were put to the test when the Australians toured Ireland. While drawing good crowds, the games highlighted problems between the two codes, namely that the professional, and much stronger, Australians were far more physical on the pitch and many commentators condemned what they saw as a violent game. Despite these problems, contacts between the two codes continued through the 1980s and 1990s, being formalised into a four-year contract in 1998 that has subsequently been renewed.[11] It is doubtful that regular contests between the professionals of an Australian game and the amateurs of the GAA was what Cusack envisaged for his games in 1884, yet the international outlet has been important in exposing the association and its players to a range of new approaches to training and fitness, as well as ensuring that the Irish code is viewed in a fresh context by a new audience.

Hurlers, because of the relatively small number of similar codes in the world, have had few international outlets in comparison to football. One of the major outlets for hurlers overseas was the Monaghan Cup, played in London from 1927 until 1975. The first game in 1927 featured Cork and Tipperary playing an exhibition game at Herne Hill in front of 9,000 spectators. The success of the exhibition encouraged Owen Ward, a London-based businessman originally from Monaghan, to present a trophy and make the event an annual occurrence. The Monaghan Cup found a steady audience among the diaspora in England, and in 1958 the decision was taken to move the match to the home of English soccer, the iconic Wembley stadium. Despite an all-time high attendance of 42,000 in 1963 to watch Tipperary and Kilkenny, the competition could not sustain its popularity into the 1970s and was eventually halted in 1975.[12]

The advent of the annual All Stars selections in 1971 afforded a new international outlet for the hurlers. It was decided that those selected would be taken, every December, to play games in North America as a means of bringing the game to the diapsora. In 1972 the first such game took place in San Francisco when the All Stars were beaten by Tipperary. Since then the games have visited every major city in the United States and Canada with a sizeable Irish population and a GAA connection. In 2008 the game returned to San Francisco to mark the opening of a new GAA facility there. The GAA president of the time, Nicky Brennan, summed up the importance of the annual tour: 'The GAA All Stars tour is not just about honouring the stars of the game in any given year but it is also very special for Irish people living in host cities as they can get a real slice of home, which is all the more special coming up to Christmas.'[13]

The only attempt at some kind of compromise game in hurling has been an annual competition against a Scottish shinty team. Similar to hurling in some ways, shinty was a traditional game of the Scottish highlands and islands and was formalised under rules in 1883. Although popular through to the early twentieth century, shinty has been in steady decline, with only forty senior teams now playing. The idea of a compromise hurling/shinty contest first emerged in the 1920s when challenge matches were played between representative sides. The British government disapproved of such contests and after the Second World War pressurised the Camanachd (shinty) Association to end such ties. The series resumed in the 1970s and is now played between a select shinty team representing Scotland and an Irish team chosen from players who have competed in the Christy Ring Cup.[14]

Of all the attempts to showcase and internationalise Gaelic games, Aonach Tailteann (the Irish Olympiad) stands out as a key undertaking in the history of the association. Little remembered today, Aonach Tailteann was a key event in the early years of the Irish Free State and one of the key moments of state formation. An ancient sporting and cultural festival dating back two thousand years, Aonach Tailteann was much admired by leading figures in the cultural revival and an attempt to revive it had been the main impulse of the 1888 American 'invasion' discussed earlier. A leading figure in GAA and Sinn Féin circles, J.J. Walsh, understood well why such luminaries as Cusack and Davin had supported a revival. He saw Aonach Tailteann as a way for Ireland to announce its presence on the world stage as an independent nation and as a means to showcase what was best about Irish culture. Throughout the period of the revolution Walsh advocated strongly for the revival of Aonach Tailteann and was rewarded with a grant of £10,000 to rebuild Croke Park so that it could host the spectacular. In the event Aonach Tailteann was staged in 1924, 1928 and 1932 and each time brought some 10,000 competitors to Dublin. A massive event featuring athletics and GAA contests, music, dancing, art, swimming, motor races and even billiards, the aim was to bring together teams from around the world who professed an Irish heritage. As such, it attracted teams from the UK, the US, Canada, Australia, New Zealand and South Africa. What is significant about the event is that it brought worldwide media attention. The staging of the first revived Aonach Tailteann in 1924 was viewed by the press exactly as Walsh had hoped: here was an independent Ireland no longer at war, but rather a nation that was displaying its sporting, artistic and cultural prowess and welcoming the world to visit the country. For the GAA the event gave them a modernised stadium and a shop window for their games, and most centrally embraced the full ideals of the association: this was not just about sport, but encapsulated so many of the cultural themes that had been identified by Cusack in 1884. It demonstrated that Irish culture, despite the years of British rule and the upheavals of the revolutionary period, was alive and well.[15]

For anyone who is involved with or has been to any event organised by the GAA, it is clear that the single most important unit is the club. It is there that teams of all ages train and play, where the women of camogie and football come to use facilities, where parents involve themselves in coaching and cheering on their children and where the community, whether rural or urban, comes together to find an identity and to express itself. A key reason for the success of the GAA across the island and among the diaspora is that it is not simply a sporting organisation. Whereas soccer can be played by all ages and both sexes, most of the passion is put into supporting and watching the élite-level teams and players of the English Premier League. This is sport at the level of consumption, and while one can visit Old Trafford, tour the stadium and stop by the megastore to buy a replica shirt or a duvet for the child's bed, it is not possible, for the vast majority of people, to be directly involved. We must simply hand over the money at the turnstile or turn on the television, cheer on United and hope that they win. This is true of most élite sporting practices at the start of the twenty-first century: they are there to be consumed. The GAA is different in that its élite players are amateurs and are visible in the local community; the key issue here is the club. Whether a footballer, hurler or camogie player, whether parent or child, the club is open to all; and centrally, given the issues at the heart of this chapter, the cultural remit of the GAA, as established in 1884, means that the club and the association is open further as it is not simply a sporting body.

At the point of origin the founders and supporters of the GAA, and their fellow travellers in a host of cultural organisations such as the Gaelic League, conceived a national identity that was wrapped up in culture. The GAA embraced this idea wholesale and promoted not simply its games but also the language, Irish manufacturing and the national culture. The most significant expression of this non-sporting identity has been the GAA's support of its cultural contest, Scór. While the GAA had always supported Irish culture in terms of dancing, singing and musicianship, this was for the most part informal relationship. Clubs, matches and the excitement about communal get-togethers were infectious and they all served as vehicles for people to express themselves and their culture. In 1969 the decision was made to formalise the links between the GAA and Irish culture with the establishment of Scór, a cultural contest organised on the All-Ireland principle of the association's sporting competitions.

The GAA is only too aware of the significance of Scór, and acknow-ledges that

> With the birth of Scór in 1969 the GAA through its clubs has become actively involved in promoting Irish culture in a meaningful and enjoyable manner. Language and culture are among the most important elements of Irish heritage. The GAA, through its many clubs throughout the country and through Scór na nÓg and Scór Sinsear, has played a significant part in the revival of our culture and heritage in creating an understanding and interest in its importance.[16]

Begining at club level, Scór annually works through a series of county and provincial championships until a national final is held in early summer. Comprising eight different events, – céilí or figure dancing, solo singing, instrumental group, recitation/storytelling, ballad group, question time (a quiz in both Irish and English), novelty act and set dancing – the fortunes of Scór have been mixed. The emergence of Irishness as something fashionable in the Celtic Tiger years however, and the associated success of the language and traditional forms of music and dance at local and national level – as evidenced by the spread of Gaelscoileanna and the international success of Riverdance and traditional musicians such as Sharon Shannon – have led to an upsurge of interest. This has been assisted further by greater amounts of screen time being dedicated to the annual finals by RTÉ.

The GAA was founded at a time when the very idea of an independent Ireland was a contested one. The 1880s was a time of innovation with respect to recapturing an ideal of what it meant to be Irish and how that might manifest itself. The GAA began with a far wider sporting *and* cultural remit than many people would now recognise. In the 125 years of its existence the GAA has managed to support this broad remit, and has developed a series of sporting and cultural events that assist, even into the twenty-first century, the creation of a national ideal. While some facets of the GAA, such as its support for athletics, may have gone by the wayside, and the inclusion of women may surprise its nineteenth-century founders, the fact that the GAA is still a sporting and cultural organisation, one that embraces traditional forms of Irish dance alongside the headline skills of the hurler, that seeks contests against similar sporting codes across the globe and that allows people to access their local club for a plethora of reasons, speaks volumes about the ways in which the original broad-church approach of the founders has been preserved.

14 The GAA as a Force in Irish Society: An Overview

GEARÓID Ó TUATHAIGH

> More than the Gaelic League, more than Arthur
> Griffith's Sinn Féin, more even than the Transport and
> General Workers' Union, and of course far more than
> the movement which created the Abbey Theatre; more
> than any of these the Gaelic Athletic movement aroused
> the interest of large numbers of ordinary people
> throughout Ireland. One of the most successful and orig-
> inal mass-movements of its day, its importance has not
> perhaps even yet been fully recognised ... it has not
> received ... serious ... sustained critical attention.[1]

In the half-century since this verdict, on the GAA's importance as a
force in the Irish social and cultural revival of the later nineteenth
and early twentieth century, was first voiced by Conor Cruise
O'Brien, significant progress has been made in remedying the neglect
of which he then complained. In addition to dedicated histories of
the association (for the production of which the centenary commemoration provided a particular stimulus),[2] a number of specialist scholarly studies have been published on the GAA's complex relationships
with forms of Irish nationalism and identity politics in modern
Ireland.[iii] The large number of club histories published has, understandably, been variable in quality, but the best have addressed
aspects of the social significance of the GAA at local level in ways
that are suggestive and frequently insightful. Detailed, scholarly case
studies of the GAA's history in the context of wider social development at a regional or indeed county or city level are still awaited,
with the notable exception of the Nolan team's fascinating work on
Dublin.[4] Meanwhile, in general histories of modern Ireland, the
social importance of the GAA remains curiously understated.[5] Most
often, it is the zealousness of the GAA's espousal of its 'national role'

22. The first surviving photograph of the central council of the GAA, taken in Dublin 1888.

in essentialist and exclusivist terms that attracts the critical comment of historians.[6]

This continuing under-valuing of the GAA's social influence may well be due to a general neglect until recent years in professional historical scholarship of the role of sport in Irish social and cultural history.[7] But it is strange, nevertheless, that a more substantial body of work has not been published on an organisation that stands second only to the Churches, and perhaps the trade unions, as a force in the associational culture of Ireland for a century and a quarter. This may seem a large claim, but it can be supported.

The GAA has some 2,600 affiliated clubs dispersed across the island of Ireland (over 2,100 in the Republic and over 400 in Northern Ireland), with a further 242 clubs among the Irish diaspora overseas. Its active adult membership was estimated in 2004 at *c*. 300,000, with more than twice that number estimated as membership and active supporters combined. It has a larger membership than any other Irish sporting organisation, and its spread of membership across age groups and social classes is broader than any other sporting body. Over 40 per cent of all sports volunteers in Ireland are GAA volunteers, with a relatively high percentage of active women volunteers, not only in the separate (but GAA-bonded) organisations concerned with camogie and ladies football, but in the core organisation dealing with male sports. The GAA owns and has developed an impressive network of grounds and club facilities, and its national stadium – Croke Park, rebuilt at a cost of some €260 million between 1992 and 2005 – is among the finest in Europe. Over 60 per cent of the total attendance at sports fixtures in Ireland are accounted for by GAA games (and in 2003, the total attendance at its summer inter-county championship series in hurling and football was just under 2 million).[viii]

The main Gaelic games – football and hurling and, increasingly, camogie and ladies football – enjoy extensive media coverage, print and broadcasting, at national and local level. The quality of its leadership and its general level of organisational competence is highly regarded by informed commentators on sports culture internationally. The leading senior players of the main games enjoy high public recognition (and, in certain occupation categories with a prominent public relations dimension, enhanced employment and career prospects), while their GAA background, as players or as high-profile officials, regularly serves as a promising launching pad for a career in politics, at local or national level.[9]

A balanced assessment of the GAA's success as a major force in Irish popular culture in the twentieth century demands some qualification of the impressive litany of accomplishments listed above. From its origins the GAA was a committed nationalist movement, and from an early date its support came almost exclusively from the nationalist community. It was not confessional in intention, but from an early stage became, *de facto*, an organisation with an overwhelmingly Catholic support base. With the emergence of two exclusive and totalising cultural identity moulds – unionist/British versus nationalist/Irish – at the turn of the twentieth century, and their consolidation into 'official' state identities with the establishment of the two states in Ireland in 1920–2, the GAA attracted no support or sympathy – but, rather, suspicion and hostility – from the Protestant unionist majority in Northern Ireland. The residual unionist community in the independent Irish state likewise found the aggressive ethnic nationalism of the GAA unappealing. The GAA's own insistence on claiming exclusive loyalty of its members – prohibiting its members from playing or attending 'foreign games'[10] – also contributed to the alienation of considerable numbers of Catholics and Protestants in the Irish state, who were comfortable in their Irish identity and reconciled, at least, to the new political dispensation, but whose sporting traditions in rugby and soccer they were unwilling to abandon. A more casually benign attitude towards Gaelic games (if not active participation) among these particular elements of Irish society was sacrificed in the interests of fortifying the resolve (and the sense of cultural self-righteousness) of those committed to the concept of 'national revival' in the terms promulgated during the cultural revival of the late nineteenth and early twentieth centuries.

The alienation of sections of the rugby-loyal middle-class Catholic and Protestant public and of the largely working-class loyal soccer followers cannot be ignored, and it was to have lasting consequences. On the debit side, also, must be counted the failure of the GAA to achieve one its most cherished aims, namely the extension of hurling to counties beyond those in which it has been traditionally strong, or to succeed even to the extent of ensuring a progressive increase in the number of counties where the numbers playing hurling and the standards being reached may be said to be improving. But, despite these failings, it must be acknowledged that the GAA did succeed from the early twentieth century in becoming the main popular sporting organisation in the country.

It not only survived the Parnell split in its early days, but was a major force for reconciliation and healing after the Irish Civil War, especially in counties where the fraternal bloodshed of the war had left poisonous wounds in local communities. It survived the disruption of all social life in the South during the 'Emergency'. The ravages of emigration inflicted real damage on the fabric of the GAA, at its basic level of local clubs. In particular, the massive exodus of the 1950s (410,000 in a decade) produced a crisis in many counties, especially in the west of Ireland: clubs found themselves unable to field teams in various grades and, in exceptional cases, were forced to dissolve.[11] The social anaemia in different parts of rural Ireland that resulted from the flight of the young in these years damaged the GAA. To the extent that it shifted the demographic balance decisively (from a rural to an urban society, from the west to the east), it has had lasting consequences for the GAA, as for Irish society as a whole. But the GAA club – its spirit and its members – was also central to later efforts at community renewal and development in the changing world of Ireland as its economy, population and social structure, and cultural landscape, all underwent transformation from the 1960s.

Discussion of the social impact of the GAA frequently revolves on the tendentious question, is the GAA an organisation or a movement? In truth, it is both. It is clearly an organisation – and a highly efficient one – for the running of games, at all levels, combining a cohort of full-time, salaried professional administrators with an army of volunteers, giving their services freely (or with no more than modest expenses) out of commitment to the games and a love of the camaraderie of the social life that involvement in the association brings. But this latter socialising function is also part of what makes the GAA a movement, in the sense that it seeks to embody and cultivate a sense of community loyalty and pride – at parish, county and national level – and deploy that 'community' sentiment in the creation of significant social capital, a network of community facilities and amenities, and a sense of discipline and civic responsibility as something to be valued by players and the wider membership. These virtues are, of course, espoused by most sporting organisations driven by idealistic volunteers: but the density of the GAA's network of clubs throughout the island, at parish or local community level, gives it a particularly influential presence in Irish social life.

The key to the GAA's achievements as a constructive force in Irish social life rests in a combination of the high calibre and constancy of its leadership and a more general capacity within the association for adaptation and change. At the highest level, four chief executives (now styled ard-stiúrthóir) in the period between 1901 and 2007 indicates remarkable continuity and stability. But more than that, the quartet were all gifted (though in different measures) with vision, dedication and formidable organisational and diplomatic skills. At other levels within the organisation the GAA found a leadership that was idealistic, honest, hard-working and utterly dedicated to the aims, and the games, of the association, and that continually demonstrated a capacity to come to terms with major currents of social change within the wider society.

The GAA, after interludes of turbulence in its early years, has functioned as a 'broad church' and force for unity and community cohesion in 'nationalist' Ireland. After its organisational structures became bedded down (notably with the establishment of the provincial councils in 1901), and its focus settled on developing the core games of hurling, football and handball (with athletics going its separate way but finding a more divisive and difficult path of development in twentieth-century Ireland), the GAA never had to endure a major or lasting split. It was never 'captured' for any extended period by any particular faction or tendency within Irish nationalist politics, neither by physical force revolutionaries in the early decades nor by any one political party within the independent Irish state after 1922. Even in the particularly difficult conditions in Northern Ireland during the recent decades of the 'troubles', though it felt the full shock of the communal strife, violence and suffering, and though it inevitably registered the political pressures, tensions and frequently bitter divisions within the nationalist community in Northern Ireland (and it was an institution exclusive to that community), the GAA in Ulster never split. This was so, despite the fact that many clubs in Ulster were badly affected by the hostile actions of both the security forces and loyalist paramilitaries (through loss of grounds, disruption of activities, imprisonment of members, and loss of life).

The emotions aroused by the moral and the political aspects of the use of violence by republicans resulted in strong differences of opinion throughout nationalist Ireland on what should be the basis for a resolution of the northern conflict. At times, GAA leaders in the Ulster Council (and rank-and-file members) felt aggrieved that, as the GAA as an association generally reflected the growing nationalist consensus in the other provinces that a peaceful accommodation of difference was the desired, indeed the only acceptable, solution, and supported constructive dialogue with unionist community leaders and British government, sections of the association in the South showed insufficient understanding of the hostility and danger which members of the GAA clubs in many parts of Northern Ireland had to endure. Yet, no split or secession occurred. And, for all the poison that had infected relations between the GAA and members of the security forces and sections of the loyalist community, when, ultimately, the moves towards dialogue and forms of accommodation (political and cultural) began to gather momentum by the mid-1990s, the GAA was ready and able to contribute constructively to the new dispensation: removing in recent years the ban on RUC participation in Gaelic games (despite the continuing misgivings of many GAA activists in Ulster, who felt it premature) and taking active steps to encourage cross-community trust and respect, through assuring members of the unionist community that they would be welcome at GAA activities.[12]

The ethos and traditions of the GAA – its history, heroes, legends, iconography, names of teams, songs, and the pictures that hang on the clubhouse walls – all firmly place it at the centre of a nationalist story in which the establishment of an independent state, a pride in all distinctive markers of Irish identity (the Irish language, traditional music, the encouraging of native industry, arts, crafts and design etc.) were all integral to a project of 'national revival' that ignited in the late nineteenth century and burned long into the twentieth. There is no question of the GAA's seeking to repudiate that story, or its own part in the narrative. But the rhetoric of ethnic nationalism frequently, and for many decades, sounded an exclusivist, essentialist note that many Irish people – including sportsmen, proud of their Irishness in an instinctive way – found too shrill and severe.[13]

The shift within mainstream Irish nationalist sentiment to versions of a more civic nationalism – acknowledging and seeking to accommodate and respect degrees of cultural pluralism, and not only in respect of the new immigrants of recent decades; respectful of differences in cultural tradition and of complexity in identity formation and affirmation – has been reflected in the GAA's recent policy developments and practices. The staging of international rugby and soccer matches involving Irish teams in Croke Park during the past two years is an immensely important symbolic statement of the new attitudes being shown by the GAA leadership. Immediately, and most obviously, the accommodations of recent years have made the GAA stadium (specifically Croke Park, but perhaps, in time, other stadiums on exceptional occasions) a more hospitable place for those, such as Ulster unionists, with a strong pan-British tradition of cultural (including sporting) affiliation; or for elements of the Protestant and Catholic upper bourgeoisie throughout Ireland, traditionally loyal supporters of rugby union and suspicious of the GAA's exclusivist claims on Irish identity embodiment; or, again, for those elements of the urban working class who are long-time supporters of soccer clubs and who in times past would have found the GAA ethos too intensely nationalist and, for some, too anti-British.

The removal of all 'bans', and the hosting (even on a temporary basis) of the international games of other codes in Croke Park, has been accompanied by other reciprocal courtesies. Competition between codes remains, but the atmosphere has changed irrevocably. It may be difficult to envisage the early prospect of joint approaches by all the main sporting organisations to either central or local government for the provision of common, shared public recreation facilities (indoor and outdoor), as part of a planned civic infrastructure to which all key organisations involved in the associational life of the community can have shared access. The GAA's tradition, and policy, of insisting on its exclusive control of its own dedicated facilities (even where it permits others to use these facilities) has served the association well in developing its impressive infrastructure, and is unlikely to be easily compromised. But the thaw in relations between the GAA and other sporting organisations (they are still competitors, but no longer culturally 'verboten'), and the emphasis on developing the games themselves as attractive spectacles and the club facilities as social amenities for the wider community, has undoubtedly increased the likelihood of a more casual, occasional attachment to GAA activities and facilities in the coming decades from elements in Irish society who never to date had bought into the more committed cultural choice offered by the traditional GAA club and activists.[14]

The GAA has reason to feel aggrieved that, to date, the main consequence of its abolition of the ban on foreign games has been the increased playing of rugby and soccer in secondary schools that were once exclusive GAA strongholds. The traditional strongholds of rugby schools, on the other hand, have not moved in any significant way to afford Gaelic games an enhanced place in their sporting activities. This applies in particular to rugby schools in the Republic. It is perhaps too early to expect Protestant schools of the unionist tradition in Northern Ireland to show a more positive attitude towards Gaelic games, to the extent of actively facilitating their promotion among their pupils; though the participation of the Northern Ireland police force in Gaelic football matches is potentially significant. Much will depend, ultimately, on the attractions of the games themselves, as the more relaxed cross-community relations permits the heavy ideological weight carried for so long by all cultural/sporting activities to lighten.

The GAA's response to socio-economic changes in Irish society in the past fifty years cannot be characterised as simply reactive, improvised or ad hoc. On the contrary, the association was probably the first voluntary body to embrace the new culture of strategic forward planning – based on rigorous analysis of firm, quantitative data, identification of emerging social trends, the setting of targets, accurate assessment of resource needs, and the adoption of actions for achieving strategic objectives – that characterised Irish public policy formulation and implementation in many spheres in the era following the Whitaker–Lemass new departure of the late 1950s. From the 1960s forward, the GAA established commissions, task forces, strategic review groups and dedicated 'delivery' structures of management for all aspects of the association's activities and development objectives. The rededication of the GAA in the 1960s as a community-based organisation, with the local club as the primary unit of the association dedicated to functioning as a vital node of community socialisation and identity, had, as its logic, in the following decades, the strong investment in club premises, pitches and facilities, the remarkable emergence of the club championship as a major national competition (in effect, replacing the inter-provincial competitions as a focus for loyalty and prestige among the association's members), and the development of a suite of cultural and social activities (Scór competitions, clubhouse cultural events – including musical events, lectures, quizzes and other events), to bring a wide spectrum of groups within the orbit of the local club and thereby strengthen its role as a cornerstone of the social life of the community.[15]

The logic of the strategic planning approach was also reflected in major ground development, of which the magnificent new Croke Park project, especially associated with Liam Ó Maolmhichíl's tenure of the post of ard-stiúrthóir, is the jewel in the crown. But ensuring the association's future in a changing socio-economic environment also involved facing up to the consequences of the continuing shift from a rural to an urban society in Ireland, the huge haemorrhage of the 1950s having a devastating effect on the vitality and activities – the very survival – of many GAA clubs in rural Ireland. New clubs had to be founded for new settlements in the expanding arc of Dublin (and, pro rata, in several other Irish cities and large towns) at an accelerating rate from the 1990s.

A common stereotyping of the GAA activists as conservative traditionalists does not sit well with the organisation's early, and confident, embrace of some of the key shifts in Irish social and cultural life in recent decades. As it had already done with radio, the GAA was prompt in engaging with the arrival and growth in cultural influence of television as a mass medium, negotiating and entering into partnership with the new medium in the interest of promoting its own games. It has continued to show a shrewd awareness of the constantly changing landscape of mass media and communications in sport and leisure, and an impressive adroitness in exploiting developments in this area in order to serve its strategic interests.

Again, the challenge of dealing with the growing importance of finance and commercial management expertise at the leadership level of all major sporting bodies in recent decades has not found the GAA wanting. The legendary GAA 'purists' have not inhibited the leaders in any way from engaging fully and confidently with the world of business and finance, in ground development (the Croke Park complex is a remarkable tribute to effective financial management, as much as to outstanding vision), corporate sponsorship, media relations and broadcasting rights, sponsorship of teams, tournaments and events at county and local level, and flexible scheduling (weekday and evening floodlit fixtures). Inevitably, this new climate has presented testing issues for a volunteer-powered, community-centred association: potential conflicts of interest, ethical issues, value-for-money criteria, balancing the instincts and ambitions of the populist rank and file with the need to attract corporate and business (and indeed government) support in acquiring the resources needed for both grounds and games development, for employing coaches as well as for bricks and mortar and the green sward. However visionary or entrepreneurial the leadership, major developments in the GAA always require the endorsement of its democratic base.

It must not be imagined that this impressive record of adaptation to change – political, socio-economic and broadly cultural – was accomplished without difficulty, doubts or debates (at times protracted, reflecting passionately held divergent views on the way forward). But the robustly democratic, and ultimately consensual, instincts of the association enabled it to embrace and manage these successive phases of change and social transformation in Irish society without damaging splits or secessions. Decisions, when democratically reached at congress (by its own, often tortuously complicated, rules and procedures), have been accepted and implemented by the vast majority of the association's members. Indeed, the association, for all its respect (indeed reverence) for tradition and the legacy of the past, has always looked and moved forward, rather than electing to dig itself in at the last ditch, on all the key issues demanding change and new directions in policy or organisational commitment. It is this forward-looking capacity of its leadership to embrace, and respond creatively to, a changing environment – within Irish society itself and in the movements of popular culture of the wider world – since the later nineteenth century that is the most striking factor in explaining the GAA's central role in the associational culture of Irish society in the past 125 years.

If, as has been argued, the success of the GAA as a sporting organisation and movement of popular culture in Ireland owes much to its capacity – at both leadership and rank-and-file level – for continual evolution and adaptation to changing circumstances, then it scarcely needs emphasising that this impressive capacity faces serious new challenges as we approach the end of the first decade of the twenty-first century. Prominent among these challenges we may identify the multiple implications of globalisation (in the patterns of popular leisure culture, including sport); the powerful salience of gender in the changing socio-economic and cultural life of Ireland; professionalism in sport, and its implications for the prospect of the GAA's retaining a credible amateur/volunteer ethos; schools and early socialisation through sport in Ireland; urbanisation; and the shifting versions or terms of debate of 'Irish identity'.

Globalisation, in the context of popular culture (its production and consumption) is a somewhat Protean concept. But in the context of the challenges facing the GAA, globalisation presents itself in a number of specific forms. Irish society is part of a particularly powerful Anglophone world of mass-media communications, where global brands of sporting codes, events, teams and symbols dominate dedicated sports channels and media outlets as well as looming large in the more variegated menu of national or mainstream broadcasters.[16] Whether it be Manchester United, Liverpool, Glasgow Celtic or other clubs, there exists a sizeable, regular, dedicated Irish 'following' for British soccer teams – whether they physically travel regularly to the grounds or attach themselves through supporters clubs and/or attendance at ritualised screenings of soccer games involving 'their' teams.

This phenomenon is not new, of course. English and Scottish soccer teams have recruited promising Irish youths for decades, and have enjoyed a loyal Irish following (generally non-travelling) for as long. But the massively powerful marketing of these cultural 'products' (as events, merchandise, icons), combined with the increased ease of relatively inexpensive travel to games in the UK, has penetrated Irish cultural consumption (both in terms of geography and social class) to an unprecedented degree during the past thirty or so years. Again, sports codes or events with a 'world' competitive dimension – as *par excellence* with soccer and, though its 'world' is rather smaller, with rugby – focus attention and loyalty on the Irish 'national' team. And, with suitably emotional choreography and symbolism (as at major international games involving Irish soccer or rugby teams, not least those staged in recent years in Croke Park), these events clearly constitute important occasions for the affirmation of 'soft' national sentiment and pride.[17] The world competitive context clearly enhances the status of these sports and their attractiveness for ambitious young Irish athletes or the larger army of supporters. And they constitute a widely shared topic of cultural reference for Irish society at large.

The GAA has been facing up to the challenges of the globalisation of popular culture (and the specific context in which Ireland is located) in a variety of ways. Since the early 1980s it has sought to develop an international dimension for its own games and élite players. This has involved compromise and experimentation, and its success to date is difficult to assess. The compromise rules series in football between Ireland and Australia (pointedly styled 'tests') has been something of a curate's egg: generally well attended, hotly contested and exciting, betimes, but on several occasions punctuated by excessive physical aggression and on-field violence, resulting in recriminations, expressions of regret, temporary suspension, public contrition and the inevitable 'new start', with tighter rules and a commitment to stricter enforcement. These tests have excited a good level of interest in Ireland, when well marketed, and the response of the participating GAA players clearly indicates that they are appreciated as a genuine 'international' recognition for Irish players otherwise confined to the domestic honours of club and county.[18] But, while these tests seem likely to continue as an international outlet for an élite cohort of Gaelic footballers, conditional on their remaining genuinely competitive while staying on the right side of physical aggression, their impact is unlikely to be decisive in either attracting or retaining the loyalty of accomplished athletes to Gaelic football or the GAA. This is true, *a fortiori*, of attempts to give hurling–shinty challenge games an international dimension. These are agreeable social occasions for the participants and, for connoisseurs of bat-and-ball skills, no doubt interesting contests, but to date they have not excited the serious interest of players or spectators to any significant degree.

A further international dimension of the GAA's socio-cultural role in Irish life relates to the Irish of the diaspora, and the ways in which the GAA can maintain a useful relationship with the Irish overseas, contribute in a meaningful way to meeting the relevant social needs of these communities, and retain the support of a sufficient number of them to form the critical mass needed for running competitions among themselves and for promoting and organising Gaelic games, in North America, Australia and the UK. Clearly the flow of emigrants will be a key variable (as it has been in the past) in determining the overall size of the pool of potential players, activists and, indeed, supporters available to GAA activities in overseas countries. Seeding the games among Irish immigrant stock – or indeed among others with no Irish connections – even in areas of long-established, heavy Irish settlement (where a social 'infrastructure', including, most likely, GAA clubs, already exists) will present daunting challenges, relating to physical, financial and human resources.

Moreover, given the strong attractions of the main indigenous sports in these countries for immigrants and their children (and the inevitable absorption of the descendants of Irish emigrants into the cultural 'mainstream' in Australia and America, in particular, though also, in more complex ways, in the UK), it is difficult to envisage a hugely expansionist future for Gaelic games among the settled, hyphenated Irish communities in North America, Britain or Australia, even with a steady flow of new young Irish emigrants and a strong marketing and promotion drive by the GAA, to sell the games on the basis of their intrinsic value and attractiveness as team games.[19] The more promising course for the GAA may be to build up a television audience for Gaelic games (largely on dedicated sports channels) in other countries, especially countries with strong Irish immigrant settlement, in order to generate an income and interest that would assist in the promotion of Gaelic games as a niche minority sport in these countries, and in order to ensure a healthy attendance, and promotional spin-off, for special exhibition games by visiting leading Irish GAA teams.[20]

The importance of gender in the overall transformation of Irish society in recent decades can hardly be exaggerated. The presiding concept here has been equality – of opportunity, access and esteem – for performance in all spheres of life in which both sexes can fully participate, including sport and leisure. For most of its history the GAA has been a male-dominated association. Its main games have been for male players, and its officials at all levels of the organisation have been overwhelmingly male.[21] In the folklore of dedication and sacrifice of volunteers, 'who have made this association what it is', women's contributions are often valorised in familiarly stereotypical terms: the quiet work behind the scenes, making the tea, washing and ironing the gear, driving the boys to games, etc. It is worth stressing, however, that women have for many decades accounted for a sizeable portion of the attendance at GAA matches, certainly at inter-county level, and that they constitute a sizeable minority of registered club members. Only in the dedicated, parallel organisations for camogie and, more latterly, ladies football, do women dominate.[22] The camogie and ladies football structures are discreet, and their games, though growing in popularity, do not enjoy the public attention or mass following that the men take for granted. It is likely that the future will see this situation change, perhaps significantly.

Women in the wider society have been advancing, albeit slowly and unevenly, in administrative, management and leadership roles across a broad spectrum of organisations in Irish society. This will happen in the GAA also, as proven managerial, administrative and leadership capacity among women eventually proves irresistible. More urgently, perhaps, the fact that women now enjoy a huge preponderance among the teaching ranks at primary school level makes it likely – and, for the GAA, necessary – that women will be more prominent as coaches and match officials at many under-age levels of Gaelic games in the years ahead than has been the case in the past. Moreover, if the GAA wishes to secure and retain the vital support of independent Irish women, across all aspects of the association's activities, it will have to ensure that the central organisation gives greater recognition and support (not least in the areas of promotion and scheduling of games) to camogie and the impressively developing ladies football competitions than has been given to them to date.

Professionalism and the challenge that it poses to the GAA (and a core element of its ethos – voluntarism) has in recent years become a more pressing and difficult issue for the GAA than the unambiguous official statements of the association's commitment to its amateur ethos would lead one to suspect. There is not available within Ireland the support base – financial or demographic – that would sustain a credible number of fully professional teams (at county or other aggregate level) for any meaningful, competitive, professional 'game' in Gaelic football, to say nothing of the less extensively supported hurling. Moreover, the divergence, were it to emerge, between the financial rewards (however sourced or described) available to a limited cohort of senior élite players and the great army of voluntary rank-and-file players and officials would carry the serious risk of discouraging or souring the efforts of some of the volunteers on whose dedicated efforts the association depends.

Indeed, the growing prominence of 'career managers' (and management teams) during the past three decades – and the persistent rumours of significant expenses packages for such management teams – has already increased the risk of 'giving scandal' to the genuine volunteers of the association and creating a degree of anxiety at the creeping professionalism which they associate with some of these 'compensation' practices of recent years. Of course, the demands of fitness, skills level and dedication that many élite players now make of themselves – and that supporters now expect, as a matter of course, on big championship days – have understandably prompted comparisons between GAA stars and élite athletes in other sports where professional incomes are the norm. The concession of out-of-pocket expenses, insurance cover, sponsored breaks and holidays, personal promotion of products, and other 'rewards' for dedication to the games – a set of welfare and recompense entitlements which have been pressed for in a systematic way by the Gaelic Players Association (GPA) established in recent years – may seem to many to have already edged some senior players in the more successful counties (to say nothing of the star managers) closer to a semi-professional status, at least for the period of their high activity in competitive games.

But the insistence of virtually all senior officers of the association (echoing the majority view of the membership) that 'pay for play' is not on the agenda and will not be permitted by the association demonstrates that the leadership recognises that the fundamental character of the GAA, as a popular, overwhelmingly volunteer-run sporting movement, would be irrevocably altered – its fundamental claims on members' loyalty fatally damaged – by any concession on the issue professionalism, in the sense of 'pay for play'. The demands of the GPA for improved conditions (including sponsorship rewards) for players will, it seems likely, continue to stretch the negotiating and diplomatic skills of the GAA's leadership, and further rewards and concessions to senior players in general (and, through dedicated sponsorship, to GPA members in particular) may be expected. But the GPA is unlikely in the foreseeable future to press for what in any case would not be conceded by the association – the payment of senior, élite players for playing hurling or Gaelic football.

The issues of urbanisation and the relationship between school and early socialisation in and through sport are closely inter-related, and are best considered together as, in effect, issues of social geography and social class. From its origins the GAA was 'mapped', so to speak, in the grid of the parish structures of rural Ireland (units of social mobilisation since the days of O'Connell's mass movements). In essence, the parish remains the basic community unit for the GAA to this day. The situation in the towns and larger cities presented challenges from an early date. This is not to say that the GAA failed to put down roots in urban Ireland: but it faced stiff competition from established middle-class rugby clubs and a firm soccer support base in the urban working class. Throughout the first half of the twentieth century – during which the GAA enjoyed the forward momentum of the nationalist sentiment that generated and permeated the independent Irish state – the GAA was to discover that while Gaelic football and hurling both succeeded (though to varying degrees) in attracting a healthy following among 'townies', both in the larger cities and in the more substantial county towns, the urban world as a whole presented the association with more numerous and more firmly embedded competitor sports, and more complex patterns of socio-spatial differentiation than was to be found in the compact country town or in the tight parochial worlds of rural Ireland. This differentiation was particularly important in Dublin, and as the twentieth century advanced Dublin (the greater metropolitan area) relentlessly increased its demographic weight (and, one might add, its cultural influence through the mass media) relative to the rest of the country. The challenges faced by the GAA in Dublin, analysed so well by Nolan and colleagues, and in urban Ireland generally as its share of the population and cultural weight continued to grow, were to prove enduring.[23]

The challenges that the GAA faces in contemporary urban Ireland – and while they are not new, they are now more pressing than in earlier generations – have to do with issues of space, social class, school loyalties and embedded sporting traditions. And, as always, the quality of organisational leadership, at national and local level, matters. Space matters in a number of ways. Both hurling and Gaelic football are space-expensive sports. Irish urban growth in recent decades – the suburban sprawl and the more recent commuter belt settlements – has not been marked by the kind of integrated environmental planning that would have provided for playing-fields or adequate community sports facilities for new or expanding communities. All sporting bodies have had to contend with these deficits as they seek to organise games and embed themselves in these new communities.

The GAA has been as successful as any organisation, with the exception perhaps of the Catholic Church, in responding and adapting to this more recent pattern of suburban development and growth, with its emergent demographics and social needs.xxiv While the influx of new settlers to dormitory towns in the past twenty or so years (in the ever-widening Dublin 'arc', with a similar if inevitably smaller-scale experience around other large cities) may well offer the prospect of a new lease of life or an enhanced population base (of players, activists and casual supporters) for an existing GAA club, the more problematic major municipal housing estates, either on the edge of relatively small cities, like Limerick or Galway, or at a greater distance from the city centre (as with Dublin and, to a limited degree, Cork) present a difficult challenge to all sports organisations:[25] deep-rooted social problems and various forms of environmental impoverishment compromise the prospects for a vibrant associational culture, even where the school and the local churches are active in generating a progressive community spirit.

The GAA must face these challenges in determining what role it can establish for itself in these communities (alongside other organisations committed to capacity-building). This has been a challenge for the GAA, one might note, since the establishment of large municipal housing estates (inner city or suburban) from the middle decades of the last century. But the size of such estates has grown significantly in recent decades, and the levels of social deprivation and the scale of the problems have also worsened, with little or no commensurate investment, from government authorities at state or local level, in facilities or social infrastructure. Among the voluntary bodies the GAA has tried hard, with limited success, in promoting its games and contributing its organisational resources to generating social capital in these deprived urban communities. However, suitable, easily accessible space for playing-fields and clubhouses with indoor facilities for communities in congested urban settlements will continue to challenge the organisational and other resources of the GAA, in common with other voluntary sports organisations. The disposition of the local schools, and established sporting traditions in these city and suburban settings, will have an important bearing on the prospects for the GAA's becoming a serious social/communal presence in these communities.

In considering the urban challenges for the GAA, space matters in other ways also. Mobility is a case in point: mobility between place of domicile and place of work or education; mobility in the pursuit of cultural and leisure activities. This mobility operates in both rural and urban settings in contemporary Ireland, and it affects the activities and social impact of all institutions of associational culture that are place-centred – in the parish, village, town, urban neighbourhood. The porosity and higher degree of anonymity of the large urban environment exaggerates the challenge of creating that strong sense of local community, as a primary focus of loyalty and a primary site of social belonging and involvement, on which the success of the GAA relies so heavily. This is not to say that 'the credit of the little village' is incapable of translation into an urban setting. But the playing pitch and club, and their embeddedness within the community, remain the key requirements. The highly contingent, and necessarily sporadic, mobilisation of large numbers of supporters for the championship run of a senior county team (the 'Dubs' in particular, but also Cork's 'rebel army') is not without its own significance, as a social phenomenon (of group identity and mobilisation – through colours, symbols, slogans, banners, chants, etc). But one has to look more closely at, for example, organised supporters clubs, as well as the regular community-based members of the GAA clubs, for evidence of the more substantial footprint in the social life of an urban community represented by the club or county team.

Schools, obviously, are a vital force in early socialisation, and this is clearly a key determinant of attachment to or involvement in sporting activities and loyalty to particular codes or organisations. Here, issues of social class and sporting tradition become pressing. The rugby tradition in the largely fee-paying upper-middle-class Irish schools, Catholic and Protestant alike (most of which were also boarding schools until recent years), resulted in Gaelic games being relegated to a very marginal status – or indeed being altogether neglected – in these schools. Over time, parents of other schools, with a similar social class profile (affluent professional and commercial middle-class), who aspire to a school ethos for their boys that is not too strongly inflected with the more recognisably nativist Irish cultural markers, especially strongly embodied in the GAA's cultural mission and in its games, have elected to install rugby as the 'school game', establishing patterns of socialisation that carry on after school into the predominantly bourgeois cultural world of Irish club rugby.

Social aspirations, combined with school tradition and the attractions of a game with a strong international dimension, are factors operating in the world of the rugby schools in all provinces. The situation in Limerick is unusual, because of its more socially diverse rugby community, and recent Munster rugby successes have given a boost to the game's popularity at all levels and throughout every corner of the province (even in traditional hurling and Gaelic football strongholds in the rural districts). The long-term consequences of this popularity for choice of codes by players remains to be seen, but the GAA cannot afford to be indifferent to this rise in rugby's popularity. Among supporters of all games in Munster, however, a more relaxed, not to say promiscuous, attitude is common. Followers of Munster rugby in all counties (and in the larger cities of Cork and Limerick) overlap with staunch supporters of GAA clubs and especially faithful followers of the senior county GAA teams in the various counties.

While the social profile of GAA activists is more varied than it is for any other code, there are, nevertheless, a number of features worth noting. Even a preliminary examination of the occupations of senior officials (including the association's list of elected presidents) and the occupational details provided for senior players involved in All-Ireland finals down through the decades indicates clearly that the officer corps of the GAA has drawn disproportionately on white-collar, middle-rank echelons of the public and private sector: teachers, local government officials, clerical and sales employees of the retail and wholesale commercial sector and, in more recent times, skilled or supervisory personnel in the manufacturing sector; with, traditionally, a sprinkling of medical doctors, engineers and solicitors. Significantly, though the Catholic archbishop of Cashel, as Croke's successor, continues to be patron of the association, and though priests frequently hold largely honorary presidencies of local clubs, no clergyman has held the office of elected president of the association, and clergy holding executive or administrative office in the association have become something of a rarity.

The player base of the association has always been more variegated, but has continued to reflect the changing structure of employment within the Irish economy and society. Thus the share of players drawn from farming or related employment has continued to fall, heavily since the 1960s, while growing employment categories in the manufacturing and, especially, service sectors of the Irish economy since that decade have been reflected in the occupation profile of the players. Significantly, the success of the GAA in establishing a strong presence throughout the rapidly expanding third-level education sector from the 1960s (both within the established universities and, most crucially, in the new institutions – the institutes of technology and the new universities, North and South) has resulted in a strong graduate cohort – across the broad spectrum of academic disciplines, vocations and graduate careers – becoming attached to the GAA, and, for some at least of that graduate cohort, becoming involved in a significant way in the running of the association. This has made available to the association an expanding pool of expertise (on a voluntary basis or through professional consultancy) in areas as diverse as business and finance, health, safety and fitness, legal and insurance liability, engineering and construction issues, as well as in the more directly games-centred aspects of the association's work.

In short, at the beginning of the twenty-first century the GAA finds itself more broadly representative of all sections of Irish society and more highly regarded, for its organisational capacity, progressive leadership and dedication to community development, than in any previous era in its history. It has also substantially shed the rhetoric (and rules and regulations) of ethnic exclusivism which critics regularly emphasised in their explanations of their antipathy towards the association or their inability to participate (or to feel at home) in its activities. A more open attitude towards the complexity of cultural traditions and identities in Ireland, and a move towards engaging with versions of a more inclusive civic nationalism (without abandoning its own special commitment to distinctive forms of Irish cultural expression), together with a commitment to contributing to cross-community tolerance, respect and, in time, shared cultural activities, including cross-community participation in Gaelic games, leaves the GAA well positioned to prosper in the more pluralist Ireland that is emerging. At a time of unprecedented change in virtually every aspect of Irish social and cultural development, no other organisation has been as impressive as the GAA in terms of its capacity to adapt and manage these changes in a manner that strengthens its own influence in Irish society.

Dedicated, visionary, politically astute and administratively able leadership, and a remarkable capacity throughout all levels of the association for adaptation, evolution and constantly devising constructive responses to the complex processes of social, economic and cultural change in Ireland: these are the virtues – in addition to the intrinsic joy, excitement and spectacle of the games themselves – that have ensured the GAA's development as the most successful community-centred voluntary sports organisation in Ireland during the past 125 years. These are also the virtues that will be needed to ensure its continuing relevance as a major force in social life in Ireland in the years ahead.

Notes

CHAPTER 1

1. Liam Ó Caithnia, *Scéal na hIomána* (Dublin, 1980).
2. See, among others, Seamus King, *A History of Hurling* (Dublin, 2005); Art Ó Maolfabhail, *Camán: 2000 Years of Hurling in Ireland* (Dundalk, 1973); Grant Jarvie (ed.), *Sport in the Making of Celtic Cultures* (London, 1999).
3. H.F. Berry, *Statutes and Ordinances and Acts of the Parliament of Ireland: King John to Henry V* (Dublin, 1907), pp.430–69.
4. C.F.C. Hawkes, 'Notes: a sporting or mythological relief-mould from Roman Britain', *Antiquaries Journal* 20 (1940), plate 1.
5. A fifteenth-century Irish grave slab provides the only known pictorial or physical evidence. For a discussion of the graves slab and its inscription, see R.A.S. Macalistér, *Corpus Inscriptionum Insularum Celticarum* (Dublin, 1949), pp.116–17, plate 48. See also W. D. Lamont, *Ancient and Medieval Sculptured Stones of Islay* (Edinburgh 1968), pp. 24–8, where similar stones are discussed.
6. The standard published edition of early Irish legal law runs to six volumes, nearly 2,400 pages of text. D.A. Binchy, *Corpus Iuris Hibernici* (henceforth *CIH*), 6 vols (Dublin, 1978).
7. Cecile O'Rahilly, *Táin Bó Cúailnge, recension I* (Dublin, 1976), ll.415–16, translation p.136. *Táin Bó Cúalnge from the Book of Leinster* (Dublin, 1967), ll.758–60, translation p.158.
8. E.G. Quin et al. (eds), *Dictionary of the Irish Language; based mainly on old and middle Irish material* (henceforth *DIL*), compact edition (Dublin, 1990), sub C, p 64.5–29.
9. O'Rahilly, *Táin*, ll.761–6, translation pp.158–9.
10. Binchy, *CIH*, p 1759.17–18.
11. Binchy, *CIH*, p 1340.10–11.
12. Binchy, *CIH*, p 202.26. See also Fergus Kelly, *Early Irish Farming* (Dublin, 1997), p.383.
13. Kuno Meyer, *The Death Tales of the Ulster Heroes* (Dublin, 1906), pp.4–5. See also R.I. Best, Osborne Bergin et al., *The Book of Leinster, formerly Lebar na Núachongbála*, 6 vols (Dublin, 1954–83), vol. ii, p.458.
14. The National Museum of Ireland, Collins barracks, presented an exhibition of such specimens in 2000. See also Art Ó Maolfabhail, *Camán*, pp.97–8.
15. Binchy, *CIH*, p 280.33–6.
16. Binchy, *CIH*, p 579.7–8.
17. Binchy, *CIH*, pp 280.36–281.14.
18. Nessa Ní Shéaghdha, *Tóruigheacht Dhiarmada agus Ghráinne* (Dublin, 1967), p.13.
19. Binchy, *CIH*, p 241.27.
20. Binchy, *CIH*, p 57.7–14.
21. Ní Shéaghdha, *Tóruigheacht*, p.13. Meyer, *Death Tales*, p.183.
22. Binchy, *CIH*, p 888.10. A similar passage is found at *CIH* 368.33–4.
23. S.H. O'Grady, *Silva Gadelica*, 2 vols (London, 1892), p.240, translation p.272.
24. E.J. Gwynn, *Metrical Dindsenchas*, 5 vols (Dublin, 1903–35), vol. xi, p.151. The term for the seating area is *forad*. It is widely attested as such. See *DIL*, sub F, p 304.25–65.
25. O'Rahilly, *Táin*, l 744, transl p 158.
26. O'Grady, *Silva Gadelica*, p.181, translation p.204.
27. Kuno Meyer, *Cath Finntrága* (Oxford, 1885), vol. i, part 4.
28. O'Rahilly, *Táin*, ll. 832–8, trans. p 160.
29. Alexander MacDonald, 'Shinty; historical and traditional', *Gaelic Society of Inverness*, 30 (1922), p.32. Ó Maolfabhail, *Camán*, p.82.
30. Binchy, *CIH*, p 945.20–40; 1347.32–40.

31. *DIL*, sub C, p. 408.3–25.
32. Binchy, *CIH*, p. 1347.32–4.
33. Meyer, *Cath Finntrága*, p.21.
34. O'Rahilly, *Táin*, l.773, transl p. 159.
35. O'Rahilly, *Táin*, l.833, transl p. 160.
36. O'Grady, *Silva Gadelica*, p.204. O'Grady translates *cluiche* as 'goals', suggesting the tally of a single game reached seven.
37. Ní Shéaghdha, *Tóruigheacht*, p.53.
38. Ibid., p.13.
39. O'Grady, *Silva Gadelica*, p.120, translation p.130.
40. Whitley Stokes, 'The voyage of Mael Dúin', *Revue Celtique*, 9 (1888–9), p.455.
41. Osborne Bergin and R.I. Best, 'Tochmarc Étáine', *Ériu*, 12 (1938), p.142.
42. Alexander van Hamel, *Compert Chon Chulainn and Other Stories* (Dublin, 1933), vol. iii, p.23.
43. Binchy, *CIH*, p 9.19–33.
44. Charles Plummer, *Betháda Náem nÉrenn: Lives of Irish Saints*, 2 vols (Oxford, 1922), vol. i, p.244, trans. ii, p 236.
45. Whitley Stokes, 'The Life of St Féchín of Fore', *Revue Celtique*, 12 (1891), p.349.
46. Sheila Falconer, 'The Irish translation of the Gregory legend', *Celtica*, 4 (1958), pp.77, 88.
47. A. O'Kelleher and Gertrude Schoepperle (eds), *Betha Colaim Chille: Life of Columcille*, compiled by Manus O'Donnell in 1532 (Urbana, 1918), pp.178–9.

CHAPTER 2

1. Paul Healy, *Gaelic Games and the Gaelic Athletic Association* (Cork, 1998); Mary Moran, *Camogie Champions* (Dublin, 1998).
2. Matthew Concanen, *A Match at Football; Or the Irish Champions. A Mock Heroic Poem, in Three Cantos* (London, 1721), p.20. The poem is printed in two further editions: *A Match at Foot-ball: A Poem* (Dublin, 1720); *The Fingallion Exercise or the Soards Match of Football* (Dublin, 1724), and is also included in the author's collection *Poems, Upon Several Occasions* (Dublin, 1722), pp.70–90.
3. Séamus Ó Riain, *Maurice Davin (1842–1927): First President of the GAA* (Dublin, 1994), pp.65–6. Ó Riain notes the existence of the Galway statute, yet maintains that football was introduced to Ireland from England in the seventeenth century.
4. Historical Manuscripts Commission [hereafter HMC], *10th Report*, appendix 5 (1885), p.402.
5. Norbert Elias and Eric Dunning, 'Folk football in medieval and early modern Britain', in Eric Dunning (ed.), *The Sociology of Sport: A Selection of Readings* (London, 1971), pp.126–9.
6. Edward MacLysaght, *Irish Life in the Seventeenth Century: After Cromwell* (Dublin, 1939), p.364.
7. Maighréad Ní Mhurchadha, *Fingal, 1603–60: Contending Neighbours in North Dublin* (Dublin, 2005), pp.164–9.
8. Jack Mahon, *A History of Gaelic Football*, 2nd edition (Dublin, 2001), pp.3–4.
9. James Sambrook, 'Concanen, Matthew (1701–1749)', in *Oxford Dictionary of National Biography* at www.oxforddnb.com/view/article/6053 (14 February 2009); Patrick Fagan, *A Georgian Celebration: Irish Poets of the Eighteenth Century* (Dublin, 1989), pp.67–77.
10. Patrick Fagan, 'A football match at Swords in the early 18th century', *Dublin Historical Record*, lvii (2004), p.223.
11. Concanen, *A Match at Football*, p.3.
12. Ibid., pp.2, 17.
13. Ibid., p.38.
14. *Sleator's Public Gazetteer*, 12 April 1759.
15. *Faulkner's Dublin Journal*, 12 February 1789.
16. *Hibernian Journal*, 20 April 1774.
17. *Universal Advertiser*, 19 March 1754.
18. *Hibernian Journal*, 10 April 1780.
19. Norbert Elias and Eric Dunning, *Quest for Excitement: Sport and Leisure in the Civilising Process* (New York, 1986).

20. Carolyn Conley, 'The agreeable recreation of fighting', *Journal of Social History*, 33, 1 (1999), pp.57–8.
21. Tom Hunt, *Sport and Society in Victorian Ireland: The Case of Westmeath* (Cork, 2007), pp.141–90; idem, 'The early years of Gaelic football and the role of cricket in County Westmeath', in Alan Bairner (ed.), *Sport and the Irish: Histories, Identities, Issues* (Dublin, 2005), pp.22–43.
22. 'The Hurling', in Edward Mandeville, *Miscellaneous Poems* (Waterford, 1798), p.53.
23. Art Ó Maolfabhail, *Camán: Two Thousand Years of Hurling in Ireland* (Dundalk, 1973), pp.1–15; S.J. King, *A History of Hurling*, 2nd edition (Dublin, 2005), pp.1–9; Liam Ó Caithnia, 'Hurling in ancient times', *The Book of Gaelic Games* (Kilkenny, 1984), pp.1–3.
24. William Shaw Mason, *A Statistical Account, or Parochial Survey of Ireland, Drawn from the Communications of the Clergy*, 3 vols (Dublin, 1814–19), vol. iii, p.207; Ibid., vol. i, p.157.
25. HMC, *10th Report*, appendix 5 (1885), p.402.
26. 7 William III, c.17; *The Statutes at Large, Passed in the Parliaments held in Ireland*, 13 vols (Dublin, 1787), vol. iii, p.315.
27. 7 William III, c.9; *The Statutes at Large*, vol. iii, pp.275–7.
28. Mr and Mrs S.C. Hall, *Ireland: Its Scenery, Character, etc*, 3 vols (London, 1841–3), vol. i, p.256.
29. Ó Maolfabhail, *Camán*, pp. 100–1; Liam Ó Caithnia, *Scéal na hIomána* (Dublin, 1980), pp.1–24, 161–289.
30. Shaw Mason, *A Statistical Account*, vol. i, p.157. For evidence of leather-covered balls, see Patrick Kennedy, *The Banks of the Boro: A Chronicle of County Wexford* (Dublin, 1875), p.90.
31. National Folklore Collection (NFC), School Notebook 221 (Delargy Centre for Irish Folklore and the National Folklore Collection, University College Dublin), p. 76.
32. A.T. Lucas, 'Hair hurling balls', *Journal of the Cork Historical and Archaeological Society* (*JCHAS*), lvii (1952), pp.99–104; idem, 'Two recent finds', *JCHAS*, lix (1954), pp.78–81; Etienne Rynne, 'Toghers in Littleton bog, Co. Tipperary', *North Munster Antiquarian Journal*, ix (1962–5), p.143.
33. MacLysaght, *Irish Life in the Seventeenth Century*, p.363. This account is supported by several records in the Irish Folklore Commission.
34. T. Ó Ciardha, *Irish Folklore Commission Manuscripts*, 107, p.58.
35. Kennedy, *Banks of the Boro*, p.90.
36. 'Common' would appear to be the phonetic spelling of *camán*, as is 'com' of *cam*.
37. Shaw Mason, *A Statistical Account*, vol. iii, p.207.
38. Hall, *Ireland: Its Scenery, Character, etc*, vol. i, p.258.
39. MacLysaght, *Irish Life in the Seventeenth Century*, p.364; Lageniensis [John O'Hanlon], 'The legend of Cullenagh', *Dublin University Magazine*, lvii (1861), p.597.
40. Ó Maolfabhail, *Camán*, pp.90–1; Ó Caithnia, *Sceal na hIomána*, pp.248–89.
41. MacLysaght, *Irish Life in the Seventeenth Century*, p.364.
42. William Hamilton Maxwell, *The Field Book: or, Sports and Pastimes of the United Kingdom* (London, 1833), p.288.
43. Kennedy, *Banks of the Boro*, p.91.
44. Hall, *Ireland: Its Scenery, Character, etc*, vol. i, p.258.
45. Kennedy, *Banks of the Boro*, p.90.
46. Liam Ó Caithnia, 'The golden age of hurling', in *The Book of Gaelic Games* (Kilkenny, 1984), pp.85–7; idem, *Scéal na hIomána*, pp.15–24.
47. St J.D. Seymour, 'Loughmoe Castle and its legends', *Journal of the Royal Society of Antiquaries in Ireland*, 39 (1909), p.74.
48. *Cork Evening Post*, 4 September 1769.
49. Richard Holt, *Sport and the British: A Modern History* (Oxford, 1989), p.15.
50. *Cork Journal*, 22 September 1755; *Faulkner's Dublin Journal*, 1 November 1770; *Finn's Leinster Journal*, 16 July 1768, 3 August 1768, 29 July 1769, 27 October 1770; *Freeman's Journal*, 4 October 1768.
51. Kevin Whelan, 'The geography of hurling', *History Ireland*, 1 (1993), p.28.
52. *Finn's Leinster Journal*, 3 September 1768, 2 July 1769, 19 July 1776; *Universal Advertiser*, 27 September 1757; Hall, *Ireland: Its Scenery, Character, etc*, p.258.
53. *Dublin Courant*, 21 May 1748, 4 June 1748.
54. *Faulkner's Dublin Journal*, 4 June 1748.

55. *Dublin Courant*, 20 May 1749.
56. *Finn's Leinster Journal*, 7 September 1768.
57. *Hibernian Journal*, 8 October 1792.
58. Ó Maolfabhail, *Camán*, pp.83–4.
59. Hall, *Ireland: Its Scenery, Character, etc*, vol. i, p.258.
60. *Faulkner's Dublin Journal*, 18 October 1755.
61. *Hibernian Journal*, 22 May 1786.
62. *Finn's Leinster Journal*, 16 July 1768.
63. *Finn's Leinster Journal*, 29 August 1770; *Dublin Evening Post*, 16 October 1792.
64. *Faulkner's Dublin Journal*, 18 October 1768; *Dublin Evening Post*, 12 August 1779. For the move towards Sabbatarianism, see Holt, *Sport and the British*, pp.41–8.
65. Arthur Young, *A Tour in Ireland: with general observations on the present state of that kingdom. Made in the years 1776, 1777 and 1778, and brought down to the end of 1779*, 2 vols (Dublin, 1780), vol. ii, p.107; [Anon], *The New Annual Register, or general repository of history, politics, and literature, for the year 1780. To which is prefixed a short review of the principal transactions of the present reign* (London, 1781), p.63.
66. R.H. Ryland, *The History, Topography and Antiquities of the County and City of Waterford; with an account of the present state of the peasantry of that part of the south of Ireland* (London, 1824), p.399; Hely Dutton, *Statistical Survey of the County of Clare: with observations on the means of improvement* (Dublin, 1808), pp.301–2.
67. William J. Baker, *Playing with God: Religion and Modern Sport* (Harvard, MA, 2007), p.117.
68. Roger Boyle, earl of Orrery to [?], 5 June 1666, in Matthew Kelly (ed.), *Cambrensis Eversus*, 3 vols (Dublin, 1848–52), vol. i, pp.22–3, n.
69. Éamonn Ó Ciardha, *Ireland and the Jacobite Cause, 1685–1766: A Fatal Attachment* (Dublin, 2002), pp. 87–367.
70. 'Deposition of Owen Sweeney', 28 July 1726, National Archives of the United Kingdom, SP 63/388, f. 41.
71. C.I. McGrath, 'The provisions for conversion in the penal laws, 1695–1750', in Michael Browne, C.I. McGrath and T.P. Power (eds), *Converts and Conversion in Ireland, 1650–1850* (Dublin, 2005), pp.37–8.
72. Eileen O'Byrne and Anne Chamney (eds), *The Convert Rolls*, 2nd edition (Dublin, 2005), pp.157, 387.
73. *Freeman's Journal*, 19 September 1769. For more on the Whiteboys see Thomas Bartlett, 'An account of the Whiteboys from the 1790s', *Tipperary Historical Record* (1991), pp.140–7; S.J. Connolly, 'Jacobites, Whiteboys and republicans: varieties of disaffection in eighteenth-century Ireland', *Eighteenth-Century Ireland*, 18 (2003), pp.63–79.
74. *Freeman's Journal*, 25 August 1764.
75. *Freeman's Journal*, 3 January 1831; Patrick O'Donoghue, 'Opposition to tithe payments, 1830–31', *Studia Hibernica*, 6 (1966), p.70.
76. O'Donoghue, 'Opposition to tithe payments', p.95.
77. *Hibernian Journal*, 17 October 1792; Hall, *Ireland: Its Scenery, Character, etc*, vol. i, p.258.
78. Holt, *Sport and the British*, p.45.
79. Whelan, 'Geography of hurling', pp.28–9.
80. 'NFC, School Notebook 221, p.78..
81. Marcus de Búrca, *The GAA: A History*, 2nd edition (Dublin, 1999), pp.10–15; Ó Maolfabhail, *Camán*, pp.48–52; Ó Caithnia, *Scéal na hIomána*, pp.654–77. For the rules of the Dublin Hurling Club (founded in 1882 by Michael Cusack) drawn up in 1883, and the GAA's first set of rules for hurling (drawn up in 1885), see Ó Caithnia, *Scéal na hIomána*, pp.759–60.
82. Ó Riain, *Maurice Davin*, pp.60–6.

CHAPTER 3

1. For an introduction to these changes see Allen Guttmann, *From Ritual to Record: The Nature of Modern Sports* (New York, 1978).
2. Mike Cronin, *Sport and Nationalism in Ireland* (Dublin, 1999) provides a good introduction to a growing specialist literature on the history of the GAA.
3. This famous letter was first published in the *Freeman's Journal*, 24 December 1884.

NOTES

4. Richard Holt, *Sport and the British: A Modern History* (Oxford, 1989), p.85.
5. Thomas Hughes, *Tom Brown's Schooldays*, 6th edition (London, 1885), p.366.
6. Cited in David Alderson, *Mansex Fine: Religion, Manliness and Imperialism in Nineteenth-Century British Culture* (Manchester, 1998), p.55.
7. Holt, *Sport and the British*, p.80.

8. Ibid., p.93.
9. For an excellent history of a national association see David Smith and Gareth Williams, *Fields of Praise: The Official History of the Welsh Rugby Union 1881–1981* (Cardiff, 1980), esp. pp.108–11.
10. Matthew Taylor, *The Association Game: A History of British Football* (London, 2007). Chapter 1 gives the most up-to-date account.
11. Tom Hunt, *Sport in Victorian Ireland* (Cork University Press, 2007), pp. 113–41.
12. Maarten Van Bottenburg, *Global Games* (Chicago, 2001), p.101.
13. Pierre Lanfranchi, Christiane Eisenberg, Tony Mason and Alfred Wahl, *100 Years of Football: The FIFA Centennial Book* (London, 2004), pp.38–41.
14. Ibid.
15. For a general social history of French sport in English see Richard Holt, *Sport and Society in Modern France* (London, 1981).
16. John MacAloon, *This Great Symbol: Pierre de Coubertin and the Origins of the Modern Olympic Games* (Chicago, 1981).
17. Philip Dine, *French Rugby Football: A Cultural History* (Oxford, 2001).
18. Holt, *Sport and Society in Modern France*, p.64.
19. Pierre-Alban Lebecq, *Paschal Grousset et la Ligue Nationale de l'Education Physique* (Paris, 1997), p. 120.
20. Benjamin Rader, *American Sports*, 4th edition (Upper Saddle River, NJ, 1999), p.46.
21. Steven Riess, *Sport in Industrial America* (Wheeling, IL, 1995), p.91.
22. Rader, *American Sports*, p.68.
23. Cited in Peter Graham and Horst Uberhorst (eds), *The Modern Olympics* (Cornwall, NY, n.d.), p.32.
24. For a full account see Bill Mallon and Ian Buchanan, *The Olympic Games of 1908: Results for All Competitions in All Events with Commentary* (London, 2000), appendix III.

CHAPTER 4

1. See, for example, John Bailey and Morgan Dockrell, *St Columba's Cricket: Not Out 150* (Dublin, 1998), *passim*, and Pat Bell, *Long Shies and Slow Twisters: 150 Years of Cricket in Kildare* (Dublin, 1993), pp.38–51.
2. W.P. Hone, *Cricket in Ireland* (Dublin, 1955), pp.21–37.
3. Marcus de Búrca, *Michael Cusack and the GAA* (Dublin, 1989), pp.30–1.
4. *The Shamrock*, 8 July 1882.
5. *The Shamrock*, 2 September 1882 and 9 October 1882.
6. *The Shamrock*, 8 July 1882.
7. De Búrca, *Michael Cusack and the GAA*, pp.36–43.
8. *Sport*, 8 October 1881.
9. R.M. Peter (ed.), *The Irish Football Annual* (1880), p.79.
10. Seán McNamara, *The Man from Carron* (Clare, 2005), p.33.
11. De Búrca, *Michael Cusack and the GAA*, pp.44–5.
12. See, for example, Cusack's article on his coat in *Celtic Times*, 16 April 1887.
13. *The Shamrock*, 8 July 1882.
14. *The Shamrock*, 9 October 1882.
15. *The Shamrock*, 17 February 1883.
16. *The Shamrock*, 24 February 1883.
17. W.F. Mandle, *The Gaelic Athletic Association and Irish Nationalist Politics 1884–1924* (Dublin, 1987), pp.1–3.
18. Minute book of the Dublin Hurling Club, Michael Cusack File, James Hardiman Library, National University of Ireland, Galway.
19. *Irish Weekly Independent and Nation*, 13 December 1902.
20. *Celtic Times*, 2 April 1887.

21. *The Shamrock*, misc. dates, including 17 February 1883.
22. Mandle, *Gaelic Athletic Association*, pp.21–3.
23. *United Ireland*, 19 December 1885.
24. *Celtic Times*, 27 November 1887.
25. *Celtic Times*, 16 July 1887.
26. *Celtic Times*, 2 and 30 April 1887.
27. *Sport*, 13 February 1886.
28. *Celtic Times*, 15 October 1887.
29. *Celtic Times*, 9 July 1887.
30. *Sport*, 6 June 1887.
31. *Celtic Times*, 19 March 1887.
32. Owen McGee, *The IRB* (Dublin, 2005), pp.164–5. Many of these verses and literary works were published later as *Poems and Ballads of Young Ireland* (Dublin, 1888) and included Hyde's 'The marching song of the Gaelic athletes'.
33. *Celtic Times*, 22 October 1887.
34. *Celtic Times*, 13 August 1887.
35. *Celtic Times*, 23 July 1887.
36. See, for example, Mandle, *Gaelic Athletic Association*, pp.1–3.
37. *Celtic Times*, 26 February 1887.
38. *United Irishman*, 4 March 1899.
39. *Celtic Times*, 30 April 1887.
40. *Celtic Times*, 26 November 1887.
41. De Búrca, *Michael Cusack and the GAA*, p.173.
42. John Cusack, undated notes on Cusack family history, Michael Cusack File, James Hardiman Library, National University of Ireland, Galway; McNamara, *The Man from Carron*, pp.72–3; De Búrca, *Michael Cusack and the GAA*, p.173.
43. *Irish Weekly Independent and Nation*, 13 December 1902.

CHAPTER 5

1. T.F. O'Sullivan, *The Story of the GAA* (Dublin, 1916), p. 1.
2. Mike Cronin, 'Fighting for Ireland, playing for England? The nationalist history of the Gaelic Athletic Association and the English influence on Irish sport', *International Journal of the History of Sport*, 15, 3 (1998), pp.36–56.
3. Mike Cronin, *Sport and Nationalism in Ireland: Gaelic Games, Soccer and Irish Identity since 1884* (Dublin, 1999), pp.70–110.
4. W.F. Mandle, *The Gaelic Athletic Association and Irish Nationalist Politics 1884–1924* (Dublin, 1987), p.221.
5. For a fascinating excavation of the details of now defunct Dublin GAA clubs, many from the early years of the association, see William Nolan (ed.), *The Gaelic Athletic Association in Dublin 1884–2000* (Dublin, 2005), pp.1,203–79. See also Mike Cronin, 'Enshrined in blood: The naming of Gaelic Athletic Association grounds and clubs', *The Sports Historian*, 18 (1998), pp.90–104 and Paul Rouse's forthcoming essay on the Fenians and the early GAA in a collection of essays on the Fenians edited by James McConnel and Fearghal McGarry (eds) *The Black Hand of Irish Republicanism* (Dublin, 2009).
6. Marcus de Burca, *The GAA: A History* (Dublin, 1999), p.44.
7. Ibid., pp.52–68.
8. *Irish Independent*, 27 January 1923.
9. Mandle, *Gaelic Athletic Association and Irish Nationalist Politics*, p.156.
10. Witness statement of Seamus Dobbyn, WS 279, Bureau of Military History (BMH), NAI.
11. Cronin, *Sport and Nationalism in Ireland*, pp.94–7.
12. Mary E. Daly, 'Less a commemoration of the actual achievements and more a commemoration of the hopes of the men of 1916', in Mary E. Daly and Margaret O'Callaghan (eds), *1916 in 1966: Commemorating the Easter Rising* (Dublin, 2007), p.50.
13. *Programme of the All-Ireland Hurling Finals*, 4 September 1966. Thanks to Carole Holohan for this reference.
14. Fearghal McGarry, *Eoin O'Duffy: A Self-Made Hero* (Oxford, 2005), p.14.
15. Peter Hart, *Mick: The Real Michael Collins* (London, 2005), pp.29–30.
16. R.V. Comerford, 'Patriotism as pastime: The appeal of Fenianism in the mid–1860s', *Irish Historical Studies*, 22 (1980–1), pp.243–4.

17. Robert Brennan, *Allegiance* (Dublin, 1950), p.34.
18. Paul Rouse, 'The politics of culture and sport in Ireland: A history of the GAA ban on foreign games 1884–1971. Part One: 1884–1921', *International Journal of the History of Sport*, 10 (1993), p.358; Mandle, *Gaelic Athletic Association and Irish Nationalist Politics*, pp.185–8; Nolan (ed.), *Gaelic Athletic Association in Dublin*, pp.147–8.
19. Michael Wheatley, *Nationalism and the Irish Party: Provincial Ireland 1910–1916* (Oxford, 2005), p.67.
20. David Fitzpatrick, *Politics and Irish Life, 1913–1921: Provincial Experience of War and Revolution* (Cork, 1977), p.112.
21. Mandle, *Gaelic Athletic Association and Irish Nationalist Politics*, pp.166–7.
22. Con Short, *Ulster Story* (Dundalk, 1984), p.61; J. Anthony Gaughan, *Austin Stack* (Tralee, 1977), p.30.
23. Short, *Ulster Story*, p.61.
24. De Burca, *The GAA*, p.97.
25. Seán O'Sullivan, 'The GAA and Irish Nationalism 1913–1923' (MA thesis, UCD, 1994), p.22.
26. Liam Deasy, *Towards Ireland Free* (Dublin, 1973), p.3.
27. Witness statement of Gerald Doyle, WS 1511, BMH, NAI.
28. For Ginger O'Connell's comments see Paul Rouse, 'Sport and the Politics of Culture: A History of the GAA Ban 1884–1971' (MA thesis, UCD, 1991), p.31, and for FitzGerald's see Desmond FitzGerald, *Memoirs of Desmond FitzGerald 1913–1916* (London, 1968), p.89.
29. Fitzpatrick, *Politics and Irish Life*, p.86.
30. Jim Cronin, *Munster GAA Story* (Ennis, 1984), pp.102–3.
31. O'Sullivan, *GAA and Irish Nationalism*, p.27.
32. *Southern Star*, 11 September 1915.
33. Peter Hart, *The IRA and its Enemies: Violence and Community in Cork 1916–1923* (Oxford, 1998), p.212.
34. Mandle, *Gaelic Athletic Association and Irish Nationalist Politics*, p.172.
35. Nolan (ed.), *Gaelic Athletic Association in Dublin*, pp.149–61.
36. Ibid., pp.149–61 and p.126.
37. De Burca, *The GAA*, pp.102–3.
38. David Fitzpatrick, *Harry Boland's Irish Revolution* (Cork, 2003), p.70.
39. Fitzpatrick, *Politics and Irish Life*, p.130.
40. Cronin, *Munster GAA Story*, p.107.
41. Fitzpatrick, *Politics and Irish Life*, p.130.
42. Michael Laffan, *The Resurrection of Ireland: The Sinn Féin Party 1916–1923* (Cambridge, 1999), p.193.
43. Peter Hart, 'The geography of revolution', in Peter Hart (ed.), *The IRA at War 1916–1923* (Oxford, 2003), p.55.
44. Laffan, *Resurrection of Ireland*, p.285.
45. Tim Carey, *Croke Park* (Cork, 2004), pp.43–4.
46. Joost Augusteijn, *From Public Defiance to Guerrilla Warfare: The Experience of Ordinary Volunteers in the Irish War of Independence 1916–1921* (Dublin, 1996), p.42.
47. Hart, *IRA and its Enemies*, p.206.
48. Ibid., pp.210–12.
49. McGarry, *Eoin O'Duffy*, p.28; Witness statement of Francis Tummon, WS 820, BMH, NAI.
50. Robert Lynch, *The Northern IRA and the Early Years of Partition 1920–1922* (Dublin, 2006), pp.15–16.
51. Marie Coleman, *County Longford and the Irish Revolution, 1910–1923* (Dublin, 2003), p.177.
52. *Clare Champion*, 22 February 1919.
53. Précis of information received in crime special branch during June 1915 in CO 904/97 in Colonial Office Papers (CO), The National Archive.
54. See Mandle, *Gaelic Athletic Association and Irish Nationalist Politics*, pp.180–1; Minutes of the Committee of the INA&VDF, MS 23,468–9, NLI and Correspondence of the INA&VDF, MS 23,464–6, National Library of Ireland.
55. Cronin, *Munster GAA Story*, p.117.
56. Chapter 5 of *Leabhar an Champa* in P 53/117 in Michael Hayes papers, UCDA.
57. C.S. Andrews, *Dublin Made Me* (Dublin, 2001), pp.190–1.
58. Witness statement of Seán Gaynor, WS 1389, BMH, NAI.
59. C.A. Munro to Max S. Green, 3 March 1921, The MacDermot to C.A. Munro, 4 March

1921, and minute by C.A. Munro, 6 March 1921, in General Prison Board 1921/1857 in GPB, NAI.

60. Frank Fahy to Piaras Béaslaí, 28 August 1918, in MS 37,917 (8) in Piaras Béaslaí papers, NLI.

61. *The Insect, No.1*, 1 September 1918, in MS 24,458 in Seán O'Mahony papers, NLI.

62. Peadar Ó hAmracháin to Henry Dixon, 12 August 1918, in MS 35,262/1 (30) in Henry Dixon papers, NLI.

63. Peadar O'Donnell, *The Gates Flew Open* (London, 1932), p.63.

64. Mandle, *Gaelic Athletic Association and Irish Nationalist Politics*, pp.183–5.

65. O'Sullivan, *GAA and Irish Nationalism*, p.43; Eoghan Corry, *Kildare GAA: A Centenary History* (Newbridge, 1984), p.114.

66. Mandle, *Gaelic Athletic Association and Irish Nationalist Politics*, pp.183–5.

67. McGarry, *Eoin O'Duffy*, p.126.

68. Corry, *Kildare GAA*, pp.114–15.

69. Mandle, *Gaelic Athletic Association and Irish Nationalist Politics*, pp.173–4; Nolan (ed.), *Gaelic Athletic Association in Dublin*, pp.99–100. For a fascinating biographical sketch of Tom Kenny which emphasises the importance of the GAA in his rise to prominence, see Fergus Campbell, *Land and Revolution: Nationalist Politics in the West of Ireland 1891–1921* (Oxford, 2005), pp.172–6. See also Úna Newall, 'The Rising of the Moon: Galway 1916,' Journal of the Galway Archaeological and History Society, 58 (2006), pp. 114–55.

70. Nolan (ed.), *Gaelic Athletic Association in Dublin*, pp.171–83; J. Gleeson, *Bloody Sunday* (1962); T. Bowden, 'Bloody Sunday – a reappraisal', *European Studies Review*, 2 (1972), pp.25–42; Miceál Ó Meára, *Bloody Sunday, 1920–1995* (Grangemockler, 1995). For a recent vivid and original account of the morning's events, see Anne Dolan, 'Killing and Bloody Sunday, November 1920', *Historical Journal*, 49 (2006), pp.789–910.

71. Witness statement of John F. Shouldice, WS 679, BMH, NAI.

72. Cronin, *Munster GAA Story*, p.120.

73. Nolan (ed.), *Gaelic Athletic Association in Dublin*, p.1,165.

74. Tom Ryall, *Kilkenny: The GAA Story 1884–1984* (Kilkenny, 1984), pp.347–50.

75. Ó Meára, *Bloody Sunday 1920–1995*, p.7.

76. Canon Philip Fogarty, *Tipperary's GAA Story* (Thurles, 1960), pp.368–9.

77. *Irish Independent*, 6 December 1922; *Freeman's Journal*, 27 March 1923.

78. *Irish Press, GAA Golden Jubilee Supplement*, 1934, p.3.

79. J.J. Barrett, *In the Name of the Game* (Bray, 1997).

80. Mandle, *Gaelic Athletic Association and Irish Nationalist Politics*, pp.207–8; Bill Kissane, *The Politics of the Civil War* (Oxford, 2005), p.146; *Freeman's Journal*, 8 January 1923.

81. Mandle, *Gaelic Athletic Association and Irish Nationalist Politics*, pp.208–9; Kissane, *The Politics of the Civil War*, p.136.

82. Breandán Ó hEithir, *Over the Bar: A Personal Relationship with the GAA* (Dublin, 1984), pp.32–3.

83. O'Neill, *Twenty Years of the GAA, 1910–1930* (Kilkenny, 1931), p.225.

84. *Freeman's Journal*, 5 June 1922.

85. McGarry, *Eoin O'Duffy*, p.126.

86. Mike Cronin, 'The Irish Free State and Aonach Tailteann', in Alan Bairner (ed.), *Sport and the Irish: History, Identities, Issues* (Dublin, 2005), pp.53–68.

87. *Irish Press, GAA Golden Jublilee Supplement*, 1934, p.3 and p.89.

CHAPTER 6

1. Dan Gallogly, *Cavan's Football Story* (Cavan, 1979); A. Ó Maolfabhail, *Camán* (Dublin, 1973); Liam Ó Caithnia, *Scéal na hIomána* (Dublin, 1979); Marcus de Burca, *The GAA: A History* (Dublin, 1980); S. Ó Ceallaigh, *Story of the GAA* (Dublin, 1978).

2. De Burca, *The GAA: A History*.

3. Ibid.

4. T.F. O'Sullivan, *The Story of the GAA* (Dublin, 1916).

5. J.J. McElholm, 'Fermanagh in at the foundation', *Fermanagh Centenary Yearbook* (Enniskillen, 1984), pp.65–9.

6. C. Short, *The Ulster GAA Story* (Monaghan, 1984).

7. Ibid.

8. W.F. Mandle, *Gaelic Athletic Association and Irish Nationalist Politics, 1884–1924* (Dublin, 1987).

NOTES

9. De Burca, *GAA*; P. Puirséal, *The GAA in its Time* (Dublin, 1982).

10. Short, *Ulster GAA Story*.

11. Ibid.

12. Marcus Bourke, 'The Early GAA in South Ulster', in *Clogher Record* (Clogher, 1969), pp.5–25.

13. Ibid.

14. M. McCaughey, *West Tyrone Board of the GAA 1931–1974* (Omagh, 1998).The Cardinal Ó Fiaich Memorial Library and Archive, Armagh City holds a comprehensive collection of Ulster Council Minutes.

15. Ibid.

16. Minutes of Ulster Council, 17 March 1917–8 October 1927.

17. McCaughey, *West Tyrone Board of the GAA*.

18. Robert Lynch, *The Northern IRA and the Early Years of Partition, 1920–1922* (Dublin, 2006), pp. 99–100.

19. Minutes of Ulster Council, 17 April 1920.

20. Short, *The Ulster GAA Story*, p.80.

21. A. Smith, 'Television coverage of Northern Ireland', *Index on Censorship*, 1:2, 15–32, p.18.

22. T. Ó hAnnracháin, 'The heroic importance of sport: The GAA in the 1930s', *International Journal of the History of Sport*, 25, 10 (September 2008), pp.1, 326–37, at pp.1,326.

23. Mike Cronin, *Sport and Nationalism in Ireland: Gaelic Games, Soccer and Irish Identity since 1884* (Dublin, 1999).

24. Minutes of GAA Annual Congress, 5 April 1931.

25. McElholm, 'Fermanagh in at the foundation'.

26. P.J. Devlin, *Our Native Games* (Dublin, 1916).

27. M. Cronin, 'Fighting for Ireland, playing for England? The nationalist history of the Gaelic Athletic Association and the English influence on Irish sport', *International Journal of the History of Sport*, 15, 3 (1998), pp.36–56.

28. Bourke, 'Early GAA in south Ulster'.

29. Cronin, 'Fighting for Ireland, playing for England?'

30. Ibid., p.42.

31. Minutes of Ulster Council's Annual Convention, 4 March 1961.

32. Ó Maolfabhail, *Camán*.

33. Quoted in the *Irish Times*, 23 April 1973.

34. D. Fahy, *How the GAA Survived the Troubles* (Dublin, 2001).

35. Minutes of GAA Annual Congress, 24 March 1979, p.14.

36. Minutes of GAA Annual Congress, 28 March 1981 (Motions 11 and 12).

37. J. Sugden and A. Bairner, *Sport, Sectarianism and Society in a Divided Ireland* (Leicester, 1993).

CHAPTER 7

1. Ciara Breathnach (ed.), *Framing the West: Images of Rural Ireland 1891–1920* (Dublin, 2007), foreword by Cormac Ó Gráda.

2. GAA books that have made the most informative use of photographs include: Eoghan Corry, *An Illustrated History of the GAA* (Dublin, 2005) and Tim Carey, *Croke Park: A History* (Cork, 2004).

3. See Charles MacKenzie, 'A Hurling Match' (Graphic) 1805, in National Library of Ireland, PD 4199 TX 1.

4. Mr and Mrs S.C. Hall, *Ireland: Its Scenery, Character, etc*, 3 vols (London, 1841–3), vol. i, p.256.

5. National Gallery of Ireland, *A Time and a Place: Two Centuries of Irish Social Life* (Dublin, 2006), pp.49–50.

6. Susan Sontag, *On Photography* (New York, 1977), p.4.

7. Edward Chandler, *Photography in Nineteenth-Century Ireland* (Dublin, 2001), p.44.

8. Seán Sexton, *Ireland: Photographs 1840–1930* (Boston, 1994), p.13; Chandler, *Photography in Nineteenth-Century Ireland*, p.41.

9. Terence Dooley, *The Decline of the Big House in Ireland* (Dublin, 2001), p.32; Edward Chandler, *Photography in Dublin during the Victorian Era* (Carlow, 1984), p.38.

10. National Photographic Archive, Clon 435.

11. *Celtic Times*, 13 March 1887.

12. Ibid.
13. See, for example, National Photographic Archive, Clon 23; 1548; 1787; 85.
14. National Library of Ireland, *Ex Camera 1860–1960: Photographs from the Collections of the National Library of Ireland* (Dublin, 1990), p.viii.
15. Golf was particularly suited to the Lawrence style as it enabled the photographer to frame the play with impressive sweeps of coastline or countryside. See, for example, Lawrence photographs of Greystones golf links, LROY 6591; or Portrush Golf Hotel, LROY 975.
16. Robert Pols, *Understanding Old Photographs* (Oxford, 1995), p.69; and *Sportscape: The Evolution of Sports Photography* (London, 2000).
17. This was the final of the 1887 hurling championship.Only five counties contested the competition and yet the final was delayed until 1888 as the fledging association succumbed to internal division and political turmoil. On the day of the final, not only were no photographs taken, no medals were presented either. In fact, the matter of providing medals for championship winners was only discussed by the GAA central executive at a meeting three weeks after the final. See Paul Rouse, 'Original red-leather day for Thurles: The 120th anniversary of the first All-Ireland hurling final', *Irish Times*, 2 April 2008.
18. Dineen did not discriminate between athletic events organised by the GAA and those held under the rules of rival athletic bodies. All were included in the *Irish Athletic Record*.
19. *The Gaelic Athletic Annual and County Directory*, no. 1 (1907–8), preface.
20. Ibid.
21. *The Gaelic Athletic Annual and County Directory*, no. 3 (1910–11), p.63.
22. Such was the confusion that had surrounded the identity of those who actually played on the Thurles team of 1 April 1888 that the captain on the day, Jim Stapleton, approaching the end of his life, felt compelled to set the record straight. The names of the players as listed by Stapleton appear in Seán Kilfeather (ed.), *P.D. Mehigan: Vintage Carbery* (Dublin, 1984), p.59.
23. The story of the first All-Ireland final was told by Paul Rouse in a lecture to the Sports History Ireland Conference, NUI Maynooth, 1 February 2006.
24. *Gaelic Athlete*, 18 May 1912.
25. Ibid.
26. Rouse, *Irish Times*, 2 April 2008.
27. See Frank Burke, *All-Ireland Glory: A Pictorial History of the Senior Hurling Championship 1887–2004* (Dublin, 2004), pp.63 and 66.
28. Padraic Ó Laoi, *Annals of the GAA in Galway 1884–1901*, vol. 1 (Galway, 1984), p.16.
29. Letter from Archbishop Croke to Michael Cusack, 18 December 1884, published in *The Nation*, 27 December 1884.
30. *Celtic Times*, 4 June 1887.
31. One of the first teams to carry a signature name on their chest was that which travelled on the so-called Invasion tour of the United States in 1888. The letters woven across their jerseys read simply: GAA. See Seamus Ó Riain, *Maurice Davin: First President of the GAA* (Dublin, 1994), pp.120–1.
32. See, for example, Burke, *All-Ireland Glory*.
33. *Gaelic Athlete*, 24 February 1912.
34. Ibid.
35. Tom Ryall, *Kilkenny: The GAA Story 1884–1984* (Kilkenny, 1984), p.28.
36. Ibid., pp.31–6.
37. *Gaelic Athlete*, 18 May 1912.
38. Ibid., 4 May 1912.
39. Ibid. In redrawing the GAA map, the *Gaelic Athlete* argued that the guiding principle should be to ensure that districts would be organised into 'counties with which they are in most direct communication'. Other changes recommended in the editorial included the division of a large territory like Cork into three or four counties, and Kerry, Tipperary, Galway, Mayo and Donegal into two each.
40. The role of the GAA in shaping county identity is discussed in John A. Murphy, 'Cork: Anatomy and essence', in Patrick O'Flanagan and Cornelius G. Buttimer (eds), *Cork: History and Society* (Dublin, 1993), pp.4–5. A similar point in relation to Offaly is dealt with in Paul Rouse, 'The Offaly Tradition: The Gaelic Athletic Association', in William Nolan and Timothy P. O'Neill (eds), *Offaly: History and Society* (Dublin, 1998), pp.889–929.
41. Richard Holt, 'The amateur body and the middle-class man: work, health and style in Victorian Britain', *Sport in History*, 26, 3 (December 2006), pp.352–69.
42. Examples include Dick Fitzgerald in Dick Fitzgerald, *How to Play Gaelic Football* (Tralee,

1914), frontispiece; Willie Hough, Limerick hurling captain, in Burke, *All-Ireland Glory*; Maurice Davin is photographed in a suit adorned by sporting medals in Ó Riain, *Maurice Davin, 1842–1927*, frontispiece.

43. Alison M. Wrynn, 'Strike a pose! Photographic representation and the construction of gender in athletic team photos, 1870–1930, *North American Society For Sport History: Proceedings and Newsletter* (1998), pp.52–3.
44. *Gaelic Annual, 1907–08*. Cited in John Sugden and Alan Bairner, *Sport, Sectarianism and Society in a Divided Ireland* (Leicester, 1993), p.29.
45. *The Gaelic Athletic Annual and County Directory, 1907–08*, p.17.
46. Comparison photographs of early rugby teams and players can be found in Edmund Van Esbeck, *One Hundred Years of Irish Rugby: The Official History of the Irish Rugby Football Union* (Dublin, 1974); a selection of early soccer team photographs can be viewed in Joe Dodd, *Leinster Senior League: 100 Years, A History* (Dublin, 1997).
47. For a more detailed account of sport and the popular press in the 1880s, see Paul Rouse, 'Sport and Ireland in 1881', in Alan Bairner (ed.), *Sport and the Irish: Histories, Identities and Issues* (Dublin, 2005), pp.7–22.
48. The *Irish Sportsman and Farmer* was first published in 1870 and ran until 1892; *Sport* appeared in December 1880 and ran until 1931.
49. Marcus de Burca, 'Michael Cusack and the Celtic Times', in *The Celtic Times: Michael Cusack's Gaelic Games Newspaper* (Clare, 2003), introduction.
50. Marcus De Burca, *The GAA: A History* (Dublin, 1980), p.34.
51. *Gaelic News*, 1, 1 (July 1897).
52. Ibid.
53. Ibid.
54. Ibid.
55. De Burca, *The GAA*, p.76.
56. Chandler, *Photography in Nineteenth Century Ireland* (Dublin, 2001), p.89.
57. *Irish Independent*, 19 January 1907; 25 January 1908; 22 February 1908; 2 January 1909; 9 January 1909.
58. Hugh Oram, *The Newspaper Book: A History of Newspapers in Ireland, 1649–1983* (Dublin, 1983), pp.100 and 106.
59. For examples of early action photographs, see Corry, *Illustrated History of the GAA*, pp.48 and 53.
60. *Gaelic Athlete*, 29 June 1912.
61. See, for example, *Freeman's Journal*, 4 November 1912; *Dublin Evening Telegraph*, 4 November 1912; *Irish Independent*, 18 November 1912; *Freeman's Journal*, 16 November 1912.
62. *Cork Examiner*, 18 November 1912.
63. *Cork Examiner*, 19 November 1912. Complaints about spectator accommodation were also carried in the *Dublin Evening Telegraph* on 18 November 1912. One letter writer to that paper remarked on how the only time they saw the ball was when it was played high in the air. He added: 'The GAA have a good following now, and if they wish to retain it, they must provide accommodation. People who pay 6d. or 1s. for admission want to see something for it.'
64. For a brilliant account of the role of illustrative material in shaping the popular experience of sport, see Michael Oriard, *Reading Football: How the Popular Press Created an American Spectacle* (North Carolina, 1993).
65. Fitzgerald, *How to Play Gaelic Football*.
66. It wasn't only the essential skills of the game that photographs were used to illustrate. One photograph was captioned 'A Piece of Foul Play i.e. "Covering the Ball"'. Fitzgerald, *How to Play Gaelic Football*, p.52.
67. See, for example, *Gaelic Athlete* 5 December 1914; 1 December 1916. The newspaper provided a minute-by-minute account of the All-Ireland football final replay between Kerry and Wexford. At 2.25 p.m., it recorded the Kerry fifteen, 'heroes of song and story, troop on the pitch, and face the cinematograph. They "look pleasant" in the approved photographic style, and also extremely fit.' The Wexford team appeared on the field a short time after and were subjected to the 'same ordeal'.
68. Gaelic Athlete, 5 December 1914.

CHAPTER 8

1. I want to acknowledge the support of NUI, Galway's Millennium Minor Project fund in carrying out the research required for this essay. Portions of this chapter first appeared in '"Shillalah Swing Time … You'll thrill each time a wild Irishman's skull shatters": Representing Hurling in American Cinema: 1930–1960', included in Ruth Barton (ed.), *Screening Irish-America* (Dublin, 2009) and 'Anticipating a postnationalist Ireland: Representing Gaelic games in *Rocky Road to Dublin* (1968) and *Clash of the Ash* (1987)' in Carmen Zamorano Llena and Irene Gilsenan Nordin (eds), *Redefinitions of Irish Identity in the Twenty-First Century: A Postnationalist Approach* (Oxford, 2009). I also want to thank Sunniva O'Flynn and the Irish Film Archive in the Irish Film Institute for their assistance in carrying out the research necessary for this work.
2. Waldemar Kaempffert, *A Popular History of American Inventions*, vol. 1 (New York, 1924), p.425.
3. Lloyd Morris, *Not So Long Ago* (New York, 1949), p.24.
4. This fight is available to view, along with other early fights filmed by Edison, at http://www.fitzsimmons.co.nz/html/rareboxingfilm.html
5. Robert Monks, *Cinema Ireland: A Database of Irish Films and Filmmakers 1896–1986* (Dublin, 1996).
6. For more on this see Seán Crosson and Dónal McAnallen, 'Portraying the Irish at play: Cinema newsreels and Gaelic games (1920–1939)', *Sport and the Arts: Construction and Reality: Proceedings of the XIIth International CESH Congress* (2009).
7. R. Boyle and R. Haynes, *Power Play: Sport, Media and Popular Culture* (London, 2000), p.xi.
8. See R. Cox, G. Jarvie and W. Vamplew, *The Encyclopaedia of British Sport* (Oxford, 1996), p.139 and Glen Jones, '"Down on the floor and give me ten sit-ups": British sports feature films', *Film and History: An Interdisciplinary Journal of Film and Television Studies*, 35, 2 (2005), pp.30–1.
9. J.H. Wallenfeldt, *Sports Movies* (New York, 1989), p. iv
10. Mike Cronin, *Sport and Nationalism in Ireland: Gaelic Games, Soccer and Irish Identity since 1884* (Dublin, 1999), pp.18–19.
11. Kevin Rockett, Luke Gibbons and John Hill (eds), *Cinema and Ireland* (Syracuse, 1988), p.6.
12. T.J. Beere, 'Cinema statistics in Saorstát Éireann', *Journal of the Statistical and Social Enquiry Society of Ireland*, 89th session (1935–1936), p.85.
13. Ibid., p.84.
14. Rockett has noted the banning of one film by the general officer commanding-in-chief of the British forces in Ireland, *Ireland a Nation* (1914), because of concerns that it might 'cause disaffection to His Majesty, and to prejudice the recruiting of His Majesty's forces'. Rockett et al., *Cinema and Ireland*, pp.14–16.
15. Ibid., p.24.
16. 'The South Bank Show', LWT programme for ITV, 1996. Documentary with Neil Jordan interview and actual footage of Michael Collins. Produced and directed by Tony Knox; edited and presented by Melvyn Bragg.
17. Rockett et al., *Cinema and Ireland*, p.24.
18. Directed by Fred O'Donovan.
19. Rockett et al., *Cinema and Ireland*, p.19.
20. Ibid., p.21.
21. Cronin, *Sport and Nationalism in Ireland*, p.87.
22. As Sarah Benton has noted: 'The hurley stick was reborn as the symbol of man's throne, and of his gun in drills.' Sarah Benton, 'Women disarmed: The militarisation of politics in Ireland 1913–23', *Feminist Review* (summer 1995), pp.148–72, at p.153.
23. B. Mairéad Pratschke, 'Gael Linn's Amharc Éireann films, 1956–64', *New Hibernia Review*, 9, 3 (2005), p.36.
24. For further on this film see Crosson, 'Anticipating a postnationalist Ireland'.
25. Seanad Éireann, 116, 14 July 1987, Adjournment Matter – Irish Film Board, http://historical-debates.oireachtas.ie/S/0116/S.0116.198707140008.html
26. Anonymous, 'Video releases', *Irish Times*, 29 July 2000, Weekend section, p.17.
27. Ibid.
28. Stephanie MacBride, '*Clash of the Ash* wins at L'Orient', *Film Base News*, 3 (Sept–Oct 1987), p.9.
29. Eamon Sweeney, 'Breaking Ball' (Motive Television for RTÉ, 2000–2006), script provided

to author by Cormac Hardagan, producer of the RTÉ series.

30. Paddy Woodworth, 'Sporting rebels', *Sunday Press*, 8 February 1987, p.1.

31. These details and those that follow are from a personal interview by the author with Tighe on 20 August 2007.

32. This information is available on the website of St Colman's College, Fermoy, http://www.stcolmanscollege.com/history.html

33. Fergus Tighe, *Clash of the Ash* (script), copyright August 1986, p.3. Held in the Tiernan McBride Library in the Irish Film Institute.

34. Ibid., p.31.

35. Neil Jordan, *Michael Collins: Screenplay and Film Diary* (London, 1996), p.126.

36. 'The South Bank Show', LWT programme for ITV, 1996.

37. Paul Bew, 'The role of the historical adviser and the Bloody Sunday tribunal', *Historical Research*, 78 (2005), p.125.

38. 'The South Bank Show', LWT programme for ITV, 1996.

39. Solange Davin, 'Tourists and television viewers: Some similarities', in David Crouch, Rhona Jackson and Felix Thompson (eds), *The Media and the Tourist Imagination: Converging Cultures* (London and New York, 2005), p.170.

40. Colin Gordon (ed.), *Power/Knowledge: Selected Interviews and Other Writings, 1972–1977 by Michel Foucault* (New York, 1980), pp.146, 155, 162, 186.

41. John Urry, *The Tourist Gaze* (London, 2001), pp. 1–2.

42. Beth Newell, 'Racial Stereotypes in Jim Sheridan's *In America*', in Kevin Rockett and John Hill (eds), *Film History and National Cinema* (Dublin, 2005), p.143.

43. V. Y. Mudimbe, *The Ideal Africa* (Bloomington and London, 1994), p.6.

44. Urry, *The Tourist Gaze*, p.3.

45. J. Culler, 'Semistics of Tourism,' *American Journal of Semiotics*, 1, 1/2 (1981), p.127.

46. So-Min Cheong and Mark L. Miller, 'Power and Tourism: A Foucauldian Observation', *Annals of Tourism Research*, 27, 2 (2000), pp. 371–90.

47. John Arundel and Maurice Roche, 'Media, sport and local identity: British rugby league and Sky TV', in Maurice Roche (ed.), *Sport, Popular Culture and Identity* (Oxford, 2000), p.84.

48. Gerry Smyth, *Space and the Irish Cultural Imagination* (Basingstoke and New York, 2001), p. 35. See also Dean MacCannell, *The Tourist: A New Theory of the Leisure Class* (London, 1976) for a discussion on the importance of 'the search for the authentic' among tourists.

49. Rockett et al., *Cinema and Ireland*, p.xii.

50. Fox Movietone and Pathé both covered the 1936 challenge game between All-Ireland hurling champions Limerick and New York as well as several other visits by Irish teams to the US. See http://www.itnsource.com for more information on matches covered and sources for surviving clips.

51. Minutes of the Meeting of the Central Council of Gaelic Athletic Association, held at Croke House on Saturday, 12 February 1938, at 8.30 p.m. at which Mr R. O'Keeffe presided. Held in the Gaelic Museum, Dublin. I want to acknowledge the assistance of Dónal McAnallen in finding information, including these minutes, relating to the reaction of the GAA to this film. A report of the Central Council meeting is also given in Anonymous, 'Unfairly treated: GAA discussion on Land Commission and playing fields', *Irish Press*, 14 February 1938, p.10. For further on these films, see Crosson, '"Shillalah Swing Time"'.

52. Martin McLoone, *Irish Film: The Emergence of a Contemporary Cinema* (London, 2000), pp.44–59.

53. Appadurai is describing here the process through which the old stabilities of place and people are more and more 'shot through with … the woof of human motion, as more persons and groups deal with the realities of having to move, or fantasies of wanting to move'. Arjun Appadurai, *Modernity at Large* (Minneapolis, 1996), p.33.

54. Ibid., p.49.

55. While both *The Quiet Man* and *The Rising of the Moon* are discussed in this chapter, another example of the juxtaposition of hurling and violence is also found in Ford and Jack Cardiff's *Young Cassidy* (1965).

56. See Joseph McBride, *Searching for John Ford: A Life* (New York, 2001), pp.577–8.

57. Luke Gibbons, *The Quiet Man* (Cork, 2002), p.91.

58. Smyth, *Space and the Irish Cultural Imagination*, pp.36–7. Smyth is quoting from Joep Leerson, *Remembrance and Imagination: Patterns in the Historical and Literary Representation of Ireland in the Nineteenth Century* (Cork, 1996), p.226.

59. McBride, *Searching for John Ford*, pp.577–8.
60. *Irish Independent*, 1 May 1956, p.13. See also *Irish Press*, 1 May 1956, p.1.
61. Anonymous, *Irish Independent*, 2 May 1956, p.12. See also *Irish Press* 2 May 1956, p.1.
62. *Irish Times*, 4 May 1956, p.1.
63. Myles na Gopaleen, 'GAATHLETES', *Irish Times*, 18 May 1956, p.8.
64. Myles na Gopaleen, 'Ford-Proconsul', *Irish Times*, 14 May 1956, p.6.
65. The name Flann O'Brien was itself a pseudonym for the author, born Brian Ó Nualláin in 1911 in Tyrone.
66. Luke Gibbons, 'Romanticism, Realism and Irish Cinema', in Kevin Rockett et al (eds) *Cinema and Ireland*, p.200.
67. This cartoon was published in the June edition of *Dublin Opinion* magazine (1956), p.106. It is included in the Lord Killanin collection in the Irish Film Institute. I want to thank Charles Barr for bringing this collection to my attention and providing me with copies of materials included in it, including this cartoon.
68. Anonymous, 'Mystery Abbey extra was – John Ford!' *Evening Press*, 8 May 1956. Included in the Lord Killanin collection in the Irish Film Institute.
69. Sandra Brennan, 'George Pollock', *All Movie Guide, The New York Times*, http://movies2.nytimes.com/gst/movies/filmography.html?p_id=106786
70. Maureen O'Hara with John Nicoletti, *'Tis Herself – A Memoir* (London, 2004), pp.27–9, 33–4.
71. Sweeney, *Breaking Ball*.
72. Seán Moran, 'Waterford associated with celebrities', *Irish Times*, 19 August 2008, http://www.irishtimes.com/newspaper/sport/2008/0819/1218868120378.html
73. An Fear Rua website, 'The darlin' of the lay-ay-dees is … Rooney-oh!', 1 January 2000, http://www.anfearrua.com/story.asp?id=156
74. Anonymous, 'Kilkenny Arts Festival', *Waterford Today*, 8 August 2007, http://www.water-ford-today.ie/index.php?option=com_content&task=view&id=962&Itemid=10172&ed=75
75. Cinema correspondent, 'Dustman's Holiday', *Irish Times*, 17 March 1958, p.6.
76. Our Film Critic, 'This Dublin scene is no travesty', *Irish Independent*, 17 March 1958, p.5.
77. Benedict Kiely, 'Cameras on Croke Park', *Irish Press*, 17 March 1958, p.6.
78. *Irish Times* reporter, 'Tourist industry has prospects of record year', *Irish Times*, 14 July 1956, p.1.
79. The Paramount Topper series began in 1951 and would last for six years, by which time shorts were being phased out by all the majors. Altogether thirty-six were made in the series, with quite a few, such as *The Littlest Expert on Football* (1951), *Touchdown Highlights* (1954) and the final film, *Herman Hickman's Football Review* (1957), taking sport as their theme. All, including *Three Kisses* – released in the US on 7 October 1955 and given an 'Excellent' rating by the *Motion Pictures Exhibitor* trade paper – were directed by Justin Herman, who is also credited as writer of *Three Kisses*. Philadelphia-born Herman, who was also a cartoonist and contributor of short stories to the *New Yorker*, worked as a 'writer, producer and director of short films at Paramount … from the late 1930s until the mid-1950s' and altogether made 118 shorts, two of which, *Roller Derby Girl* (1949) and *Three Kisses*, were nominated for academy awards. Anonymous, 'Justin B. Herman dead at 76; Writer and producer of films', *New York Times*, 10 December 1983, http://query.nytimes.com/gst/full-page.html?res=9C04E3DE1638F933A25751C1A965948260&sec=&pagewanted=print
80. Even though the film was described in the press on its release as a 'documentary', the subject matter itself is clearly fictionalised, as the above narrative summary indicates.
81. Barry trained fourteen Cork teams (thirteen in hurling and one in football (1946)) and one Limerick hurling team (1934) to All-Ireland victory between 1926 and 1966. See Jim Cronin, *Making Connections: A Cork GAA Miscellany* (Cork, 2005), pp.55–63.
82. This information was kindly supplied to the author in an interview with Jimmy Brohan, one of the Cork players depicted in the film.
83. Anonymous, 'First showing of two films about Ireland', *Irish Times*, 19 July 1956, p.1.
84. Anonymous, 'Film and the Irish tourist industry', *Irish Independent*, 19 July 1956, p.8.
85. Benedict Kiely, 'The tourists and the screen', *Irish Press*, 23 July 1956, p.6.
86. The Cinema Correspondent, 'The business jungle', *Irish Times*, 23 July 1956, p.6.
87. Dean MacCannell, 'Staged authenticity: Arrangements of social space in tourist settings', *American Journal of Sociology*, 79, 3 (1973), p.595.
88. Anonymous, 'Dublin letter: Too much "Blarney"', *Cork Examiner*, 19 July 1956, p.6.

NOTES

CHAPTER 9

1. Seán Moran, 'President rules out rumours', *Irish Times*, 14 March 2000.
2. 'Poots addresses GAA conference', *Irish Times*, 20 October 2007.
3. See Liam P. Ó Caithnia, *Micheál Cíosóg* (BÁC, 1982), pp.115–75.
4. Máirtín Ó Murchú, *Cumann Buan-Choimeádta na Gaeilge: Tús an Athréimnithe* (BÁC, 2001), p.84, n.1. See also Ó Caithnia, *Micheál Cíosóg*, pp.17–18.
5. See Ó Murchú, *Cumann Buan Choimeádta*, pp.83–4.
6. W. F. Mandle, *The Gaelic Athletic Association and Irish National Politics 1884–1924* (Dublin, 1987), p. 20.
7. 'Weekly meeting of the Gaelic League', *Irish Independent*, 27 November 1893.
8. 'Gaelic League', *Freeman's Journal*, 15 December 1893.
9. 'Gaelic League', *Freeman's Journal*, 5 January 1894.
10. Douglas Hyde, 'The necessity for de-Anglicising Ireland', in Breandán Ó Conaire (ed.), *Language, Lore and Lyrics* (Dublin, 1986), p.168. Hyde later claimed to be a founding member of the GAA. See Brendan Fulham, *The Throw-in: The GAA and the Men who Made It* (Dublin, 2004), p.90. See also Marcus de Búrca, *The GAA: A History*, 2nd edition (Dublin, 1999), pp.20 and 167.
11. Mandle, *Gaelic Athletic Association and Irish Nationalist Politics*, p.161. For Hyde's 'expulsion' as patron from the GAA see de Búrca, *GAA*, pp.166–70.
12. See Marcus de Búrca, *Céad Bliain ag Fás: Cumann Lúthchleas Gael 1884–1984*, translated by Tomás Tóibín (BÁC, 1984), p.92. See also de Búrca, *The GAA*, pp.141–3.
13. See de Búrca, *Céad Bliain ag Fás*, pp.93–4. The establishment of Gael Linn's pools caused tension between the two bodies as they competed for public donations. See Breandán Ó hEithir, *Over the Bar* (Dublin, 1991), p.152.
14. 'A Man and a Giant', http://www.anfearrua.com/story.asp?id=755 ie (29 September 2008). Ó Caithnia, *Micheál Cíosóg*; *Scéal na hIomána* (BÁC, 1980); *Báirí Cos in Éirinn* (BÁC, 1984).
15. R.F. Foster, *Modern Ireland 1600–1972* (London, 1988), p.446.
16. F.S.L. Lyons, *Ireland Since the Famine* (London, 1989), pp.226–7.
17. Diarmaid Ferriter, *Transformation of Ireland* (New York, 2007), p.101.
18. J.J. Lee, *Ireland 1912–1985* (Cambridge, 1998), pp.80–1.
19. Ferriter, *Transformation of Ireland*, p.98.
20. See Philip O'Leary, *Gaelic Prose in the Irish Free State* (Dublin, 2004), pp.1–89. For Coimsún na Bealtaine see Aindrias Ó Muineacháin, *Dóchas agus Duainéis* (Cork, n.d), pp. 17–23.
21. Ibid., p.101.
22. Fintan O'Toole, 'Diary', *London Review of Books*, 6 September 2007.
23. Mandle *Gaelic Athletic Association and Irish Nationalist Politics*, p.161.
24. See http://ulster.gaa.ie/culture/irish-language-course/ (7 October 2008).
25. *Official Guide* (Central Council of the Association, June 2008) (internet version), p.4.
26. Ibid., p.3.
27. 'GAA open to questions', *Mirror*, 16 March 2004.
28. Moran, 'President rules out rumours'. See also Dáil Éireann debates, vol. 529, 30 January 2001, p.692.
29. Eugene McGee, 'Anyone give a focal? Appeals to DRA panels making for a farcical situation', *Irish Independent*, 12 November 2007.
30. Address by Nioclás Ó Braonáin, Uachtarán CLG (GAA president) at Congress 2008 in Sligo, 12 April 2008. http://www.kerrygaa.ie/index.php?option=com_content&task=view&id=151&Itemid=74 (24 September 2008).
31. Eamonn Sweeney, *The Road to Croker* (Dublin, 2004), p.148.
32. Brian McDonald, 'Concern at "racism" in GAA', *Irish Independent*, 20 December 2007. See also Cóilín Duffy, 'Broadcaster quits GAA over "racism" against Irish', *Irish News*, 19 December 2007. Both McGee and Breathnach frame their complaints within a Celtic Tiger discourse and voice their concerns for the 'New Irish' when they participate in Gaelic games.
33. Marcus Ó Buachalla, 'Translating names', *Irish Times*, 23 April 1999.
34. Ó Braonáin, Congress 2008, 12 April 2008.
35. See 'Home truths about hurling', *Sunday Independent*, 8 July 2007.
36. De Búrca, *GAA*, p.185.
37. Ó hEithir, *Over the Bar*, p.153.

38. Ciarán Dunbarrach, 'Hard to find the Gaelic in the GAA', *Irish Independent*, 3 August 2007. The San Francisco GAA site is bilingual in English and Spanish.
39. Gearóid Ó Colmáin, 'The New Irish', *Metro Éireann*, 9 August 2007.
40. Ibid. The site is, however, linked to the excellent site of Coiste Gaeilge Laighean chaired by Liam Ó Néill in conjunction with Máire Ní Cheallaigh, Vivian Uíbh Eachach, Ciarán Ó Feinneadha, Micheál Mac an Bhaird and Cathal Seoige.
41. Mark Gallagher, 'RTÉ set to retain GAA contract', *Irish Examiner*, 2 February 2001.
42. Concubhar Ó Liatháin, 'Lack of Gaelic games on TG4', *Irish Times*, 24 June 2008.
43. 'Camogie fury over TG4 "Discrimination"', *Irish Independent*, 3 March 2007.
44. Ibid. In 2008 TG4 provided coverage of All-Ireland championship camogie, under-21 hurling and ladies Gaelic football. See 'Super Saturday on TG4', http://www.hoganstand.com/ArticleForm.aspx?ID=99865
45. 'GAA tells RTE to stay in the past', http://www.hoganstand.com/ArticleForm.aspx?ID=35995
46. Tim O'Brien, 'GAA urged to find its cultural, radical past', *Irish Times*, 13 August 2002.
47. See Danny Lynch, 'GAA: A mirror image of society, subject to law of land', *Sunday Independent*, 14 November 2004.
48. Brian Walker, '"Opening" of Croke Park', *Irish Times*, 26 April 2005. See also letter from 'Protestant Irish speaker', 'It's Irish for themselves alone', *Belfast Telegraph*, 13 March 2008. See also 'Protestants being culturally cleansed', *Belfast Telegraph*, 1 August 1996. For responses to Walker's letter, see *Irish Times*, 29 April 2005. See also 'Freagra CLG ar ghearáin Campbell', *Lá Nua*, 18 September 2008. It should be noted that the Camanachd Association who promote shinty in Scotland are happy to engage with the GAA.
49. Mike Cronin, *Sport and Nationalism in Ireland: Gaelic Games, Soccer and Irish Identity since 1884* (Dublin, 1999), p.190.
50. Gearóid Ó Tuathaigh, ' The Irish-Ireland idea: Rationale and relevance', in Edna Longley (ed.), *Culture in Ireland: Division or Diversity?* (Belfast, 1991), p.68.
51. Darragh McManus, *GAA Confidential* (Dublin, 2007), p.162.
52. Colm Keys, 'The times, they are a-changin', *Mirror*, 23 January 2002.
53. 'The Danny years', *Irish Examiner*, 8 September 2008.
54. See 'Dearcadh aisteach an "GAA" i leith na Gaeilge II', http://igaeilge.wordpress.com
55. Paul Rouse, 'GAA: Fianna go bráth', *Village*, 12 November 2004.
56. John A. Murphy, 'The subtle and everyday legacy of Irish-Irelanders', *Sunday Independent*, 27 August 2006.
57. Sweeney, *Road to Croker*, p.147.
58. 'TG4's live coverage of Gaeltacht football tournament', http://www.hoganstand.com/ArticleForm.aspx?ID=47038
59. Sweeney, *Road to Croker*, p.147.
60. Martán Ó Ciardha, 'Bua mórtais', *Foinse*, 8 June 2008.
61. See http://www.gaa.ie/files/pdf/inside_gaeilge_sa_chlub.pdf
62. 'Novel Comórtas idea looks sure to cause a stir', *Western People*, 15 February 2006.
63. Tomaí Ó Conghaile, 'Iarratas as an úr do chomórtas peile na Gaeltachta', *Lá Nua*, 23 November 2006.
64. See *Clár Oifigiúil: Comórtas Peile na Gaeltachta 2006*, p.101. Clann Choláiste Mhuire contested the 1984 and 1991 junior final.
65. 'Fear Rua clicks with GAA fans', *Irish Times*, 20 January 2007.
66. See Colm Mac Séalaigh's series of articles, www.beo.ie. Notable Irish-language print commentators include Seán Óg de Paor, Dara Ó Cinnéide, Mac Dara Mac Donncha and Mártan Ó Ciardha.
67. Finbarr Bradley, 'Innovation and rural knowledge communities: Learning from the Irish Revival', *Irish Review*, 36, 7 (2007), p.113.
68. Ibid., p.118.
69. Ibid.
70. Ó hEithir, *Over the Bar*, p.153.
71. Ó Braonáin, Congress 2008, 12 April 2008.
72. Diarmait Mac Giolla Chríost, *The Irish Language in Ireland: From Goídel to Globalisation* (London, 2005), p.203.
73. Pádraig Ó Riagáin (edited by Caoilfhionn Nic Pháidín and Seán Ó Cearnaigh), *New View of the Irish Language* (BÁC, 2008), p.64.
74. Ó Braonáin, Congress 2008, 12 April 2008.

75. 'Home truths about hurling', *Sunday Independent*, 8 July 2007.
76. Colm Keys, 'Final diary - speaking of the all-Irish team', *Mirror*, 21 September 1999.
77. The author is indebted to the following for their advice and knowledge: Seosamh Mac Donncha, Martán Ó Ciardha, Páid Ó Neachtain, Breandán Delap, Seán Clancy, Breandán Feirtéir and Jimmy Ó Conghaile.

CHAPTER 10

1. 'Carbery', *Famous Captains: Gaelic Football Leaders from 1887 to 1946* (Tralee, 1947), p.85; *Derry Journal*, 5 January 1943. See also *Winnipeg Tribune* (unknown date, 1914), cited in *Gaelic Athlete*, 15 August 1914 ('the largest amateur athletic body in the world'); Thomas J. Kenny, *Tour of the Tipperary Hurling Team in America, 1926* (London, 1928), p.59 ('the greatest Amateur Athletic Association in the world'); *Frontier Sentinel*, 1 May 1943 ('the world's greatest amateur association'); *Irish Independent*, 27 January 1947 (quoting future GAA president Séamus McFerran: 'the greatest amateur athletic association in the world'); 'Terence Casey' [Pádraig S. de Búrca], 'What the GAA has done for Ireland', *Capuchin Annual*, 1960, p.214 ('the greatest amateur sporting body in the world'); and *Irish Independent*, 13 March 2008 (GAA patron, Archbishop Dermot Clifford: 'the greatest amateur organisation in the world').
2. The Gaelic Athletic Association for the preservation and cultivation of national pastimes, *Rules of the Gaelic Athletic Association*, 1885, pp.20–1.
3. *Celtic Times*, 6 August 1887. From 1886, however, the GAA disallowed money prizes for athletes. See Séamus Ó Riain, *Maurice Davin (1842–1927): First President of the GAA* (Dublin, 1994), p.94; Pádraig Griffin, *The Politics of Irish Athletics 1850–1990* (Ballinamore, 1990), pp.20–1).
4. Jeffrey Hill, *Sport, Leisure and Culture in Twentieth-Century Britain* (Basingstoke, 2002), p.36. The argument that the GAA adopted British sporting models – see W.F. Mandle, 'The GAA and popular culture, 1884–1924', in Oliver MacDonagh, W.F. Mandle and Pauric Travers (eds), *Culture and Nationalism in Ireland 1750–1950* (Canberra, 1983), pp.105, 113, 115; and Mike Cronin, *Sport and Nationalism in Ireland: Gaelic Games, Soccer and Irish Nationality since 1884* (Dublin, 1999), pp.106–12 – has, alongside texts on amateurism in other sports, inspired a fallacy that GAA amateurism was a relic of the Victorian English 'gentleman amateur' ethos. But the latter hinged on class exclusion (Tony Mason, *Sport in Britain* (London, 1988), pp.37, 39; Richard Holt, *Sport and the British: A Modern History* (Oxford, 1989), p.104), while the GAA's amateurism opposed class division.
5. Gaelic Athletic Association, *Official Guide*, 1907, 1908, 1909, pp.234, 235.
6. Charles J. Kickham, *Knocknagow, or The Homes of Tipperary*, 13th edition (Dublin, 1887), p.461. Mat actually makes this statement during a sledge-throwing contest, after a hurling match.
7. *Belfast Morning News*, 23 December 1882.
8. The first GAA rule book did, however, contain a detailed article, 'Hints on training for athletes' – probably written by Maurice Davin – aimed at individual track-and-field athletes rather than teams. See Gaelic Athletic Association, *Constitution and Rules, Official Copy*, 1889, pp.42–4.
9. Noel O'Donoghue, *Proud and Upright Men* (Indreabhán, 1986), p.180.
10. Holt, *Sport and the British*, p.281, makes a similar point about English county cricket.
11. Dick Fitzgerald, *How to Play Gaelic Football* (Cork, 1914), p.15.
12. Paul Rouse, 'The politics of culture and sport in Ireland: A history of the GAA ban on foreign games 1884–1971. Part One: 1884–1921', *International Journal of the History of Sport*, 10, 3 (December 1993), pp.341–2; Brendan Mac Lua, *The Steadfast Rule: A History of the GAA Ban* (Dublin, 1967), pp.23, 25.
13. Neal Garnham, 'Accounting for the early success of the Gaelic Athletic Association', *Irish Historical Studies*, 34, 133 (May 2004), pp.71–2.
14. Ibid., pp.74–5.
15. Holt, *Sport and the British*, pp.109–10, 117.
16. Michael Cusack declared it a victory for 'democratic Christian socialism' when the public was allowed to play hurling in the Phoenix Park, Dublin, in the 1880s (*Celtic Times*, 30 April 1887). The GAA has been credited with bringing a separatist democratic culture to the Irish countryside; see F.S.L. Lyons, *Ireland since the Famine* (London, 1971),

pp.226–7; John Hutchinson, *The Dynamics of Cultural Nationalism: The Gaelic Revival and the Creation of the Irish Nation-State* (London, 1987), pp.289–90.

17. Joe Lennon, *Towards a Philosophy for Legislation in Gaelic Games*, 3 vols (Gormanstown, 1999), vol. i, pp.117, 133–5.
18. Ó Riain, *Maurice Davin*, p.183. See also Marcus de Búrca, *The GAA: A History*, 2nd edition (Dublin, 1999), p.7; idem, *Michael Cusack and the GAA* (Dublin, 1989), pp.165, 170, 173; and W.F. Mandle, *The Gaelic Athletic Association and Irish Nationalist Politics 1884–1924* (London, 1987), p.70.
19. GAA, *Constitution and Rules*, 1889.
20. Lennon, *Towards a Philosophy for Legislation*, vol. iii (*Part 1: A Comparative Analysis of the Playing Rules of Football and Hurling 1884–2000*), pp.641–3.
21. See GAA, *Constitution*, 1889, p.5 for a complaint by patron Archbishop Croke about publicans at games. See also *Celtic Times*, 10 September 1887, for bookmakers at a Dublin athletic meeting under GAA rules.
22. Padraic Ó Laoi, *Annals of the GAA in Galway, vol. 1, 1884–1901* (Galway, 1984), pp.10, 19, 22.
23. *Leinster Leader*, 25 August 1894, cited in Eoghan Corry, *Kildare GAA: A Centenary History* (Naas, 1984), pp.52, 102, 164.
24. See D.J. Vaughan, *Liffey Gaels: A Century of Gaelic Games* (Dublin, 1984), p.157 for a club game in Dublin in 1895, for a £10 bet, ending prematurely.
25. Paddy Dolan and John Connolly, 'The civilising of hurling in Ireland', *Sport in Society*, 12, 2 (March 2009), pp.193–208; idem, 'The civilising and sportisation of Gaelic football in Ireland: 1884–2008', conference paper, Conference of the European Association of Sociology of Sport, 22–25 May 2008.
26. See Tom Hunt, *Sport and Society in Victorian Ireland: The Case of Westmeath* (Cork, 2007), p.203 for a commercial cup donation in 1904; and Rev. John Mulligan, *The GAA in Louth: An Historical Record* (Dundalk, 1984), p.134 for a similar donation in 1921.
27. P.J. Corbett, 'The Limerick Commercial Football Club: Its history', *The Gaelic Athletic Annual and County Directory for 1910–11*, p.55. Similarly, the 1891 Kerry (Ballyduff) hurling team paid a hefty train fare of 16 shillings per man to the All-Ireland final in Dublin (Micheál Ó Ruairc, 'The early days of athletics, football and hurling in Kerry', *Kerry GAA Yearbook*, 1977, pp.3–4).
28. Paul Rouse, 'The first All-Ireland final: 1 April 1888', a lecture delivered at Birr library in March 2008. See also *Irish Times*, 2 April 2008.
29. *Sport*, 13 April 1895.
30. Hunt, *Sport and Society*, pp.150–1, 209–10.
31. Mandle, *Gaelic Athletic Association*, pp.112, 116; R.T. Blake, *How the GAA was Grabbed* (n.p., 1900), p.13. Similar allegations were made about, for example, an Ulster Council gatekeeper in the 1900s (*Irish News*, 4 October 1909); a Wexford county secretary in the 1930s (Conor Foley, *Legion of the Rearguard: The IRA and the Modern Irish State* (London, 1992), p.203); and a Monaghan club treasurer in the 1930s (Peter Kavanagh, 'Kavanagh country – poet in the sticks', in Larry Meegan, *The Inniskeen Story: A History 1888–1988* (Inniskeen, 1988), pp.80–1; Patrick Kavanagh, 'Gut Yer Man', ibid., p.88).
32. *Gaelic Athlete*, 29 March 1924.
33. Donnchadh Mac Con Uladh, 'Ulster and the GAA' in *GAACD for 1908/09*, p.20. See also Bulmer Hobson, *Ireland Yesterday and Tomorrow* (Tralee, 1968), pp.32, 35; J. Anthony Gaughan (ed.), *Memoirs of Senator Joseph Connolly (1885–1961): A Founder of Modern Ireland* (Dublin, 1996), pp.38–9. For a micro-study of the impact of cultural nationalism on the GAA in the 1900s, see Hunt, *Sport and Society*, pp.190–9, 204.
34. *United Irishman*, 23 January 1904.
35. *United Irishman*, 17 December 1904. Rev. James B. Dollard, 'A word about the GAA' in *GAACD, 1907–08*, p.19 stated that 'the ideal Gael' should be 'a matchless athlete, sober, pure of mind, speech and deed, self-possessed, self-reliant, self-respecting, loving his religion and his country with a deep restless love, earnest in thought and effective in action'.
36. See *Anglo-Celt*, 3 December 1904, for the Ulster Council legislating against players fielding under the influence of alcohol. In 1903 bookmakers were banned from games and sports meetings (GAA, *Official Guide*, 1907, 1908, 1909, p.71). Some members were suspended for betting (Pádraig Puirséal, *The GAA in its Time* (Dublin, 1982), pp.134, 136). The rule was later strengthened, inviting members to inform 'the local police' about bookmakers at games – gambling was illegal under the law of the land – even though policemen could not join the GAA (GAA, *Official Guide*, 1912–13, p.77). But even in the GAA's main

ground from 1913, Croke Park, it took some time to remove the gambling fraternity.

37. Dollard, 'Word about the GAA', p.18.
38. T.F. O'Sullivan, *The Story of the GAA* (Dublin, 1916), p.186.
39. Tim Horgan, *Cork's Hurling Story: From 1890 to the Present Time* (Dublin, 1977), p.34.
40. O'Donoghue, *Proud and Upright Men*, pp.190, 191.
41. Eoghan Corry, *Catch and Kick: Great Moments of Gaelic Football 1880–1990* (Dublin, 1989), pp.64–5; idem, *Kildare GAA*, pp.73, 80.
42. O'Donoghue, *Proud and Upright Men*, pp.176–82.
43. Fitzgerald, *How to Play Gaelic Football*, pp.66–7.
44. Cahir Healy, 'To combat the Gaelic games: The Ulster bribe', *GAACD*, 1907–8, p.33.
45. F.J. McCarragher, 'Antrim in the early days up to 1915', *Ar Aghaidh Linn: Clár Oifigeamhail, Ath-Thógáil Pháirc Uí Chorragáin, agus Cúrsaí Gaelacha i gConndae Aondroma C.L.–C.G.* [Corrigan Park Reconstruction week programme] (*c.* 1947), pp.7, 9. The victorious Monaghan team of 1914 got medals instantly, however (*Irish News*, 1 October 1914; *Anglo-Celt*, 3 October 1914).
46. *Derry People and Donegal News*, 16 September 1905.
47. *United Irishman*, 14 July 1900.
48. Tom Ryall, *Kilkenny: The GAA Story* (Kilkenny, 1931), pp.28–9.
49. *United Irishman*, 21 March 1903.
50. *Kilkenny Journal*, 13 August 1910.
51. Mac Con Uladh, 'Ulster and the GAA', p.19.
52. Ibid. See Holt, *Sport and the British*, pp.144–5 for similar concerns about 'spectatorism' in England in the 1880s.
53. *Kilkenny Journal*, 13 August 1910.
54. *Gaelic Athlete*, 31 May 1913. See also Neal Garnham, *Association Football and Society in Pre-Partition Ireland* (Belfast, 2004), p.81.
55. Norman Gardiner, *Greek Athletic Sports and Festivals* (London, 1910), pp. 2–7 describes how physical fitness was essential to ancient Greek citizens, as potential soldiers for Greece's continual wars with its neighbours; but over time, an overemphasis on bodily excellence and athletic success made sport more the monopoly of an élite class, and the general populace became less active, degenerating into an 'unathletic crowd' enjoying sport 'by proxy'. Gardiner argues that 'the decline of Greek athletics is an object-lesson full of instruction' for modern England, with its similar 'tendency to specialisation and professionalism', 'hero-worship of the athlete' and the growth of the unhealthy crowd. See also pp.2–7, 80–2, 122, 124, 126–7, 130, 134, 135, 146, 148, 186, 188–9.
56. *Kilkenny Journal*, 13 August 1910.
57. Garnham, *Association Football*, pp.88, 99.
58. Mac Con Uladh, 'Ulster and the GAA', p.19.
59. *Derry People and Donegal News*, 27 May 1905. The gate money, another local GAA advocate suggested, went 'to support the Orange faction in Ulster' (*Derry People and Donegal News*, 30 May 1908).
60. *Kilkenny Journal*, 16 December 1911.
61. Healy, 'Ulster bribe', pp.31–2. See also *Derry People*, 13 October 1906, 10 November 1906. During this period some GAA clubs in Ulster turned over to soccer, and vice versa, so inducements were expected to catalyse the process.
62. Ulster secretary's report to Ulster convention of the GAA, 1920, Cardinal Ó Fiaich Library and Archive, Armagh; Eoin O'Duffy, 'Days that are gone', in Séamus Ó Ceallaigh (ed.), *Gaelic Athletic Memories* (Limerick, 1945), pp.169, 171.
63. *United Irishman*, 6 January 1900.
64. *United Irishman*, 10 September 1904. Anonymous, 'Buillí in airde' in *GAACD*, 1908/09, p.45, wrote that '[t]he borrowing, procuring or "purchasing" of players is despicable … defeating the very aim of the GAA.'
65. See Newmarket-on-Fergus Hurling Club, *A Proud Past: Highlights of the Newmarket-on-Fergus Hurling and Football Story 1885–1973* (Ennis, 1974), p.28 for an 1889 team wearing medals. Some officials, disliking the apparent obsession with medals, argued that Irish educational books should be awarded to winners instead (O'Sullivan, *Story of the GAA*, pp.198–9).
66. Rev. Philip Canon Fogarty, *Tipperary's GAA Story* (Thurles, 1960), p.91.
67. *Limerick Leader*, 22 January 1913; Séamus Ó Ceallaigh and Seán Murphy, *The Mackey Story* (Limerick, 1982), p. 36. I am grateful to Michael Maguire, Limerick City Library, for this reference.

68. Holt, *Sport and the British*, pp.105, 248–9.
69. *Freeman's Journal*, 17 April 1893.
70. GAA, *Official Guide*, 1907, 1908, 1909, p.27.
71. Fogarty, *Tipperary's GAA Story*, pp.100–1. This decree resulted in the seizure of the personal property of GAA secretary Luke O'Toole.
72. *Cork Sportsman*, 15 August 1908.
73. See, for example, Ryall, *Kilkenny*, p.26; O'Donoghue, *Proud and Upright Men*, p.190; *Anglo-Celt*, 15 February 1908.
74. Gaelic Athletic Association, *Official Guide*, 1922–3, p.65.
75. *Cork Sportsman*, 15 August 1908. Although six hurlers from two Kilkenny–Cork games in 1908 got a total of £7 in compensation, there was bad feeling over a Cork delegate's opposition (on the basis that all six players played to the end) to any payment.
76. *Cork Sportsman*, 15 August 1908.
77. *Cork Sportsman*, 22 August 1908.
78. Corry, *Kildare GAA*, p.93.
79. *Freeman's Journal*, 14 January 1892. In 1893 it was also decided to appoint a paid secretary to assist the honorary secretary, at a yearly salary of £25 (ibid., 17 April 1893). By 1896 the honorary secretary received 15 per cent of gross receipts (ibid., 11 May 1896). By 1899 this yielded over £100 per year for him (O'Sullivan, *Story of the GAA*, p.140). In 1902 the rate was re-fixed at 10 per cent of receipts (ibid., p.156).
80. *Freeman's Journal*, 11 May 1896.
81. In 1925 the Munster secretary became the first provincial officer to receive a defined salary, at £200 plus 10 per cent of receipts up to £2,000 (Jim Cronin, *The Munster GAA Story* (Ennis, 1986), p.130).
82. The Louth county secretary got a grant of £5 from 1907, £10 from 1910, £20 from 1917, and £35 from 1926. In 1907 the treasurer got a maximum of £5 to meet incidental expenses (Mulligan, *GAA in Louth*, pp.77, 89, 122, 152). The assistant secretary was allowed expenses of £10 and the registrar a sum of £5 in 1926 (ibid., p.152).
83. A motion to license and pay referees was lost at 1902 congress (O'Sullivan, *Story of the GAA*, p.156).
84. *Freeman's Journal*, 9 January 1905; GAA, *Official Guide*, 1907, 1908, 1909, pp.70–1.
85. 'Celt' [P.J. Devlin], 'Goals and points: a monologue on many things', *GAACD*, 1910/11, p.44.
86. O'Sullivan, *Story of the GAA*, p.91. See also ibid., p.97.
87. Eamonn Fitzgerald (ed.), *Dr Crokes' Gaelic Century 1886–1986* (Killarney, 1986), p.35; Tom Looney, *Dick Fitzgerald: King in a Kingdom of Kings* (Dublin, 2008), pp.39–41. A quartet of Cork players who made a similar trip in 1909 included a star player named Charlie Paye (*Cork Sportsman*, 30 October 1909).
88. William Fletcher, 'Athletics in America', *GAACD*, 1910–11, p.10.
89. Paul Darby, 'Gaelic games, ethnic identity and Irish nationalism in New York city c.1880–1917', *Sport in Society*, 10, 3 (May 2007), pp.355–8; Seamus J. King, *The Clash of the Ash in Foreign Fields: Hurling Abroad* (Cashel, 1998), pp.101, 105.
90. King, *Clash of the Ash*, pp.101, 106, 111.
91. Minutes of the Annual Congress of the GAA, 8 April 1928.
92. King, *Clash of the Ash*, pp.114–15.
93. Mulligan, *GAA in Louth*, p.107. See also Corry, *Catch and Kick*, pp.91–2.
94. *Gaelic Athlete*, 28 June 1913.
95. Ibid., 10 October 1914.
96. Fitzgerald, *How to Play Gaelic Football*, pp.66–7.
97. Ibid., p.15.
98. Letter from J. Duggan, 28 September 1914, in Bob O'Keeffe collection, GAA Museum, Croke Park. See also *Irish Times*, 28 August 1995, cited in Ollie Byrnes, *Against the Wind: Memories of Clare Hurling* (Cork, 1996), p.30.
99. The first training grants (£25 each) were paid to the Kerry and Kildare football sides in 1905.
100. De Búrca, *GAA*, p.91. O'Toole was only nominally part-time ard-rúnaí early on (from 1901), but the workload put a great burden on him, as he struggled to run his private businesses and rear eight children (Pádraig O'Toole, *The Glory and the Anguish* (Loughrea, 1984), pp.27, 126).
101. *Gaelic Athlete*, 2 August 1913. See also ibid., 19 July 1913, 26 July 1913.
102. *Anglo-Celt*, 30 March 1929; GAA congress minutes, 20 April 1930.

103. Patron Michael Davitt paid £400 from his own pocket so that GAA athletes could return from America in 1888 (Mandle, *Gaelic Athletic Association*, pp.71–2, 123, 149). See also Fearghal McGarry, *Eoin O'Duffy: A Self-Made Hero* (Oxford, 2005), p.14.

104. *Anglo-Celt*, 26 January 1907; Con Short, *The Ulster GAA Story 1884–1984* (Rassan, 1984), p.71.

105. Interview with James McQuaid, Dungannon, on 15 November 2008. The interviewee's father was said to have refused to claim for expenses in three decades as a Central Council delegate for Tyrone.

106. Mandle, *Gaelic Athletic Association*, pp.152, 158.

107. Minutes of the Central Council of the GAA, 19 December 1914. See also *Freeman's Journal*, 13 April 1914, 21 December 1914.

108. P.D. Kearns, *Scéal Chluain Dáimh: The Clonduff Story 1887–1984* (n.p., 1984), p.98. See also Minutes of the Armagh County Board of the GAA, meeting of 21 July 1935, CÓFLA.

109. Dan O'Neill with Liam Horan, *Divided Loyalties: The life and times of a Mayo man who, in 1957, won an All–Ireland title with Louth* (Ballinrobe, 2008), pp.37–9.

110. Lennon, *Towards a Philosophy for Legislation in Gaelic Games*, vol. iii, pp.714, 722.

111. Tommy Doyle, *A Lifetime in Hurling – as told to Raymond Smith* (London, 1955), pp.42–4.

112. Val Dorgan, *Christy Ring: A Personal Portrait* (Swords, 1980), pp.185–8; Tim Horgan, *Christy Ring: Hurling's Greatest* (Cork, 2007), p.5.

113. Horgan, *Christy Ring*, pp.42–3. See also Ryall, *Kilkenny*, p.47.

114. See 'Joseph Anelius' [Joseph Hanly], *National Action: A Plan for the National Recovery of Ireland*, 2nd edition (Dublin, 1943); and Tadhg Ó hAnnracháin, 'The heroic importance of sport: The GAA in the 1930s', *International Journal of the History of Sport*, 25, 10 (September 2008), p.1,333.

115. McDevitt, 'Muscular Catholicism', p.271.

116. GAA congress minutes, 1 April 1923.

117. Mandle, *Gaelic Athletic Association*, pp.142–3, uses this description for the 1900s period, but it is probably better merited for the 1920s onwards.

118. De Búrca, *GAA*, pp.210–21; idem (ed.), *Gaelic Games in Leinster: Forbairt agus Fás* (Comhairle Laighean, 1984), pp.28, 29, 31.

119. As one leading advocate put it, the GAA policy should be to 'outrage … business tenets and endow the weak and unprofitable at the expense of the strong and remunerative' (P.J. Devlin, 'Native games and athletics', *Catholic Bulletin*, 17, 3 (March 1927), p.299).

120. Griffin, *Politics of Irish Athletics*, pp.76–80. See also John [Seán] McKeown, [unpublished] autobiography and memoirs, Linen Hall Library, Belfast, pp.58–9, for an account of the NACA's efforts to 'gain unity for clean amateur sport', against the gambling industry. Towards the same end, in 1949 GAA congress barred horse and greyhound racing from its grounds (GAA, *Official Guide*, 1950, p.93), but it was not expunged from Newbridge until 1964 (Corry, *Kildare GAA*, p.338).

121. Ryall, *Kilkenny*, p.320.

122. Joseph Hanly, *The National Ideal: A Practical Exposition of True Nationality Appertaining to Ireland* (Dublin, 1931), pp.204–5.

123. McGarry, *Eoin O'Duffy*, pp.156–62.

124. Devlin, 'Native games and athletics', p.99.

125. P.J. Devlin, *Our Native Games* (Dublin, 1934), pp.61–3.

126. Devlin, 'Native games and athletics', p.894.

127. Hanly, *National Ideal*, pp.204–5. See also *An Camán*, 10 September 1932, for Séamus Upton again recounting the role of professional sport in the decline of Greece. As before, Upton's writings reflected recent literature on classical times. See E. Norman Gardiner, *Athletics of the Ancient World* (Oxford, 1930), pp.2–3, 99–105, 115–16.

128. *An Camán*, 3 December 1932. Just as he had written over twenty years before, Upton again berated the English obsession with money-making (*An Camán*, 15 October 1932).

129. GAA congress minutes, 5 April 1931. McKeown saw 'no greater moral power outside religion than the GAA'. See also O'Duffy, 'Days that are gone', p.191.

130. McKeown, *Autobiography*, pp.112, 113.

131. Horgan, *Christy Ring*, p.90; Tom Williams, *Cúchulainn's Son: The Story of Nickey Rackard* (Dublin, 2006), p.32.

132. Seán Óg Ó Ceallacháin, *Seán Óg: His Own Story* (Dublin, 1988), pp.138, 214; Breandán Ó hEithir, *Over the Bar: A Personal Relationship with the GAA* (Swords, 1984), pp.176–7.

133. The inter-provincial Railway Cup competitions flourished as annual St Patrick's Day fixtures, but later withered when the dates changed. Inter-varsity Gaelic competitions, boasting many of the top players, never attracted large crowds like certain American and British collegiate contests did.

134. *Pathé Gazette*, 14 May 1931 [footage of 1930 All-Ireland football final], www.british-pathe.com, 771.20. See also Dónal McAnallen and Seán Crosson, 'Portraying the Irish at play: British cinema newsreels and Gaelic games, 1920–39', in Laurent Daniel (ed.), Proceedings of the twelfth international CESH congress, 20–22 September 2007, *Sport and the Arts: Construction and Reality* (Lorient, 2009).

135. William Nolan (ed.), *The Gaelic Athletic Association in Dublin 1884–2000*, vol. i, p.143 (Dublin, 2005).

136. Corry, *Kildare GAA*, p.148.

137. Ibid., pp.342–3. This comment was made after a Kildare versus Westmeath game.

138. Corry, *Catch and Kick*, p.113; idem, *Kildare GAA*, pp.126–7.

139. Corry, *Kildare GAA*, p.155.

140. Leinster Council minutes, meeting of 3 March 1929. I am grateful to John Connolly (DCU) for this reference.

141. Ulster Secretary's Report (for 1947) to Ulster Convention, 1948, p.11.

142. Brendan Mac Lua, 'Betting in Gaelic games', *Cuchulainn Annual*, 1969, reported that a player in the 1968 All-Ireland football final had bet on the outcome.

143. The 'allowances' from Central Council to the Galway and Meath teams for the 1951 National League finals in New York, for instance, amounted to £1,717, apart from travelling and hotel expenses (Audited Accounts for GAA Central Council for 1951, contained in General Secretary's Report to Annual Congress, 1952, p.A9).

144. *Anglo-Celt*, 16 August 1947. See also General Secretary's Report, 1959, p.A21.

145. Martin Codd, *The Way I Saw It: Nickey Rackard Leads Wexford to Hurling Glory* (Enniscorthy, 2005), p.217.

146. *Anglo-Celt*, 18 October 1947.

147. Horgan, *Christy Ring*, p.41. Some county boards tried to avoid hotel stays for teams before finals, believing that players' larks in hotels upset prior team displays (McKeown, *Autobiography*, pp.28–9).

148. The scheme was hampered by less serious (and some spurious) claims. Decades later it evolved into a comprehensive Players' Injury Scheme.

149. Mary Moran, *Cork Camogie's Story* (Cork, 2001), p.34.

150. *An Phoblacht*, 5 November 1926.

151. *Kilkenny Journal*, 5 February 1927.

152. See, for example, *Gaelic Athlete*, 14 February 1925; and *Kilkenny Journal*, 2 April 1927.

153. GAA congress minutes, 17 April 1927.

154. GAA congress minutes, 8 April 1928.

155. After years of sporadic awards, fixed rates were set (but often exceeded in practice, primarily when championships were prolonged). The official rates were as follow: £100 for finalists and £50 for semi-finalists by 1930 (GAA, *Official Guide*, 1930, p.125); £200 and £100 respectively by 1950 (ibid., 1950, pp.104–5); £300 and £150 by 1956 (ibid., 1956, p.104–5); £600 and £300 from 1963 (ibid., 1966, pp.106–7); £1,000 and £500 by 1978 (ibid., 1978, pp.94–5). The figures were then removed from rule and left at the discretion of Central Council. Provincial councils also gave grants to their champion teams annually, Cronin, *Munster GAA Story*, pp.111, 115, 121; Tony Conboy, 'The forties', in Tomás Ó Móráin (ed.), *Stair CLG Chonnacht: History of Connacht GAA 1902–2002* (2002), pp.60, 63.

156. Minutes of the Leinster Council of the GAA, meeting of 27 March 1927, in Áras Laighean, Portlaoise.

157. For example, in 1932 Westmeath County Board paid £3 *ex gratia* to an inter-county hurler for clothes lost during a game (Tom Hunt, 'Cusack Park, Mullingar: the conception, difficult gestation and spectacular delivery of a GAA venue', *Ríocht na Mídhe: Journal of the Meath Archaeological and Historical Society*, 17 (2006), p.279).

158. See *Dundalk Democrat*, 18 October 1913, for the presentation of a 'purse of sovereigns' to a recent All-Ireland winner, Eddie Burke of Louth, by his club colleagues, on the occasion of his departure.

159. Seán O'Neill, 'The turbulent thirties', *Kerry GAA Yearbook*, 1984, p.52; Minutes of the Annual Congress of the GAA, 18 April 1954.

160. *Sunday Independent*, 20 December 1953; *Sunday Press*, 10 January 1954.

161. *Sunday Independent*, 20 December 1953; GAA congress minutes, 18 April 1954.
162. Jack Mahon, *The Game of My Life: In Conversation with the Giants of the GAA Past and Present* (Dublin, 1993), p.76.
163. *Irish Independent*, 7 April 1947.
164. Interviews with Gerry Murphy (Keady), Jack Bratten and John Hanratty (Armagh), 1953 Armagh panellists, on 8 November 2008. See also Joe Ó Muircheartaigh and T.J. Flynn, *Princes of the Pigskin: A Century of Kerry Footballers* (Cork, 2007), p.167 for similar practice in Kerry.
165. Mahon, *Game of My Life*, p.76.
166. Interviews with G. Murphy and J. Hanratty, 1951 Armagh minor panellists, on 8 November 2008.
167. General Secretary's Report, 1940, p.15; ibid., 1941, p.14.
168. GAA congress minutes, 6 April 1947.
169. General Secretary's Report, 1947, p.17; Raymond Smith, *Decades of Glory* (Dublin, 1966), pp.96, 221. Evidently, though, most players enjoyed the camps (Jack Mahon, *A History of Gaelic Football* (Dublin, 2000), p.89).
170. *Sunday Independent*, 31 January 1954.
171. GAA congress minutes, 18 April 1954.
172. *Sunday Independent*, 20 December 1953.
173. *Sunday Independent*, 18 April 1954.
174. General Secretary's Report, 1954. See also *Irish Press*, 30 November 1953.
175. *Sunday Independent*, 27 December 1953.
176. *Sunday Press*, 3 January 1954.
177. Ó Muircheartaigh and Flynn, *Princes of the Pigskin: A Century of Kerry Football* (Cork, 2007), p.189.
178. Éamon N.M. O'Sullivan, *The Art and Science of Gaelic Football* (Tralee, 1958), p.26.
179. *Sunday Press*, 18 April 1954. See also GAA congress minutes, 21 April 1946.
180. GAA congress minutes, 18 April 1954, Croke Park.
181. Cumann Lúithchleas Gaedheal, *Treoraí Oifigiúil*, 1956, pp.58, 59.
182. *Irish News*, 6 January 1925.
183. Hunt, 'Cusack Park', pp.275, 277–8, 282.
184. See, for example, Anonymous, 'The new field: The story of an achievement', in Joe Bailie (ed.), *Programme for the Opening of Davitt Park, Lurgan, 1 June 1947*, pp.3–7; and 'Lists of Subscriptions', ibid., pp.95–114.
185. Voluntary labour was sometimes sought by public appeal. See Síghle Nic An Ultaigh, *Ó Shíol go Bláth: An Dún – The GAA Story* (n.p., 1990), p.221, for a newspaper advertisement in Newry in 1945: '50 Volunteers Wanted (with shovels and spades), in the Gaelic Field … on Wednesday evening next … Lend a Hand to Aid the Good Work.'
186. 'J. McQ.' (John McQuaid), 'The O'Neill Park: The realisation of a dream', in *Programme for the Official Opening of O'Neill Park, Dungannon, 29 June 1947*, p.44. See also Frank O'Neill, 'Three Years Hard-' in *Programme for the Opening of Cardinal MacRory Memorial Park, Coalisland, 19 June 1949*.
187. *Anglo-Celt*, 21 October 1933. 'Communism is finding root amongst the working classes of the world. Let us, at least, not sow the seed amongst our own.'
188. Jimmy Smyth, 'Memoir of a hurling life', in *In Praise of Heroes: Ballads and Poems of the GAA* (Dublin, 2007), p.23; Dorgan, *Christy Ring*, p.187.
189. Smyth, 'Memoir of a hurling life', p.25.
190. John Mulligan, S.M., *Dundalk Young Irelands GFC: An Historical Record of the Green and Blacks* (Dundalk, 2004), p.174.
191. See, for example, Malachy Fitzgerald, *Derrytresk Fir an Chnoic 1903–2003* (Derrytresk, 2006), pp.4, 81–2.
192. *Irish Independent*, 3 May 1927, 9 May 1927, 10 May 1927, 12 May 1927. See also *An Phoblacht*, 5 May 1934.
193. McGarry, *Eoin O'Duffy*, p.147. Similarly, town teams comprising talented 'blow-ins', mainly working in middle-income jobs, were taunted by their rural opponents, as the 'League of Nations' (George Cartwright, *Up the Reds: The Cornafean Achievement* (Cavan, 1990), p.86).
194. *Dundalk Democrat*, 13 February 1915.
195. Ibid., 3 January 1927.
196. Cartwright, *Up the Reds*, p.86.
197. Owen McCrohan, *Mick O'Dwyer: The Authorised Biography* (Waterville, 1990), p.36.

198. *Dundalk Democrat*, 14 May 1927.
199. Williams, *Cúchulainn's Son*, p.32; Ó Muircheartaigh and Flynn, *Princes of the Pigskin*, p.195.
200. *Freeman's Journal*, 5 April 1915. This resolution was apparently not written into rule. See, for example, *Gaelic Athlete*, 16 August 1913, for a sports day with cash prizes in Kerry.
201. Michael McCaughey, *The West Tyrone Board of the GAA (1931 to 1974)* (Coiste Chontae Thír Eoghain, 1998), pp.52, 82. See also Fintona Pearses GAC, *Céiliúradh Céad Bliain: A Century of Gaelic Games in the Donacavey Parish*, pp.98–9, for a prize of 10 shillings a man at a 1941 tournament; Phil McGinn, *Armagh Harps 120 Years* (Armagh, 2008), p.167, for a £100 team prize at a tournament in Co. Derry; and *Mid-Ulster Mail*, 4 August 1956.
202. Cartwright, *Up the Reds*, pp.99–100.
203. Codd, *The Way I Saw It*, pp.121–2.
204. Williams, *Cúchulainn's Son*, p.149.
205. General Secretary's Report, 1955, p.A17, CÓFLA.
206. General Secretary's Report, 1959, p.A23, CÓFLA.
207. General Secretary's Report, 1961, p.A15, CÓFLA.
208. Johnny Joyce, 'The "Dubs" in the rare ould times', in Nolan, *Gaelic Athletic Association in Dublin*, pp.479–80. This 'coming together' produced 'a new-found camaraderie', and a belief that 'we were the best and we were going to prove it'.
209. Joe Lennon, *Fitness for Gaelic Football* (1969), p.vi.
210. Willie Smyth, 'Wearing the light blue for UCD (1962–1968)', in Nolan, *Gaelic Athletic Association in Dublin*, p.608.
211. Mahon, *Game of My Life*, p.209; Michael Foley, *Kings of September: The Day Offaly Denied Kerry a Five in a Row* (Dublin, 2007), p.22.
212. *Gaelic Weekly*, 14 January 1967.
213. Mick O'Connell, *A Kerry Footballer* (Cork, 1974), pp.16–17, 63–6.
214. Ibid., pp.9, 63.
215. Joyce, 'The "Dubs" in the rare ould times', p.473, details how a leading player retired from inter-county football at twenty-six, when given an ultimatum by his employer about evening work.
216. O'Sullivan, *Art and Science of Gaelic Football*, p.26.
217. GAA congress minutes, 30 March 1980.
218. Report of the Commission on the GAA (Dublin, 1971), p.95; Horgan, *Christy Ring*, p.249.
219. Dorgan, *Christy Ring*, pp.5–6, 221–2; Ó hEithir, *Over the Bar*, p.186; Jay Drennan, 'Micko the master', *Our Games* annual, 1970, p.21.
220. Billy Rackard, *No Hurling at the Dairy Door* (Dublin, 1996), p.229.
221. Ulster Secretary's Report to Ulster Convention, 1964, CÓFLA.
222. *Irish Times*, 27 March 1967. See also Séamus McRory, *The Voice from the Sideline: Famous GAA Managers* (Dublin, 1997), p.2.
223. Minutes of the Ulster Convention of the GAA, 14 March 1964, CÓFLA.
224. *The Downman: The Magazine of the Down Association of Gaelic Sportsmen*, no. 1, p.2. I am grateful to Michael Anderson, Poyntzpass, for this reference.
225. Joseph Lennon, *Coaching Gaelic Football for Champions* (Poyntzpass, 1964). The book actually carried an endorsement from the previous GAA president, Hugh Byrne (1961–4) on its dust cover.
226. *Sunday Independent*, 23 May 1971. See also *Irish Press*, 14 May 1971, 16 May 1971.
227. *Sunday Independent*, 23 May 1971; GAA, *Official Guide*, 1973, pp.3–4. The rule read: 'The Association is an Amateur Association. Payment or other material reward (officially approved trophies excepted), for participation in games and pastimes under the control of the Association, is expressly forbidden. Full-time training is inconsistent with the amateur status of members of the Association and such members are, accordingly, prohibited from participating in training of this type.'
228. Report of the Commission on the GAA (Dublin, 1971), p.116.
229. Peter McDermott, *Gaels in the Sun: A Detailed Account of Meath's Historic Trip to Australia* (Drogheda, 1968). Kerry teams also went on holidays to Australia from the 1970s, and an official international compromise rules series between Ireland and Australia began in the mid-1980s.
230. For example, Offaly footballers on the 1972 All-Stars trip to America demanded an increased *per diem*. Whether players' wives would be included in touring parties was once a thorny topic; the inclusion of girlfriends even more so.

NOTES

231. King, *Clash of the Ash*, p.121.
232. Pat Spillane and Seán McGoldrick, *Shooting from the Hip: The Pat Spillane Story* (Dublin, 1998), pp.74, 77–9.
233. *Sunday Press*, 29 November 1987.
234. Liam Hayes, 'The Payola game ... is here to stay', *Gaelic Review*, 2, 4 (July 1988), p.4.
235. Keith Duggan, *The Lifelong Season: At the Heart of Gaelic Games* (Dublin, 2004), pp.193, 204, 211–13; Paul Darby, 'Gaelic games and the Irish immigrant experience in Boston', in Alan Bairner (ed.), *Sport and the Irish: Histories, Identities, Issues* (Dublin, 2005), p.97.
236. Patrick Madden, 'Professionalism – the new approach', *Gaelic World*, 1, 9 (May 1980), p.15.
237. This reflected contemporary use of these words in the English language generally. See J.B. Sykes (ed.), *The Concise Oxford Dictionary of Current English*, 6th edition (Oxford, 1976).
238. Eoghan Corry, *Kingdom Come: A Biography of the Kerry Football Team 1975–1988* (Dublin, 1989), pp.170–3. The Cork football team was induced to wear one firm's sportswear in the mid-1970s, but was suspended by its own county board for six months for doing so. See also Spillane and McGoldrick, *Shooting from the Hip*, pp.171–4.
239. Corry, *Kingdom Come*, pp.230–2.
240. O'Connell, *Kerry Footballer*, pp.97–104; *Sunday Press*, 18 January 1987.
241. Hayes, 'Payola game', p.4.
242. Cumann Lúthchleas Gael, Report of the Rules Revision Committee, Marta, 1985, p.12.
243. GAA, *Official Guide*, 1986, p.4. The rule now read: 'The Association is an Amateur Association. No player, team, official or member shall accept payment in cash or in kind or other material reward in connection with his membership of the Association, nor shall be associated with any commercial enterprise in connection with membership of the Association. Expenses paid to all officials, players and members shall not exceed the standard rates laid down by the Central Council. Members of the Association may not participate in full-time training. This rule shall not prohibit the payment of salaries or wages to employees of the Association. Penalty: Six months' suspension or expulsion.'
244. Director-General's Report to Annual Congress, 1986, p.5; GAA congress minutes, 5 April 1986, pp.41–4; *SP*, 18 January 1987.
245. GAA congress minutes, 27 March 1988, pp.107–9. See also *Irish Times*, 28 March 1988.
246. GAA congress minutes, 28 March 1987, pp.47–52. See also *Irish Times*, 30 March 1987.
247. *Sunday Press*, 18 September 1988.
248. Ibid.
249. Liam Hayes, *Out of our Skins* (Dublin, 1992), p.140.
250. Foley, *Kings of September*, pp.110–11. A Kerry player of this era admitted that playing inter-county games 'opened up doors for you. People did business with you because of it. It was always good for your profile to be prominent. If you look at all the prominent players of that era, they did well.' Another referred to having it 'in the back of my mind that this would be good for business. I'd get an article in the paper and a bit of publicity ... We all went a bit individualistic to get some recognition'.
251. John Callinan, 'Gaelic Players' Association', in *University College Cork Fitzgibbon Cup programme*, 20–21 February 1982, pp.50–1.
252. *Sunday Press*, 17 January 1988; Liam Hayes, 'GAA money matters', in *Maynooth College Sigerson Cup programme*, 4–6 March 1988.
253. GAA Central Council, *Eadrainn Féin: Information Bulletin for County Officials*, 6, 9 (Márta, 1989), pp.2–4.
254. Michael Frain, 'The professionalisation of sport in an Irish context: The Gaelic Athletic Association and the process of professionalism' [working title], (MSc thesis, UCD, 2009). See also Eric Dunning and Kenneth Sheard, *Barbarians, Gentlemen and Players: A Sociological Study of the Development of Rugby Football*, 2nd edition (London, 2005).
255. General Secretary's Report, 1955, p.A17, COFLA.
256. General Secretary's Report, 1955, p.A19. See also ibid., 1955, p.A14
257. *Programme for the opening of Cardinal MacRory Memorial Park, Dunmoyle* (1956), pp.33–4, 14, 27; reprinted in Dermot McCann and Tommy Trainor, *The Gaelic Fields of Errigal Kerrogue* (Omagh, 2006). See also Michael Frawley, 'The playing fields of Emly 1886–1968', in Michael O'Dwyer (ed.), *The Parish of Emly: A History of Gaelic Games and Athletics* (Emly, 2000), pp.273–80.
258. Pádraig Ó Caoimh, 'The Gaelic Athletic Association progress', *Capuchin Annual*, 1960, p.231.

259. Ibid., p.232.
260. *Sunday Press*, 5 June 1955. 'Lurgan rallied round the club to a man, teachers left their schools and brought their pupils along after hours to lend a hand, chemists and dentists mixed mortar, and businessmen trimmed the costs – not for their own reward, but for a great cause.' See also *Gaelic Echo*, December 1954; Clann Éireann GAC, *Mórtas Chlann Éireann: Programme for the Official Opening of the Hurling Field* (1990), pp.4–5, 74. See also 'J. Anelius', *National Action*, p.112, for an earlier idea for such a project.
261. Marcus de Búrca, 'Women and the GAA', in *The Book of Gaelic Games* (1984), part 7, pp.178–80.
262. GAA, *Official Guide*, 1966, p.11. This article is still carried at the time of writing (ibid., 2008, p.3).
263. Smith, *Decades of Glory*, p.368.
264. Hill, *Sport, Leisure and Culture*, pp.130, 137. Hill, p.181, even suggests that sporting voluntarism, and the '"amateur" ethos of self-help and improvement' was 'peculiarly British'.
265. Pat John Rafferty, 'Gleanings from the Treasurers' reports', in Patrick J. Campbell (ed.), *The Carrickmore Tradition* (Carrickmore, 1982), p.351.
266. This was the unofficial prize for the Lavey Provincial Tournament in Co. Derry (interview with Michael Hasson, Rasharkin, Co. Antrim – who played in it – on 27 October 2008).
267. GAA, Official Guide, 1966, pp.104-5. This rule was later amended to allow non-cash prizes of up to £10 in value (ibid., 1973, pp.83–4), and then prizes equivalent to £50 in value (ibid., 1986, p.36).
268. There were exceptions, however. A seven-a-side event in Co. Westmeath in the mid-1970s had a prize of £50 per man (Foley, *Kings of September*, p.23). Guest players at the unofficial 'Fisher Cup' at Cookstown, Co. Tyrone, in the 1970s were reputedly well paid; hence some played in it rather than train with their county teams on the eve of championships.
269. *Gaelic Weekly*, 14 January 1967.
270. Director-General's Report to Annual Congress, 1989, p.7. Some managers or trainers were reputedly receiving up to IR£20 or £30 a session for clubs in the late 1980s (Hayes, 'Payola game', p.5).
271. Tom Humphries, 'The tradition of volunteerism', in programme for the All-Ireland football final, 16 September 2007, pp.88–9.

CHAPTER 11

1. The author acknowledges the support of the staff of a number of archival institutions in the research of this essay and in particular the staff of the Tipperary Local Studies Department at the Source in Thurles, the National Library, the National Archives and the Valuation Office. Bobby Roche in the latter institution was ultra-patient with my numerous requests for the valuation list books. A number of individuals provided invaluable support and advice in identifying individuals and families in localities. These included Dr Frank Sweeney of the Maynooth Local History Group; Tipperary men Pat Bracken, Liam O'Donoghue, Seamus King and Seamus Leahy had words of wisdom regarding Tipperary hurlers; Ned O'Keeffe of Mooncoin and Edward Kennedy of Freshford were equally insightful in matters relating to Mooncoin and Tullaroan; Jim Fogarty, Kilkenny County Librarian, sent me in all the right directions. Martin Morris, joint-archivist of counties Longford and Leitrim libraries played a similar role. Dan Purcell in Clonea helped identify hurlers and footballers from that parish. Errors, of course, remain my sole responsibility.
2. *United Irishman*, 4 March 1898.
3. Tom Hunt, *Sport and Society in Victorian Ireland; The Case of Westmeath* (Cork, 2007), p.1.
4. The database was compiled using a variety of sources, primarily Denis Kinsella (ed.), *The Mooncoin Story* (Mooncoin, 1990), p.132; Jim Fogarty (ed.), *Two Mile Borris 1900 All-Ireland Hurling Winners: A Souvenir History* (Two Mile Borris, 2000); Liam Ó Donnchú (ed.), *Horse and Jockey All-Ireland Hurling Champions, 1899* (Horse and Jockey, 1999), pp.11–16. Peter Meskell, *Suir View Rangers, 1895–1898* (Thurles, 1998), pp.28–49; John G. Maher, *Tobberadora, The Golden Square Mile* (1995); Michael J. Hughes, *Caherlistrane GAA and 150 Years of Parish Life* (Caherlistrane, 1990), pp.38–9; *Celtic Times*; Seán Ó Suilleabhán, *Scéal Club Colmcille: Colmcille's GAA Story, The First*

Hundred Years (Longford, 1984), pp.9–11; Seán Kierse, *History of Smith O'Brien GAA Club Killaloe 1886–1987* (Killaloe, 1991), pp.65–83; *Longford Independent*; *Westmeath Examiner*; Éamonn Fitzgerald (ed.), *Dr Crokes' Gaelic Century* (Killarney, 1986); Antóin Ó Dúill, *Famous Tullaroan 1884–1984* (Tullaroan, 1984); Michael Lydon, *Dunmore McHales: A History of Football in Dunmore Parish* (Dunmore, 1983); Baile-Ui-Duib Ioctor 1884–1987 (Ballyduff, County Waterford, (1987).

5. *Census of Ireland, 1901*, general report with illustrative maps and diagrams, tables and appendix; 1902, Cd. cxxix.1.

6. This division of occupations into categories is broadly based on the system used by Guy Ruth, *Occupations and Pay in Great Britain 1906–1979* (London, 1980) and is similar to the one used by Peter Hart in his analysis of Volunteer membership in *The IRA at War 1916–1923* (Oxford, 2003).

7. Tom Looney, *Dick Fitzgerald: King in a Kingdom of Kings* (Blackrock, 2008), p.17.

8. Hunt, *Sport and Society*, pp.248–55.

9. Ó Donnchú, *Horse and Jockey*, pp.11–12. Jim O'Keeffe won three All-Ireland senior hurling medals in a row with three different clubs, Tubberadora (1898), Horse and Jockey (1899) and Two Mile Borris (1900); Fogarty, *Two Mile Borris*, p.66; Looney, *Dick Fitzgerald*, p.9.

10. Peter Hart, *The IRA and its Enemies: Violence and Community in Cork 1916–1923* (Oxford, 1998), p.156.

11. Dermot Keogh, *The Rise of the Irish Working Class: The Dublin Trade Union Movement and Labour Leadership 1890–1914* (Belfast, 1982), pp.73–6.

12. Tony Farmer, *Ordinary Lives: Three Generations of Irish Middle Class Experience, 1907, 1932, 1963* (Dublin, 1991), pp.22–3.

13. See Hunt, *Sport and Society*, pp.158–61 for an account of the social activities associated with early GAA clubs and for an insight into the variety of clubs that young commercial men joined.

14. W.F. Mandle, *The Gaelic Athletic Association and Irish Nationalist Politics 1884–1924* (Dublin, 1987), p.7.

15. Marcus de Búrca, *The GAA: A History of the Gaelic Athletic Association* (Dublin, 1980), p.101.

16. I am indebted to Liam O'Donoghue, Thurles and Thurles Sarsfields GAA club for providing me with this information.

17. The final of 1900 was not played until 26 October 1902.

18. *Census of Ireland, 1901*. Part 1. Area, houses and population. 1902. Volume 11. Province of Munster, No. 5 County of Tipperary [Cd. 1058 – IV], p.121.

19. *Census of Ireland, 1901*, pp.16–17.

20. *Westmeath Nationalist*, 5 November 1891.

21. *Westmeath Nationalist*, 19 and 26 May 1892, 6 June 1892.

22. Fogarty, *Two Mile Borris*, p.3.

23. Looney, *Dick Fitzgerald*, p.61.

24. Royal Commission on Labour: the agricultural labourer. 1893–94 Vol. IV Ireland. Part II [C.6894..XIX], p.27.

25. Denis O'Gorman, 'The 1887 All-Ireland', *Tipperary GAA Yearbook 1987* (Thurles, 1987), p.41.

26. Padraig O'Toole, *The Glory and the Anguish* (Loughrea, 1984), pp.26–7; Seán O'Donnell, *St Mary's Hurling Club, Clonmel, 1925–89* (Clonmel, 1990), pp.20–1.

27. Maher, *Golden Square Mile*, p.6; *Sport*, 18 and 25 February 1899.

28. See Hunt, *Sport and Society*, pp.158–61 for descriptions of the social scene associated with Westmeath GAA clubs in the 1890s.

29. Mike Huggins, *The Victorians and Sport* (London, 2004), p.107.

30. Hunt, *Sport and Society*, pp.135–40.

31. Myrtle Hill, *Women in Ireland: A Century of Change* (Belfast, 2003), p.21.

32. The age of the player was calculated on the scheduled year of the competition and on the first reference to the player in the competition.

33. Fogarty, *Two Mile Borris*, p.64.

34. Five players in the number were married and only three non-Catholics were evident.

35. Timothy W. Guinnane, *The Vanishing Irish: Households, Migration and the Rural Economy in Ireland, 1850–1914* (Princeton, 1997), pp.193–240.

36. *Census of Ireland, 1901*, p.114. Based on calculations from detail on conjugal status of different age groups.

37. Peter Meskell, *Suir View Rangers*, pp.15–16.

38. Ibid., pp.8–10. Tubberadora also competed in that championship but withdrew when John Maher suffered a broken leg in a training accident. Tubberadora didn't become part of the Boherlahan-Dualla parish until 1903. Prior to that date Tubberadora had been part of the Moycarkey parish.

39. Maher, *Golden Square Mile*, pp.4–7. Tubberadora suffered their only defeat in a Croke Cup match against Clare champions Tulla when the team was short several regulars.

40. Ibid., p.2.

41. See Margaret Leahy, 'Tubberadora Mill, 1918: a forgotten industry', *Boherlahan-Dualla Historical Journal*, 8 (2005), pp.7–18 for an insight into the workings of the mill in 1918.

42. Maher, *Golden Square Mile*, p.14.

43. Ibid., p.6.

44. Ibid., pp.44–5.

45. *An Déiseach*, '74, Waterford GAA Yearbook (Dungarvan, 1984), pp.95–6. Peter Lovesey, *The Official Centenary History of the AAA* (Enfield, 1980), p.186. Joe Ó Muircheartaigh and T.J. Flynn, *Princes of the Pigskin: A Century of Kerry Football* (Cork, 2007), pp.11–12. Percy Kirwan captained Waterford against Kerry in the 1903 Munster football championship. Rody was selected on the Kerry team on that day but refused to line out 'against his own', probably the only occasion a Waterford footballer refused a position on a Kerry team.

46. Edward Kennedy, *The Land Movement in Tullaroan, County Kilkenny, 1879–1891* (Dublin, 2004), p.1.

47. Ó Dúill, *Famous Tullaroan*, p.26.

48. Michael O'Dwyer, *The History of Cricket in Kilkenny: The Forgotten Game* (Kilkenny, 2006), pp.225–31.

49. Kinsella, *Mooncoin Story*, p.132.

50. Jack Burtchaell, 'The south Kilkenny farm villages', in William J. Smyth and Kevin Whelan (eds), *Common Ground: Essays on the Historical Geography of Ireland, presented to T. Jones Hughes* (Cork, 1998), pp.110–16.

51. Ibid., p.112

52. Ibid., p.120.

53. Ibid., pp.117–20.

54. Kinsella, *Mooncoin Story*, p.132.

55. Keogh, *Irish Working Class*, p.69; Farmer, *Ordinary Lives*, p.22.

56. William Nolan (ed.), *The Gaelic Athletic Association in Dublin 1884–2000* (Dublin, 2005), vol. i, p.32. This is a quote from a pamphlet produced for the playing of the Kickham cup *c*.1956.

57. Ibid., pp.32–3.

58. Ibid; D. Vaughan, *Liffey Gaels: A Century of Gaelic Games: 1884–1984* (Dublin, 1984), p.55.

59. Jim Cronin, *Making Connections: A Cork GAA Miscellany* (Cork, 2005), p.310.

60. *An Deiseach*, pp.97–9.

61. Keogh, *Irish Working Class*, p.76.

62. Micheal Ó Ruairc, 'The early days of athletics, football and hurling in Kerry', in Michael Lyne (ed.), *Kerry GAA Yearbook 1977* (Valentia, 1977), p.7.

63. Nolan, *Gaelic Athletic Association in Dublin*, pp.34–5.

64. Ibid., pp.23–5.

65. *Sport*, 18 February 1899. This was the 1897 final.

66. Nolan, *Gaelic Athletic Association in Dublin*, pp. 1189–90.

67. Des Donegan (ed.), *The Complete Handbook of Gaelic Games* (Dublin, 2005), p.119, 328.

68. Cronin, *Making Connections*, pp.310–15.

69. Michael Leyden, *Dunmore MacHales: A History of Football in Dunmore Parish* (Dunmore, 1983), pp.21, 30, 51.

70. Cronin, *Making Connections*, pp.323–5.

71. Neal Garnham (introduction), *The Origins and Development of Football in Ireland: Being a Reprint of R.M. Peter's Irish Football Annual of 1880* (Belfast, 1999), p.172.

72. Rouse, *Politics and Culture of Sport in Ireland*, p.348.

73. Hunt, *Sport and Society*, pp.190–215.

74. Timothy G. McMahon, *Grand Opportunity: The Gaelic Revival and Irish Society 1893–1910* (Syracuse, 2008), p.88.

75. *Roscommon Herald*, 22 September 1902.

76. Hunt, *Sport and Society*, pp.198.

77. Nolan, *Gaelic Athletic Association in Dublin*, p.81.

78. Ibid., pp.1,241, 1,202, 1,213.
79. Jimmy Wren, *Saint Laurence O'Toole GAC 1901-2001: A Centenary History* (Dublin, 2001), p.3.
80. Eoghan Corry, *Oakboys: Derry's Football Dream Comes True* (Dublin, 1993), pp.56–7; Garnham, *Origins and Development*, p.172.
81. Nolan, *Gaelic Athletic Association in Dublin*, p.69.
82. Huggins, *Victorian Sport*, p.46.

CHAPTER 12

1. Irish Department of Foreign Affairs, Press Release, 24 June 2008.
2. This study will be published as a book provisionally entitled *Gaelic Games, Nationalism and the Irish Diaspora in the United States* by University College Dublin Press in 2009.
3. Kerby A. Miller, *Emigrants and Exiles: Ireland and the Irish Exodus to North America* (New York, 1985).
4. Frank D'Arcy, *The Story of Irish Emigration* (Cork and Dublin, 1999).
5. T.J. O'Gorman, *A History of the Irish Fellowship Club of Chicago: 1901–2001* (Chicago, 2001).
6. R.A. Burchell, *The San Francisco Irish: 1848–1880* (Manchester, 1979).
7. W.C. Abbott, *New York in the American Revolution: 1763–1783* (New York and London, 1929); Brian McGinn, 'A century before the GAA: Hurling in eighteenth-century New York', *Journal of the New York Irish History Roundtable*, 11 (1997), pp.12–16.
8. R.C. Wilcox, 'The shamrock and the eagle: Irish-Americans and sport in the nineteenth century', in George Eisen and David Wiggins (eds), *Ethnicity and Sport in North American History and Culture* (Westport, CN and London, 1994), pp.54–74.
9. *Alta California*, 4 May 1853.
10. See Paul Darby, 'Emigrants at play: Gaelic games and the Irish diaspora in Chicago, 1884–c.1900', *Sport in History*, 26, 1 (2006), pp.47–63; 'Gaelic games and the Irish immigrant experience in Boston', in Alan Bairner (ed.), *Sport and the Irish: Historical, Political and Sociological Perspectives* (Dublin, 2005), pp.85–101; 'Gaelic Sport and the Irish Diaspora in Boston, 1879–90', *Irish Historical Studies*, 33, 132 (2003), pp.387–403.
11. See Paul Darby, '"Without the aid of a sporting safety net?" The Gaelic Athletic Association and the Irish émigré in San Francisco (1888–c.1938)', *International Journal of the History of Sport*, 21, 1 (2009), pp. 63–83; 'Gaelic games, ethnic identity and Irish nationalism in New York city c.1880–1917', *Sport in Society*, 10, 1 (2007), pp.347–67.
12. J. Byrne, 'The New York GAA, 1914–1976', in D. Guiney (ed.), *The New York Irish* (Dublin, 1976), pp.6–24.
13. *Annual Congress GAA Minutes*, 6 April 1947.
14. Ó Caoimh noted in his report to Central Council (13 December 1947) that the arrangements for the sale of tickets might also have negatively impacted on the attendance. In their desire to prevent the tickets being bought by black-marketeers and sold on at inflated costs, the organising committee had decided not to use the services of the city's ticketing agencies and instead only sold tickets from a single location, controlled by the GAA.
15. Pádraig Puirséal, *The GAA in its Time* (Dublin, 1982).
16. *Central Council GAA Minutes*, 21 November 1952.
17. Ibid., 8 December 1952.
18. For example, the last hurling final played under the auspices of the National Council of the GAA between Chicago and New York drew a crowd of 10,000 to Chicago's Shewbridge field (*Chicago Daily Tribune*, 10 June 1956).
19. *Central Council GAA Minutes*, 21 November 1952.
20. The principal players in the push for a national body included John O'Brien and Henry Cavanagh in Cleveland, Jack Courtenay and Fr Peter Quinn in Buffalo, Michael Cavanaugh of Philadelphia and Dan O'Kennedy of Detroit (*Irish Emigrant*, 22 November 1999).
21. Interview with author, Brighton, MA, 15 August 2000.
22. The NACB sought county board status by encouraging affiliated delegates to put forward motions at a number of GAA congresses in the early 1960s. This status was eventually granted by Central Council in 1993 (North American County Board, *Our Story Retold: 1884–1997* (North American County Board, 1997)).
23. The 1921 Quota Act established the US's first immigration quotas. This was followed in 1924 by the Immigration Act that set an annual immigration limit of almost 155,000 per annum and allocated countries a quota based on its US population as determined by the 1920 census.

24. C. B. Keely, 'Effects of the Immigration Act of 1965 on selected population characteristics of immigrants to the United States', *Demography*, 8, 2 (1971), pp.157–69.
25. F. E. Cochrane, 'The end of the affair: Irish migration, 9/11 and the evolution of Irish America', *Nationalism and Ethnic Politics*, 13, 3 (2007), pp.335–66; D.M. Reimers, 'An end and a beginning', in R.H. Bayor and T.J. Meagher (eds), *The New York Irish* (Baltimore and London, 1997), pp.275–300.
26. The rules governing the import of players from Ireland to NACB clubs were as follows: Players wishing to play for an NACB club in the regular season had to be registered with that club before a cut-off date (normally in early April). These players would be considered 'home-based' and there were no limits on the numbers who could sign for a club. In addition, clubs were permitted to sign 'sanction' players from Ireland by a further cut-off date (normally in late July). However, only three of these players could be on the field at any one time. These rules were abused by NACB clubs and players. For example, three inter-county Roscommon footballers received lengthy suspensions from the GAA for playing illegally for the Galway club in Boston (Seán Moran, 'McHugh among 20 banned by GAC', *Irish Times*, 10 January 1997, p.15).
27. For example, at the NACB's convention in 2000, a motion was proposed to increase the number of sanction players permitted to be on the field of play at any one time. Opposition to this motion came primarily from the north-east and western divisional delegates who argued that, if passed, it would undermine the promotion of Gaelic games to players already resident in the US, including those who were coming through the various youth programmes (E. Kelly, 'North American County Board 2000 Convention Report', www.NAGAA.org/agm2000.htm).
28. Ian O'Riordan, 'GAA moves to block players' exodus to US', *Irish Times*, 18 July 2002, p.23.
29. See, for example, Mike Cronin, *Sport and Nationalism in Ireland: Gaelic Games, Soccer and Irish Identity Since 1884* (Dublin, 1999): W.F. Mandle, *The Gaelic Athletic Association and Irish Nationalist Politics, 1884–1928* (London and Dublin, 1987); John Sugden and Alan Bairner, *Sport, Sectarianism and Society in a Divided Ireland* (Leicester, London and New York, 1993).
30. Darby, '"Without the aid of a sporting safety net"'; 'Emigrants at play'; 'Gaelic games and the Irish immigrant experience in Boston'; 'Gaelic games, ethnic identity and Irish nationalism in New York city'.
31. Mike Cronin, 'Enshrined in blood: The naming of Gaelic Athletic Association grounds and clubs', *Sports Historian*, 18, 1 (1998), p.96.
32. *Irish Echo*, July 1888; *The Gael*, May 1887.
33. *The Advocate*, 3 September 1914.
34. L. J. McCaffrey, *Textures of Irish America* (Syracuse, NY, 1992), p.154.
35. Irish Northern Aid was established ostensibly to collect money in the US to support the families of republican prisoners in Northern Ireland. However, the American, British and Irish governments came to the conclusion that its primary function was to raise funds to arm the IRA and as such the organisation was proscribed by all three governments.
36. Brian Hanley, 'The politics of NORAID', *Irish Political Studies*, 19, 1 (2004), pp.1–17.
37. *The Advocate*, 6 May 1972, 24 June 1972, 1 July 1972.
38. *Ulster Gaelic Football Club*, Constitution.
39. Interview with Joe Duffy, former Ulster GFC chairman, San Francisco, CA, 28 August 2006.
40. Des Fahy, *How the GAA Survived the Troubles* (Dublin, 2001).
41. Interview with author, Brighton, MA, 15 August 2000.
42. North American County Board, *Official Programme for the NACB Finals* (Washington, 1998).
43. Interview with author, San Francisco, CA, 27 August 2007.

CHAPTER 13

1. F.A. Fahy, *A Gaelic League Catechism* (Dublin, n.d.), p.4.
2. Douglas Hyde, 'The necessity for de-Anglicising Ireland', in Arthur Mitchell and Pádraig Ó Snodaigh (eds), *Political Documents 1869–1916* (Dublin, 1989), p.85.
3. For a discussion of the literary issues and the contested nature of the debate see, for example, Declan Kiberd, *Inventing Ireland: Literature of the Modern Nation* (London, 1997)

and R.F. Foster, *The Irish Story: Telling Tales and Making it Up in Ireland* (Oxford, 2004).

4. For an overview of the language issue and its fortunes in a literary context see the works of Philip O'Leary, *The Prose Literature of the Gaelic Revival* (Pennsylvania, 2004) and *Gaelic Prose in the Irish Free State, 1922–39* (Dublin, 2000).

5. T.J. McElligott, *The Story of Handball* (Dublin, 1984), p.9.

6. For a survey of handball alleys and their demise, see the Irish Handball Alley project, http://irishhandballalley.blogspot.com/

7. Alice Gomme, *The Traditional Games of England, Scotland and Ireland*, 2 vols (London, 1898).

8. Marcus de Búrca, *The GAA: A History* (Dublin, 1980), pp.30–1.

9. For coverage of athletics see P. Griffin, *The Politics of Irish Athletics, 1850–1900* (Leitrim, 1990) and Pearse Reynolds, 'The Split: Divisions in Irish Athletics, 1920–40', (MA thesis, De Montfort University, 2008.

10. For the history of the first Meath tour see Mike Cronin, '"When the world soccer cup is played on roller skates": The attempt to make Gaelic games international: The Meath–Australia matches of 1967–68', *Immigrants and Minorities*, 17, 1 (1998), pp.170–86; and Peter McDermott, *Gaels in the Sun : A Detailed Account of Meath's Historic Trip to Australia, March 2–24, 1968* (Louth, 1968).

11. For a general overview of the Australian connection see Jack Mahon, *A History of Gaelic Football* (Dublin, 2000), pp.170–7.

12. Seamus J. King, *A History of Hurling* (Dublin, 1998), pp.234–5.

13. Hogan Stand website, 'Touring All Stars finalised', 26 November 2008, www.hoganstand.com/allstars/ArticleForm.aspx?ID=104127

14. For a history of shinty and details of the contacts with hurling see Hugh Dan MacLennan, *Not an Orchid* (Inverness, 1995).

15. For details on Aonach Tailteann see Mike Cronin, 'The state on display: The 1924 Tailteann art competition', *New Hibernia Review*, 9, 3 (Fómhar/Autumn 2005), pp.50–71; and Mike Cronin, 'Projecting the nation through sport and culture: Ireland, Aonach Tailteann and the Irish Free State, 1924–32', *Journal of Contemporary History*, 38, 3 (2003), pp.395–411.

16. Background to Scór on GAA website, http://www.gaa.ie/page/scor.html

CHAPTER 14

1. Editor's Introduction to Conor Cruise O'Brien (ed.), *The Shaping of Modern Ireland* (London, 1960), p.16.

2. Marcus de Búrca, *The GAA: A History*, 2nd edn (Dublin, 2000) is the standard account; but for lively comments see also Eoghan Corry, *An Illustrated History of the GAA* (Dublin, 2005).

3. See, in particular, Mike Cronin, *Sport and Nationalism in Ireland* (Dublin, 1999). Also W.F. Mandle, *The Gaelic Athletic Association and Irish Nationalist Politics 1884–1924* (Dublin, 1987); John Sugden and Alan Bairner, *Sport, Sectarianism and Society in a Divided Ireland* (Leicester, 1993); Alan Bairner (ed.), *Sport and the Irish: Histories, Identities, Issues* (Dublin, 2005).

4. William Nolan (ed.), with contributions by Jim Wren, Marcus de Búrca and David Gorry, *The Gaelic Athletic Association in Dublin 1884–2000*, 3 vols (Dublin, 2005). For a recent rich case study, see Tom Hunt, *Sport and Society in Victorian Ireland: The Case of Westmeath* (Cork, 2007).

5. Though Diarmaid Ferriter, *The Transformation of Ireland 1900–2000* (London, 2004) offers critical commentary. A concise, perceptive treatment of certain aspects of sport in Irish identity discourse is R.V. Comerford, *Ireland: Inventing the Nation* (London, 2003), pp.212–35.

6. See, for example, essays by Alan Bairner: 'Civic and ethnic nationalism in the Celtic vision of Irish sport', in Grant Jarvie (ed.), *Sport in the Making of the Celtic Cultures* (Leicester, 1999), pp.12–25; 'Sport, nationality and postcolonialism in Ireland', in John Bale and Mike Cronin (eds), *Sport and Postcolonialism* (Oxford and New York, 2003), pp.159–74, and references in note 3 above.

7. A point made by Mike Cronin, in reviewing Nolan et al, note 4 above, in *Irish Economic and Social History*, 33 (2006), pp.143–5.

8. The statistics (relating to the years 2003/2004) are contained in Liam Delaney and Tony Fahey, *Social and Economic Value of Sport in Ireland* (Dublin, 2005), pp.11–13. The GAA has a high ratio of members to players; its total adult male playing population is lower than that of soccer.

9. For an outstanding example, see Dermot Keogh, *Jack Lynch* (Dublin, 2008).

10. The specific games (often described as 'garrison games') 'banned' were rugby, soccer, hockey

and cricket. The ban was not abolished until 1971. The fact that Sunday was selected as the day for Gaelic games (a democratic instinct, to allow the working man participate on his free day) offended conscientious, mainly Protestant, Sabbatarians.

11. For the emigration experience, see, most recently, Mary E. Daly, *The Slow Failure: Population Decline and Independent Ireland, 1920–1973* (Madison, WI, 2006), and Enda Delaney, *The Irish in Post-War Britain* (Oxford, 2007).

12. Tours of the facilities at Croke Park provide an easy, non-threatening introduction to the association. The overtly Catholic rituals of earlier decades – team captains kneeling to kiss the bishop's ring and the singing of the hymn 'Faith of our Fathers' before the start of major games – had been discontinued by the mid-1960s.

13. The GAA's language of ethnic Irish nationalism – with its frequently essentialist and hyperbolic rhetoric – that many commentators find 'dark' and divisive should be read in the context of the rhetoric of cultural superiority and the civilising mission characteristic of British imperial discourse, to which Irish cultural nationalism in the late nineteenth and early twentieth century was, in considerable measure, a reaction. See J.A. Mangan (ed.), *Pleasure, Profit, Proselytism: British Culture and Sport at Home and Abroad 1700–1914* (London, 1988); Richard Holt, *Sport and the British: A Modern History* (Oxford, 1989).

14. The possibility of players playing different games at different stages of their careers or on an occasional basis is now considered principally in terms of its feasibility – e.g. the physical demands, scheduling, time commitments, level of competition – rather than being described in the more emotive language of 'rejection', suspension and expulsion, familiar in an earlier era.

15. One might note here the introduction of squash courts and other 'generic' fitness facilities in GAA club premises, and the staging of large concerts – mainly 'pop' concerts – in GAA grounds, including Croke Park, both for revenue purposes and in the interests of establishing the 'venue' as hospitable to varieties of youth cultural events.

16. For an introduction, see Richard Giulianotti and Roland Robertson (eds), *Globalization and Sport* (Oxford, 2007).

17. Michael Holmes and David Storey, 'Who are the boys in green? Irish identity and soccer in the Republic of Ireland', in Adrian Smith and Dilwyn Porter (eds), *Sport and National Identity in the Post-War World* (London and New York, 2004), pp.88–104.

18. There is an irony in the eclipse of the province as a unit for competitions with a popular following in Gaelic games at the time when it has emerged as the crucial unit for aggregate loyalty and support in the new professional era in rugby.

19. Though the popularity of Irish-dancing competitions and the traditional music scene largely under Comhaltas Ceoltóirí Éireann auspices among Irish emigrant stock – and among others attracted by these cultural 'products' – may hold promise for a stronger GAA imprint in these overseas countries than this essay allows.

20. For a recent discussion of the complexity of the assimilationist 'pull' in sport, as it affects the Irish, see Mike Cronin, David Doyle and Liam O'Callaghan, 'Foreign fields and foreigners on the field: Irish sport, inclusion and assimilation', *International Journal of the History of Sport*, 25, 8 (July 2008), pp.1,010–30.

21. In recent years women have begun to emerge more in the communications or public relations side of GAA administration.

22. Delaney and Fahey, *Social and Economic Value of Sport in Ireland*, provide statistics for women's participation. Organised camogie games date from 1903; the women's football organisation from 1974.

23. Limerick's 'exceptionalism', because of the strong working-class element in its rugby base, is well known. Soccer also has deep roots in the city. For a glimpse of the difficulties of a centre-city GAA club in the rugby heartland, see Tony Williams (ed.), *The Boys in Blue: History of St Munchin's Parish GAA 1886–1987* (Limerick, n.d. but c.1988).

24. The expanding *Gaelscoileanna* network would, one suspects, map closely to the formation and growth of new GAA clubs in these new communities for more than two decades.

25. This emerges in Delaney and Fahey, *Social and Economic Value of Sport in Ireland*, p.75.

Index

INDEX

291

INDEX

INDEX